The ill-Logic of Islamophobia

How Stereotypes of Muslims
Foment Hatred,
Fuel Extremism on All Sides,
and Endanger Us All

Zane K. Asadi

The ill-Logic of Islamophobia

How Stereotypes of Muslims Foment Hatred, Fuel Extremism on All Sides, and Endanger Us All

Zane K. Asadi

ISBN 978-1-952290-13-8

Library of Congress Control Number
2022923848

Published by:

Tahrike Tarsile Qur'an, Inc.

Publishers and Distributors of The Qur'an

www.koranusa.org

Printed in Canada

Table of Contents

Introduction

Islamophobia is an irrational and overblown fear of or hatred towards Islam or Muslims. Despite George W. Bush's assertion that The War on Terror was not a war against Islam but rather against a small group that had "hijacked" the religion, in the popular imagination, it has become increasingly difficult to discern the "good" Muslim from the "bad" one. As such, in the aftermath of the September 11 attacks and the European refugee "crisis," Islamophobia morphed rather quickly from a mere chronic though harmful stereotype into an increasingly mainstream form of virulent racism that is readily exploited by politicians for votes and by the media for profits. In the post-communist world, Islamophobia became the new lifeblood of the military-industrial complex and national security industries.

Islamophobia is underpinned by very simplistic and stereotyped notions of Muslims as a homogeneous population of rigidly fanatical, innately violent, and virulently misogynist people. Such stereotypes lead to the marginalization of minority Muslim populations and justifies the use of military force against any perceived threat emanating from the Muslim world. The perception of Muslims as fundamentally irrational and seeking nothing but martyrdom leads to the erroneous conclusion that there are no valid grievances to be addressed and that diplomatic solutions could never work. As seen in Iraq and Afghanistan, the use of military force only exacerbates problems and fuels extremism among both Muslims and Islamophobes alike. Considering that Islam today has 1.8 billion followers living peacefully in societies across the globe, a military solution to Islam, Muslims, or even Islamic extremism hardly makes rational sense. Similarly, a narrow and heavily stereotyped conceptualization of Muslims does nothing to capture the cultural, linguistic, intellectual, and sectarian diversity of Muslim populations.

What I seek to do in this book is to dissect the racialized stereotypes and rhetorical tools that denigrate Islam and drum up xenophobia targeting Muslims. In many instances, it will be apparent that Islamophobia parallels what has been seen with other current or historically marginalized groups, such as African Americans and Catholics in the United States, Jews in Nazi Germany, or colonial subjects under European dominion. Part I will focus on the portrayal of Muslims as terrorists and Islam as an inherently violent religion. Part II will consider the perceived religio-cultural threats Muslims pose to western societies. These are explored across two dimensions—first, the concept that Muslims are antithetical to core western values such as freedom of speech and tolerance of conflicting ideas; second, the belief that Islamic attire, food, and architecture pose distinct social perils and hence need to be curtailed. Part III will explore stereotypes of Muslim men as lascivious chauvinists and rapists who are empowered by Islam to subjugate women. Given my aversion to "mansplaining" sensitive topics on gender and my belief that Muslim women should take the lead in tackling such issues, I invited my sister, who is currently studying anthropology, to author this section of the book. Finally, Part IV will address fears that Muslims constitute an inherently backward population that will invariably subvert democratic societies and impose "shariah law" through immigration, procreation, and non-assimilation. The book will conclude with the dangers inherent in anti-Muslim bigotry and how a brighter future based on mutual understanding and accommodation is preferable to fearmongering and conflict.

At the end, the logic (or ill-logic, so to speak) of Islamophobia falls under "armchair theorizing" or more specifically what the sociologist W. E. B. Du Bois condemned as "car-window" sociology.[1] Armchair theorizing starts with the assumption that Muslims are exactly as stereotyped and then looks for explanations as to why this is. If Muslims are presumed to be violent, then one seeks the cause of this violence. Perhaps it can be found in a handful of the Quran's 6,349 verses. Maybe sifting through dozens of volumes of hadith—recordings of the sayings and deeds of the Prophet (S), the members of his household, and his early followers—will provide an explanation. Possibly some juristic edicts found tucked away among hundreds of volumes of *fiqh* can explain their violence. But in all these cases, that Muslims are innately and uniquely prone to violence or terrorism is somehow assumed; any factual or textual evidence to the contrary is simply ignored.

In this sense, Islamophobes and Islamic extremist groups like Al-Qaeda and ISIS share a very similar impression of Islam as a religion with a singular focus on jihad. Where they differ is that the former assume that all or at least all "real" Muslims are like the terrorists they see on television, whereas the latter lament why it is so hard to recruit Muslims to join their cause. Such a narrow focus on violence betrays a deeper understanding of the richness of Islam (Islam is not just jihad) and the reality that violent jihad plays no role in the lives of virtually all Muslims. It is no surprise that ISIS recruits order books like *Koran for Dummies* and *Islam for Dummies* from Amazon prior to joining their ill-fated "jihad,"[2] and that the most highly educated Muslim scholars are never to be found among the ranks of terrorists.

Another stereotype that is central to Islamophobia is that Muslim men are the epitome of toxic masculinity. All that is needed is a single word in the Quran or some hadith to explain Muslim patriarchy, as if Muslims hold a monopoly on misogyny. As such, cultural practices such as female genital cutting become conflated with Islam; the fact that Christians and other non-Muslims in the same geographic regions perform these same practices is ignored, as it fits neither the stereotype nor the narrative.

Du Bois' concept of "car-window sociology" entails superficial observations that are made by driving through a neighborhood, with these observations serving only to reinforce pre-existing stereotypes. An Islamophobe might bravely venture out to observe a woman wearing a niqab that covers her face. Her attire is seen as proof that Muslim women are helplessly oppressed and hence in need of feminist western men and women to save them from their Muslim male oppressors. Her own voice is of no consequence; the highly presumptive conjectures of someone from a different religio-cultural background are paramount.

Part of what fuels Islamophobia among the far-right is the belief that Muslims are determined to achieve world domination through migration, marriage, and procreation. In this context, even the smallest sign of Muslim existence in the west is seen not in terms of cultural diversity or the benefits immigrant communities bring to their host societies, but rather in terms of the takeover and defeat of native populations. This explains the overhyped reaction to seemingly inconsequential events such as a mosque or minaret being under construction or halal meats being stocked in the local grocery store. The extreme emotional reactions are attributed to Muslims offending natives, as opposed to being seen as a symptom of societal racism. As such, the "Ground Zero Mosque" controversy is perceived by many Americans as yet another instance of Muslim troublemaking rather than as an example of intolerance within American society.

On a final note, one must be careful not to confuse Islamophobia with intellectual criticism of Islam, individual Muslims, groups of Muslims, or Muslim societies. Open discussion of the status of women in Islam, the rights of religious minorities in a shariah-based society, the role of *hudud* punishments in the modern world, and Islam's views on the use of violence in political disputes are absolutely critical. Indeed, open debates on jurisprudential topics have always had an important place within Muslim communities, as Islamic jurisprudence has very little that is considered to be of juristic consensus (*ijma*) among scholars. One can only hope that these issues continue to be addressed objectively and with an open mind among Islamic scholarly circles, Muslim civil society groups, interfaith organizations, and societies at large.

A Few Stylistic and Definitional Notes

For ease of reading, Anglicized versions of Arabic words are typically used; symbols indicating proper Arabic spelling and pronunciation have generally been omitted. Given my belief that race and ethnicity are human constructs, I chose to use lowercase letters for words such as black, brown, white, west, and western. Capitalizing these words would grant them more legitimacy than they deserve. I am aware that a term such as "white" can be defined in various manners, but throughout this work a commonplace definition of a Christian or Jew of European descent has been utilized. This is not to deny that native white European Muslims exist but rather to stick to the common cultural concept of a white person.

I have similarly used commonplace conceptualizations of words like "extremism" and "terrorism," even though I am well aware that these words can be prejudicial and that any definition of these words unravels upon closer inspection. Similarly, even though the term is by no means ideal, "Islamophobia" is used to connote bigotry targeting racialized conceptualizations of Islam and/or Muslims. The use of the phrase "ill-logic" is deliberate; it is not to say that all racist polemics are completely illogical as in lacking in any logic, but rather to highlight the sick and perverted logic that is repeatedly utilized in race-baiting discourse.

Out of respect, "(S)" has been added after references to the Prophet Muhammad (S), and "(AS)" has been used after references to others who are highly revered by Muslims. These stand for "may God's prayers and peace be upon him and his family," and "peace be upon him," respectively. Also, dates and centuries cited are based on the Gregorian calendar.

Acknowledgements

I am greatly indebted to the numerous friends and family members who have debated these topics, who have assisted with sourcing specific reference material, who have aided with translations, and who have helped review and edit this work.

Glossary of Arabic Terms

Adhan	The Islamic call to prayer
Allah	God
Allahu Akbar	"God is greater," used as a proclamation in a variety of contexts
Burqa	Technically, a head-to-toe covering worn by women in Afghanistan, but often referring to any Muslim garb that similarly covers a woman
Daesh	Acronym for ISIS in Arabic
Dhimmi	The legal status of non-Muslims in a Muslim state
Diya	Financial recompense for injuries or death
Fatwa	A formal legal opinion issued by a jurist
Faqih	An expert on Islamic jurisprudence
Fiqh	Islamic jurisprudence
Fitna	Discord, civil strife, sedition, social distress, tribulations
Hadd	A specified punishment for a crime
Hadith	A narration that describes a saying or deed of the Prophet (S), his companions, or his family members
Hajj	An obligatory pilgrimage to Mecca
Halal	Permissible
Haraam	Prohibited
Hijab	Clothing that provides a sense of Islamic decency; in common usage, an article of clothing that covers a woman's head
Houri	A maiden of paradise
Hudud	Plural of *hadd*

Ijtihad	A expert scholar's use of the Quran, hadith, *fiqh* literature, and juristic principles to derive jurisprudential opinions
Imam	In both Sunni and Shia contexts, the one who leads prayers; in the Shia context, a divinely appointed successor to the Prophet (S)
Jihad	A struggle; in common use, holy war
Jizya	A poll tax placed on *dhimmis*
Kharijite	A sect that believes that committing a major sin causes one to leave Islam
Khums	A one-fifth tax stipulated on certain gains
Madrasa	School; in common western usage, a place where children undergo Islamist indoctrination
Mihrab	A niche in the wall of a mosque that is closest to Mecca, denoting the direction of prayer
Minaret	A tall, slender structure adjacent to a mosque from which the *adhan* is traditionally recited
Mujtahid	A scholar who is qualified to perform *ijtihad*
Niqab	A face covering worn by some Muslim women
Qisas	Retributive punishment (e.g., an eye for an eye)
Quran	Islam's holy book revealed to the Prophet Muhammad (S)
Salafi	Referring to any one of a number of relatively modern Sunni groups that call for what they consider to be a strict and puritanical approach to Islam
Shariah	The religious precepts of Islam
Shia	A sect of Islam that believes in divine appointment of the Prophet's (S) successors
Sunnah	The practices and customs of the Prophet (S)
Sunni	A sect of Islam that denies that the Prophet's (S) successors are divinely appointed and believes in the political legitimacy of caliphates
Takfiri	Someone who declares those who disagree with his or her interpretation of Islam as apostates and infidels

Taqiyya	Dissimulation; hiding one's true beliefs to save one's life and/or property at times of persecution
Tazir	A discretionary punishment handed out by an Islamic judge for a crime that has no specific, pre-ordained punishment
Umra	A voluntary pilgrimage to Mecca
Wahhabi	A Salafi branch that predominates in Saudi Arabia
Wudu	An ablution performed prior to rituals such as prayer
Zakat	A charitable tax that is mandatory for Muslims

Part I

Fear of Islamic Terrorism

Chapter 1

Islamophobia as a Form of Racism

There are two main problems when discussing racism in the context of Islamophobia: first, few people admit to being racist; second, Islam is claimed not to be a race. Even though hardly anyone openly claims to being racist, racism somehow manages to be pervasive throughout society. This phenomenon is what Duke Sociologist Eduardo Bonilla-Silva has termed "racism without racists."[1] To study racism, therefore, one must demonstrate how racism manifests itself in the form of persistent stereotypes and analyze differences in social outcomes between different ethnic groups.

When we imagine racism in America, African Americans are often the first who come to mind. Racism targeting blacks today does not focus on dark skin color, since that would be overtly racist. Rather, what racists allude to are the alleged high crime rates of black neighborhoods, the imagined poor work ethic of black employees, or the perceived propensity of "welfare queens" (somehow always imagined to be people of color) to abuse the "welfare state." With respect to Muslims, it is similarly not their stereotyped brown skin color that's the issue, it is just that we need to keep our country safe, we ought to protect women's rights, and we must preserve our liberties. Racism is perpetuated through passively accepting the stereotypes underlying these narratives and behaving both personally and politically as if they are true.

Since calling someone a racist is seen as an insult, pointing out racism is often seen as offensive and irksome. As Robin DeAngelo points out in *White Fragility*, there is an expectation that any discussion of racism has to be carried out delicately such as not to offend those who are perpetuating the racist social structure.[2] At the end, "White fragility functions as a form of bullying; I am going to make it so miserable for you to confront me—no matter how diplomatically you try to do so—that you will simply back off, give up, and never raise the issue again. White fragility keeps people of color in line and 'in their place.'"[3]

It is pretty much seen as rude to point out racism because you can't point out racism without insinuating that someone is racist and thereby insulting them. This reality hampers academic debate, popular discussion, and cultural sensitivity training over issues of race and ethnicity. It is no surprise that even the most vehement Islamophobes repeatedly claim, "I'm not a racist; I'm not an Islamophobe; I just have valid concerns about Islam and Muslims."

Race as a Social Construct

With respect to Islam, a thought-terminating cliché is that Islam is not a race but rather a religion, and as such denigrating Islam or Muslims cannot be racist. On the surface, this appears plausible. However, there is plenty of anti-Hispanic racism in the United States, even though Hispanic is not a race but an ethnic classification covering diverse populations. Sure, plenty of Hispanics fit the commonplace stereotype of someone with brown skin and shorter stature. However, I have also known Hispanics with blonde hair and blue eyes (who may be subject to far less racism) as well as Asian Hispanics whose ancestors moved from Japan to Mexico and Brazil decades ago and who have adopted the languages and cultures of the latter countries. It is also not rare to see black Hispanics who are the descendants of African slaves brought to the New World. Despite the racial diversity of the Hispanic population, Hispanics are generally clumped together into one racialized stereotype. Similarly, despite their racial diversity, Muslims have been clumped together in the popular imagination as "non-Hispanic brown" people from the Middle East. When making a meme, adding a beard for men and head covering for women helps complete the stereotype.[4] This is despite

Muslims ranging in complexion from black to redheads with green eyes and contrasts with the reality that most Muslims are not Middle Eastern but rather of Asian, South Asian, or African descent.

It is also often assumed that all Muslims are "some type of Arab," even though Muslims are racially, ethnically, linguistically, and culturally diverse. Even within a single Muslim-majority country, there is significant ethnic diversity. It might be surprising that Iran has greater ethnic and linguistic heterogeneity than the United States. That the Persians, Turks, Kurds, Gilaks, Lurs, Bakhtiaris, Baluchis, Arabs, and others who comprise Iran's population are not only seen as effectively the same but also considered to be essentially the same as the populations inhabiting neighboring countries highlights the racialized homogenization of Muslim-majority populations in the western imagination. Indeed, Arabs themselves are a religiously diverse population comprised of followers of Islam, Christianity, Judaism, and many other faiths. Muslim and Arab are hardly synonymous.

It must be stated that race is not a biological reality but rather a social construct. No specific gene has been found that defines race, and race is not qualitative in nature. As one travels upstream along the Nile or eastwards along the Silk Road, there is a gradual shift from stereotypically Caucasian towards more stereotypically African and Asian racial features, respectively. There is no point at which a specific line can be drawn defining two distinct races. Stark differences only appear when voluntary or forced migration bring people from vastly different geographies into contact with one another.

With race being a social construct, the question is who creates race? Does the dominant social group create and assign race, or is it the subordinate and disenfranchised groups that create racial identities for themselves? In *Toward a Political Philosophy of Race,* Falguni Sheth, a professor at Emory University, explains racialization as a process that is used by the sovereign power to manage the "unruly" segments of society that are deemed to be "unpredictable, undependable, or threatening" by the prevailing sociopolitical order.[5] Racializing a population requires an already vulnerable group that can be pointed out through some distinguishing feature. A distinguishing feature can be something visible, like differences in skin color, or it can be entirely imagined, such as when the Nazis created a distinct race of Jews despite difficulties in visually distinguishing Jews from "Germans." While caricaturized hooked noses might have worked in cartoons, forcing Jews to wear yellow stars became about the only way to tell the two ethnic groups apart in person.[6]

That racialization is imposed by the dominant social group is apparent not only in how German Jews had to be forced to wear yellow stars but also in how blackness became defined in the United States. Considering the frequency with which white slave masters took liberties with black women and girls, a progressively whiter "black" population emerged. As physical differences proved increasingly inadequate in defining race, the definition of blackness and hence enslavability and later marginalizability had to be progressively altered. Being black went from requiring one-quarter African descent to one-eighth and one-sixteenth; eventually, a single drop of "black" blood became sufficient to establish blackness in some jurisdictions. With the end of slavery, many "blacks" tried to move up the race-based caste system by "passing" as white. If the concept of race was embraced by blacks as opposed to imposed by whites, these one-droppers would have been anxious to hold on to their black "identity." This also applies on a national level. Turkey spent decades on a project of forced Europeanization and de-Islamization, yet no matter how hard it tried, it was not to be admitted to the European Union. They could dress European, write in a Latin script, and have Sundays off instead of Fridays, but none of this could change their racialized perception among Europeans from Islamic to western. Turkey's accession to the EU remains permanently stalled. Meanwhile, the EU only allowed the Greek half of Cyprus to join the union, despite the majority of Turkish Cypriots voting for reunification of the island prior to EU accession. Similarly, the accession of Bosnia-Herzegovina remains a pipe dream, while Croatia and Slovenia were granted entry. Hence, racialized identity is ascribed by the dominant group. Accordingly, Iranian nationalists can think of themselves as white and Aryan (after all, they claim, Iran means "land of the Aryans"), but within racialized western frameworks, they fall within the same homogenized ethnicity assigned to their Semitic/Arab neighbors; their own racial claims are entertained as no more than amusing ramblings about "ancient history."

Racialization is not merely a neutral form of categorizing people so that they would be known geographically, linguistically, or ethnically but then judged on an individual level. That kind of ethnic neutrality is reflected in the Quranic verse, "O mankind! We have created you from a male and a female and have made you into nations and tribes so that you may know one another. Surely the most noble of you to God is the best of you in conduct."[7] Rather, racialization is a process by which groups of people are singled out for differential treatment based on their ascribed racialized identity.

According to Sheth, liberal societies believe that they uphold the universal ideals that they claim, such as "all men are created equal" and "liberty and justice for all." Yet, they invariably exclude significant segments of their populations from benefiting to the same extent as others from these ideals. Racialization allows "exceptions" to be made to the general rules so that "outcaste" groups can be excluded, while society can go on feeling proud of the ideals they claim to uphold.[8] This is why historically the United States could go on professing to be a bastion of "life, liberty, and the pursuit of happiness," while carrying out genocides against native societies, holding large swathes of its population as slaves, and preventing non-white immigrants and emancipated blacks from pursuing happiness through acquiring American citizenship. There may be ideals such as one-man one-vote, equality before the rule of law, and capitalist individual property rights, yet voter restriction laws, racial inequality in the criminal justice system, and race-based red-lining, deed restrictions, and land acts have ensured that these ideals have been mostly reserved for one segment of society—white men. Outcaste groups are seen as undeserving of these rights and privileges through some fault of their own, not because of any shortcoming of the liberal democratic order. Dismissing outcaste populations as lacking sanity or rationality means that they do not deserve to be treated the same as everyone else. After all, how can people who are not "human-like-us"[9] deserve the exact same human rights as we do? By dehumanizing a group of people and stripping them of their rationality, it becomes easy for society to accept the political, economic, and social marginalization of a racialized community.

Through racialization, the power structure justifies excluding large segments of the population from various benefits of liberal society at any given time, while making them subject to the most draconian implementation of the law that is conceivable. Simply put, outcaste groups are subject to the prohibitions of the law but not its protections.[10] This is evident in the roles the police plays in African American neighborhoods, ICE plays in Hispanic communities, and the FBI plays in Muslim establishments.

According to Sheth, liberal societies invariably have racialized outcaste groups not as an exception but as "an intrinsic element."[11] Yet, these societies have an amazing ability to dismiss this fundamental flaw as merely a series of historical flukes. It is easy to look back on slavery, Jim Crow laws, or the internment of Japanese as past mistakes, while we continue to brazenly deprive minority groups of the full benefits of citizenship in ever-evolving ways. The stated ideal is what defines society in its own mind; the past is ancient history; current outcaste groups are justifiably set aside for differential treatment because they *are* different and hence deserve differential treatment. Thus, structural racism perpetuates itself as a constant fixture, not as an aberrance, of liberal democracies.

Once a racialized population is created, the entire group is widely accepted as fundamentally problematic. As such, strong-arm policing becomes justified against blacks; constitutionally questionable drug busts seem sensible when the targets are Hispanic; and phishing for terrorist connections seems reasonable when dealing with Muslims. According to Sheth,

> If the American state convincingly renders Muslims a new race of "evildoers" with an inherent psychology of terrorism, then it can constitute Muslims as some kind of

"exception" population, a population that is simultaneously subject to the law, but not entitled to its protection.[12]

Based on the acts of nineteen men on September 11, 2001, all Muslims came to be seen as potential terrorists. This is hardly surprising when one considers that belonging to a racialized group is equated in the popular imagination with constituting a potential threat to safety and security. This paradigm justifies the exclusion of racialized groups from certain rights and privileges and singling them out for the use of force or other forms of social control. Stop and frisk seems like a sensible policy when targeting black and brown men, as does additional screening for Muslims at the airport. Constructing a race and depriving the racialized group of the rights and privileges that others enjoy become widely accepted as entirely natural and completely just phenomena, since the entire process is blamed on innate flaws within the racialized group.

Muslims as Objects of Intersectional Discrimination

For any one individual, racialization and discrimination do not necessarily operate on a single dimension like skin color. Individuals can be subject to the intersection of multiple forms of racialization; this can result in compound forms of discrimination that operate quite distinctly from each form in isolation. This was first described by Kimberlé Crenshaw in 1989.[13] Crenshaw noted how the courts would throw out employment discrimination claims from African American women when the workplace hired both black men (e.g., for manufacturing jobs) and white women (e.g., for secretarial positions). The courts would rule that no claim could be made on counts of discrimination based either on race or sex, even though black women were excluded from employment. They did not consider how being subject to a combination of two racialized categories would create a form of discrimination that is distinct from its two components. Crenshaw demonstrated how intersectionality can lead to discrimination that is greater than and different from the sum of its constituent parts.[14]

As such, a Muslim man from Somalia moving to Minneapolis can find himself at the intersection of racial (black), religious (Muslim), and linguistic (Somali accent) discrimination. A woman from Syria can find herself at the intersection of gender (female), ethnic (Arab), religious (Muslim), and linguistic (Arabic speaker) discrimination.

Furthermore, Muslims can be subject to categorization based on being undocumented immigrants who are subject to deportation, or refugees who are subject to arbitrary repatriation when the host country deems the nation of origin to be "safe," regardless of whether that is actually the case for that individual. Millions of Muslims from Myanmar, Palestine, India, and elsewhere are also subject to the particular challenges posed by statelessness, as they are denied the rights of citizenship afforded to others. Muslims can also be subject to ethnic or sectarian discrimination and persecution within Muslim-majority countries.

It is worth noting that the specific stereotypes experienced by a Muslim woman can vacillate between being seen as a helpless maiden trapped in misogyny on the one hand and a cunning terrorist plotting jihad from behind a veil—the stereotypical "Jihad Jane"—on the other. A Muslim woman wearing hijab can be subject to further discrimination based on assumptions that she is an extremist or that she is trying to make a subversive political statement through her choice of clothing. Hijab is transformed from personal attire based on religious observance to a distinguishing feature that enables further stereotyping and racialization.

The Long History of Islamophobia in the West

In some ways, Islamophobia has been part of western discourse for centuries. In medieval Europe, Islam was seen as an alien, non-Christian, and hence demonic force. In 807, the Abbasid Caliph Harun al-Rashid sent a brass water clock to Charlemagne that featured twelve horsemen. Each hour, a window would open and a horseman would appear, with the total number of visible horsemen indicating the hour of the day. At the completion of twelve hours, the horsemen would withdraw back into their respective windows, and the cycle would repeat.[15] The clock alarmed some of the Christians who were convinced that it represented a piece of diabolical Mohammedan sorcery.[16] The demonic view of Muslims is exemplified in the medieval English story *The King of Tars*, which was written around 1330. Dr. Rachel Moss who teaches history at the University of Northampton said,

> In this story, the daughter of the Christian King of Tars offers to marry the Muslim Sultan of Damas in order to end war between their kingdoms. She falls pregnant, and the child she bears her new husband is born as a dark lump of flesh. Only after her husband allows her to christen the lump does it turn into a (white!) infant. Impressed by the power of the Christian God, the sultan also converts, and on his baptism his skin changes from black to white. In this romance, the product of a Christian-Muslim marriage is a child that is no child: it is a formless, lumpen thing that cannot really be classed as human. Only Christian people are human, the romance suggests—and Christian people are white.[17]

Humphrey Prideaux's 1697 book, *The True Nature of Imposture Fully Displayed in the Life of Mahomet*, became the prime source through which the English-speaking world understood Islam. He recycled medieval Christian polemics portraying Islam's founder as an impostor who used false religious pretexts to achieve political and sexual domination over Arabia.[18] The mistaken concept that Muhammad (S) is to Muslims as Jesus (AS) is to Christians gave rise to the derogatory name "Mohammedanism" for Islam, and necessitated that "imposter" be applied to any reference of Muhammad (S), notwithstanding the Muslim rejection of the divinity of either.[19] These derogatory caricatures formed the backdrop through which Islam was perceived by eighteenth century Europeans and Americans. In 1736, Voltaire wrote a five-act play named *La Fanatisme* (*Fanaticism*) or *Mahomet le Prophète* (*Mahomet the Prophet*), in which he portrayed the founder of Islam as a deceitful and lustful tyrant who manipulated the fanaticism of his followers.

Thomas Jefferson, one of the Founding Fathers of the United States, used Islam as an example of just how far religious tolerance would go in the new republic. Islam was seen as the quintessential other, the true antithesis of American Protestantism.[20] A state that would tolerate Muslims would constitute the epitome of tolerance itself. He presumably did not imagine that the United States would someday actually have to tolerate a Muslim population. He also seemed oblivious to the fact that Islam had already had a long history in the United States, carried over with African slaves, some twenty percent of whom are estimated to have been Muslim.[21]

Edward Said, whose book *Orientalism* is often considered to have given birth to the field known as postcolonial theory, describes how the colonization of Muslim lands was facilitated by pre-existing stereotypes of Muslims. "To say simply that Orientalism was a rationalization of colonial rule is to ignore the extent to which colonial rule was justified in advance by Orientalism, rather than after the fact."[22] The stereotype held that "the Oriental is irrational, depraved (fallen), childlike, 'different'; thus the European is rational, virtuous, mature, 'normal.'"[23] The Napoleonic invasion of Egypt of 1798 allowed for the "truly scientific appropriation of one culture by another,"[24] through a lens of "cultural strength"[25] that contrasted "the familiar (Europe, the West, 'us') and the strange (the Orient, the East, 'them'),"[26] thereby granting western superiority "the status of scientific truth."[27] Indeed, "the major component in European culture is precisely what made that culture hegemonic both inside and outside Europe: the idea of European identity as a superior one in comparison with all non-European peoples and cultures... reiterating European superiority over Oriental backwardness."[28] Western stereotypes of the "Orient" have persisted to this day. It is worth noting that Said was an Anglican Palestinian; had he been

Muslim, his writings on the treatment of Islam in the west would most likely have received no serious academic attention.

In the United States, the Naturalization Act of 1790 limited citizenship to "any alien, other than an alien enemy, being a free white person, who shall have resided within the limits and under the jurisdiction of the United States for the term of two years."[29] In 1891, the Supreme Court highlighted simmering American antipathy towards Muslims when its ruling made note of the "intense hostility of the people of Moslem faith to all other sects, and particularly to Christians."[30] In 1913, a South Carolina court refused citizenship to a Lebanese Christian because his skin was similar in color to a "walnut." In 1942, Ahmed Hassan was denied citizenship on the basis that an Arab like him could not be expected to "be assimilated into our civilization."[31] Between 1921 and 1965, the National Origins Formula was used to impose quotas on immigration based on the proportionate share each country had among the foreign-born population of the United States. This effectively ensured that immigration would be limited to people from Western Europe. In 1968, this system was finally replaced by one that allowed 170,000 immigrants from the Eastern Hemisphere annually, opening the door to increased immigration from Asia.

Despite these simmering negative attitudes towards Muslims, Islamophobia's most virulent manifestations have spread relatively recently and over a short period of time, arguably in the wake of the September 11, 2001 attacks. Muslims, who had already been racialized and heavily stereotyped, were instantly cast as the main threat to national and global security. Every Muslim turned into a potential terrorist or at the very least a potential terrorist supporter or sympathizer. As stated by Professor Saher Selod, a sociologist at Simmons College in Boston, "It has nothing to do with their actual status as a threat—their religious identity in and of itself marks them as potential suspects."[32]

As such, the post 9/11 world ushered in a period of increased scrutiny of Muslims that was almost instantaneously seen as justified. Thousands of Muslims were detained on thin or non-existent pretexts. With the War on Terror, the racialized discourse portraying Muslims as terrorists became globalized and has continued to justify violence targeting Muslims around the world. Equating Muslims with terrorists underpins the reasons given for military action in Chechnya,[33] the persecution of Uyghurs in China,[34] and the ethnic cleansing of Rohingyas in Myanmar.[35] Even Muslim-Hindu romance has come to be seen as "love jihad" waged by Muslim men on behalf of international terrorist organizations.[36] The stereotypes of Muslim men as eternal jihadists beholden to shadowy foreign organizations and Muslim women as baby factories churning out the next generation of jihadists constitute the common denominator for these and many other Islamophobic narratives.

Media Portrayals of Muslims

Racialized stereotypes are ubiquitous in media portrayals of Muslims and exposure to such caricaturized imagery starts early in life. A child watching Walt Disney's *Aladdin* will hear in its opening lyrics, "Oh, I come from a land—from a faraway land— where the caravan camels roam... It's barbaric, but hey it's home." A vast region is defined as innately barbaric in contrast to the presumed civility of other lands, particularly western ones. The good Arabs like Aladdin are fair-complected, have small noses, and speak with American accents, whereas the villainized characters are darker-complected, have hooked noses, and speak with foreign-sounding accents.[37]

These portrayals hardly improve over one's lifetime. The news invariably shows Muslims as "a large anonymous mob, deindividualized, dehumanized."[38] Once in a while, a Muslim or Arab is actually brought onto television to provide his (the person invited, all too often, is a man) perspective on current events. This person is typically going to speak heavily accented and highly ineloquent English, driving home the foreignness of this individual and his ideas. Especially in the context of the Israeli-Palestinian conflict, the Israeli guest almost invariably speaks flawless and unaccented American English in contrast to the Palestinian guest whose points are lost to the fact that his accent is reminiscent of how the bad guys on *Aladdin* speak. These exchanges highlight the issue of "relatability" in racial contexts. One group, comprised of white Christians of European descent, is held as the objective and ideal standard against which all other groups must be contrasted.[39] Given the way Muslims are consistently portrayed, it is hardly shocking that a 2017 poll found that only 28% of Americans have a favorable opinion of Islam.[40] This is, as explained by Edward Said, because "there is no influential countervailing view of Islam in the media."[41] According to Rice University's Craig Considine,

> Jack Shaheen... spent his career analyzing the way that Arabs have been portrayed in American film and television over the last century. In 2006, his book *Reel Bad Arabs* showed that Hollywood depicts Arabs as "brute murderers, sleazy rapists, religious fanatics, oil-rich dimwits and abusers of women." Shaheen's research documented well over 1000 films depicting Arabs and subsequently found that 932 films depict them in a stereotypical or negative light. Only 12 films have a positive depiction. He also cites films that portray Arabs as cold, money hungry Muslims or inept villainous terrorist[s] that seek to destroy "Western civilization." ... By reinforcing stereotypes of the Middle East as a place of extremism and Muslims as terrorists, these representations produce support for policies that have dire consequences... These caricatures of Arabs and Muslims also provide a popular "permission to hate," which often unfolds through a synthesis of racial and religious discrimination.[42]

According to Shaheen, "The word 'sheikh' means, literally, a wise elderly person, the head of the family, but... instead of presenting sheikhs as elderly men of wisdom, screenwriters offer romantic melodramas portraying them as stooges-in-sheets, slovenly, hook-nosed potentates intent on capturing pale-faced blondes for their harems."[43] Meanwhile, Arab women are portrayed as either eroticized belly-dancers and members of harems, or they are conversely shrouded in black and relegated to silence.[44] This contrasts sharply with the wide range of attire and roles Arab women are found in in the real world—they are teachers, nurses, doctors, engineers, activists, politicians, and yes, housewives too. Over a dozen Muslim women have served as heads of state. Pakistan, Bangladesh, and Turkey have had female prime ministers, whereas the United States is yet to elect a single woman as president.

What is missing is virtually any portrayal of Arabs and Muslims as heroes or even as normal people with jobs, families, and admirable ambitions. The negative stereotypes persist in the media due to general social silence, the dearth of contravening voices within the media industry, the absence of an organized and effective lobby, and the reality that "bash-the-Arab movies make money."[45] This is not to say that the situation is hopeless. As explained by Shaheen, "Ethnic stereotypes do no die off on their own, but are hunted down and terminated by those whom the stereotypes victimize." African Americans, Asian Americans, and Jewish Americans have strived hard to combat negative stereotypes within the film industry and have made significant inroads.[46] In more recent years, negative stereotypes of Muslims are more commonly pointed out by left-leaning activists and journalists, and I anticipate that over time, the promulgation of these stereotypes will be seen as ever more distasteful.

Hate Crimes Against Sikhs

The racialized image of a Muslim is reflected in the outbreaks of hate crimes targeting Sikhs. Unlike Christianity, Judaism, and Islam, Sikhism is neither an Abrahamic nor a Middle-Eastern faith, having originated in India's Punjab region. However, the brown skin color, beards, and turbans traditionally worn by Sikh men fit the racialized image commonly associated with Muslim men. Sikhs have thereby become prime targets for Islamophobic attacks, culminating in the deadly 2012 attack on a Sikh temple in

Oak Creek, Wisconsin. The attack, which led to seven deaths, was carried out by 40-year-old Wade Michael Page, a white supremacist US Army veteran.[47] This incident highlights just one example of how Sikhs are subjected to racialized violence. According to the Sikh Coalition,

> In the first month after the 9/11 attacks, the Sikh Coalition documented over 300 cases of violence and discrimination against Sikh Americans throughout the United States... 69% of turban-wearing Sikh students in the Bay Area of San Francisco have suffered bullying and harassment because of their religion... 30% of them had been hit or involuntarily touched because of their turbans. These attacks occur because the Sikh articles of faith—in particular, the turban—are associated with terrorism and 9/11... At some airports in the United States, Sikhs are subjected to secondary screening 100 percent of the time by Transportation Security Administration (TSA) personnel. TSA consistently refuses to audit its screening policies to determine whether Sikh travelers are being profiled.[48]

It hardly matters that Sikhs are not Muslim; what matters to a hate criminal or a federal TSA agent is that they fit the stereotype of one. Once racialization is achieved, it becomes difficult to see nuance. Considering that Sikhism and Islam are conflated in the popular imagination, one cannot overlook the challenges that lie ahead in replacing broad racialized caricatures in favor of appreciating the significant differences that exist among Muslims and "Muslim-appearing" individuals.

Chapter 2

Why Are All Terrorists Muslim?

One of the most common Islamophobic tropes is that, even though most Muslims might not be terrorists, virtually all terrorists are Muslim. Furthermore, considering that Muslim terrorists carry out their acts in the name of Islam while chanting *"Allahu Akbar,"* it is evident that Islam has something to do with terrorism. Hence, the safety of western countries hinges on strictly limiting Muslim immigration, impinging on the civil liberties of Muslims, and eyeing Muslims both collectively and individually with suspicion. The problem with this very commonplace line of thought is that its basic assertion is patently false. According to the European Network Against Racism,

> A survey conducted by the Center for Research and Globalization found that the terrorists (sic) acts perpetrated by Muslim extremists constitute only 2.5% of all terrorist attacks on U.S. soil between 1970 and 2012. In 2013, 152 terrorist attacks occurred in Europe with only 1 attack being religiously motivated while 84 were motivated by ethno-nationalist or separatist beliefs. The massive media coverage of Muslims extremists' acts contributes to feeding the myth that all terrorist acts are perpetrated by Muslims. Far-right movements are also a form of extremism present in Europe, which poses a similar threat to society and peaceful coexistence.[1]

The perception that Muslims hold a monopoly on terror persists because of the commonplace definition of terrorism as an act of violence perpetrated by a Muslim combined with increased media attention given to any attack that is carried out by Muslims. Even prior to 9/11, it was difficult for some people to imagine a terrorist act without the perpetrator being Muslim. Immediately after the 1995 Oklahoma City bombing, Steve Emerson, a self-proclaimed terrorism expert, appeared on CBS to explain, "Oklahoma City, I can tell you, is probably considered one of the largest centers of Islamic radical activity outside the Middle East." The bombing, he claimed, "was done with the intent to inflict as many casualties as possible. That is a Middle Eastern trait."[2] A Jordanian American man who happened to have a flight to Jordan that day was detained, handcuffed, strip-searched, and paraded about to great publicity,[3] until the authorities found out that the perpetrator was not him but rather Timothy McVeigh, a white "all-American" man of Catholic-Irish descent.

When an act of violence occurs, if the perpetrator is Muslim, the act is perceived as terroristic in nature, otherwise it is not. Furthermore, the religion and ethnic background of the perpetrator is only newsworthy when the terrorist is Muslim. West and Lloyd took real news stories and presented them to participants as either having been carried out by Muslim or non-Muslim perpetrators. What they found, unsurprisingly, was that an act was more likely to be seen as terroristic if the perpetrator was presented as Muslim.[4] Similarly, Huff and Kertzer from Harvard University's Department of Government conducted an experiment in which they presented participants with a series of randomly generated events. They found that an event was significantly more likely to be categorized as terroristic in nature if the perpetrator was Muslim.[5]

Furthermore, when a violent act is carried out by a Muslim, it is all too often seen as a sign of Islamic radicalization and proof that Islam itself and Muslims collectively are at fault, since it is assumed that terrorism is intrinsic to Islam and Muslim societies. Political instigators (e.g., the Israeli occupation, the War on Terror), cultural concerns (e.g., westernization), social causes (e.g., marginalization and poverty), and personal deficiencies (e.g., mental illness) are seen as secondary factors at best.[6] As such, the act is seen as a sign of Islamic piety, even when the perpetrators lack any signs of religious devotion. The attacks of 9/11 were seen as "Islamic" acts of terrorism even though the four pilots and several of their co-conspirators "rented cars in Las Vegas and visited several striptease clubs where they received lap dances, smoked hashish, drank alcohol and also visited a topless bar and an adult video rental shop."[7] These are hardly signs of piety. Yet, it is assumed that Islam is what motivated their attack. Furthermore, Muslim violence is invariably seen as malevolent, whereas as pointed out by Edward Said, "the notion that American military power might be used for malevolent purposes is relatively impossible within the consensus."[8]

If an act of violence is carried out by a white Christian male, it is the result of having been subjected to too much bullying in middle school, suffering from mental illness, playing too many video games involving graphic violence, or some other quasi-legitimate grievance such as sexual deprivation (e.g., the "incel" movement), the ongoing takeover of their country by immigrants, or a desire to rid the nation of Islamic influence. Even overt religious genocide, such as when carried out by Christian Serbs against Bosnian Muslims (who are also ethnically Slavic) is not seen as having to do with Christianity. If Bosnians were massacring Serbs, on the other hand, it would be seen as somehow related to Islam. The repeat terrorist attacks carried out against civilian targets by the Irish Republican Army did not perpetuate the belief that being Irish or Catholic constituted causes of terrorism. The conflict was seen in a historical and nationalistic context in a way that acts of terrorism carried out by Muslims are not.

The same line of thinking permeates societal reaction to crime. In the aftermath of Hurricane Katrina, blacks were described as "looting" grocery stores, whereas whites doing the exact same thing were merely said to be "finding food."[9] The act is innately malevolent when carried out by racialized individuals and intrinsically benign when carried out by whites. This is the same mentality that explains why Muslims are constantly berated for not condemning and apologizing for terrorism enough. If terrorism was merely seen as the sin of one individual or a group of specific individuals, there would be no need for collective apology. But when terrorism is seen as the collective and "original" sin of Islam and Muslims, then no amount of apology for or denunciation of terrorism can suffice. The expectation of apology is highly racialized; there is no expectation that individual whites ought to be apologizing for colonial genocides or brutal postcolonial military interventions in developing nations (e.g., Vietnam, Central America, Iraq, and Afghanistan), even when these actions enjoyed broad-based support in democratic countries in a way that terrorism does not within Muslim ones. Craig Considine, a professor at Rice University, points out that the Planned Parenthood shooter is referred to in the media as a "gunman" and not a terrorist. Similarly, the murder of three Muslim students at the University of North Carolina Chapel Hill was described as a "shooting" and not a terrorist attack. He explains,

> Imagine if the "terrorism" label was used in cases of White Christian men. America would have a serious problem. The entire "war on terror" narrative would collapse; Muslims wouldn't be the only terrorists anymore. The "terrorists" are right here living among us. We'd have to deploy the might of the American military to squash them. Words like "terrorist" and "terrorism" are used by media as propaganda terms to manufacture anti-Muslim sentiment, which in turn "justifies" worldwide military adventures to dominate other countries. Muslims have to be painted in a scary and violent light because doing so creates hysteria and fear of the Other. That's the only way that wars can be justified.[10]

A major reason Muslims are perceived as terrorists is because of the outsized media attention given to terrorist attacks when they are carried out by Muslims. Erin Kearns and colleagues, in a study of media coverage of Muslim terrorist attacks, found that, "when the perpetrator is Muslim... the

increase in coverage among major [media] sources is 758%."[11]
The fear of Muslims generated by the media is akin to the
irrational fear of sharks created by movies like *Jaws* and the
inevitable reporting of shark attacks even when they occur in
faraway lands and lead to minimal injuries. This creates an
illusion that sharks are constantly attacking humans. Movies like
Open Water feed into the stereotype of sharks as calculated,
relentless, and ruthless killing machines. In reality, worldwide,
there were 9 fatal shark attacks in 2021.[12] In contrast, humans
kill approximately 100 million sharks a year.[13] The belief that
sharks pose a constant danger fosters indifference towards
environmentally catastrophic fishing practices. Similarly, despite
falling crime levels in the United States over the past fifty years,
the media creates a false image of rising and rampant urban crime.
This creates a widespread sense of insecurity, fuels racism (crime,
after all, is perceived as a black and brown problem), and
contributes to the expansion of a highly racialized prison-
industrial complex.

There is also a discrepancy in the emotional response
when heart wrenching savagery is carried out by Muslims as
opposed to followers of other religions. The beheading of
journalists and the massacre and mass rape of Yazidis by Daesh
(ISIS) rightly led to widespread expressions of disgust
worldwide. This should be contrasted with the 1982 Sabra and
Shatila massacre in Lebanon, which has largely been forgotten.
Israeli troops, in an operation directly overseen by defense
minister Ariel Sharon, surrounded the two Palestinian refugee
camps. All entrances and exits were blocked and Israeli Defense
Forces were stationed on high points along the perimeter of the
camps. Some 1,500 Lebanese Christian militiamen, riding in
Israeli-supplied jeeps, were allowed into the camp to carry out a
brutal massacre of its civilian population. Over a period of three
days, they slaughtered some 3,000 to 3,500 civilians.[14] Ariel
Sharon later served as foreign minister and prime minister of
Israel and was warmly welcomed in western capitals. Now
imagine if Hezbollah fighters were, hypothetically, to surround
and seal off a Jewish or Christian town and to allow in ISIS

fighters to massacre the trapped civilians. Islam would be widely seen as the culprit in a way that Christianity and Judaism are not in an analogous but real scenario.

Defining Terrorism

The fact remains that there is no universal definition of terrorism. The FBI defines international terrorism as "violent, criminal acts committed by individuals and/or groups who are inspired by, or associated with, designated foreign terrorist organizations or nations."[15] As such, terrorism is not defined by an act, but rather by its perpetrators and their sponsors. Islamic militants fighting the Soviet occupation of Afghanistan with CIA backing are brave freedom fighters; the exact same individuals fighting the American occupation of Afghanistan are terrorists. Palestinians and Iraqis making Molotov cocktails to use against occupying forces is terrorism; Ukrainians doing the same when the occupiers are Russian is patriotism and courage. Alex Schmid, in his work *The Routledge Handbook of Terrorism Research*, notes,

> There are hundreds of definitions of terrorism in use... 'Terrorism' may well be the most politicized term in the political vocabulary these days. Used as a label for a certain form of political violence, it reflects, if it 'sticks', negatively on a political opponent, demonizing him and de-legitimizing his conduct... Used as a rhetorical device, the term 'terrorism' threatens to become a mere invective in political debates... Those involved in the definition debate have often tried to mould definitions in a way that suites their needs. In other words, definitions generally tend to reflect the political interests and the moral judgment (or lack thereof) of those who do the defining.[16]

By this token, terrorism is merely a matter of perspective. French Partisans fighting the German occupation of France were

seen as freedom fighters by the Allies but considered to be
terrorists by the Nazis; Hezbollah fighters combating the Israeli
occupation of Lebanon were seen as freedom fighters by many
Lebanese but considered to be terrorists by Israel and many of its
western allies. The absurdity of official western definitions of
terrorism is best highlighted by how Nelson Mandela was on the
US terrorism watch list until 2008 because he would not
renounce violence as a means to end the white supremacist
apartheid regime in South Africa. As is commonly said, one
man's terrorist is another's freedom fighter.

Trying to define terrorism as a specific type of action
would be problematic, as nearly any such definition would leave
the United States exposed to Noam Chomsky's charge that it is
the leading state sponsor of terrorism.[17] In 1976, CIA-backed
Cuban exiles blew up Cubana Flight 455 in mid-air with full
knowledge of the American government. Addressing the
atrocities that have been carried out by Contras in Nicaragua, by
the *paramilitares* in Colombia, and by the numerous other
extremist right-wing organizations acting with utter impunity
with the full backing of the United States would make a book by
itself. As Edward Herman, a professor of finance at the
University of Pennsylvania, said,

> The reason for the western misperception is that *the
> powerful define terrorism*, and the western media loyally
> follow the agenda of their own leaders. The powerful
> naturally define terrorism to exclude their own acts and
> those of their friends and clients... As the United States
> and its clients, like South Africa, El Salvador, and
> Guatemala, do not (by definition) engage in terrorism,
> their attacks on their enemies require alternative words...
> The gap has been filled by the concept of
> "counterterror." ... The massacres of peasants carried out
> by the Guatemalan state to root out any opposition (i.e.,
> "terrorists") is counterterror.[18]

As such, terrorism in common western usage is simply an act of violence that the United States and its allies neither like nor approve of. Any other act of violence, no matter how savage or to what extent it targets civilians, is not terrorism. The commonplace acceptance of this type of definition of terrorism feeds into the racist narrative of the "peaceful westerner" versus the "terrorist Muslim." By definition, we do not engage in acts of terror; only they do. This mindset has allowed colonial and neocolonial powers to justify carnage while simultaneously both feeling victimized by and purporting to be the saviors of the exact populations that they are brutalizing.

For the sake of this book, the common racialized definition of terrorism hardly needs to be refined. It stands on its own as a clear example of the pervasiveness of racism. But if I were to venture a definition, terrorism would be violence that directly targets civilians or that shows disregard to civilian life, as well as violence that, in the absence of war or foreign occupation or a struggle for equal rights, targets military personnel or infrastructure.

Blaming Acts of Terror on Islam

When terrorist attacks are carried out by purported Muslims, it is invariably assumed to be the fault of Islam because Islam allegedly nurtures ideas of violent holy war. Furthermore, when Muslims carry out attacks in the name of Allah, then one is expected to conclude that Islam is the motivating cause of terrorism.

The logic linking terrorism to Islam is discriminatory because acts of violence carried out by Christians in the name of Christianity are seen to reflect neither on Christianity as a religion nor on Christians as a people. The Lord's Resistance Army is a perfect example. Its stated goal is to establish Christian rule in Uganda, and in the name of God, its members have abducted countless children for use as child soldiers and sex slaves; they have looted and torched villages; and they have tortured and maimed countless civilians. Their attacks led to the displacement of some two million innocent civilians.[19] Currently, predominantly Christian anti-balaka fighters are engaged in the ethnic cleansing of Central African Republic's Muslim civilian population. Yet, most people do not see this brutality as a reflection of Christianity. In the United States, the Army of God serves as a Christian terrorist organization whose members have carried out a number of attacks targeting abortionists. Eric Rudolph carried out multiple bombings initially targeting abortion clinics and later the 1996 Atlanta Summer Olympics. The terrorist attacks were part of his confessed quest to "embarrass the Washington government in the eyes of the word for its abominable sanctioning of abortion on demand."[20] Even though many Christians vehemently oppose abortion, it is widely assumed that this type of radical extremism is hardly representative of Christians in general.

Similarly, the Christchurch shooter who gunned down 91 people in a mosque in New Zealand did so because he was obsessed with the belief that Christians must remove Muslim occupiers. The purported racist and religionist reasons for his act are not seen as indicative of a flaw with Christianity, Christians, or western civilization in general. The repeated mass shootings in the United States carried out predominantly by white Christian men is similarly not seen as a flaw of Christianity or as necessitating apologies by Christians or white men. It is ironic that Anders Breivik, who violently bombed and then gunned down over 70 people in Norway, wrote a manifesto complaining that Islam is intrinsically violent and that peaceful Muslims are just the ones who ignore Islamic injunctions to kill wantonly.[21]

When Baruch Goldstein, a physician who opened fire on Palestinians praying in Hebron, killed 29 and injured 125, this was not seen as an issue with Judaism or Old Testament scriptures. *The New York Times*, in fact, found his ethnic cleansing ideology to be acceptable mainstream discourse when it published his letter to the editor in 1981 saying that Israel "must act decisively to remove the Arab minority from within its borders."[22] According to the Anti-Defamation League, "Since

2008, there have been repeated attacks carried out by extremist Israeli Jews against Israeli Arabs and Palestinians... These attacks, which are frequently labeled 'price tag' incidents, target mosques, churches, Arab and Jewish homes and property, Israeli military bases and vehicles, as well as other Israeli Jews."[23] The same acts carried out by Islamic extremists would be called terrorism, but when they are carried out by Jewish extremists, they are referred to as "attacks" or "incidents." The word "incident" makes it appear as if such things just happen without premeditated human involvement.

If someone claims that these terrorists aren't Christian or Jewish but are just deluded about their faiths, then the same ought to be said about Muslim terrorists. Terrorist attacks by atheists (e.g., communists) are also somehow not seen as indicative of a fundamental problem with secularism or atheism. Islam is somehow singled out as the only religion that causes terrorism.

When one considers that Nazi soldiers' belts were inscribed with *Gott mit uns* (God is with us), and rifle scopes used to kill Iraqis and Afghans were inscribed with references to biblical verses,[24] it is evident that invoking religious beliefs during conflict is rather common and not something that only Muslims partake in. Believing that one will die and go to heaven if killed in combat is not a belief unique to Islam; if every American and European soldier killed in battle was presumed to go to hell as opposed to heaven or to simply perish, it would not help armed forces' recruitment efforts.

Furthermore, the basic concept that Islam is the cause of terrorism is hard to accept when one considers the fact that Islam has been around for around 1,400 years but Muslims carrying out suicide bombings has only been around since the 1980s.[25] In a country like Iraq, suicide bombings and the ethnic cleansing of the Christian population were not the result of Islamic indoctrination, but rather the fruit of the American invasion. Iraq had a thriving population of 1.5 million Christians of various denominations who had prospered in Iraq since the dawn of Christianity and through fourteen centuries of nominal Muslim rule. In the span of two decades of American occupation, at most a few hundred thousand remain, the rest have been forced into a global diaspora.[26]

We also seem to ignore the reality that residents of Muslim-majority countries are less likely to support military or non-military attacks on civilians as compared to residents of non-Muslim majority nations. In stark contrast to the 19% of people in the Middle East and North Africa who believe that military attacks on civilians may be justified, 49% of Americans and Canadians support the use of military force targeting civilian populations. As stated by Gallup, "Americans are the most likely population in the world (49%) to believe military attacks targeting civilians is sometimes justified, followed by residents of Haiti and Israel (43%)." Such obscenely high numbers must be contrasted with the 3% of Egyptians and Qataris, 7% of Kuwaitis, and 8% of Iraqis who believe that military attacks on civilians can ever be justified.[21] Yet, the association of Islam with violence is so omnipresent that artificial intelligence models asked to complete prompts or to create stories about Muslims generate violent narratives 66% of the time.[27] This merely reflects the obsession with Muslim violence in English-language media.

American popular support for the targeting of civilians has provided tacit support for the relentless drone bombing campaign that has resulted in innumerable extrajudicial killings, including that of many innocent civilians as well as American citizens living abroad. As Noam Chomsky put it,

> Remember the worst terrorist campaign in the world by far is the one that's being orchestrated in Washington. That's the global assassination campaign. There's never been a terrorist campaign of that scale... That's exactly what it is. Over large parts of the world, the United States is systematically, publicly, openly... carrying out regular campaigns to assassinate people who the US government suspects of intending to harm it someday... And when you bomb a village in Yemen, say, and you

kill somebody—maybe the person you were aiming at maybe not—and other people who happened to be in the neighbourhood—how do you think they are going to react? They're going to take revenge.[28]

Indeed, the largest gifts to Islamic extremist organizations were the invasions of Afghanistan and Iraq and the drone campaign that killed countless civilians. A quest to combat perceived global injustice, a desire to defend Muslim women and children, and a craving for revenge for killed family members and friends served as motivators for disillusioned Muslims to join their ranks.

Calls for Reform

A common Islamophobic claim is that with so many attacks carried out in the name of Islam, we would be better off without Islam or that Islam is in dire need of reform. It is often alleged that every major religion has undergone reform except for Islam. Underlying this thought is the Orientalist assumption that Muslims are a people stuck in the past, a relic of ancient times, completely impervious to change or modernity. In reality, Islam's success has been in the fact that it has always been a living religion. Islam is not the imposition of the past on the present or the Arabian Desert onto the world. Islam has been adapted to a wide range of cultural, geographic, and temporal realities. The diversity of theological, jurisprudential, and sectarian views and their evolution over time has made it impossible for one restrictive ideology to hold a monopoly over the faith. In the absence of a papacy in Islam, there is no role for a Martin Luther to institute a Reformation. Reform Judaism deemphasizes rigid adherence to Jewish rituals and laws. In Muslim society, there is no such formality—people vary in terms of personal devotion and adherence to the law. Some people are obsessive with ritual purity, wake up in the middle of the night to offer supererogatory prayers, and make sure to pay ever last penny of their *khums* and *zakat*; others don't fret "minor" things, sleep through their morning prayers, and never pay their religious dues. Individual Muslims make these decisions without the need for an entire movement in which someone from above dictates what they are to do now.

The argument that wars or violence carried out in the name of something is a fault of that thing and that we would be better off without it or with it reformed or changed so as to no longer be recognizable seems to only resonate on a societal level when talking about Islam. In the name of freedom and democracy, the United States has been involved in over one hundred wars in its two hundred year history. Should we do away with or reform freedom and democracy? Perhaps the answer is yes, but it is hard to imagine how freedom will be reformed such that it can no longer be cited as a pretext for conflict. Similarly, there is no rational way to make verses of the Quran, works of hadith, or books of jurisprudence disappear or to edit out the parts some people don't like as if they are Wikipedia entries. What we can do, however, is openly discuss the meaning and contexts of Quranic verses, the validity of each hadith, the accuracy of juristic rulings, and the active role of *ijtihad* in deciding how Islamic principles are best applied to current issues.

There is also a large disconnect between popular western portrayals of Islam and Muslim impressions of their own religion. The western media appears obsessed with the thought that Muslims who blow themselves up in terrorist attacks are guaranteed seventy-two virgins in paradise. Yet, from the perspective of the vast majority of Muslims, those who terrorize innocent and almost invariably Muslim civilians—we see this all too often with bombs placed in marketplaces and mosques that predominantly kill Muslim women and children—are not martyrs but rather fall into the category of "those who wage war against God and His Prophet and spread evil through the land," whose Quranic punishment is execution, crucifixion, amputation, or exile.[29] A true martyr is one who dies from faith-based persecution, defending his homeland from enemies, or fighting in a war directly ordained by a divinely-appointed prophet or imam (who are simply not present today). In fact, the entire concept of martyrdom has become highly racialized. Asking a Muslim, "Would you die as a martyr?" is hardly different than asking a US Marine, "Would you sacrifice yourself for your country?" Martyrdom being seen as an honor is no different than the respect shown in non-Muslim countries to their war dead. The claim that Muslims only seek martyrdom effectively becomes a justification for the use of force against Muslims. After all, is it really wrong to kill people who actually want to be killed? Yet, we do not think of Patrick Henry, one of the Founding Fathers, as a suicidal maniac for having proclaimed, "Give me liberty, or give me death!"

As for the seventy-two virgins, it is based on a tradition cited by Tirmidhi according to which a martyr will be wed to seventy-two wives from among the *houris*.[30] This is neither newsworthy nor relevant specifically to martyrdom when one considers another hadith in the same collection that says, "The lowest of the people of paradise are those with eighty thousand servants and seventy-two wives."[31] Indeed, the tradition has done more to mesmerize western imagination than to establish Islamic precepts. If anything, western media has turned itself into an advertisement tool for militant extremists. A Muslim child growing up in the west on a steady diet of television, radio, and social media will imagine that terrorism is what Islam preaches since it is the most consistent message he hears.

In terms of violence and martyrdom, there are two basic lines of attack on Islam, one from the Christian and one from the atheist. The Christian attack on Islam tends to boil down to rhetorical claims that Christianity is a religion of peace and love, whereas Islam is a religion of war and hate. This will be addressed in the next chapter. The atheist, conversely, sees religion as a fundamentally troublesome entity that only leads to conflict and war. Indeed, many wars have been fought in the name of religion, but the decline of religion has not ended war. This is most evident in Europe, where it became unfashionable to fight wars in the name of religion, so instead they were fought in the name of nationalism by citing any number of grievances or festering border disputes. Religion gave way to fascism that ushered in some of the largest religious and ethnic genocides seen in human history. Communism, as godless as it gets, led to horrific loss of life in Russia, China, and throughout much of the world. After World War II, liberal democracies have been engaged in forever-wars in every corner of the planet. In this context, Islam as a cause of war is hardly a blip on the radar.

The Rise of Modern Islamic Extremism

The rise of Islamic extremism of the nature that is often fretted over in the west today is rooted in the Cold War. Prior to the Soviet invasion of Afghanistan, there were violent uprisings based on Islamist ideologies, but these were typically in the form of local anti-colonial movements such the Mahdist Uprising in Sudan. There was no globalized militancy among Muslims, and even efforts to recruit Muslims to join the causes in Palestine and Kashmir were rather unsuccessful.[32]

To counter the communists, the United States overtly and covertly promoted, trained, and armed transnational Muslim militants to fight in Afghanistan. A radical Islamic revival was seen as a firewall against further Soviet expansion. A narrative was pushed that Muslims have a religious obligation to fight infidels on Muslim soil and that militants carrying out such missions are the truest of Muslims. These anti-Soviet militants were actively cheered on by the west. Countries like Saudi Arabia were happy to send off their disgruntled youth to die in Afghanistan,[33] but there was little forethought as to what this would engender when that conflict would someday be over.

After the Soviet withdrawal, these militants saw nothing but American military bases in Saudi Arabia, a prolonged occupation of the West Bank and Gaza, and political leadership of Muslim-majority countries in the hands of corrupt and oppressive tyrants propped up by the west. That they would seek new targets for their militancy is hardly shocking. Nor can it be surprising that the clandestine systems of financing and arming these entities would persist after the initial Soviet and subsequent American withdrawals from Afghanistan.

In more recent times, one can readily see how western military interventions create extremist entities such as Daesh (ISIS), which arose from the ashes of the western devastation of Iraq. A country that was upended by two invasions led by the United States and an intervening genocidal United Nations sanctions regime became ripe for extremist violent ideologies.

That western military intervention leads to increased extremism is also evident in how in 2001 Al-Qaeda was holed up in Tora Bora, but after the wars in Afghanistan and Iraq, their offshoots spread like wildfire and continue to wreak havoc on regions spanning from Central Asia to the Sahel. In the breakdown of social order that follows the devastations of war, the most violent elements of society become its most prominent ones. The solution to Islamic extremism is not reforming Islam but rather de-escalating the cycles of violence that drive extremism. Without the Soviet takeover of Afghanistan, the American invasions of Iraq and Afghanistan, an indefinite Israeli occupation of Palestinian territories, and fanning the flames of civil war in Libya, Syria, and Yemen, there hardly would be terrorism within the Muslim world.

One would assume that the United States would have learned that it is best not to arm extremist groups, but instead it repeatedly falls for "the enemy of my enemy is my friend" trap. Some reports indicate that in 2012, the US Ambassador to Libya was killed in Benghazi while he was trying to help purchase weapons and recruit fighters for terrorist groups operating in Syria. According to an article in *Socio-Political-Journal*,

> Ambassador [John Christopher] Stevens himself played a central role in recruiting jihadists to fight Assad's regime in Syria, according to Egyptian and other Middle Eastern security officials. Stevens served as a key contact with the Saudis to coordinate the recruitment by Saudi Arabia of Islamic fighters from North Africa and Libya.

The jihadists were sent to Syria via Turkey to attack Assad's forces, said the security officials.[34]

According to an article written in the *Washington Times* by syndicated columnist Andrew Napolitano, "What I saw has persuaded me beyond a reasonable doubt and to a moral certainty that Mrs. [Hillary] Clinton provided material assistance to terrorists and lied to Congress... Some of the groups that received the arms were on the US terror list."[35]

Finally, it cannot go unmentioned that even secular laws of war do allow for self-defense. Yet, when Muslims in occupied and colonized countries fight back in their own lands, it is seen as illegitimate acts of terror, not legitimate acts of defense. This has become more plainly evident as the right of Ukrainians to arm themselves, to make Molotov cocktails, and to use anti-tank and anti-aircraft weaponry against Russian occupying forces has been widely hailed in the west, whereas any protestation by Palestinians of their decades-long occupation is seen as terrorism, even if it constitutes something as trivial as throwing a pebble.

At the end, for something to be moral, it ought to be universalizable. If the occupation of Iraq by the United States is moral on the basis that Iraq allegedly had weapons of mass destruction, then so would be the occupation of the United States by Iraq on the basis that it has weapons of mass destruction. If the blockade of Gaza is moral, then so would be a blockade of Israel. The fact that these scenarios seem unthinkable is reflective of the extent to which certain types of aggression have been completely normalized when carried out by western nations and their allies. In the Global South, however, such hypocrisy is rather evident and fuels resentment. A brighter future is not one in which we accept extremist terrorism or state brutality, but rather one in which we use the same standards that we use against extremist violence to denounce all forms of violence and hegemony.

Chapter 3

Is Islam a Religion of Peace or War?

It is common to hear Christianity painted as a religion of love and peace, while Islam is portrayed as a religion of hate and war. Christian Islamophobes often point to Jesus (AS) not having fought in any wars as opposed to Muhammad (S) who engaged in numerous battles. They take Quranic verses, typically truncated and completely out of context, as proof of Islam's innate violence. This sort of reasoning sits well with a western audience that feels that they are a peaceful and loving people, even when they are citizens of democratic nations that are at constant war and even when they personally vote for political parties that spew hate.

Quranic Verses Enjoining War

Verses of the Quran pertaining to war can be broken down into a few categories. First are those that tell Muslims to fight back against those who attack them, such as, "Fight in the way of God those who fight against you."[1] Second, there are verses that encourage Muslims to join the fight when the outbreak of war is imminent, such as "O Prophet! Urge the believers to war."[2] Third, there are those that urge victory during war. Perhaps the most commonly cited one in this category is, "Slay the idolaters wherever you find them and take them as captives and besiege them and lie in wait for them in every place of ambush."[3] Although this might seem harsh, it is basically how war is fought—you kill, capture, besiege, or ambush an enemy.

A similar verse often quoted by Islamophobes reads, "slay them wherever you find them."[4] This phrase makes for a great soundbite, as it is made to appear that Muslims are being ordered to kill nonbelievers every chance they get. The only problem is that, in its Quranic context, the verse reads very differently: "Fight in the way of God those who fight against you but do not transgress; verily, God does not love the transgressors. And slay them wherever you find them and expel them from whence they expelled you."[5] The next verse adds, "And if they cease [hostilities], God is Forgiving, Merciful."[6] As such, this is not a blanket command to ceaseless violence against disbelievers, but rather an exhortation to fight in self-defense against those who have started hostilities, with the caveats that Muslims are not to escalate the conflict by transgressing the level of violence shown by the enemy and that they must cease hostilities as soon as the enemy desists. Even the aforementioned verse, "slay the idolaters wherever you find them," starts with, "So when the sacred months have passed, slay the idolaters..." showing that the verse pertains to one specific conflict, as those sacred months passed some fourteen centuries ago.

Avoiding escalation is an extremely central concept in Islam's approach to warfare, as it constitutes the slippery slope to ever-more-savage cycles of violence. The attacks of September 11, as condemnable as they were, led to two countries being invaded in retaliation for two buildings being destroyed. According to the Quran, there is no place for this type of escalation in a civilized world. Indeed, the entire concept of *qisas*—often thought of as "an eye for an eye"—is about not escalating but rather tempering any desire for revenge. The Quranic concept of *qisas* goes even further, "Yet whoever forgoes [retaliation] out of charity, that shall be an expiation [of sin] for him."[7] According to the Quran, forgiveness is best, non-escalatory retaliation is acceptable, and escalation is forbidden.

Another Quranic verse that is often quoted by Islamophobes reads, "So kill the leaders of disbelief."[8] This is similarly taken out of context. The entire verse reads, "And if they break their oaths [of peace] with you after their [peace] treaty [with you] and attack you for your religion, then fight the leaders of disbelief, as indeed, their oaths are nothing to them; so that they might desist." The verse is not a blanket order to fight or kill all non-Muslim leaders, as is often alleged, but rather a command to fight against those who have broken their peace treaties with Muslims and who have come out to fight Muslims because of their faith, and to do so only until they desist from hostilities. Furthermore, it is not their beliefs but rather their military aggression that is the reason for war. It should be mentioned here that the verbs for "to kill" and "to fight" are the same in Arabic, which is why the truncated version of the verse is typically translated as "kill the leaders of disbelief" to further dramatize things.

Perhaps the verse most commonly used to claim that Islam is a proponent of never-ending wars is, "Fight them until there is no more *fitna* (persecution, oppression, discord) and religion is entirely for God."[9] This is often presented as a command for Muslims to fight until there is no religion but Islam. Yet, in classical Islamic literature, this verse is not taken in the way that Islamic extremists and Islamophobes understand it. *Sahih Bukhari*, the leading Sunni work of hadith, addresses this verse by saying, "Islam used to be weak; a man would be persecuted, killed, or tortured for his religion. Later, Islam became more powerful and the *fitna* (persecution) ceased."[10] It also clarifies that "this [verse] does not pertain to your fighting for the sake of power."[11] Clearly, the verse is understood to enjoin Muslims to combat religious persecution but not to continue warring when the persecution ceases. Shia traditions regarding this verse, conversely, take it to refer to apocalyptic events at the end of time, not to the beginning of Islam or to current times. Hence, "the time for this verse has not yet arrived."[12]

There seems to be endless debate over whether Islam is a religion of peace or of war, with many Muslims pointing out that "Islam," as a word, simply means "peace." In reality, these verses capture the essence of war in Islam, which involves fighting against aggression, injustice, and persecution only to the degree that is absolutely necessary and without escalation. As a religion that is meant to be for all times and places, Islam must address both peace and war. As such, Islam is not a pacifist religion in that it does not outlaw war, but it similarly is not a militaristic religion that ordains war as the preferred state of affairs. Martyrs have a special place in Islam, but hadith teach us that "the ink of the scholar is more precious than the blood of the martyr."[13]

Such Islamic precepts can be generalized to outside what is typically seen as the Islamic context. When it comes to combating oppression, there is a role for a warrior like Nelson Mandela, a martyr like John Brown, and a scholar like Frederick Douglass. If someone were to take Islam as a pacifist religion that forbids all acts of war, they'd be incorrect; similarly, anyone who imagines Islam as a particularly war-like religion would be quite misguided. The Quran condones neither pacifism nor militarism, but rather calls for a "moderate" nation that avoids either extreme.[14] Nevertheless, both Islamic extremists and Islamophobes are intent on taking snippets of Quranic verses out of context and turning them into soundbites that equate Islam with perpetual holy wars against infidels, heretics, blasphemers, and hypocrites.

War in the Bible

In the eyes of the Islamophobe, the Quran is the world's quintessential problem. As Boris Johnson, the former British prime minister, put it,

> To any non-Muslim reader of the Koran, Islamophobia—fear of Islam—seems a natural reaction, and, indeed, exactly what that text is intended to provoke... Judged purely on its scripture—to say nothing of what is preached in the mosques—it is the most viciously sectarian of all religions in its heartlessness towards unbelievers.[15]

I somehow doubt that Boris Johnson has read the Quran, and if he has, he just skimmed it for verses that would support his foregone conclusions. The American Southern Baptist televangelist Jerry Falwell demonstrates a similar suspense of reality when he said,

> Muhammad was a terrorist. I read enough of the history of his life written by both Muslims and non-Muslims [to know] that he was a violent man, a man of war. In my opinion... Jesus set the example for love, as did Moses. And I think that Muhammad set an opposite example.[16]

As for these Christians who claim theirs is a religion of peace, the Bible states otherwise:

> In the cities of the nations the Lord your God is giving you as an inheritance, do not leave alive anything that breathes. Completely destroy them—the Hittites, Amorites, Canaanites, Perizzites, Hivites and Jebusites—as the Lord your God has commanded you. Otherwise, they will teach you to follow all the detestable things they do in worshiping their gods, and you will sin against the Lord your God.[17]

Similarly, the Lord ordered, "Now go, attack the Amalekites and totally destroy all that belongs to them. Do not spare them; put to death men and women, children and infants, cattle and sheep, camels and donkeys."[18] These are a quite extreme forms of religious genocide, as even the animals are to be slaughtered. In all fairness, other vanquished groups were to be treated more leniently: "When the Lord your God delivers it into your hand, put to the sword all the men in it. As for the women, the children, the livestock and everything else in the city, you may take these as plunder for yourselves."[19] As for Babylon, "Happy is the one who seizes your infants and dashes them against the rocks."[20] Just imagine what the Islamophobes would say if the Quran had a verse suggesting that suckling infants should be yanked from their mothers' bosoms and smashed against rocks. Indeed, there is not one verse of the Quran that calls for killing innocent civilians, women, children, or even enemy combatants who are captured in war.

The end of times, when Christianity manifests in its full glory, isn't exactly a very welcoming time for non-Christians: "But the cowardly, the unbelieving, the vile, the murderers, the sexually immoral, those who practice magic arts, the idolaters and all liars—they will be consigned to the fiery lake of burning sulfur."[21] So much for Christian love. Indeed, this is the fate of the vast majority, "for small is the gate and narrow is the road that leads to life, and few will be they who find it."[22]

As for peace, Jesus is quoted as having said, "Do not suppose that I have come to bring peace to the earth. I did not come to bring peace, but a sword. For I have come to turn a man against his father, a daughter against her mother, a daughter-in-law against her mother-in-law—a man's enemies will be the members of his own household."[23] As for hate, Jesus is claimed to have said, "If anyone comes to me and does not hate his own father and mother and wife and children and brothers and sisters, yes, and even his own life, he cannot be my disciple."[24] According to Reza Aslan, the author of *Zealot: The Life and Times of Jesus of Nazareth*, the Romans realized that Jesus was about to lead an armed rebellion to drive them out of Jerusalem so they decided to crucify him.

In response to such biblical quotes, one can anticipate a number of retorts. First, it can be asserted that these are taken out of the greater contexts of the scriptures and the religions as a whole. In that case, the same could be said about the Quranic verses taken out of context. Second, it can be argued that Christians and Jews no longer follow these biblical precepts. If the precept being referred to is war, then one finds countries with Christian and Jewish majorities to be constantly at war. One would also find that their wars carry significant public backing, especially among the most purportedly religious segments of society. Third, if it is argued that current western wars are different because Muslims engage in holy war, then I would point out that western war is never claimed to be unholy. When Bush went to war in Iraq claiming it was the Battle of Gog and Magog, the argument that western wars are somehow not based on religious fanaticism falls flat.[25] Finally, one hears the tiresome refrains of Christians who talk about turning the cheek while they walk around with loaded guns, join the military, and spew hate. If it is argued that these are not true Christians, well, why would anyone assume that terrorists are true Muslims? In all fairness, I do not believe that Judaism and Christianity are any more a religion of peace or war than Islam. However, the widespread belief that the Quran is inherently violent in a way that the Bible is not is simply absurd.

The Problem with Quoting the Quran

The problem with quoting a verse of the Quran to establish an Islamic injunction is that a literal take on a verse is simply not how Muslims are meant to understand the Quran. To understand a Quranic verse, one must take into account whether it is decisive (*muhkam*) or ambiguous (*mutashabih*), whether it is abrogating (*nasikh*) or abrogated (*mansukh*), whether it is general (*'amm*) or particular (*khass*), and whether it enjoins (*amr*) or forbids (*nahy*). To know this, one needs quite a bit of understanding of the circumstances of revelation (*asbab al-nuzul*) of each verse to know which specific individuals and circumstances a verse pertains to. To complicate things further, some Muslim sects contend that the Quran has an exoteric (*zahir*) and an esoteric (*batin*) meaning.

Verses enjoining war for the Prophet's (S) companions are meant for wartime during his life; verses enjoining peace are meant for times of peace. To take verses pertaining to a specific war and generalize them to include peacetime would be doing gross injustice. This is not some sort of modern, moderate, or washed-down understanding of Quranic interpretation; this is how traditional Muslim understanding of the Quran has been for centuries. That verses of the Quran are not to be taken literally is apparent to even a novice; otherwise, one must imagine that Moses (AS) and the Pharaoh spoke in Arabic. Indeed, the Quran warns Muslims against the dangers of taking its verses literally:

> In it are decisive (*muhkam*) verses, they are the principle [verses] of the Book, while other [verses] are ambiguous (*mutashabih*). As for those in whose hearts there is perversity, they follow the part of it that is ambiguous, seeking to cause discord (*fitna*) and seeking to give it [their own] interpretation.[26]

Based on this verse, someone who wants to take the Quran literally would literally have to not do so. Furthermore, Muslims have never advocated reaching juristic verdicts based on taking Quranic verses at face value. If that were the case, the verse, "When you come out of *ihram* (i.e., finish your *hajj* and *umra* rituals), then hunt,"[27] would mean that Muslims are obligated to go hunting after their pilgrimage to Mecca. In reality, the verse is lifting the prohibition on hunting that remains in place during the pilgrimage. Moreover, in the following verse, what appears like permission to walk between Safa and Marwa during the pilgrimage is widely accepted as a mandate: "Safa and Marwa (two hills near the Kaaba) are among the symbols of God; so whoever performs *hajj* or *umra* pilgrimages to the House, there is no fault with him if he walks back-and-forth between them."[28] At face value, this verse seems to say that it is merely permissible to walk between Safa and Marwa, but in reality the verse is enacting an absolute mandate to do so. The verse is not addressed to today's Muslims, but to the Prophet's (S) companions who were concerned about whether Muslims can walk between the two hills in light of their pre-Islamic tribal traditions. Without a comprehensive knowledge of jurisprudence and the ḥadith explaining this verse, the wrong conclusion could be easily reached.

Verses such as "kill them wherever you find them"[29] and "strike [your wives]"[30] cannot be taken as general commands but rather as pertaining to extremely specific situations that are unlikely to arise within one's lifetime. Taking these verses as decisive (*muhkam*) and general (*amm*) as opposed to ambiguous (*mutashabih*) and of limited scope (*khass*) would lead, as the Quran says, to discord (*fitna*). Given the possibility of misinterpretation, the Quran is clear that many miscreants are misled by its verses as opposed to being guided by them.[31] As a rule of thumb, if anyone quotes a verse of the Quran to prove a point, one should seek out the voluminous works of Sunni and Shia Quranic commentary (*tafsir*) to ensure that the verse has been understood and presented in the proper context.

The concept of *sola scriptura* adopted by some Protestant denominations has been squarely rejected by mainstream Muslims who weigh Quranic verses in light of voluminous and often contradictory or unreliable hadith narrations and scholarly interpretation. The complexities involved lead to many permutations of opinions, and this has ensured Islam's rich theological and jurisprudential diversity. It is said that the most decisive (*muhkam*) of the Quran's verses is the verse of ablution (*wudu*), which reads, "When you rise to pray, wash your faces and hands to the elbows and wipe your heads and your feet to the ankles."[32] It is said that there are nearly one hundred distinct ambiguities in this verse,[33] which has led to different *wudu* customs. To claim that any specific verse can only be interpreted in one way—the way of the Islamophobes and extremists—is simply absurd. Quranic verses cannot, in any fairness, be used to stereotype Muslims, as there will always be a diversity of opinions vis-à-vis any contentious verse. As pointed out by Sumbul Ali-Karamali, "Many Western non-religionists are equally conditioned to believe that, whereas Jews and Christians contextualize and engage with their texts, Muslims must take every word of their text literally (or else they're 'picking and choosing')."[34]

It is worth noting that Islam is not alone in rejecting the concept of *sola scriptura*. The Catechism of the Catholic Church states that the church "does not derive her certainty about all revealed truths from the holy Scriptures alone. Both Scripture and Tradition must be accepted and honored with equal sentiments of devotion and reverence."[35]

Considering the complexities of contextualizing the meaning and determining the practical implications of Quranic verses, the problems are compounded when dealing with hadith, which are reports of the sayings and deeds of the Prophet (S), his early followers, or members of his family. Aside from contextual analysis, each hadith is subject to scrupulous analysis of its chain of transmission to determine its validity. Hadith is best seen as one person's questionable report. Quoting hadith is similar to quoting a scientific study—it is easy to find conflicting reports and questions of validity and reproducibility are always central.

Nevertheless, one repeatedly sees isolated hadith quoted to prove something about Islam, even though these narrations are subject not only to the types of contextualization required when interpreting Quranic verses but also to questions of authenticity. Hadith were passed down through oral narrations that were recorded in writing decades or centuries later. This has created ample room for errors in transmission and the deliberate invention of fake narratives for political or theological gain. Islamic scholarship focuses heavily on determining the validity of hadith, and only a small handful of *mutawatir* traditions—those that have been narrated through numerous independent chains of transmission—are universally accepted as valid. Books of hadith commonly group together traditions that make opposite claims, and it is understood that it is up to a scholar to make determinations based on expert analysis of conflicting information. That this is an imprecise science—akin to determining historical events based on conflicting reports—is what contributes to the diversity of juristic and theological opinions in Islam.

Why Don't Muslims Love Their Enemies?

In *Tea with Hezbollah: Sitting at the Enemies' Table*, Ted Dekker and Carl Medearis detail their travels through the Middle East.

They had one specific mission in mind—to find out whether people in the Middle East had heard of the parable of the Good Samaritan. He basically set out to ask people out of the blue if they had heard of the parable and if they had not, he would conclude that all the conflicts and enmities in the Middle East are caused by their lack of Christian values. As for the parable, it goes as follows:

> [A man] asked Jesus, "And who is my neighbor [whom I am to love]?" In reply Jesus said: "A man was going down from Jerusalem to Jericho, when he was attacked by robbers. They stripped him of his clothes, beat him and went away, leaving him half dead. A priest happened to be going down the same road, and when he saw the man, he passed by on the other side. So too, a Levite, when he came to the place and saw him, passed by on the other side. But a Samaritan, as he traveled, came where the man was; and when he saw him, he took pity on him. He went to him and bandaged his wounds, pouring on oil and wine. Then he put the man on his own donkey, brought him to an inn and took care of him. The next day he took out two denarii and gave them to the innkeeper. 'Look after him,' he said, 'and when I return, I will reimburse you for any extra expense you may have.' Which of these three do you think was a neighbor to the man who fell into the hands of robbers?" The expert in the law replied, "The one who had mercy on him." Jesus told him, "Go and do likewise."[36]

The moral is that the neighbor one ought to love is the one who shows mercy—that is, in this case, the Samaritan—not one's coreligionists who show no signs of humanity. This parable is particularly meaningful when one considers the enmity that raged between the Jews and the Samaritans at the time. In the context of interfaith cooperation, it highlights that we must value universal moral precepts over nominal group affiliation with people who are devoid of morality.

The authors go on to confront a number of Muslims who don't recognize the parable by name. The authors insinuate that their social problems arise from their lack of understanding of the teachings of Jesus (AS). Of course, they manage to find a Christian Arab to interview also, but they hand-picked a peace activist, so it wasn't too difficult to make him look peaceful in contrast to the Muslims who don't even know of the parable. The conclusion? If only they had Christian values, they wouldn't be so hateful, there wouldn't be so much conflict in the Middle East, and the world would just be a better place. The book joins an endless line of rhetoric that promotes the same stereotype of hateful Muslims devoid of Christian moral values. If only they would accept Jesus (AS) as their lord and savior...

The entire argument falls flat for many reasons. First, the parable speaks of loving a *good* Samaritan, yet it is hard to see how, for example, the Lebanese would find the Israelis or Americans to be "good" Samaritans as opposed to the guys in the parable who beat the man and left him for dead in the first place. Jesus (AS) does not seem to be preaching love for *bad* Samaritans.

Second, the author appears somewhat oblivious to the fact that Christians are perfectly capable of hate. Whereas Muslims universally love and revere Jesus (AS), it takes a stretch of the imagination to see how the Christian nationalists in the United States and Europe love either Muhammad (S) or his followers. Furthermore, the hatred for Muslims and Islam that permeates mainstream western discourse and the hatred that led to disastrous military campaigns in Afghanistan and Iraq somehow seem irrelevant.

Third, the assumption that Muslims lack a universal code of morality that allows them to transcend narrow religious beliefs or mere tribalism is simply misguided. As the Prophet (S) said, "I have been sent to bring perfection to noble qualities."[37] The Quran defines righteousness not as being overly ritualistic but as being charitable, freeing slaves, keeping promises, and being patient through adversity:

Righteousness is not that you turn your faces toward the
east or the west [when praying], but [true] righteousness
is [found in the] one who believes in God, the Last Day,
the angels, the Book, and the prophets and who gives
wealth, out of love for Him, to relatives, orphans, the
needy, the wayfarer, and to those who ask [for help], as
well as for the freeing of slaves; and who establishes
prayer and who gives in charity; and [those who] fulfill
their promise when they make one; and [those who] are
patient in tribulations and adversities and in times of
distress. Those are the ones who have been sincere, and
it is those who are the pious.[38]

Fourth, the Quran admires the good personal qualities of
Muslims and non-Muslims alike: "Among the People of the Book
is he, who if you entrust him with a treasure, will return it to
you."[39] The Quran also acknowledges that though many non-
Muslims are sinners, "among them are people on a just course."[40]
Nor are non-Muslims universally damned: "Surely those who
believe [in Islam] as well as those who are Jews and Sabians and
Christians—as for any who believe in God and the Last Day and
who do good deeds, no fear shall be on them and they shall not
grieve."[41]

Fifth, Islam is not a religion that is hell-bent on angry
revenge. Quite to the contrary, when it comes to retribution for
injuries and death,[42] disagreements that arise during divorce,[43]
and handling distressed loans,[44] the Quran urges putting
forgiveness, kindness, and generosity ahead of demanding one's
maximum personal rights. Even when dealing with those who
hate Muslims, the Quran does not call for violence, but rather for
persevering in justice: "Do not allow a group's hostility towards
you to cause you to deviate from justice."[45] No matter how others
wrong Muslims, it is never to be used as a justification for
Muslims to "transgress."[46]

Finally, Muslims absolutely love Good Samaritans. I am
eternally grateful to people of all faiths and convictions who help
the destitute, who resettle refugees, and who fight for social

justice. I admire peace activists in the United States and Israel, environmentalists who live in trees to save them from being chopped down at the altar of insatiable corporate greed, and healthcare workers who leave their posh western lifestyles to bring medical care to remote parts of Africa, Asia, and Latin America. I have no doubt that there will be a great reward for their devotion to humanity. Muslims all over the world love them while they despise nominally Muslim Daesh terrorists, western-backed despots, and CIA-trained torturers. This is, to me, what following the parable entails.

Comparing Quranic and Biblical References to Violence

Tom Anderson, a software engineer, set out to empirically determine whether terrorism carried out in the name of Islam reflects something inherently and distinctly violent about Islam's holy book as compared to those of other religions. He found that the Bible scored higher for anger and much lower on trust than the Quran. As for violence,

> Killing and destruction are referenced slightly more often in the New Testament (2.8%) than in the Quran (2.1%), but the Old Testament clearly leads—more than twice that of the Quran—in mentions of destruction and killing (5.3%).[47]

Philip Jenkins, a historian at Penn State University, conducted a study analyzing the use of war in the Bible and Quran. He concluded:

> Much to my surprise, the Islamic scriptures in the Quran were actually far less bloody and less violent than those in the Bible... The laws of war that are laid down by the Quran are actually reasonably humane... Then we turn to the Bible, and we actually find something that is for many people a real surprise. There is a specific kind of

warfare laid down in the Bible which we can only call genocide.[48]

Nevertheless, the assumption that Muslims are innately hateful creates narratives such as George W. Bush's assertion that, "They hate our freedoms: our freedom of religion, our freedom of speech, our freedom to vote and assemble and disagree with each other."[49] In reality, most Muslims respect western political freedom and the freedoms of religion and speech. What they hate are wars that cause loss of life and widespread destruction of civilian infrastructure, the needless suffering and starvation of innocent civilians due to brutal economic sanctions, and the aggressive diplomatic and military support western nations provide to autocrats who rule over Muslim-majority nations with iron fists.

The claim that "Muslims hate us for our freedoms" suffers two problems. First, it assumes that Muslim hate America in contrast to everyone else who adores it. Second, the purported reason requires pervasive historical amnesia. When Iranians chanting "death to America" stormed the US embassy in Tehran and took American citizens as hostages, the image that became permanently seared onto the western imagination was that of an angry Muslim mob. It is imagined that the mob is angry by nature; historical causes of anger that would require some soul-searching are ignored. The fact that Iranian attempts at democratization were quashed by a CIA-backed coup that forced an unpopular and brutal despot back onto the throne is beside the point. The humiliating Capitulations Agreements signed by the Shah that caused an uproar among Iranians was seen as irrelevant. Ayatollah Khomeini reflected the popular sentiment regarding these agreements when he said,

> They have reduced the Iranian people to a level lower than that of an American dog. If someone runs over a dog belonging to an American, he will be prosecuted. Even if the shah himself were to run over a dog belonging to an American, he would be prosecuted. But if an American

cook runs over the shah, the head of state, no one will
have the right to interfere with him.[50]

It is also imagined that the revolutionary zeal that took
over Iran epitomizes all Muslims of all times and in all places. An
angry mob has thereby become a timeless and indelible part of
the dehumanizing stereotype of Muslims. Indeed, the stereotype
of Muslims as a people boiling over with perpetual and unabated
rage requires a belief that the west features so prominently in the
daily lives of ordinary Muslims as to preoccupy them in lieu of
more mundane issues like studying for an exam, balancing a
checkbook, quarreling with a spouse, counting the days till the
next episode of a favorite television show, or planning a weekend
get-together with family and friends. It cannot be stressed
enough that the vast majority of Muslims have more important
priorities in life than hating on others.

The attacks on 9/11 further seared the image of Muslim
anger onto the western and particularly the American racialized
mindset. Such attacks were and continue to be seen as occurring
in a historical vacuum, arising merely from the ethnic and
religious background of the perpetrators. What has happened in
the Greater Middle East to evoke such anger is generally ignored.
Forgotten are America's ongoing support for Israeli occupation,
American invasions of Somalia and Iraq, unpopular American
military outposts throughout the Middle East, western backing
for any number of unpopular dictatorships, and UN-imposed
sanctions starving hundreds of thousands of Iraqi children to
death.

My argument is not that terrorist attacks are morally
justified. Rather, aggressive western interventions create
terrorism as a sociological phenomenon. Without these historical
and contemporary aggravations, Islamic extremism and terrorism
targeted at the west would not exist. If the alleged hatred was for
western freedoms as opposed to actions, terrorists would be just
as likely to target Brazil as the United States.

Historical amnesia is a key ingredient to the perpetuation
of racial injustice. In racialized power dynamics, the atrocities of

the past are deemed irrelevant by those wielding power. As such, any negative emotions encountered in marginalized groups are seen in vacuous contexts and hence as innate to those populations. Muslims are seen as hateful, African Americans as resentful, American Indians as resigned, and feminists as angry. It is as if their hate, resentment, resignation, and anger are innate to them, as opposed to being natural reactions to the frustrations they have faced in their struggles for social justice.

Bernard Lewis, in his article in *The Atlantic* titled, "The Roots of Muslim Rage," entertains but readily dismisses as possible causes concerns about western "tyranny and exploitation," colonialism, imperialism, support for dictatorial regimes, support for Israel, two world wars, the Cold War, slavery, and economic systems that have engendered poverty. Instead, he states, "There is something in the religious culture of Islam which inspired, in even the humblest peasant or peddler, a dignity and a courtesy toward others never exceeded and rarely equalled in other civilizations. And yet, in moments of upheaval and disruption, when the deeper passions are stirred, this dignity and courtesy toward others can give way to an explosive mixture of rage and hatred."[51] Thus, Muslim anger is not due to extrinsic circumstances that would make anyone angry but rather due to something intrinsic to the Muslim person.

As with other racialized contexts, when frustrations boil over and "mob" violence breaks out, it is seen as an unruly population that is out of control and that needs to be quashed with force, not as a symptom of a broken and unjust system that has left no effective peaceful recourse. After all, why should blacks be resentful when they were freed over 150 years ago and they can sign up for welfare and enjoy the benefits of affirmative action? That "reasonable" appearing people ask such questions and believe that the solution lies in ever-more militarized policing requires a combination of historical amnesia and present-day myopia.

Even though plenty of non-Muslims resent western colonialism and interventionism, passionately hating the west is a stereotype assigned specifically to Muslims. When non-Muslim "mobs" protest western hegemony and corporate imperialism, they are not seen as hateful; they are merely dismissed as pesty "anti-globalization protesters."

Muslim Hospitality

Postcolonial Muslim grievances, though real, tend to remain on an abstract political level, with the vast majority of Muslims resentful of the harmful acts of western governments and their allies but not resentful of individual westerners. Indeed, people from the west traveling through Muslim countries are far more likely to meet the most hospitable and loving people they have ever encountered rather than to meet any antagonism or hostility. This contrasts with the disdain that those who dress visibly Muslim commonly encounter on the streets of western cities. As such, visitors to Iran who often fear that the nation will live up to its media representations will be shocked to find themselves "traveling through a place where you're invited into strangers' homes, offered free food and drinks, and [where] the taxi drivers refuse to take money from you."[52] Richard Gunderman, an American physician visiting Sudan, a country that spent a good while on the US State Department's list of state sponsors of terrorism, wrote,

> As a visitor from a far-off land and an adherent of another faith, my own experiences in Sudan attested to the importance of hospitality in the Islamic tradition. Even people who were clearly in need went out of their way to make me as their guest feel comfortable, providing their best food and drink and offering their home as a place to stay. I had the sense that my Muslim hosts saw hospitality not as a duty they were required to comply with but as an opportunity to shine at something that they cared deeply about... My experiences in Sudan led me to think that hospitality and generosity are far more characteristic of the Islamic faith than extremism and

terrorism... I do not know much about worldwide terrorist threats and I have no access to government intelligence on same. I do know, however, what real hospitality and generosity look like, and I am very grateful to have received a refresher course through the graciousness of my Sudanese hosts.[53]

Inherent Racism in How the Debate is Posed

Finally, it must be said that the question, "Is Islam a religion of peace?" that provides a popular topic for debates[54-56] is inherently prejudicial because the question itself assumes that Islam ought to be singled out for questioning and placed on trial. The question assumes that acts of terror are innately linked with Islam in a way that they are not with respect to other religions or political ideologies. What is it about Islam that creates events like 9/11? Well, what is it about Hinduism that makes mobs tear down mosques? What is it about Buddhism that makes monks burn down entire villages and drive out their residents? What is it about Christianity that has its adherents repeatedly dragging the world through war, gang raping Bosnian women, and using brutal scorched-earth policies in Vietnam? What is it about Judaism that makes Israel turn Palestinians into second-class citizens and deprive Palestinian refugees of the right to return to their homes? These questions are rarely, if ever, asked because we can somehow in our minds see the conflicts as political, economic, or even ethnic and not innately linked to their adherents' religious faiths. That Islam is somehow seen as deserving to be singled out in this context is due to inherently Islamophobic stereotypes.

Anyone can become his or her own prosecutor, go online and search for fragments of evidence that explains why Islam is guilty as charged. Perhaps a fragment of a verse taken out of context or an obscure tradition hardly anyone has heard of can explain why Muslims are so hateful and violent. Whether they are truly more hateful or violent than anyone else in the same situation is hardly seen as relevant.

In the end, the question boils down to whether it is possible to have peace with Muslims when the Quran and other Islamic texts contain sentence fragments that appear to condone violence. Yet, there are no debates about whether we can have a peaceful planet with Christians, Jews, Europeans, and Americans around given what their sacred texts say and given their long history of violence, warfare, and indeed terrorism. The question of whether we can have a peaceful society with Muslims around is no different than asking whether it is possible to have a crime-free society with blacks around or if we can ever reduce greed with Jews around. Each question carries an innately racist, fundamentally inaccurate, and indeed cringeworthy underlying assumption that is somehow apparent when dealing with groups other than Muslims. The real answer to "Is Islam a religion of peace?" is that the biggest obstacle to peace is not Islam but rather Islamophobia; it is not religion but rather racialized hatred that drives perpetual conflict.

Chapter 4

Why Don't Muslims Condemn Terrorism?

That Muslims do not condemn terrorism against civilians has almost become a cliché in western societies. As Bobby Jindal, the former Republican governor of Louisiana and presidential candidate, put it, "Let's be honest here, Islam has a problem." He further elaborated by saying,

> If Islam does not support what is happening in the name of Islam, then they need to stand up and stop it... Many Islamic leaders argue that these are the acts of a radical few. If they refuse to say this, then they are condoning these acts of barbarism. There is no middle ground.[1]

This line of thinking is problematic for several reasons. First, the basic assumption that Muslims do not condemn terrorism enough is not true. Part of the issue is that you would not know that Muslims are condemning terrorism when their condemnation is not reflected in western media. According to Ontario Consultants on Religious Tolerance, an interfaith organization,

> A common complaint among non-Muslims is that Muslim religious authorities do not condemn terrorist attacks. The complaints often surface in letters to the editors of newspapers, on phone-in radio shows, in Internet mailing lists, forums, etc. A leader of an evangelical Christian para-church group, broadcasting over Sirius Family Net radio, stated that he had done a thorough search on the Internet for a Muslim statement

condemning terrorism, without finding a single item. Actually, there are lots of fatwas and other statements issued which condemn attacks on innocent civilians. Unfortunately, they are largely ignored by newspapers, television news, radio news and other media outlets.[2]

There was near universal condemnation of the 9/11 attacks from across the Muslim world as well as from all major Muslim organizations in the United States. Even the Islamic Republic of Iran, which has been demonized in the west since its revolutionaries seized the US embassy in Tehran, condemned the attack. Iran's president, Mohammad Khatami, declared, "On behalf of the Iranian people and the Islamic Republic, I denounce the terrorist measures, which led to the killing of defenseless people, and I express my deep sorrow and sympathy with the American people." Iranians held a candlelight vigil for the attack's victims.[3] Nevertheless, the chorus of Muslim solidarity against terrorism was drowned out by reports of isolated celebrations in the West Bank. This was despite the fact that *The New York Times* reported that most of the West Bank was quiet and non-celebratory. While, according to the *Times*, some Palestinians expressed a sense of revenge—"Let the Americans know the meaning of death"—this was clearly placed in the context of political realities and not in terms of theological imperative. As a Palestinian plumber put it, "The Americans give the Israelis Apache helicopters to bomb our houses... They give them diplomatic support and intelligence help on how to kill us." A desire for anything that would shake up the intolerable status quo was evident in comments such as, "We don't hate the American people, we just want to solve the problem."[4] Nevertheless, these isolated incidents became equated with widespread Muslim celebration of the 9/11 attacks.

The fact that rumors of Muslims celebrating on 9/11 gained so much traction highlights the reality given to racialized stereotypes. Since Muslims are hateful and hate us, the argument goes, it only makes sense that they would widely celebrate 9/11. These celebrations need not even occur to be perceived as real, as demonstrated by Donald Trump's assertion in a 2015 campaign rally in Birmingham, Alabama that, "Hey, I watched when the World Trade Center came tumbling down. And I watched in Jersey City, New Jersey, where thousands and thousands of people were cheering as that building was coming down. Thousands of people were cheering." When challenged by ABC's George Stephanopoulos, he said, "It was on television. I saw it... It was well covered at the time, George." He went on to tell New Hampshire news network NH1, "If you look at for instance where I said the thousands of Muslims were cheering. It turned out to be true." Yet, there were no televised celebrations of the sort at the time, ABC News was unable to find any footage of such celebrations, and indeed no one has been able to confirm the false rumors.[5] This lack of evidence does little, however, to dispel the myth that American Muslims publicly celebrated 9/11; to western societies it just makes sense that they would celebrate.

Muslims Standing up to Terrorists

The second problem with the claim that Muslims don't condemn terrorism enough is that it overlooks the reality that it is often Muslims who are the ones standing up to terrorists during attacks. If there was mass support for terrorism, one would expect Muslims caught in the crossfire to either join or express sympathy towards the attackers. Yet, this appears never to be the case. To the contrary, when it comes to risking one's life to combat terror, Muslims are often the ones on the front lines. This is evident in Ahmed Merabet, a French policeman of Algerian descent,[6] who bravely confronted the *Charlie Hebdo* attackers, trying to block their escape. They shot him, first in the groin and then in the head, at point blank range.[7] The irony is that he gave his life to support the freedom of the French to insult his religion.

In 2015, members of the Somali group al-Shabaab attacked a bus in Kenya with sixty passengers on board. One of the attackers boarded the bus and demanded that the passengers disembark and form two groups, one comprised of Muslims and the other of non-Muslims. The Muslims on the bus started handing articles of faith, such as hijab, to the non-Muslims to help them pass as Muslim.[8] The Muslims then flatly refused to separate into two groups, demanding the militants "kill them together or leave them alone."[9] Unfortunately, two people were killed, one of whom was shot while trying to escape. Nevertheless, the courage and self-sacrifice of these Muslims saved many lives. That this event is under-reported in the western media and that pretty much no one other than a handful of interfaith activists seem to talk about it is because it does not fit the narrative of tacit Muslim complicity in acts of terrorism.

In Egypt, Muslims chanting the slogan, "We either live together, or we die together," served as human shields to protect the 2011 Coptic Christmas Mass from possible extremist attacks.[10] Much of the tension at that time had stemmed from multiple cases of female Coptic converts to Islam being forcibly returned to their abusive husbands who then made them convert back to Christianity. Ordinary Muslims wanted to do their best to prevent exploitation of these charged events by extremists.

That people who terrorize civilians are not particularly welcomed as part of the Muslim fold is further highlighted by the fact that the Muslim Jama Masjid Trust refused an Islamic burial to the nine militants who participated in the 2008 Mumbai attacks. One of the organization's trustees declared, "People who committed this heinous crime cannot be called Muslim."[11] Needless to say, this was not widely reported.

Collective Guilt

The third problem with the claim that Muslims don't condemn terrorism enough is that it assigns collective guilt only to Muslims, while expecting no one to assign collective guilt when non-Muslim westerners commit deliberate acts of violence targeting civilians. When Robert Lewis Dear shot up a Planned Parenthood in Colorado Springs in 2016, his guilt was not collectively assigned to all Pro-Lifers. Similarly, when Floyd Perkins walked into the conservative Family Research Council in 2013 to gun down people because they opposed gay marriage, there is no expectation that every homosexual ought to condemn his attack.[12] In such cases, it is simply assumed that guilt is confined to the perpetrators.

In 2006, American troops rounded up 11 civilians in the Iraqi town of Ishaqi. Five of the detainees were five years old or younger and another four were women, one of whom was 74 years old. The soldiers handcuffed them, and then proceeded to shoot them execution-style in the head. The US government did its best to cover up the incident. Eventually, WikiLeaks released diplomatic cables in which Philip Alston, United Nations special rapporteur on Extrajudicial, Summary, or Arbitrary Executions, raised concerns about the incident.[13] For his role in such leaks, the US has been actively trying to extradite WikiLeaks founder Julian Assange to the United States, where there is ample concern he could face the death penalty.[14]

Whereas Muslims are criticized for not constantly apologizing for attacks in which they played no role, there is no expectation that every American ought to apologize for such a heart-wrenching terrorist act. Indeed, one cannot ignore the contrast between how Muslims line up to apologize for terrorist attacks perpetrated by self-proclaimed Muslims, whereas the US government routinely covers up and denies sadistic acts carried out by its uniformed soldiers. In fact, perpetrators of the Ishaqi massacre were "cleared" of all "misconduct" by the U.S. military.[15]

In the Haditha massacre, US Marines killed 24 unarmed civilians. A taxi driver and four students were ordered out of the car and shot dead in the street. The troops then went door to door into civilian homes, killing nineteen people in three adjacent homes. The Marine Corps quickly blamed the incident on Muslim terrorists. They alleged that a terrorist bomb killed fifteen civilians, after which eight insurgents were killed by brave Marines. A statement by the US military said,

A US marine and 15 civilians were killed yesterday from the blast of a roadside bomb in Haditha. Immediately following the bombing, gunmen attacked the convoy with small arms fire. Iraqi army soldiers and marines returned fire, killing eight insurgents and wounding another.[16]

Needless to say, there was no meaningful judicial process, and not a single perpetrator was imprisoned. These are but two of the hundreds of examples of war crimes, extrajudicial executions, and rapes carried out by western forces in Iraq, Afghanistan, and elsewhere. The purpose of highlighting such atrocities is to point out that it is somehow seen as rational to assign communal blame to all Muslims for savage acts carried out by a select few, whereas there is no sense of communal blame when it comes to atrocities carried out by westerners. Furthermore, while Muslims do not cover up atrocities committed by extremists, there is a huge coverup of the brutalities committed by western "heroes" who are supposedly fighting to spread freedom. The concept of communal blame is central to racialization; any crime committed by a member of a racialized group can be ascribed to a fundamental flaw of the entire group, whereas any crime committed by a member of a dominant group is seen, at most, as an error or fluke.

In contrast to the American government doing its utmost to cover up crimes against humanity committed by its troops, Muslims have actively exposed possible threats arising from within their populations. The father of Umar Farouk Abdulmutallab, commonly known as the "Underwear Bomber," contacted the US Embassy prior to the attack to warn them of the potential danger his son might pose.[17] When Craig Monteilh, an undercover FBI agent, tried to recruit congregants in an Orange County mosque to Islamic extremism, the mosque obtained a restraining order against him and informed the FBI.[18] Abdelhamid Abaaoud, the Belgian-Moroccan terrorist who organized the November 2015 Paris attacks was caught thanks to a call to the police by a Muslim woman whose identity has been revealed only as "Sonia."[19] In all these instances, the Muslims feel no affinity towards terrorism and do their utmost to foil terrorist plots.

The Dangers of Communal Blame

The fourth problem with the claim that Muslims don't condemn terrorism enough lies in the dangers of accepting the concept of communal blame. On the one hand, communal blame stigmatizes all Muslims within western societies, contributing to their marginalization. On the other hand, it serves as a boon for extremist groups like Al-Qaeda who thrive off casting blame for the political and military atrocities of western nations collectively onto all westerners, thus justifying their use of violence against civilian targets. This same ill-logic is seen among non-Muslim extremists also. When Dylann Roof, a white supremacist terrorist, murdered nine African Americans who were peacefully worshiping at the Emmanuel AME Church in Charleston, South Carolina, he justified his attack through assigning collective guilt to all blacks. He claimed, "I have to do it... You rape our women and you're taking over our country, and you have to go."[20]

In Italy, Pamela Mastropietro, an 18-year-old heroin addict, was stabbed to death one day after she chose to leave an inpatient drug rehabilitation program, where she had been admitted for months.[21] The assailant was Innocent Oseghale, a Nigerian who, having been refused asylum, turned to drug dealing. The killing of a white woman by a black "illegal" man became the Italian version of Willie Horton, exploited by right-wing politicians to pander for votes. In response to the outrage surrounding the homicide, a neo-Nazi fascist named Luca Traini went on a shooting spree in which he shot six African immigrants who had nothing to do with the crime. Traini was a former local candidate for Matteo Salvini's Northern League political party, which is notorious for promoting hate speech targeting minorities. This highlights how inflammatory statements by politicians fuel racist violence.[22]

On a larger scale, communal blame justifies grotesque responses that devastate civilian populations. This is evident in the repeat attacks on Gaza that entail widespread destruction of civilian infrastructure—houses, kindergartens, and hospitals—in response to rocket attacks carried out by very specific entities such as Palestinian Islamic Jihad. Extensive devastation of civilian targets was similarly unleashed against Falluja in response to four Americans being killed in the city. The use of white phosphorus, a highly controversial incendiary chemical weapon, against a civilian population hardly received attention in the United States.[23] Historically, the Nazis carried out a devastating pogrom known as *Kristallnacht* (The Night of Broken Glass) in response to a 17-year-old Polish Jew assassinating a German diplomat in Paris. Within hours, hundreds of German synagogues were demolished, thousands of Jewish businesses were ransacked, and tens of thousands of innocent Jewish men were sent to concentration camps. These examples highlight why it is imperative to have a zero-tolerance policy towards communal blame.

Only Western Lives Matter

The fifth problem with the claim that Muslims don't condemn terrorism enough is that it effectively implies that only western lives matter. Muslims are perceived as the sole perpetrators and westerners as the sole victims of terrorism. The reality is that Muslims constitute the number one victim of extremist Islamic terrorism worldwide. Indeed, the prime targets of extremist Islamic groups are Muslim civilian populations and Muslims who do not agree with their politico-religious views.[24] In this context, to blame Muslims and Islam for terrorism is simply victim-blaming; and to construe "Islamic" terrorism as something carried out by Muslims that primarily targets "infidels" is simply ludicrous.

In effect, terrorism only seems to matter if the victims are western or non-Muslim. This is evident when one looks at the vociferous reaction to the November 2015 attacks in Paris as compared to the muted response to the deadly attacks carried out just a day earlier in Beirut. Everyone across the globe rushed to drape their Facebook pages with French flags, whereas it is hard to tell if anyone in the west really cared about the Lebanese civilians who had just been ruthlessly massacred. To expect Muslims worldwide to come out to condemn deaths in France while the French hardly seem concerned about the plight of civilians in their former colonies is a symptom of the reality that only white lives matter. Meanwhile, when "third world" citizens die due to western military intervention, it is dismissed as unfortunate but inevitable "collateral damage," akin to ants inevitably getting crushed when one goes gardening.

Considering the interconnected world we live in, the reality is that westerners won't be able to live in security until there is universal respect for the right of every civilian anywhere on earth to live in peace. This became clear in light of the refugee crises that unfolded after the NATO military intervention in Libya and western support for rebels in Syria. The resulting instability in these two countries resulted in the destabilization of Europe in terms of surging ethnonationalism and xenophobia, a drastic rise in despotism and the erosion of democratic safeguards in countries like Hungary and Poland, the breakup of the European Union in the wake of Brexit, and the increased popularity of politicians who offer nothing but hateful rhetoric as a recipe for their nations' problems. Whether the lesson was learned remains to be seen, but it is evident that safety and security in Europe is dependent on the security of Muslim-majority nations in the Middle East and North Africa. Similarly, if the United States is serious about not having "refugee caravans" from Central America, they need to invest heavily in the stability and prosperity of the region. We will all be much better served by choosing collective security over collective guilt.

Why Are Minorities such a Problem?

The final problem with the claim that Muslims don't condemn terrorism enough is that it perpetuates the narrative that minority groups invariably constitute a "problem" for society. The eminent scholar and sociologist W. E. B. Du Bois explained it as such:

> All, nevertheless, flutter round it. They approach me in a half-hesitant sort of way, eye me curiously or compassionately, and then, instead of saying directly, How does it feel to be a problem? they say, I know an excellent colored man in my town; or, I fought at Mechanicsville; or, Do not these Southern outrages make your blood boil? At these I smile, or am interested, or reduce the boiling to a simmer, as the occasion may require. To the real question, How does it feel to be a problem? I answer seldom a word. And yet, being a problem is a strange experience, — peculiar even for one who has never been anything else...[25]

> It was a phase of this problem that caused the Civil War... All nevertheless knew, as we know, that the question of Negro slavery was the real cause of the conflict... Peremptory military commands this way and that, could not answer the query; the Emancipation Proclamation seemed but to broaden and intensify the difficulties; and the War Amendments made the Negro problems of to-day.[26]

Du Bois describes blacks as being seen as a problem in America when, in reality, the problem is not them but rather the racist structure of American society—a constitution that enshrined chattel slavery, an effective white national consensus that turned the hope of Reconstruction into the despair of Jim Crow, and the denial of racial equality to this day. Yet, African Americans continue to be seen as a societal problem, as unruly troublemakers.

Similarly, it is not Islam and Muslims that are the problem. The problem is two centuries of colonialism that ensured prosperity for the Global North and destitution for Global South, a postcolonial political order that has perpetuated conflict in previously colonized societies, a neoliberal economy that has exacerbated income disparity, and military adventurism that has perpetuated insecurity and violence.

That Muslims are seen as a problem is phrased neither hesitantly nor indirectly as described by Du Bois. Donald Trump quite bluntly proclaimed, "We have a problem in this country, it's called Muslims."[27] Louisiana's former governor Bobby Jindal, a Hindu-turned-evangelical who has pandered to the far-right by brandishing his Islamophobic credentials, said, "Let's be honest here, Islam has a problem."[28] Boris Johnson believes that the solution to the Muslim problem requires "disposing of the first taboo, and accepting that the problem is Islam. Islam is the problem."[29] He also explains that, "to any non-Muslim reader of the Quran, Islamophobia—fear of Islam—seems a natural reaction."[30] As always, the problem is not bigotry but its victim. To the Nazis, Jews are the problem; to the KKK, blacks are the problem; to the Know Nothings, Catholics are the problem; to the white settler, Native Americans are the problem; and to the Islamophobe, Muslims are the problem.

The problem with stereotypes is that they easily become self-fulfilling prophecies. When women were barred from higher education because they were deemed to lack the required mental faculties, there were no educated women to be found; the fact that there were no educated women only reinforced the belief that women were not intelligent enough to be educated. The stereotype of the black criminal leads to discrimination in employment, which results in increased poverty, which in turn contributes to crime. Furthermore, the stereotype ensures that they are far more likely to be arrested for and convicted of minor offenses; the higher conviction rate only serves to reinforce the initial belief that they are more prone to crime. Similarly, Muslims facing marginalization because they are collectively treated like potential terrorists only contributes to radicalization and extremism.

For a sensible way forward, we need a universal expectation of transparency when civilians are targeted regardless of the perpetrator; we need a media that aggressively investigates and provides equal coverage to such atrocities regardless of the national, ethnoracial, or religious identities of the perpetrators and victims; we need equally broad condemnation of attacks against civilians, be they Afghan, American, French, Iraqi, or Lebanese; and we need a recognition that no people or faiths or cultures are a particular problem, but rather the problem is to be found in faulty sociopolitical structures and in self-fulfilling racist narratives.

Chapter 5

Racial Profiling of Muslims

A 2014 Zogby poll found that 42% of Americans believe that law enforcement is justified in using racial profiling to target Muslim Americans and Arab Americans.[1] The post-9/11 "see-something, say-something" mindset cast every American into the role of a potential racial profiler in the War on Terror. As such, when four friends—two Bangladeshis, one Arab, and one Indian Sikh—were traveling together on an American Airlines flight from Toronto to New York in 2016, they were forced off the plane because their presence made the crew feel uncomfortable. They were asked to "just be peaceful," as if there was any reason to believe they wouldn't be. As the four victims were removed from the plane, passengers clutched their children as they hurled racist slurs at the men.[2]

In the same year, Khairuldeen Makhzoomi, a senior at the University of California Berkeley, was kicked off a flight because one of the passengers overhead him speaking Arabic on his cell phone. He was calling his uncle to tell him about an event he had attended that included a speech by United Nations Secretary General Ban Ki-Moon.[3] In 2019, American Airlines cancelled a flight because the "crew didn't feel comfortable" flying with two Muslim men on board. One of them, apparently, had been heard flushing the toilet twice, an act that could only be perceived as constituting a mortal threat to an airplane when carried out by a Muslim-appearing man.[4] Such incidents became so common that they became referred to as "flying while brown."[5]

Incidents like these are not limited to flying. In 2018, a Muslim man was kicked off a Greyhound bus traveling from

Michigan to Ohio for speaking Arabic on his cell phone.[6] In a separate incident, a Punjabi Sikh refugee in Texas was forcibly held down by passengers until fifteen police officers arrived with their guns drawn. They dragged him off the bus, ripped off his turban, and detained him. The alleged crime was that one of the passengers claimed to have overheard him talking about bombs in Arabic. In reality, he was speaking in Punjabi to a Pakistani man who happened to be on the same bus. As he put it, "The only crime I committed was wearing a turban, having a beard, and speaking in a different language to another brown man on a bus."[7] To imagine that everyone who "looks" Muslim speaks Arabic and that anyone speaking Arabic would only be plotting terrorist attacks is how Islamophobic stereotypes play out in the real world.

This is exactly why racial profiling has no place in combating extremist terrorism. It puts the "comfort" of racists ahead of the civil liberties of racialized communities. In many instances, the victims of racism are further victimized by representatives of the transportation industry and/or law enforcement. Excluding Muslims from transportation to provide an illusion of comfort and security to other passengers is equivalent to how blacks were excluded from restaurants, theaters, and swimming pools to make white patrons feel more comfortable. Excluding and discriminating against minorities is not the path to a safe society. Indeed, we have no duty to make racists feel comfortable and secure by pandering to their bigotry.

Racial profiling has no tangible societal benefits. Its best example is "driving while black," which results in the needless death of innocent and unarmed African American men and women, leads to what should be illegal searches of a disproportionately black and brown population based on mere hunches, and creates an endless supply of arbitrarily selected minorities to feed the prison-industrial complex.

In any case, racial profiling of Muslims won't help address terrorism because Muslims do not constitute one race that fits the "Muslim" stereotype. Among American Muslims, 30% describe themselves as white, 23% as black, 21% as Asian,

6% as Hispanic, and 19% as other or mixed race.[8] This hardly lends itself to stereotyping based on physical appearance. I myself, the son of a Chinese American convert and an Iranian American father of mixed Persian, Turkish, and Mizrahi ethnicities, don't exactly stand out as a stereotypical "Muslim." Furthermore, converts to Islam are considerably overrepresented in the exceedingly small portion of Muslims who are drawn to extremism and terrorism.[9] In the United States, 28% of Muslims charged with terrorism-related crimes are converts.[10] These converts would phenotypically and linguistically blend in with non-Muslim members of society and hence not stand out as stereotypically Muslim.

Racial profiling also leads to targeting of the wrong groups. This is why Sikhs are so often held up at airports, whereas white Danes face little scrutiny when they travel to join Daesh (ISIS) in Syria. Even targeting the most stereotypical of Muslims—the Arab—misses the reality that many Arabs are not Muslim. It is worth noting in this context that Christian Zionists in the United States seem to completely overlook the fact that Arab Christians constitute a sizeable portion of the Palestinian population. In Israel, Christians have gone from constituting 21% of the Arab population to 2% of the Israeli population now, in what Georgetown University's Reverend Drew Christiansen dubbed "a quiet ethnic cleansing."[11] To this day, Christians who have been able to remain in Jerusalem are subject to spitting attacks, verbal abuse, and acts of vandalism carried out by hardline Jews.[12,13] The Christian right empathizes more with the ethnic policies of the Israeli right than the plight of Christian Palestinians.

Marginalizing, tormenting, and criminalizing ethnic minority groups will only drive disenchanted Muslim youth into the open arms of extremists who tell them that westerners are the enemy of Islam and Muslims. It is not shocking that some African Americans were drawn to Elijah Muhammad's message that whites are the "devil;"[14] in the experience of American blacks, this was hardly far from the truth. To formally condone racist law enforcement tactics only feeds resentment and makes the hateful speech of extremists all the more appealing. Racial profiling also antagonizes the very Muslim citizenry whose cooperation is most needed in combating Islamic extremism and terrorism. As discussed in the previous chapter, Muslims are often the ones who turn in terrorists.

Accepting racial profiling also opens the door to far-right political groups who offer empty solutions based on increased discrimination and securitization without offering any genuine solutions to socioeconomic or sociopolitical challenges. It is not surprising that a peddler of snake oils like Donald Trump was an outspoken advocate for the racial profiling of Muslims. He believed that profiling Muslims made "common sense;"[15] he advocated for the effective creation of a Muslim registry;[16] he called for a "total and complete shutdown of Muslims entering" the United States;[17] and he repeatedly gloated about the dubious story of General John Pershing gunning down Filipino Muslims with bullets dipped in pigs' blood.[18] In an interview with CBS, he said, "Profiling is something we're going to have to start thinking about as a country."[19] His call for a Muslim registry ignored the fact that the Bush administration had tried this previously through its NSEERS program, which created bureaucratic nightmares for countless Muslims and tore apart numerous families without catching a single terrorist.[20]

In fact, Trump has had a long personal history of supporting racialized state brutality. In 1989, when a 28-year-old white woman was assaulted and raped while jogging in New York's Central Park, four black and one Hispanic teenagers were convicted and imprisoned based on forced confessions. Trump placed a half-page ad in *The New York Times* which said, "BRING BACK THE DEATH PENALTY. BRING BACK OUR POLICE!... Criminals must be told that their CIVIL LIBERTIES END WHEN AN ATTACK ON OUR SAFETY BEGINS!" In 2002, another convicted rapist serving a life sentence admitted to the crime and DNA evidence exonerated the five convicted teenagers.[21] Nevertheless, as late as 2019, Trump remained insistent that New York should have executed these five innocent boys since they had "admitted their guilt."[22]

The only thing these men were guilty of was carrying the presumed guilt inherent in being black or brown, a racialized "original sin" that can never be atoned for or repented from. Racial profiling is the antithesis of principles such as "liberty and justice for all" and "innocent until proven guilty." Racial profiling merely creates illusions of the exact problems it purports to solve—instead of reducing crime, it creates fake criminals; instead of reducing terrorism, it creates faux terrorists.

Manufacturing Terrorists

When one considers the bloated post-9/11 homeland security and antiterrorism budgets, the security apparatus felt pressured to show results. As such, they wiretapped phones, surveilled mosques, spied on halal restaurants, and detained countless Muslims on mere suspicion. What do you do when you are tasked with catching terrorists but cannot find any? You resort to creating them.

It is worth noting that catching fake terrorists is hardly an American prerogative. In Colombia's "false-positives scandal," the American-backed and trained army found it was quite difficult and risky to kill actual "terrorist" rebels. Instead, they either kidnapped innocent teenagers (over 6,400 of them[23]) from urban slums or lured them with promises of work. They would then take them out to the jungle where they would be gunned down. These "brave" soldiers would then collect the $500-a-head bounty the government paid out for hunting terrorists.[24] The government would present the shot-up corpses to the public as shining examples of its glorious successes in the war against narco-terrorism.

The FBI used similar tactics in the United States. The strategy was simple. You look for a mentally disturbed and economically vulnerable Muslim man who lacks the capacity to carry out any terrorist attack, pressure him into participating in some imagined terrorist plot, then arrest him and claim a victory in the War on Terror. According to an article in *The Intercept*,

FBI undercover agents or informants personally led the terror plots in question in at least 49 cases. The FBI would manipulate these men into placing a fake bomb, accepting money for carrying out an imagined crime, or purchasing tickets to join Daesh.[25] Trevor Aaronson, author of *The Terror Factory: Inside the FBI's Manufactured War on Terrorism*, said,

> The FBI is responsible for more terrorism plots in the United States than any other organization. More than al Qaeda, more than al Shabaab, more than the Islamic State, more than all of them combined. This isn't likely how you think about the FBI. You probably think of FBI agents gunning down bad guys like John Dillinger, or arresting corrupt politicians. After the 9/11 terrorist attacks, the FBI became less concerned with gangsters and crooked elected officials. The new target became terrorists, and the pursuit of terrorists has consumed the FBI. Every year, the Bureau spends 3.3 billion dollars on domestic counterterrorism activities. Compare that to just 2.6 billion dollars combined for organized crime, financial fraud, public corruption and all other types of traditional criminal activity. I've spent years poring through the case files of terrorism prosecutions in the United States, and I've come to the conclusion that the FBI is much better at creating terrorists than it is at catching terrorists.[26]

Tamer Elnoury, the pseudonymous author of *American Radical: Inside the World of an Undercover Muslim FBI Agent*, describes the tactics he used to befriend Chiheb Esseghaier, a maladjusted Tunisian graduate student who allegedly wanted to derail a train travelling between the United States and Canada. Needless to say, Chiheb lacked the money, expertise, tools, or explosives that would be required for such a plot. All these would have to be provided by the FBI agent. Chiheb's accomplice, Raed Jaser, a Palestinian consumed with antisemitism, considered the train plot to be pointless as it would only kill ordinary "sheep" instead of the wealthy Jewish "wolves" whom he preferred to target. Both were arrested and charged with terrorism. It is noteworthy that Raed's father had previously sought help in combating his son's burgeoning extremist views.[27] The book ends with concern that the two were arrested before the FBI agent could determine if there was a sleeper agent in the United States. Perpetual fear of "sleeper" cells creates a reason for eyeing every Muslim with suspicion and provides a justification for security agencies to demand over-bloated budgets to chase down imaginary threats. After all, there is no way to prove that a sleeper cell does not exist or that any one Muslim is not part of an underground sleeper cell.

The documentary *The Newburgh Sting* perhaps did more than anything to bring the FBI's tactics to popular attention. The federal government alleged that a group of Muslim terrorists planned to bomb two synagogues and to shoot down military cargo planes bound for Afghanistan. In a plot that is fit for Hollywood, Shaheed Hussain, a fraudster-turned-FBI-informant, offered James Cromitie, a 42-year-old convert to Islam who barely attended any mosque services, $250,000, a BMW, and a barber shop if he would carry out the attacks. Months later, after he lost his job, Cromitie took some interest in the plot but insisted that the synagogues be bombed at night when they would be empty because he did not want there to be any loss of life. Under pressure, he recruited three of his Muslim convert friends to join the ill-fated scheme. Judge Colleen McMahon, while imposing the mandatory minimum 25-year sentence, wrote,

> I believe beyond a shadow of a doubt that there would have been no crime here except the government instigated it, planned it, and brought it to fruition... I am left with the firm conviction that if the government had simply kept an eye on Cromitie, and moved on to other investigations, nothing like the events of May 20, 2009, would ever have occurred.[28]

In another case, a Kurdish refugee names Yasin Aref, who barely spoke English, was sentenced to 15 years in prison for allegedly shrugging his shoulders when told by an FBI informant that there was an impending terrorist attack on New York City. There was no proof of the incident other than the testimony of a fraudster-turned-informant who needed to catch terrorists for the FBI to make his own legal troubles go away. He claimed that he had accidentally dropped his recorder and hence had no objective proof of the incident, yet the jury was sufficiently appalled to return a guilty verdict.[29] After all, when it comes to Islamic terrorism, the legal standard is guilty until proven innocent and a Muslim does not actually need to be part of a terrorist plot to be convicted of terrorism. In reality, resources that should be expended on reducing extremism are instead wasted on creating terrorists to fill up prison cells, to earn accolades for government bureaucrats, and to feed the hysteria that Muslim terrorists abound to justify further counterterrorism funding.

The FBI phishing for terrorists has become part and parcel of Muslim life in America. In 2006, FBI agents planted an informant in an Orange County, California mosque to gather as much information as possible on the congregants, particularly those who appeared devout. Needless to say, no terrorism charges or convictions resulted from this waste of time.[30] However, such adventurism is not harmless. It has a chilling effect on religious practice, making many Muslims prefer to pray at home rather than to attend service at a mosque; it reduces charitable contributions from potential donors who want to avoid governmental scrutiny; and it curtails the exercise of free speech in mosques.

The FBI specifically targets Muslims with immigration or legal problems to serve as informants, promising them that their problems would vanish if they would help the FBI identify and catch terrorists.[31] These informants are presumably under tremendous pressure to find extremists who simply don't exist. The entire premise boils down to treating every Muslim as a suspect in a crime that has not yet occurred and never will. The

Fourth Amendment prohibitions on illegal and warrantless searches and seizures are waived when it comes to Muslims. As with any racialized group, Muslims are singled out for the law's punishments but not its protections.

In my local mosque, someone showed up to evening prayers a few years ago proclaiming himself to be "the ambassador of Caliph al-Baghdadi of the Islamic State of Iraq and Syria," and called out for recruits to join the cause. A group of Muslims cordoned him off so he wouldn't be beaten up by the congregation, many of whom are Iraqi immigrants and refugees who loathe Daesh. When the police arrived, he turned out to be an FBI undercover agent. The sheer level of institutional ignorance involved in sending a purported Sunni extremist into a predominantly Shia mosque to recruit people to go to Iraq and Syria to join a barbaric Sunni-Salafi-Takfiri group that loves to kill Shias defies belief. This operation was about as smart as sending fake KKK recruiters to an NAACP meeting or sending neo-Nazi recruiters to a synagogue as part of an investigation into white supremacy.

At the end, such racialized tactics only undermine the cooperative approaches based on mutual trust and a shared desire for security that are needed for effective counterterrorism. It is quite unfortunate that Islamophobia reigns supreme at the heart of counter-terrorism operations. According to the Southern Poverty Law Center, which monitors hate and extremist groups in the United States,

> [Robert] Spencer is one of the most prolific anti-Muslim figures in the United States. An incessant blogger, author, and activist, he insists, despite his lack of academic training in Islam, that the religion is inherently violent and that extremists who commit acts of terror are simply following its most authentic version... Spencer has given seminars on Islam and jihad to the U.S. Central Command, Army Command and General Staff College, the Army's Asymmetric Warfare Group, the FBI, the Joint Terrorism Task Force, and the U.S. intelligence

community. He also appears regularly on Fox News Network.[32]

Among the FBI's recommended reading list for new recruits was Robert Spencer's book *The Truth About Mohammed: Founder of the World's Most Intolerant Religion* and Raphael Patai's *The Arab Mind*. New recruits were taught that "Arabs only understand force," and that "Arab minds" are "swayed more by words than ideas and more by ideas than facts."[33] This mirrors the racialized tactics that are used in the War on Crime. Even though KKK leaders are not formally brought in to train the police, their racist ideas permeate law enforcement and have led to what Michelle Alexander terms "the new Jim Crow."[34] As Malcolm X put it, "A hundred years ago the American white men used to put on a white sheet and use a bloodhound against Negroes. Today they have taken off the white sheet and put on police uniforms and traded in the bloodhounds for police dogs, and they're still doing the same thing."[35] That Islamophobic tropes are taught as mere facts and constitute the basis of policy initiatives from FBI field offices to the Oval Office only highlights the widespread acceptance of anti-Muslim bigotry and should raise alarm bells regarding the misguided policies that are being implemented across the political spectrum.

Part II

Fear of Islamic Culture

Chapter 6

Freedom of Speech

The question of how tolerant Islam is of freedom of speech gained prominence after the 1988 publication of Salman Rushdie's *The Satanic Verses*, which included offensive descriptions of the Prophet (S). Protests broke out in Muslim countries that led to several deaths. In response, Ayatollah Khomeini issued a fatwa declaring Salman Rushdie's blood forfeit. This event put the word fatwa into western parlance and raised questions about the limits of Islam's tolerance for free speech. In 2004, the Dutch filmmaker Theo van Gogh was assassinated by Mohammed Bouyeri, a Dutch-Moroccan extremist, for producing a ten-minute film called *Submission*, which uses inflammatory and highly stereotyped depictions to portray Muslim women as victims of toxic Islamic misogyny.[1] The 2005 publication of cartoons depicting the Prophet (S) in a derogatory manner in Denmark led to protests across the Muslim world and a boycott of Danish goods, hurting the bottom line of companies like Arla Foods and Novo Nordisk that had nothing to do with the cartoons.[2] In 2010, Kurt Westergaard, a Danish cartoonist, was the victim of an attempted axe attack for his cartoon depicting the Prophet Muhammad (S) with a bomb in his turban.[3] These and other incidents have fed the narrative that Muslims are inherently opposed to free speech.

Charlie Hebdo

Charlie Hebdo, a satirical French weekly newspaper, has published numerous offensive cartoons of the Prophet (S) and has defended doing so in the name of free speech. Its November 2, 2011 edition listed the Prophet (S) as its editor-in-chief, and its cover carried a caricature of him saying, "One hundred lashes if you don't die of laughter." The issue was filled with cartoons depicting various Islamophobic stereotypes of Islam, Muslims, and shariah law, particularly domestic violence, amputations, stoning of adulterers, and brainwashing of children. In 2012, the newspaper's website was hacked and its office was firebombed.

In light of the firebombing, Muslims lined up to condemn the attack. The head of the Paris Mosque, Dalil Boubakeur, told a news conference, "I am extremely attached to freedom of the press, even if the press is not always tender with Muslims, Islam or the Paris Mosque." Abderrahmane Dahmane, a Muslim former presidential adviser on religious diversity, said, "We have a sense of humor in the world of Islam... what we sometimes say about Islam and the prophet, among ourselves and in the presence of imams, is worse than what *Charlie Hebdo* wrote."[4]

In 2012, *Charlie Hebdo* went on to publish a series of cartoons with lewd depictions such as one "entitled 'Mohammad: a star is born,' [which] depicted a bearded figure crouching over to display naked buttocks and genitals, a star covering his anus."[5] On January 7, 2015, masked gunmen attacked *Charlie Hebdo*'s offices, killing twelve people and injuring eleven others. The dead included five staff cartoonists and two editors. The two gunmen were identified as French Muslim brothers of Algerian descent. Instantly, "*je suis Charlie* (I am Charlie)," became a slogan of support, chanted at rallies and emblazoned across social media platforms.

It was maintained that the exercise of the right to free speech effectively requires insulting Islam and that any form of Muslim protest indicating dislike of being insulted simply serves as proof that they lack French values, cannot truly be integrated into French society, are trying to force shariah law onto French citizenry, and are in dire need of cultural reeducation. In fact, some French Muslims came out in support of this notion of free speech. Mohammed Moussaoui, president of the French Council of the Muslim Faith, told the *Agence France-Presse*, "The freedom to caricature is guaranteed for everyone."[6]

Yet, the outpouring of "*je suis Charlie*" isn't without problems. Considering that the Muslim population of France is generally poor and marginalized, pushed into ghettoes, and systematically discriminated against, taking pride in insulting the religious beliefs of these people is hardly something to be proud of. Do we really want millions proclaiming, "I am a racist," and taking a stand with cartoonists who insult the sacred beliefs of minority populations? If someone walks into a black or Hispanic neighborhood, goes around referring to everyone in some racial slur, and ends up getting beaten up, anyone sensible would criticize his idiocy for needlessly insulting people and figure that he got what was coming. This does not mean that anyone sensible would carry out the beating or even find the beating to be sensible; rather, we know the consequences of wantonly insulting others.

Some in Iran countered by hosting an international Holocaust denial cartoon contest to point out western hypocrisy when it comes to freedom of speech. Considering that denial of the Holocaust is, perhaps rightly, a crime in many European countries, these nations do not espouse the blanket freedom to insult or incite that is often claimed. In France, the 1990 Gayssot Act made it illegal to question crimes against humanity, including the Holocaust,[7] with a presumed, though unstated, exemption carved out for French colonial atrocities. Are Holocaust denial cartoons the answer to *Charlie Hebdo*? Beyond pointing out a double-standard, it is hard to see how cartoons denigrating Jews and belittling their suffering in Europe will add anything constructive to the plight of marginalized Muslim communities in France. Iran's foreign minister at the time, Mohammad Javad Zarif, distanced the government of President Hassan Rouhani from sponsorship of the cartoons, saying,

> Why does the United States have the Ku Klux Klan? Is the government of the United States responsible for the fact that there are racially hateful organizations in the

United States? ... Don't consider Iran a monolith. The Iranian government does not support, nor does it organize, any cartoon festival of the nature that you're talking about.[8]

Pope Francis perhaps explained the situation best when he said that if someone "says a swear word against my mother, he's going to get a punch in the nose."[9] Sure, you're free to insult, but don't act like the victim if someone responds. The Pope is essentially pointing out how certain forms of speech constitute incitement and hence deserve neither celebration nor freedom from consequence. If you run around referring to African Americans, women, and homosexuals using derogatory terms and end up getting a good beating, you only have yourself to blame. You can't complain about the intolerance of specific groups when you actively go out of your way to offend them. If there was one thing I learned reading J. D. Vance's *Hillbilly Elegy*, it's that you should never insult a "hillbilly's" mother unless you're ready to get a good beating. Different groups may have different sensibilities depending on their cultural or religious values, and not violating these sensibilities does not constitute censorship but rather basic respect. One cannot be surprised that racialized communities get upset when they are specifically targeted and actively provoked, such as when someone paints a swastika on a synagogue, dumps a pig's head in a mosque, or places a noose outside a black church. These acts, indeed, are done for the sole purpose of eliciting a reaction. In the case of a magazine, there is the added benefit that the greater the reaction, the higher the profits. This is not to say that we should encourage violent reactions to insults, but rather that those who go around insulting and offending can't act like victims when they are the instigators of the violence. Regardless, given the cultural stereotype of Muslims as innately intolerant and violent, the violent reactions to offensive cartoons only plays into the hands of the far-right Islamophobes and reinforces their bigoted views of Muslims.

The Beheading of Samuel Paty

On October 16, 2020, Samuel Paty, a French school teacher, was beheaded for showing cartoons of the Prophet (S) naked with his genitals exposed to a classroom full of young teenagers.[10] President Macron was quick to say, "Our compatriot was killed for teaching children freedom of speech."[11] Meanwhile, widespread condemnation of the murder was heard from across the Islamic community.

The real issue is not whether beheading Paty is justified, as it is hard to point to any meaningful support for the murder aside from fringe extremists. The issue is whether he was teaching students freedom of speech. The basic assumption is that Muslims come from societies in which any criticism of religion is non-existent, that Muslims living in western countries lack an understanding of freedom of speech, and that exposing them to insults will help address these facts. The problem is that all these premises are fallacious. First, Muslim societies are not monolithic, and the majority of Muslims grow up surrounded by people with various degrees of religiosity, from ultra-pious to outright areligious. Secular thoughts would not be as foreign to the average Muslim as some might imagine.

Second, Muslims living and growing up in France are certainly not sheltered in some imagined Islamic bubble, impervious to the influences of the wider society. Any Muslim in a western country is quite aware of their minority status and cultural and religious differences. It is hard to imagine that they are oblivious to the concepts of freedom of speech or of the press and need education through condescension. They are also quite aware that this freedom is often one-way, permitting the ridicule of Islam and Muslims with the expectation that the insulted Muslims show deference to freedom of speech. Meanwhile, Muslim speech, even on political subjects where the right to free speech ought to be most strictly protected, is not tolerated. In 1961, French police killed 200-300 peaceful protesters who were marching against French colonial atrocities in Algeria. Some were beaten to death by police batons; others drowned after being shoved into the Seine River. Actions speak louder than words when it comes to the meaning of liberty and free speech.

Third, teaching freedom of speech is not best achieved through inflammatory and bigoted cartoons. Imagine trying to teach an African American middle schooler about freedom of speech by forcing her to look at racist cartoons depicting people of African descent as apes. I invite the reader to peruse the website of Ferris State University's Jim Crow Museum of Racist Memorabilia. While, thankfully, most of the cartoons are cringey relics of the past, some are quite recent, like a cartoon with the quote "Obama in '08" under a picture of Curious George holding a peeled banana. We would find it idiotic to teach Jewish teenagers freedom of speech by showing them pictures of swastikas, Nazi cartoons denigrating Jews, and white pride literature. No one would think of teaching freedom of speech in these ways to non-Muslims, yet perfectly intelligent-appearing people believe that Muslim youth need to be taught freedom of expression through obscene cartoons that insult them. This typifies how Islamophobic racism promotes discriminatory standards for dealing with Muslims. The basic argument is that Muslims get offended because they don't understand freedom of speech, whereas in reality it has nothing to do with being Muslim; it is normal for people to get offended when you deliberately offend them. That a small minority reacts violently to this offense is effectively irrelevant when one considers that only one person takes violent action out of millions who are potentially offended. If anything, this shows a general antipathy of Muslims towards reacting violently, not their proclivity to violence.

Fourth, if the attacks on *Charlie Hebdo* and the assassination of Samuel Paty show that Muslims lack an appreciation for freedom of speech, then one would have to conclude that westerners, including Americans, also lack such an appreciation. The firebombing of the office of Edward Said at Columbia University[12] and the assassinations of Martin Luther King and Malcolm X for their exercise of the right to speech demonstrate that silencing one's critics is hardly limited to

Muslims. White supremacist vigilante groups use intimidation to suppress the civil liberties of Muslims, whether in the form of heavily armed thugs congregating outside a mosque in Irving, Texas, vandals desecrating a mosque in Pflugerville, Texas with feces and torn pages from the Quran, or arsonists setting a mosque in Ontario ablaze.[13]

Fifth, governments do restrict freedom of speech even when they are not inciteful. For example, in the United States, HIPAA regulations prohibit healthcare workers from divulging the private health information of their patients. Similarly, a fraudster won't get far in court claiming that he was merely exercising his freedom of speech when he defrauded people of all their savings, and perjury charges won't be dropped just because someone claims it was their right of free speech to lie in court. There is no meaningful opposition to such limitations on speech. Anwar al-Awlaki, a US citizen, was assassinated in a premeditated drone strike ordered by Barack Obama without any due process of law and despite never having been charged with any crime. Rather than proceeding through the judicial process, capital punishment was doled out simply because Obama disliked his preaching. Aside from some grumblings from human rights organizations, [14] this drone strike was widely condoned across the political spectrum.

Sixth, everyone knows that there is really no such thing as free speech. In North Korea, you're technically free to proclaim what you really think of Kim Jong-un in a public square; what makes speech there seen as not free are the consequences you will suffer as a result. In the United States, you're free to tell your teachers, employers, customers, clients, and business associates whatever you want; it's the consequences that make you bite your tongue instead. It could be argued that the difference lies in whether the government is the one inflicting the consequences, but that there are dire consequences remains the same. Considering that European cartoonists are not suffering from state persecution, what Islamophobes are arguing for is not actually free speech but freedom from any consequences that might arise from their exercise of speech. They expect a type of free speech that no one enjoys anywhere. Does absolute freedom of speech include the freedom to insult the Prophet (S), blacks, Jews, etc.? Yes, absolutely. Yet, that is not the real question. We have an absolute right to go up to a perfect stranger on the street and say something horribly disrespectful, but anyone with the slightest amount of decency would cringe at the thought. The freedom of speech that constitutes a cornerstone of liberalism should not be confused with an obligation to offend. Nor should the media feel that it has an obligation to provide a platform for hate speech.

This call for decency is not a call for government censorship of the media. Rather, it is a call for the media to stop spewing racist rhetoric, whether in prose or in depictions, and to stop perpetuating disdainful portrayals of minority communities. It is a call for the media to fact-check bigoted rhetoric and to question the credentials of so-called experts who perpetuate fallacious stereotypes. It is a call to trade in the right to offend for the more sacred privilege of living in harmony. Secularism, at its best, is the freedom to worship as one pleases or not to worship at all, not the wanton exercise of the legal right to insult other faiths using inflammatory rhetoric.

It is worth noting that *Charlie Hebdo* is not an automaton that publishes anything that is insulting. They have an editorial board that also chooses what not to publish. The magazine was quick to fire Maurice Siné, who had served as one of its cartoonist for two decades. His offense was publishing a cartoon insinuating that Jean Sarkozy, who at the time was the son of the French president, was going to convert to Judaism to marry Jessica Sebaoun-Darty, a wealthy Jewish heiress. His caption read, "He'll go a long way in life, this lad!"[15] That the cartoon was offensive and antisemitic goes without question but the degree of offensiveness can hardly compare to that seen in lewd depictions of the Prophet (S).

Finally, it should be noted that, as pointed out by Stanley Fish in his essay *There's No Such Thing as Free Speech*, freedom of speech is an illusion, and merely reflects social norms set by dominant groups. He writes,

> Despite the apparent absoluteness of the First Amendment, there are any number of ways of getting around it, ways that are known to every student of the law. In general, the preferred strategy is to manipulate the distinction, essential to First Amendment jurisprudence, between speech and action. The distinction is essential because no one would think to frame a First Amendment that began "Congress shall make no law abridging freedom of action," for that would amount to saying "Congress shall make no law."
> ... First Amendment theorists and jurists fashion a distinction within the speech/action distinction: some forms of speech are not really speech because their purpose is to incite violence or because they are, as the court declares in *Chaplinsky v. New Hampshire* (1942), "fighting words," words "likely to provoke the average person to retaliation, and thereby cause a break of the peace." The trouble with this definition is that it distinguishes not between fighting words and words that remain safely and merely expressive but between words that are provocative to one group (the group that falls under the rubric "average person") and words that might be provocative to other groups, groups of persons not now considered average.[16]

This passage explains the process through which freedom of speech maintains a dominant group's social norms while depriving minority groups of similar rights. While speech that is deemed to fall within proper bounds is tolerated, what falls beyond the pale is seen as inciteful. As such, speech inciting to some specific war is celebrated as patriotic, whereas speech inciting to some specific "jihad" is seen as extremist and subject to censorship. Considering that there are only three options—tolerating all speech, tolerating some speech while censoring other speech, and censoring all speech—every society falls into the same category of tolerating some but not all speech. This is why, in some societies, cartoons denigrating the Prophet (S) are tolerated, whereas a woman wearing hijab in a public space is not. Considering the fact that hijab is seen as most offensive when it is purported to constitute political speech that renounces the liberal order in favor of an "Islamist" one, the hollowness of free speech rhetoric becomes apparent. The conceptualization of free speech as something that permits freedom only within the bounds set by the norms of a dominant group goes back to John Milton, whose 1644 polemical essay *Areopagitica* served as the foundational essay of the free speech tradition.[17] In it, he says,

> I mean not tolerated Popery, and open superstition, which as it extirpates all religions and civil supremacies, so itself should be extirpated, provided first that all charitable and compassionate means be used to win and regain the weak and the misled: that also which is impious or evil absolutely either against faith or manners no law can possibly permit, that intends not to unlaw itself: but those neighboring differences, or rather indifferences, are what I speak of, whether in some point of doctrine or of discipline, which though they may be many, yet need not interrupt the unity of Spirit.[18]

According to Milton, freedom of speech is the freedom to preach Protestantism to lost Catholic souls and the freedom to debate, within a limited framework, competing but tolerable Protestant ideas, but not the freedom to promote Catholicism. Similarly, John Locke, in his "Letter Concerning Toleration," urges respect for individual conscience, while stressing that the "[Catholic] Church can have no right to be tolerated."[19] While the modern liberal concept of free speech is more expansive, it is nevertheless innately limited in scope. At the very least, liberal democrats are wary of autocrats, communists, or Islamists using free speech and electoral means (i.e., what is sacred to a liberal democracy) to subvert the liberal democratic order. This ill-logic is used against Muslims in Europe and the US by alleging that they will eventually subvert western liberal democracies in favor of a shariah-based state. "Islamism" is singled out as a universal threat to democracy, as if the Christian right and ultra-Orthodox Jewish communities have no voice in American and Israeli politics, respectively. This reasoning is also used to deprive "Islamists"—Muslims who believe that the political structure should reflect religious ideology—of the right of political participation in Muslim autocracies; their call for representative democracy is dismissed as simply a means to usurp power and then demolish the democratic bridge that got them there. Autocracy, with avid support of the west, is hailed as the only way to prevent an Islamist takeover of Muslim countries.

It is not that Muslims don't want more accountable governance; it is that they are not seen as capable of handling it. When Palestinians voted for Hamas, the United States and Israel unleashed punitive measures that have primarily affected the civilian population. In some sense, Muslims are hardly alone in this regard as they constitute but one segment of the Global South. When Chileans voted for Salvador Allende as their president, Kissinger and Nixon saw the matter as too important to be left to the Chilean people to decide. The CIA orchestrated a coup led by Augusto Pinochet that led to Allende "committing suicide." This was followed by years of vicious atrocities unleashed against Chilean civilians to punish them for exercising their freedom of speech and freedom to vote for a candidate of their choosing.

As an aside, it can be said that an Achilles heel of liberal democratic idealism is that the system, in contrast to the theoretical system promoted by Islamists of various types, is not universalizable. Only a small minority of Americans and Europeans would be okay with a world order in which borders are erased and everyone on the planet is granted free speech and one vote. It is hardly surprising that reinforcing borders and creating further obstacles to immigration and citizenship are sure ways to garner votes in democratic nations. If voting is so great, then why not let "undocumented" immigrants and refugees vote as well?

Free Speech as a Tool of Racist Social Domination

What is perhaps lost upon dominant ethnic groups is that caricaturizing marginalized communities is a form of domination and social control. It is a narrative that is controlled entirely by one group at the expense of another and it does not lend itself to fruitful debate or meaningful mutual understanding. Freedom of speech becomes a one-way street in which colonizers can portray their restless subjects as terrorists and enslavers can portray their enslaved as rightfully exploited beasts. Would it be legal to publish cartoons that portray straight white men of European descent as terrorists and apes? Yes, but considering the racist structure of contemporary society, such cartoons would fall flat. At one point, cartoons depicting the Irish as apes did exert cultural influence,[20] but at that point Irish immigrants constituted a racialized minority community. Only in depicting the racist stereotypes that underpin the existing hierarchy do such cartoons exert any cultural influence, shape the contours of societal debate, and generate sizeable profits.

This gets to the heart of the question of why it is perceived that Muslims are "so sensitive" to their prophet being insulted, why African Americans are "so sensitive" to racist microaggressions, and why women are "so sensitive" to sexual harassment. It is because people are tired of not being left alone to just be. The socially dominant caste feels compelled to repeatedly belittle others to maintain its own status. As Asma Barlas, a retired professor of politics put it,

> What we condemn is not the idea that people should be free to speak but the use of speech to dominate and degrade the already marginal or vulnerable. Defending domination in the name of freedom just confirms that not

all conceptions of freedom are equally worth defending.[21]

The slogan *"je suis Charlie"* is completely counter-productive as far as freedom of speech goes. It is a thought-terminating cliché that sets a "you're with us or you're against us" dichotomy, stifling dissenting voices as inherently unpatriotic. *"Je suis Charlie"* becomes a rallying cry to further ostracize Muslims who are seen as inimical to the core French value of *liberté*. Yet, true *liberté* requires society to accept the dissenting voices of others, including those who condemn the dissemination of distasteful and insulting cartoons that promote ethnic strife.

In many western societies, freedom of speech has turned into an obligation to perpetuate racist rhetoric. As such, starting in 2012, American courts forced local transit authorities to run Islamophobic advertisements in buses and subways. The ads, put out by Pamela Geller's American Freedom Defense Initiative, read, "In any war between the civilized man and the savage, support the civilized man. Support Israel. Defeat Jihad." *The Washington Post*'s editorial board published a piece claiming that, "The bottom line is that censorship is even more distasteful than the ad. And it's plainly unjustified, even on a temporary basis, to reject [the ad]."[22] That Pamela Geller has the legal freedom to preach hate is conflated with a legal obligation for others to provide platforms to help disseminate her hate speech.

Yet, when free speech is seen as offensive to the dominant racial group, restrictions are quickly put in place. In France, a photograph of a man wiping his bottom with a French flag won a prize in a photo contest in Nice in 2010. The French government quickly mobilized, passing a law making it illegal to insult the French flag in any public setting. The crime is now punishable by a 1,500 euro fine.[23]

That there is no tolerance for insulting the sensibilities of the French public is highlighted by *Hara-Kiri*, *Charlie Hebdo's* predecessor. In 1970, following the death of French World War II hero Charles de Gaulle, it published a cartoon satirizing the amount of attention given to the death of one Charles de Gaulle as compared to the 146 mostly young men and women who had just died in a fire at a discotheque in Saint-Laurent-du-Pont. This was seen as such an affront to the French nation's sensibilities that the French interior minister forbade the magazine's publication and *Hara-Kiri* was thereby shuttered.[24]

The criticism that Muslim nations lack freedom of the press is not entirely without merit. However, there is a discriminatory fixation on cases in which Muslims are the censors as opposed to the ones being censored. Edward Said pointed out this hypocrisy when he said, "There was widespread outrage routinely expressed at the absence of freedom of the press in Saudi Arabia. (How many feelings of outrage were expressed about Israeli rules against Arab newspapers, schools, and universities on the West Bank?)"[25] Accordingly, Israel is seen as enjoying a free press, even though its forces have killed at least 47 journalists between 2000 and 2022 with no one being held to account.[26] Furthermore, such criticism presupposes that western press is truly free—free from government interference, the influence of commercial interests, societal racism, and any sociopolitical agenda. As Edward Herman and Noam Chomsky point out in *Manufacturing Consent: The Political Economy of the Mass Media*, mainstream American media, though nominally free, functions merely as a propaganda tool of the US government.

In conclusion, a far more powerful slogan than "*Je suis Charlie*" is "*je suis Ahmed*," which unfortunately few have heard of. Ahmed Merabet was a French Muslim police officer who was killed in the *Charlie Hebdo* massacre. He gave his life defending the office of *Charlie Hebdo* against the gunmen. As one tweeter put it, "I am not Charlie, I am Ahmed the dead cop. Charlie ridiculed my faith and culture and I died defending his right to do so."[27] The story of Ahmed highlights the integration of Muslim immigrants into western societies and the willingness of Muslims to die to protect liberal values. That the attackers get so much more attention than Ahmed does is because the attack fits racialized stereotypes of Muslims far more than Ahmed's sacrifice does.

Chapter 7

Apostasy and Blasphemy in Islam

In traditional Islamic jurisprudence (*fiqh*), apostacy—the act of publicly leaving Islam—and certain forms of blasphemy, in particular insulting God or the Prophet (S), are punishable capital offenses. Apostacy laws affect only Muslims and ex-Muslims, whereas blasphemy laws can affect Muslims and non-Muslims alike. Alongside controversies over freedom of speech, these issues were brought to the fore in western consciousness when Salman Rushdie was condemned to death by Iran's spiritual leader, Ayatollah Khomeini, for apostacy and blasphemy charges arising from his book, *The Satanic Verses*. The subject is likely to receive renewed attention in light of the recent stabbing attack on the book's author.

The Quranic Perspective

The Quran does not propose any earthly punishment for apostacy. Rather, apostacy is seen in terms of being spiritually lost: "Verily, those who disbelieve after believing [in Islam], then go on to increase their disbelief, their repentance will not be accepted, and they are the ones who are astray,"[1] and "Indeed, those who have believed then disbelieved then believed then disbelieved, then increased in disbelief, God will not forgive them and guide them to the [right] path."[2] The punishment for apostacy is in the hereafter: "And for he who apostatizes and dies while a disbeliever... they are the companions of the Fire, to remain therein in perpetuity."[3]

Ridiculing Islam and Muslims is not something new, as Muslims have faced ridicule since the first days of Islam. The Quran includes words derived from the root *h-z-a* and *s-kh-r* (to ridicule) over forty times, typically in reference to unbelievers mocking Muslims and their religious beliefs and practices. It is often alleged that Muslims are not used to criticism of their prophet, yet anyone reading the Quran can hardly overlook the fact that it reflects many of the insults the pagans hurled at Muhammad (S)—that he was an insane[4] poet[5] and sorcerer[6] whose revelations were merely things taught to him by others[7] and whose message amounted to nothing but old fables.[8] Considering that highly-educated people in the twenty-first century use the same hackneyed diatribes to describe the Prophet (S), it appears that Islamophobic discourse has hardly evolved over the past fourteen centuries.

When confronted with ridicule of Islam, the Quran doesn't exactly advise pulling out one's sword or suicide vest as might be assumed from popular portrayals of Islam. Instead, it advises, "When you hear the revelations of God denied and ridiculed, do not sit with them until they engage in some other conversation."[9] The Quran does not consider ridicule to be a constructive form of dialogue and as such expects Muslims not to ridicule or insult other faiths: "Do not insult those whom they worship other than God."[10] In contrast to ridicule, the Quran calls for civilized debates on matters of faith: "Invite to the way of your Lord with wisdom and beautiful preaching, and debate with them in a manner that is best."[11]

Furthermore, non-believers are welcome to learn about Islam and are perfectly free to choose not to convert; they are not to be harassed in any manner and must be assured complete safety in this regard: "And if any one of the pagans seeks your protection, then grant it to him so that he may hear the Word of God. Then deliver him to his place of safety."[12] Considering this verse is in the ninth chapter (*sura*) of the Quran, which has some of the harshest verses about dealing with the polytheists of Arabia, it becomes clear that people were free to accept or reject Islam in complete peace and security throughout the prophetic mission. After all, "if they accept Islam, they have become guided; if they turn away, your duty is only to preach;"[13] a Muslim's duty is not to force people to convert.

Some scholars, in light of the Quranic principle that "there is no compulsion in religion"[14] and given juristic disagreements in terms of the conditions under which blasphemy and apostacy laws are to be administered, have advocated for complete freedom of religion.[15] This goes along with Quranic verses such as, "The Truth is from your Lord; let him who wishes believe and let him who wishes disbelieve,"[16] and "For you is your religion and for me is my religion."[17] Nevertheless, traditional texts of *fiqh* do take a harder line against apostacy and blasphemy.

Anti-Blasphemy Laws

Anti-blasphemy laws are not limited to Muslim nations. According to Pew Research, such laws can be found in countries like Austria, Finland, Greece, Italy, Poland, and Russia.[18] That restrictions on religious practice are not limited to Muslim countries is also obvious in the myriad ways in which European countries restrict the practice of Islam—from anti-hijab laws to restrictions on halal slaughter to prohibitions on building mosques. According to Pew, in 2019, 98% of European governments harassed religious groups, 91% interfered in worship, and 42% used force against religious groups. Virtually all European countries were rated as moderate to high in terms of government restrictions on religion. Countries like Saudi Arabia and Iran rank lower in terms of religious hostility than Germany, the United Kingdom, and Spain, defying the stereotype of people in Muslim countries as innately intolerant of other faiths.[19]

Reading through compilations of hadith, one runs across numerous instances in which a heretic (*zindiq*) would challenge Islamic beliefs or Quranic verses. Invariably, they would be debated and enlightened, but not dragged out and killed. It seems like the application of such laws was restricted to specific instances in which social or political instability was feared, not merely to intellectual disagreements. As such, there is no clear case of someone who was executed for mere apostasy or blasphemy during the Prophet's (S) lifetime. Furthermore, Imam Ali (AS), the first Shia Imam and the fourth Sunni caliph, did not persecute the Kharijites whom both Shias and Sunnis have considered to be apostates. The Kharijites vociferously condemned Ali (AS), considered him to be an apostate, militarily threatened his rule, and eventually assassinated him. He only acted against them when they openly rebelled by forming an army and going out in battle. As such, one must consider the exact circumstances under which apostasy and blasphemy laws was to be applied, and whether these crimes were seen as distinct from open rebellion.

Islam's purported stance on apostasy and blasphemy has been used to cement the stereotype of Muslims as particularly intolerant. Moderate Muslim voices are allegedly silenced out of fear, and Muslims are purported to be incapable of assimilating into western countries that value freedom of religion. As Bill Maher put it, "[Moderate Muslims are] afraid to speak out because they're the only religion that acts like the mafia, that will f--king kill you if you say the wrong thing, draw the wrong picture, or write the wrong book."[20] Yet, within Muslim societies, "moderate" Islam is the norm; extremists generally have to tread carefully. Across the Muslim world, prisons are not full of "moderate" Muslims who said the wrong thing. Rather, they're the abode of extremists who are seen as political and ideological threats to the political system.

Concern about Islamic restrictions on apostasy and blasphemy is an overblown problem. An official in the United States Commission on International Religious Freedom, an advisory board created by Congress, cited only four known cases of executions for apostasy between 1985 and 2006.[21] This should be compared to a single drone strike killing over forty civilians attending a wedding in Afghanistan.[22] When it comes to what kills people, worrying about Muslim apostasy laws would rank quite low, especially when one considers that an average of thirteen people a year die by getting crushed by vending machines.[23] Nevertheless, one has to lament incidents such as the one in which a mob in Pakistan lynched a mentally ill man who burnt pages of the Quran. Pakistan's prime minister, Imran Khan, announced that his government had "zero tolerance for anyone taking the law into their own hands," and that "mob lynchings will be dealt with full severity of the law." Tahir Ashrafi, Pakistan's special representative on religious harmony, said, "Who could possibly justify the barbaric act of stoning to death a mentally ill person?" and added, "This is not the religion of my prophet, to kill people under your own interpretation of religion."[24]

Despite the relative rarity of these fringe events, there is a cottage industry of ex-Muslims on social media touting the dangers of leaving Islam. Considering they're all pretty much well and thriving and always begging for more financial support, it seems like the danger is a bit exaggerated. This is not to say that the danger is absolutely zero. It is theoretically possible that some fanatic will go after them, but their chances of getting killed by a shark attack during a trip to the beach would be substantially higher. Considering that Mercedes Morr, a model and social media influencer in Houston, was strangled to death by a stalker,[25] it seems like there are far more dangerous jobs out there than being an ex-Muslim vying for attention on YouTube.

Comparative Perspectives

Apostasy laws should be compared to treason laws that are virtually universal. Section 18 § 2381 of the US Code clearly states, "Whoever, owing allegiance to the United States, levies war against them or adheres to their enemies, giving them aid and comfort within the United States or elsewhere, is guilty of treason and shall suffer death."[26] At the time of the Prophet (S), when Muslims in Medina faced the constant threat of extermination by their enemies, apostasy effectively entailed "adhering to their enemies," which by modern standards would constitute a treasonous act. Similarly, Section 885 of Title 10 of the US Code, states, "Any person found guilty of desertion or attempt to desert shall be punished, if the offense is committed in time of war, by death."[27] These laws are clear that freedom of association and speech are by no means universal but rather tightly bound by the norms set by the system of power.

Muslim intolerance is often alleged to arise directly from the Quran, in contrast to western tolerance which arises from European Christian or Judeo-Christian values. Yet, it is hard to find tolerance for apostasy in either the Old or New Testament. From the Ten Commandments exhorting, "Thou shalt have no gods before me," and "Thou shalt not take the name of the Lord thy God in vain," freedom of religion and speech were curtailed. In case someone were to leave the religion, the laws were quite clear, as reflected in the following three passages:

> If your very own brother, or your son or daughter, or the wife you love, or your closest friend secretly entices you, saying, "Let us go and worship other gods...," do not yield to them or listen to them. Show them no pity. Do not spare them or shield them. You must certainly put them to death. Your hand must be the first in putting them to death, and then the hands of all the people.[28]

> If a man or woman living among you... has worshiped other gods... take the man or woman who has done this evil deed to your city gate and stone that person to death.[29]

> All who would not seek the Lord, the God of Israel, were to be put to death, whether small or great, man or woman.[30]

The New Testament affirms the Old Testament edict that apostates should be killed:

They exchanged the truth about God for a lie, and worshiped and served created things rather than the Creator—who is forever praised. Amen... They know God's righteous decree that those who do such things deserve death.[31]

The Islamophobic narrative assumes that Muslims not only are distinctly intolerant of heretical beliefs, but also derive their extreme intolerance directly from the Quran. Yet, in contrast to the Bible, the Quran does not explicitly call for any worldly punishment for the apostate or blasphemer. Furthermore, Islam is hardly the only religion that prohibits deserting the religion. For better or for worse, the peace-loving Amish shun their children who stop practicing the faith far more than many Muslims do. In fact, I have known plenty of ex-Muslims, but none of them have suffered any tangible consequence from their loss of faith.

Portraying Islam as a Cult

The purported dangers of leaving Islam helps fuel the image of Islam as a dangerous cult that chases down and beheads any deserters. Gerard Batten, who served as the leader of the UK Independence Party (UKIP) in 2018 and 2019, called Islam a "death cult," sought a ban against mosque construction in the UK, and called for Muslims to sign a document renouncing parts of the Quran that are not to his liking.[32] Perhaps he got his "death cult" idea from Sam Harris' article titled, "It's real, it's scary, it's a cult of death."[33] That the *Los Angeles Times* would publish an article with this overtly bigoted title shows how Islamophobic stereotypes are widely accepted and disseminated by mainstream media.

Kim Kimberley-Blackstar, a UKIP city council candidate in Newcastle, called Islam a "barbaric satanic cult," and said that he would "never trust a Muslim."[34] Ron Ramsey, who served as Tennessee's Lieutenant Governor from 2007-

2017 claimed that he is "all about freedom of religion," but clarified, "Now you could even argue whether being a Muslim is actually a religion, or is it a nationality, a way of life, or cult—whatever you want to call it. We do protect our religions, but at the same time, this is something that we are going to have to face."[35]

The cult narrative serves several purposes. First, it further marginalizes a quarter of the world's population by delegitimizing their religion and lowering its status from that of religion (i.e., the sort of thing followed by rational people) to that of a cult (i.e., something that only irrational, brainwashed people join). Second, it enables the position that "cult" activities can be legally curtailed, as cults are potentially exempt from the freedom of religion extended to "real" religions. Third, it insults the Prophet (S), since a cult is, almost by definition, a group of people brainwashed by a charlatan and an imposter. Fourth, it validates all the stereotypes of Muslims—that they are fanatical and rigid, that they are not allowed to question anything about their faith, that they cannot be reasoned with because they're irrational and brainwashed, and that many of them remain Muslims out of fear of being killed if they were to leave the faith. Finally, it has to be pointed out that the cult narrative reveals more about the prevalence of Islamophobic stereotypes and assumptions than it does about Muslims themselves, who are a culturally, intellectually, theologically, and juristically diverse group with no universal leadership or organization. In reality, Islam is about as far from a cult as any religion gets.

Is Allah the Same as God?

From the perspective of the west, Muslims are often seen as a foreign people worshiping a foreign deity, speaking a foreign language, and following foreign customs. Islamophobes often refer to *Allah* with much emphasis—when Muslims take over, they will impose *Allah's* will and force us to worship *Allah*; when Muslims carry out terrorist attacks, they do so in the name of

Allah; and it is *Allah* who tells Muslims to beat their wives. Replacing "Allah" with "God" in these contexts would drastically blunt the rhetoric.

Simply put, *Allah* means upper-case God, while *ilah* means lower-case god. In reference to Jews and Christians, the Quran says, "Our god (*ilah*) and your god are the same and we are in submission to Him."[36] Pope John Paul II affirmed this assertion when he told an audience of Muslims in Casablanca, Morocco, "We believe in the same God, the one God, the living God, the God who created the world and brings his creatures to their perfection."[37] In Islam, Allah is the God of Adam, Noah, Abraham, Moses, and Jesus (AS). In fact, the word for God for Arabic-speaking Jews and Christians is Allah. The claim that "Muslims believe in Allah" is thus nominally true, but misses the point that Allah is not considered by Muslims to be a different deity than the one worshiped by Jews and Christians. It would be like saying that Hispanics don't worship God but *el Dios*. In common discourse, Persians refer to God as *Khoda* and not Allah, highlighting the fact that Muslims, like people of other faiths, commonly use words from their native languages when referring to God.

Theologically, some Christians assert that Allah cannot be the Christian God because Allah does not beget a son. It is certainly true that Islam is a strictly unitarian religion that rejects the trinity and apotheosis, while it affirms the virgin birth of Jesus (AS). However, Jews would just as easily claim that their God does not beget children and hence the trinitarian Christian God could not be the same unitarian God that they worship. Circumventing this issue altogether, Arab Christians use terminology such as *Allah al-ab* (God the Father), *Allah al-ibn* (God the Son), *Allah al-ruh al-qudus* (God the Holy Spirit).[38]

Nevertheless, the word "Allah" has led to needless controversies. In Malaysia, a decades-long legal battle has pitted Christians who want to use the word Allah for the God they worship against a group of Muslims who claim that only Muslims have the right to use the word. In their defense, the Christians argued that they had been using the word Allah to refer to God for centuries. Finally, in 2021, Malaysia's high court overruled lower court rulings and established that Christians also had the right to use the word Allah in their publications.[39]

In the United States, when Larycia Hawkins, a tenured professor at Wheaton College in Illinois professed that Muslims and Christians "worship the same God," she was suspended and later terminated from her position.[40] Among evangelical missionaries, there is a raging debate about whether the word Allah can be used when evangelizing Muslims and when translating Christian works or Judeo-Christian Scriptures. Missionaries with experience in Muslim countries often argue in favor of using the word Allah since they understand that it means God, whereas those living in the west feel like converting Muslims to Christianity necessitates that they stop believing in *Allah*, which they perceive as a deity foreign to their Christian faith.[41]

Chapter 8

Secularism: Freedom of Religion or Freedom from Religion?

American concepts such as "all men are created equal" and French mottos such as *liberté, egalité, fraternité* (liberty, equality, and fraternity) and *laïcité* (secularism) typify fanciful liberal ideals that fall flat upon close inspection. In 1852, Frederick Douglass was asked to speak on the occasion of the Fourth of July, a day that symbolized independence for whites and slavery for blacks. This invitation was particularly offensive in light of the Southern custom of holding slave auctions on the Fourth of July. He chose the 5th of July instead to deliver his speech entitled, "What to the Slave, is the Fourth of July." He said,

> Are the great principles of political freedom and of natural justice, embodied in that Declaration of Independence, extended to us? ... The rich inheritance of justice, liberty, prosperity and independence, bequeathed by your fathers, is shared by you, not by me. The sunlight that brought light and healing to you, has brought stripes and death to me. This Fourth July is yours, not mine. You may rejoice, I must mourn. To drag a man in fetters into the grand illuminated temple of liberty, and call upon him to join you in joyous anthems, were inhuman mockery and sacrilegious irony.[1]

The American Declaration of Independence asserts as a self-evident truth that all men are created equal with unalienable rights. This makes for good propaganda and great fodder for patriotic egos. If only other countries were like America where everyone is treated equal. Yet, reality hardly stands up to such ideals. The founding fathers did not include any women, any Native Americans, any African Americans, any slaves, or any non-whites in their concept of "all men." The fight for legal equality has dragged on for generations, and for everyone to be treated equally seems quite fanciful even today.

Nevertheless, it cannot be denied that, as history has unfolded, the United States has shown commendable de jure tolerance for a wide array of religious practices. This was not necessarily a secular concept, as its greatest proponents were some Anabaptist and Baptist denominations. In contrast to Roman Catholics who baptize their infants shortly after birth, these Protestant groups oppose infant baptism and believe that a confession of faith upon reaching maturity is a prerequisite to a valid baptism. In contrast to infant baptism, which can be forced upon an individual, a valid confession cannot be coerced, as faith must be openly embraced. As such, they strongly asserted that religion cannot be assigned by the state. Furthermore, many of the Protestant denominations residing in the American colonies had escaped religious persecution in Europe and wanted to ensure that the new republic would not persecute them again. Narrow Protestant theological and political concerns morphed into a system that has generally respected the right to practice one's religion. It should be noted that, far from being a strictly secular manuscript, issues of concern to Protestant denominations can be found throughout the Constitution. For example, when the Constitution lays out the wording of the "Oath or Affirmation" of a new president, it starts with, "I do solemnly swear (or affirm)..." This precise wording was used to cater to Quakers who refuse to "swear" to tell the truth but are willing to "affirm" the truth.

The American concept of freedom of religion must be contrasted with the French concept of *laïcité*, which is not really freedom *of* religion but rather a freedom *from* religion—i.e., an individual's rights to religious practice are subservient to society's expectation that religion be left out of the public sphere.

As such, secularism has been used to justify an active assault on religious liberties, primarily targeting Muslims.

Hijab Bans

In 1989, three schoolgirls in France were suspended when they refused to remove their headscarves. The controversy simmered until 2004, when the Law of Secularity and Conspicuous Religious Symbols outlawed religious head coverings in schools and government buildings. On September 14, 2010, the French parliament passed Law 2010-1192, "Act prohibiting concealment of the face in public space." This targeted the estimated 2,000 Muslim women in France who wear niqabs covering their face as part of their cultural traditions and/or religious beliefs. Niqabs conflate two different stereotypes of Muslim women: the oppressed woman forced behind a veil and the sinister terrorist—the Jihad Jane—whose plots to terrorize and take over the world are shrouded behind the anonymity provided by a niqab.

It is worth mentioning that niqabs are not in widespread use among Muslim women worldwide and are alien to most Muslim societies, although the spread of Salafi ideology has made niqabs more commonplace in countries in which they were previously unheard of. Some people, including some Muslims, report feeling uncomfortable with the personal alienation they feel when someone's face is hidden. Nevertheless, freedom of religion is the freedom to be bothered by the religious garb others choose to don so long as one leaves them free and unhindered to dress as they choose in accordance with their religious beliefs. Being able to see someone else's uncovered face is not a fundamental human right, as became evident with widespread mask mandates that unfolded in the name of public health during the COVID-19 pandemic.

More recently, the French Senate voted on bills that outlaw any girl under the age of 18 from wearing clothing that implies female subordination (i.e., hijab) in public, that prohibit "burqinis" in public swimming pools, that ban hijabi mothers from chaperoning school fieldtrips,[2] and that bar hijab from sports competitions.[3] Such laws have the effect of further marginalizing France's Muslim population, especially the Muslim women they are purportedly trying to emancipate. Furthermore, the French government's pressuring of Muslim imams to sign a "charter of republican values" presses home the discriminatory message that Muslims are unique in fundamentally lacking French mores. As such, Muslim imams can be obliged to accept same-sex marriage, whereas Catholic priests would not be.[4]

It must be acknowledged that most societies do not leave humans fully free to determine what they wear. Dress codes and obscenity laws are near universal in human societies and maintain a minimum standard for what is societally considered decent. The opposite of decency laws would be ones that force people to uncover themselves in a manner they personally find indecent. Such laws are sexually degrading and have no role in any free society.

The conversation surrounding the issue of hijab follows the discourse of liberation, the unending burden of Europeans to liberate all others from the yokes of their backward cultures and religions. It is assumed that women who wear hijab are forced to do so by men, not that they are free agents who choose what to wear. Fadela Amara, a Muslim who served as a junior minister in the French government, declared, "The veil is the visible symbol of the subjugation of women," and therefore has no place in a secular public school system.[5] If she were to speak to ordinary Muslim women, she might find that they indeed do not feel truly free to choose whether to wear hijab or not. Western societal stigmatization mean that many Muslim women forgo the hijab due to external pressure. Hijab is not a sign of subjugation, but rather reflects what the New Testament, advises: "Do not adorn yourselves outwardly by braiding your hair, and by wearing gold ornaments or fine clothing; rather, let your adornment be the inner self with the lasting beauty of a gentle and quiet spirit, which is very precious in God's sight."[6] Hijab is a sign of religious devotion, not subjugation. It is also not a political statement. It

should be seen as akin to a nun's habit. It is an attire that is freely
and consciously embraced by a woman, not one that is forced
upon her.

In Iran, during the reign of Reza Shah Pahlavi, hijab bans
were implemented in the name of modernity. My great
grandmothers sequestered themselves at home, venturing
outdoors only on occasion in the dark of night. Was this due to
the tyranny of their husbands and sons? No. One of my great
grandmothers was orphaned and widowed and her one son
hardly stood as a beacon of religiosity. It was her own personal
choice to cover despite the patriarchal monarchic order to unveil.

As was the case with countries like Iran and Turkey, hijab and
niqab bans in Europe are likely to make devout Muslim women
not want to leave their homes; as with other instances in which
the west purports to "liberate" less enlightened races, the end
result is captivity, not freedom. On the eve of the 1979 Iranian
Revolution, after decades of so-called "modernization," 60% of
Iranian women were illiterate. A quarter century after the
revolution, women constituted 58% of public universities
enrollees.[7] This is hardly surprising. Devout young women are
far more likely to attend a university if their religious attire is
respected than if they have to forgo their religious observances in
order to pursue secular education.

Echoes of Colonialism

Restrictions on hijab cannot be seen outside of their colonial
contexts. As pointed out by Catherine Phipps, rescuing Muslim
women from Muslim men became an integral claim of the French
mission civilisatrice (civilizing mission) in North Africa. Mocking
the veiling of women, comparatively lower marital ages, and
customary gender seclusion became a way to glorify a French
colonial regime that carried out pervasive atrocities for the sake
of economic exploitation and the political hegemony of European
men.[8] European feminists took an active role in "saving" Muslim
women from the oppression of Muslim men, helping to mask the

oppression of both Muslim men and women under colonial rule. The freedom Muslim women yearned for was not from their fathers, brothers, husbands, and sons but from the yoke of colonial oppression. Even if they were somehow to be "freed," they were not to be granted self-determination. Western feminism merely served to justify the ongoing violent oppression of Muslim women and men at the hand of the colonial regime. The fruits of this type of European "enlightenment" of their female Muslim subjects is reflected in the fact that a staggering 98% of Algerian women lacked literacy in 1954 by French educational standards.[9]

During the Algerian struggle for independence, the French carried out "unveiling" ceremonies, in which Algerian girls and women were coerced into collectively undonning— and, in more dramatic instances, burning—their hijabs. Family members would be arrested and tortured, only to be freed once their daughters would agree to such displays of "enlightenment." This was the fate of the more fortunate girls; countless others were viciously and repeatedly raped by French soldiers.[10] In one example, a 14-year-old child named Kheira was gang raped by French soldiers. When they found out that she had become pregnant, they viciously and repeatedly beat her to make her abort her child. She eventually gave birth to a son who suffered his entire life from birth defects sustained as a result of these beatings.[11]

Frantz Falon was born in Martinique in 1925, completed his education in France, and served as a psychiatrist in Algeria. He wrote an article entitled, "Algeria Unveiled." In it, he describes the particular wrath with which the French colonizers viewed the veil, as it symbolized that which lay beyond the reach of the European. "Every face that offered itself to the bold and impatient glance of the occupier, was a negative expression of the fact that Algeria was beginning to deny herself and was accepting the rape of the colonizer." He added, "This woman who sees without being seen frustrates the colonizer."[12] Indeed, much has been made by Islamophobes of the necessity of seeing someone's face in society, as if it is the right of the observer to lay eyes on whichever parts of a woman he feels entitled to. Yet, the absolute necessity to see people's faces instantly vaporized as mask mandates pushed all faces behind a veil during the pandemic.

Perhaps what makes forced unveiling feel like emancipation to westerners is that a typical woman of European descent cannot imagine voluntarily wearing a burqa, a niqab, or a headscarf. They imagine what it would take to make them dress like that. They conjure a strict tyrannical paternalistic system, threats of violence and honor killings, the external imposition of unbearable shame, and the internalization of immeasurable guilt. It is assumed that women who dress differently than they do must be forced to do so and must be eagerly awaiting emancipation so that they would have the freedom to be just like western women. It is somehow hard to imagine that someone would choose to live and dress differently, to be proud of their distinct religious or cultural attire, and to see liberty as freedom from harassment when they dress as they please. Anti-hijab activism has managed to ostracize the women it is trying to "save," while empowering and mainstreaming Islamophobic discourse and handing extremists a narrative that westerners are the enemies of Islam. It is also overlooks the fact that hijab is not merely a choice, a political statement donned in opposition to liberal western society, but rather a religious obligation donned in submission to divine will.

French freedom being served at gunpoint is not a relic of some long-gone past. Quite recently, four armed French officers forced a Muslim woman on a public beach in Nice to remove her burqini. Another woman was fined for wearing leggings, a tunic, and a headscarf on a beach in Cannes. She was technically ticketed for not wearing "an outfit respecting good morals and secularism."[13]

A group of "Muslim Rosa Parks" has emerged who have staged swim-ins in public pools in the French city of Grenoble. These pools have banned burqinis in the name of "hygiene and security."[14] Similarly, in the name of "hygiene," men are not allowed to wear American-style swim shorts but rather must wear Speedo-style swimwear that clings to their genitals.[15] These guidelines effectively target Muslim men who generally prefer more modest swimwear.

From a public health standpoint, these regulations are absurd. Clothing is not what brings pathogens to pools. In any case, the pools are presumably chlorinated so that pathogens would not be transmitted. Hygiene is simply a racist way to say that Muslims are unwelcome at French pools. This is reminiscent of the banning of African Americans from public pools, beaches, and lakes in the United States. The perception of black bodies as being innately prone to transmitting contagious diseases as well as being sexually threatening to white women turned pools and beaches into some of the most segregated spaces in America.[16] Subsequent desegregation of public swimming pools led whites to desert public pools altogether and to move to the suburbs, where they could build private ones instead.[17] Across the South, public pools were cemented up. If desegregation meant equal access, then no one having access to pools was seen as better than everyone having access to them. In the meanwhile, YMCAs proliferated so that, as private entities, they could cater to a white-only clientele, until they were forced to desegregate in the 1970s.[18] Such incidents highlight the absurdity of the racist and xenophobic claim that minorities do not want to integrate; in reality, it is the dominant ethnic group that actively shuns them.

It is worth nothing that the concept of racialized populations posing an infectious disease threat is hardly new, but within the context of the COVID-19 pandemic, this has taken on expanded dimensions. While Sinophobes used phrases like "China virus" and "kung flu" to describe the pathogen, in India, the concept of "corona jihad" became prevalent and led to boycotts of Muslim-owned businesses and repeated acts of violence targeting Muslims.[19] In the United Kingdom, numerous fake social media posts claimed that Muslims were congregating in defiance of social distancing regulations. Invariably, the photographs used were found to have been taken from before any public health restrictions had been announced.[20]

Imposition of Western Norms

Burqas are a regional form of attire, and their recent spread has perhaps been aided by media portrayals equating burqas with Islamic piety. Burqas are neither universal in Muslim societies, nor exclusively worn by Muslims. In Israel, some ultra-orthodox Jewish women have adopted the "Jewish burqa," or *sal*, to conform to traditional Jewish concepts of modesty.[21] Indeed, burqa-style garments were commonly worn by Jewish women until the mid-twentieth century.[22] In 2009, when the State Department allowed Yemeni Jews to resettle in the US, Americans were shocked to find that the female refugees arrived wearing niqabs.[23] Other forms of Muslim hijab also find parallels in non-Muslim societies. A headscarf similar to ones worn in Iran is rather commonplace among older Greek women. A Catholic nun's habit closely resembles the *roopoosh* and *maghna'eh* worn by Iranian schoolgirls. The fact that hijab bans effectively constitute a ban on Islam and not the attire itself is evident in how nuns are free to enjoy French beaches in their habits, whereas Muslims wearing equally modest "burqinis" are not.[24] Indeed, covering a woman's hair was commonplace among early Christians, and covering the head in church is still prevalent in many denominations. This is because the New Testament says that it is a "disgrace" for a woman to pray with her head uncovered.[25] In light of the fact that one is to "be constant in prayer,"[26] many Anabaptist women (e.g., Amish) cover their head.

Cultural hegemony has created a standard according to which dressing exactly as westerners do is considered freedom, enlightenment, and progress, whereas uncovering or covering any more than they typically do is equated with savagery and barbarism. If men and women in hunter-gatherer tribes go naked or topless, they are seen as backward savages. If women from Gulf states are completely covered, they are somehow also seen as backward savages. Yet, if a woman wears a bikini at the beach, a tank top at a picnic, a t-shirt at her boyfriend's house, and a strapless dress at a dinner party, she is supremely civilized and enlightened.

When it comes to feminine attire, Muslims might be more tolerant of differences in dress and culture than French and other Europeans are. One can hardly point to a Muslim living in France who demands that French women wear a headscarf, a burqa, a niqab, or a burqini. Indeed, these Muslims epitomize the liberty the French so liberally talk about by donning clothing of their choice despite societal backlash, while at the same time not expecting others to dress in a manner similar to them. This is the true meaning of secularism and freedom. Yet, given the racialized context, freedom for the French means freedom to be "French," whereas freedom for Muslims means freedom from Islam as the French perceive it. In this context, white men requiring Muslim women to undress to their liking is seen as a cure for patriarchy and a recipe for freedom.

In July 2021, the European Court of Justice ruled that employers can forbid their staff from wearing visible symbols of religious or political belief, including headscarves, in order to present an image of "neutrality."[27] Neutrality, of course, is defined by purely western standards with any other faith, culture, or ethnicity representing a deviation. Neutrality is not neutrally accepting the diversity of human traditions but rather a narrow concept of whites and white culture as normal and every other person and culture as some type of anomaly. Forcing Muslim women to choose between their job and their faith leads to nothing but marginalization, poverty, and limited career options—exactly what the Islamophobes accuse Muslim men of imposing on women.

Western obsession with what women wear in other cultures is hardly limited to Muslims. British colonists were appalled at the amount of flesh left exposed by the saris worn by many Hindu women. Depending on geographic location and caste, these saris would completely expose or only partially cover the breasts, with only the higher caste women wearing a breast band. The British mandated a lengthening of the saris and the addition of blouses and petticoats. Servants were expected to dress in western attire, and this was seen by colonial overlords as a generous privilege. Of course, this was hardly out of British cultural generosity; huge profits were to be reaped from forcing the population to purchase overpriced English textiles.[28]

The 1943 Zoot Suit Riots in the United States are an example of how racialized violence can target minority groups based on attire. Zoot suits, which had become popular among African American and Hispanics, were loose-fitting suits that required more fabric to produce. When wartime restrictions were placed limiting the use of fabric for civilian clothing, wearing zoot suits became equated with a lack of patriotism and innate criminality. American servicemen left their Los Angeles barracks to carry out savage mob attacks targeting innocent minority men. They stripped them of their clothes, beat them viciously, and even used a knife to gouge out the eye of a black defense plant worker.[29]

In such instances, attire merely serves as a proxy or "distinguishing feature" for race. Someone wearing racialized attire is seen as particularly offensive, as the act indicates a voluntary and public rejection of white cultural norms. Whereas one does not have a choice in terms of one's skin color, one does have a choice in terms of what one wears. Wearing racialized articles of clothing such as hijab is seen as particularly offensive when it is perceived to be a political statement in favor of repudiating dominant cultural power. If the dominant cultural power is replaced, it is presumed that hijab will become forced on everyone else as the new cultural norm. This explains the vehemence with which hijab has been treated not only in the west where it is conflated with an impending Muslim takeover but also in nominally Muslim countries like Turkey, where hijab restrictions remained in place for decades.

The emotionally charged vehemence with which some people oppose the right to wear hijab culminates in violence targeting Muslim women. Marwa el-Sherbini, a young Egyptian woman and national handball champion, was stabbed to death in the middle of a German courtroom by an unemployed Russian bigot who riled against her hijab. In plain view of her three-year-old son, her husband, the judge, and the entire courtroom, he plunged his knife into her no less than 18 times. When Marwa's husband tried to save his dying wife, courtroom police opened fire on him, assuming, rather unsurprisingly, that the perpetrator must be the Arab and not the white man. This incident unfolded just days after former French president Nicolas Sarkozy gave a speech denouncing the burqa. [30]

Burqa bans have become a rallying cry for western politicians from across the political spectrum to pander for votes while leaving a thin veneer that covers bigotry with a façade of feminism. Even "centrist" politicians adopt anti-burqa policies to help their electoral prospects. Former German Chancellor Angela Merkel, after being accused by right-wing opponents of presiding over the Islamization of German society, called for a burqa ban "whenever legally possible." [31] In these instances, the voice of the Muslim hijabi woman is ignored, her freedom of religion is curtailed, her freedom of speech is silenced, and her humanity is forgotten.

Chapter 9

Bans on Islamic Architecture

Bans on visible icons representing Islam can include prohibitions on hijab for women, stereotypically Islamic beards for men, Muslim rosaries (*misbahah* or *tasbih*), and even Islamic works of architecture such as mosques and minarets. There are three points worth mentioning here. First, considering that these can be thought of as visual representations or icons of Islam, such restrictions effectively amount to a societal ban on the free practice of Islam. Islam is only to be tolerated insomuch as it is not seen. Second, such restrictions hinder the integration of Muslims into multicultural societies. This is both due to the message that emblems of Islam and hence the Muslims who accompany them are unwelcome in society, as well as due to the fact that some Muslims will choose personal devotion over social integration. Third, in addition to the bans on visual representations endorsed by Islam, there is often a concomitant celebration of offensive visual icons that are banned by Islam. Hence, bans on hijab often go hand-in-hand with defending, if not endorsing, offensive caricatures of the Prophet (S). Considering that aniconism when it comes to prophetic images is widely though not universally adopted by Muslims, cartoons portraying him in a positive light are hardly to be found. The cartoons become doubly offensive through both disrespecting Muslim aniconism and lewdly insulting a revered figure. Aniconism is hardly restricted to Islam, with early Buddhism, Judaism, and the Protestant Reformation all including notable aniconic tendencies. The Taliban's destruction of the 6th century Buddhas of Bamiyan, which had survived over thirteen centuries of Muslim rule, paled in comparison to the widespread destruction of European Christian art at the hands of Calvinists.

Islamic art includes a wide range of fields, including calligraphy, textiles, glasswork, ceramics, and quite notably architecture. Many mosques are adorned with domes and minarets, which are tall, slender towers that serve both as a visual reference point to the mosque as well as a place from which the call to prayer (*adhan*) can be broadcast. Whereas domes can be found in churches, palaces, and other structures, minarets are exclusively associated with mosques and hence have become a target of anti-Islamic activism.

In 2005, the Turkish cultural association in Wangen bei Olten, a town of about five thousand residents in northern Switzerland, applied for a permit to build an 18-foot-high minaret on the roof of its community center. The town's residents fought the construction through legal means. On final appeal, the Federal Supreme Court rejected their claims and the minaret was built. Right-wing politicians seized on the issue and pushed through a referendum banning the erection of minarets in Switzerland. Despite the Swiss government and the Catholic Church urging citizens to vote against the ban, 57.5% of voters supported the constitutional amendment, and hence the building of minarets became illegal.

The campaign for the constitutional amendment made heavy use of posters depicting a cartoon of a veiled woman wearing a niqab juxtaposed on minarets shaped like missiles rising up from the Swiss flag. The text reads, "Stop. Yes to the minaret ban."[1] In effect, the building of minarets and the wearing of hijab were equated with Switzerland being turned into a base for Islamic militancy and extremism. Right-wing propagandists claimed that minarets symbolize Islamic conquest: when Muslims conquer a land, they erect minarets as a sign of their victory and domination. Funding for the minarets would allegedly come from shadowy foreign sources trying to export a subversive ideology,[2] and such structures would become an abode of foreign-trained imams.[3]

Foreign-Trained Imams

Allegations in which local religious minorities subvert a host country by serving sinister and clandestine foreign entities is a common feature of bigotry targeting religious minorities. Examples include allegations that Catholics are mere pawns of papal influence, that Jews are determined to infiltrate society on behalf of George Soros or Israel or the "Elders of Zion," and that Bahais merely serve Russian or British colonial and neocolonial interests. Nevertheless, the issue of foreign imams raises a number of points.

First, the absence of locally trained imams is not part of a conspiracy. They simply do not exist because western countries do not provide adequate avenues for Islamic theological education. Anyone seeking advanced learning in Islamic theology or jurisprudence would invariably have to spend some years abroad. This is not any different than someone seeking a doctoral degree in Spanish architecture spending some time in Spain.

Second, there is an inherent double-standard at play with respect to foreign funding or foreign training when Muslims are involved. As Edward Said put it, "When Muslim countries donate money to American universities for Arab or Islamic studies, a great liberal outcry arises about foreign interference in the American university, but when Japan or Germany donates money no such complaint can be heard."[4]

Third, foreign-trained imams are not ideal for many immigrant Muslims as a cultural chasm exists between imams who are often older, foreign-born, and relatively new to the host country and a younger generation that is typically more fluent in the host country's language and more acclimated to western culture. They simply cannot relate as well to someone who does not share their second or third generation immigrant experience. This alienation is compounded by the fact that it is exceedingly difficult to speak eloquently in a non-native tongue, which makes sermons far less compelling. More recently, there has been an increase in western-raised Muslims obtaining religious education in the Middle East or elsewhere and returning to their communities. Their ability to deliver fluent sermons in western languages makes them far more accessible to the younger generation who would otherwise just play on their iPhones while someone delivers a sermon in a language they barely understand. This generation of imams can play a significant role in promoting the integration of younger Muslims, as a sense of alienation from both one's country of residence and one's ancestral lands can be a contributing factor to being drawn to extremism.

Finally, there is definitely some validity to the concern that this theological vacuum creates an opening for Saudi Arabia to provide grants and scholarships to young imams to study in Saudi seminaries and to subsequently spread Wahhabi ideology. It would be foolish to pretend that has not been happening throughout much of the Muslim world. The way to counter extremism, however, is not banning visible emblems of Islam, but rather through the de-marginalization of Muslim communities in a way that allows a diversity of Islamic thought to flourish. All Muslims and indeed Islam itself being painted with the brush of extremism only normalizes radicalized voices that otherwise would be seen as fringe. Western media does a fabulous job of portraying a truly devout Muslim as one who would be ready to be a martyr for any fringe extremist group. This type of messaging does more to drown out moderate voices than Saudi funding. Furthermore, many ordinary Muslims adopt silence because they don't want to find themselves on the side of Islamophobes. A less toxic social environment would do more to empower "moderate" Muslim voices.

In all fairness, some of the proponents of the minaret ban pay lip service to the concept that "moderate" Muslims are welcome in Switzerland.[2] What is unclear is who constitutes a moderate Muslim. A Muslim who eats pork, drinks alcohol, wholeheartedly adopts western dress and customs, constantly demonstrates shame and remorse in response to any bad act any Muslim commits anywhere on earth, and strives to blend in completely would presumably be seen as quite moderate.

Perhaps not as moderate but still tolerable would be one who prays in seclusion at home but shows no visible signs of being Muslim. What is, by inference, not moderate and hence not welcome is any visible or audible emblem that distinguishes a Muslim from others.

The absence of visible signs of racialized minorities makes it easy for a dominant ethnic group to delude itself into thinking that it leads a tolerant and free society. This is how small, uniformly white New England towns feel quite liberal and racially tolerant in contrast to the Southern whites who are seen as racist. As soon as blacks, Hispanics, Muslims, and other immigrants move into town, the innate intolerance of these communities becomes more apparent. Yet, they never admit to being racist—it is just that other ethnic groups create problems. In effect, by bringing race and ethnicity to the community, they carry with them the "problem" of race. Whiteness, of course, is assumed to be the default state of humanity and the mere absence of race. A Greek friend once told me that Greeks used to imagine that Americans were horribly racist for the way they have treated African Americans. Once African refugees and migrants crossed into Greece, xenophobia and racism flourished, and the problem of course was not seen as Greek racism, but rather as the presence of Africans.

The question is why minarets anger people to the point of wanting to change their constitutions, impinge on the religious freedoms of others, and create seemingly needless controversy. There were four minarets in place in Switzerland at the time of the vote, and it is unclear how they caused any problems. Yet, there is no denying that a minaret does raise fears in native communities. The realization that minority communities are growing and here to stay raises fears of population replacement, a topic that is discussed in chapter 27. Visible vestiges of minority presence in a neighborhood could raise fears of property devaluation and the specter of white flight. The existence of young minority men might raise fears of terrorism or concerns that that they would seek white girlfriends and wives. The presence of an imam in clerical robe could raises fear that shariah law is here to take over. Given such racialized fears, it is hardly surprising that a poll found that 56% of Germans would not want a mosque in their neighborhood. This compares to 17% who would not want a Christian church and 25% who would not want a Jewish synagogue or Buddhist temple nearby.[5]

Since racist fears are posed as reasonable concerns, the problem is invariably seen to lie within the minority group. In a world in which Donald Trump—who refers to African countries, Haiti, and El Salvador as "s--thole countries"—can claim during a presidential debate that he is "the least racist person in this room," and his claim actually resonates with much of the population, we must consider what being racist even means any more. As pointed out by Robin DiAngelo in *White Fragility*, our bar for racism has effectively been set to where short of wantonly using racial slurs or joining the KKK, one can claim not to be a racist.[6] Having spoken with the office building's black janitor once in the elevator, "adoring" the Salvadoran maid who so immaculately cleans one's home, and relishing the cultural enrichment of a summer trip to Japan are seen as signs that one is clearly not racist. As such, racism is not to be found in the open confession of racists, but rather ought to be pointed out in the stereotypes that underlie discourse and in disparities in socioeconomic outcomes that reveal how racism persists as an omnipresent social force in liberal societies.

What minarets symbolize is not a military takeover of a western nation, but rather the existence of a safe space for a religious and cultural minority community where they feel unjudged practicing their own traditions. This might simply be a space where they can freely speak their native tongue, recite the poetry of their nation of origin, and be guaranteed a halal meal. It is not a space to exclude others; any Islamic center I know of openly welcomes the community to learn about Islam and to engage with Muslims, even though they might be wary of how their customs can readily be twisted by the media. A video of Muslim children in a Dearborn mosque learning to recite the Quran can easily be portrayed on social media and on Fox News as analogous to a Taliban *madrasa*. The racially charged atmospheres many Muslims live in lend every small act to sinister interpretations.

The "Ground Zero Mosque" Controversy

In the United, States, resistance to building mosques and Islamic schools has been pervasive. Kathleen Foley, a fellow at the Institute for Social Policy and Understanding, said,

> Conflicts over mosque development in American cities and suburbs were local affairs that rarely garnered attention beyond the municipalities in which they were proposed. Opponents tended to focus their critiques on such land use issues as parking, traffic, and noise, even if those stated reasons veiled their true intent to exclude Muslims from the neighborhood. Zoning and planning boards frequently yielded to public pressure and denied the necessary permits. As a result, Muslim American communities often spent years searching for developments sites before finally succeeding. In fact, it was not unusual for them to settle for parcels that were undesirable but more likely to be approved, or to make considerable compromises on their original plans.[7]

Those who oppose local mosque construction in their neighborhoods are rather vocal and often get their way. That people would want a mosque not to be built in their neighborhood is hardly surprising when one considers how pervasive negative stereotypes of Muslim are in western societies. A mosque would simply bring more troublesome characters, extremists, and future terrorists to the neighborhood, and its school would serve as a *madrasa* (the two words are synonymous, after all). Who wants that in their backyard?

When Muslims are barred from building adequate prayer spaces for their congregations, Friday prayers often extend out of cramped prayer rooms and onto the surrounding public streets, which can affect pedestrian and vehicular traffic. This then creates calls for bans on praying in public streets. In 2011, former French interior minister Claude Guéant outlawed street prayers in Paris.[8] Rather limited and easily avoidable inconveniences caused by Muslims are thus cracked down on, whereas repeated and highly disruptive acts in the form of transit strikes, street protests, and civil disobedience by whites are tolerated as freedom of speech and assembly.

Whereas most of these issues are fought out at the local level, controversy over construction of the "Ground Zero Mosque" became a rallying cry of the American right. Cordoba House was designed to be a 13-story Islamic community center and mosque at the Park51 location in Lower Manhattan, which is two blocks from the former World Trade Center. It was intended to provide a forum for interfaith dialogue within the community. An outcry from Islamophobes like Pamela Geller and Robert Spencer, founders of Stop Islamization of America, brought the issue to national attention. Talk radio host Rush Limbaugh echoed the equation of Islamic architecture with a Muslim takeover when he declared, "They want to build a victory monument."[9] A Pew study found that 62% of Americans believe that "Muslims should have the same [legal] rights as other groups to build houses of worship in local communities," but that only 34% believe that an Islamic center should be allowed to be built near the site of the former World Trade Center.[10] The "Ground Zero Mosque" controversy has provided a venue for right-wing polemics. The issue is no longer about freedom of religion but a zero-sum cultural war against the encroachment of a dangerous and antagonistic foreign ideology.

In fact, the most banal of activities can be seen as sinister when carried out by Muslims. Take the controversy whenever a group of Muslims plays paintball. The NYPD has wasted countless taxpayer dollars investigating whether whitewater rafting and paintball serve as a cover for terrorist training among Muslim college students, while keeping detailed logs of how many times a day each student prayed.[11] At Embry-Riddle Aeronautical University, an aviation school in Florida,

Mahmoud Khatib, a former president of its Muslim Student Association (MSA), had to publish the following disclaimer:

> The Embry-Riddle MSA is not affiliated with ANY terrorist organization and does not support or engage in ANY terrorist activity, period. Our MSA paintball trips, as with all of the recreational activities we host (BBQ, soccer,   beach   trips,   go-karting,   etc.)   are EXCLUSIVELY FOR THE PURPOSE OF FUN.[12]

This was written in response to published allegations that the MSA was engaged in terrorist training based on a paintball outing. In fact, association with an MSA is commonly used in Islamophobic smear campaigns. When Dr. Abdul El-Sayed ran for governor of Michigan, Republican state senator Patrick Colbeck asserted that he was part of a "civilizational jihad" to take over America. He claimed that since El-Sayed had served as the vice president of his college's MSA, he must have ties to the Muslim Brotherhood.[13] Something as banal as joining an officially sanctioned college religious organization is conflated with being part of a hyped-up international Islamist conspiracy.

A Slippery Slope

The danger with allowing bans on visible emblems of Islam such as hijab, mosques, and minarets is that they serve as the first step on a dangerous journey towards greater exclusion, cultural genocide, and ethnic cleansing. In 2014, authorities in Karamay, a city in Xinjiang, a predominantly Muslim region in Western China, banned people with Islamic attire or "large" beards from traveling on public transportation.[14] In 2017, a law was passed that banned veils and beards in any public space in Xinjiang, prohibited enrollment in private schools, and outlawed the refusal to watch state television programming.[15] Quickly enough, this expanded into the forced internment of millions of Muslim Uyghurs in "re-education" camps, where they are forced to eat pork and drink alcohol.[16] They are barred from speaking their native language. Female detainees are forcibly sterilized and repeatedly raped.[17] Golden domes and minarets are demolished or replaced with Chinese style roofs. A razed historic mosque in Hotan is now to become a Hilton Hampton Inn.[18] Freedom of religion is re-defined as the freedom to pray in seclusion in one's home.[19] Muslim-owned stores and restaurants are required to sell and serve alcohol and cigarettes and to promote them in "eye-catching displays."[20] China defends its policies by claiming they are needed to fight "the three evils of extremism, separatism and terrorism."[21] One cannot be so complacent as to overlook the reality that the same exact arguments used in Europe to promote minaret and hijab bans are used to justify genocide in Xinjiang.

An even more harrowing reality has unfolded just south of China in Myanmar. In Rakhine State, on the country's western coast, anti-Muslim rhetoric led initially to the shuttering of all mosques. In 2012, mosques in the state were systematically burnt down by Buddhist nationalist mobs spearheaded by Buddhist monks. Like the Swiss proponents of minaret bans, they denigrated Muslims as an expanding and dangerous foreign entity.[22] It hardly matters that the Rohingya have called the area home for over a millennium; they are still seen as foreign. The flames of ethnic cleansing were fanned through Facebook, which was eager to capitalize on the profits to be made in the Burmese market. Facebook posts such as, "We must fight them the way Hitler did the Jews,"[23] went viral. Buddhist mobs methodically torched Muslim homes and villages, culminating in the largest displacement of civilians in Asia since the Vietnam War.[24] Facebook, which acknowledges the role its platform played in the genocide, has recently been sued for $150 billion in American and British courts.[23]

The fact is that ethnic genocide starts with racist rhetoric that is allowed to proliferate in the name of freedom of speech or freedom of the press, moves on to seemingly trivial restrictions on "unusual" or "offensive" attire or behavior, and then can rapidly culminate in genocide carried out by a dominant population that has been primed to hate. This is why it is imperative to confront any vestige of ethnoreligious stigmatization.

Silencing the Muslim Call to Prayer

Bans on Muslim architecture and attire help reduce visible vestiges of the Muslim presence. As British broadcaster Julia Hartley-Brewer put it, "[We are] just tired of having Islam thrust in our faces day in, day out."[25] She, like other Islamophobes, just wants to live in a world where she doesn't have to see anything that reminds her of Islam. Her desire, in her mind, somehow trumps the right of others to live in peace and to practice their religion freely. As a lived experience, religion encompasses all the senses. Visual icons, including the architecture of churches, mosques, and temples, the visible features that signify an altar or *mihrab*, and the presence or absence of various forms of artwork adorning houses of worship, contribute to a visual experience. The humming of prayers, beating of drums, ringing of bells, singing of choirs, and recitation of holy texts form part of the auditory experience. The smell of incense, perfumes, or rosewater add olfactory stimuli. Ablutions, genuflecting and prostrating, and holding rosaries form part of the tactile and proprioceptive sensations associated with worship. Serving communion, eating eggnog, or consuming foods culturally associated with Ramadan or Muharram or other religious observances contribute to a gustatory experience.

One of the most stereotypical Hollywood portrayals of Muslim lands is that the *adhan* (call to prayer) can be heard in the background as the sun rises. This, of course, is rather inaccurate, as the morning *adhan* is at twilight, approximately an hour and a half prior to sunrise. Nevertheless, since the *adhan* has come to symbolize Islam, restrictions on the *adhan* serve to limit the auditory perception of Islam within a society. Accordingly, numerous countries and municipalities have placed restrictions on whether the call to prayer can be broadcast, what language it can be recited in, whether loudspeakers can be used, and what times of day or days of the week the call can be made.[26-27] The same type of people who are strongly in favor of freedom of speech when it comes to offensive Islamophobic cartoons are the ones petitioning local and national governments to restrict the rights of Muslims to publicly recite their call to prayer.

Restrictions on the *adhan* are hardly limited to the west. For nearly two decades, Turkey banned the *adhan*'s recitation in Arabic as part of Ataturk's "modernization" policies.[28] Modernization, of course, was not in the form of granting meaningful political and religious freedoms but rather in the form of Islamophobia; the only path to modernity would be through ridding society of any vestige of Islam.

In 2015, Duke University announced that the Muslim call to prayer would be announced from the bell tower of Duke Chapel. There was an immediate outcry from the Christian right. Reverend Franklin Graham, a right-wing evangelist, called on alumni to withhold donations from the university until it reversed its policy.[29] He posted on Facebook,

> The Muslim call to prayer that has been approved to go out across the campus of Duke University every Friday afternoon for three minutes includes "Allahu Akbar"— the words that the terrorists shouted at the onset of last week's massacre in Paris.

The university backed down, saying, "Duke remains committed to fostering an inclusive, tolerant and welcoming campus for all of its students... However, it was clear that what was conceived as an effort to unify was not having the intended effect."[30] Basically, Muslim students at Duke were to be held to account for terrorist attacks carried out in Paris and to be punished for the Islamophobia prevalent among the university's wealthy and predominantly white donors. Appeasing racists should not be a university's goal. Rather, a university priding itself on diversity should eagerly support equal rights of citizenship regardless of ethnicity, gender, and religion. "Allahu Akbar" being associated with terrorism in the west is due to the silencing of the Muslim voice and the amplification of that of the terrorist. To Muslims, the phrase is so commonplace that it is not associated with acts of violence but rather with spirituality, prayer, or mere excitement.

College campuses have turned into an unwelcome environment for many Muslim students. According to CAIR California's "Campus Climate Report," 40% of Muslim students experienced harassment or discrimination, over one-half experienced bigoted comments from other students, and a third experienced such comments from professors and instructors. "Students who advocated on behalf of pro-Palestinian issues were subjected to particularly egregious or persistent forms of harassment and discrimination."[31] According to a report by *The Guardian*,

> Students protesting against Israeli occupation frequently find themselves accosted by a powerful array of well-funded adversaries—some backed by the Israeli government itself—armed with a battery of cyber tools... At the University of Michigan... pro-Palestinian activists have been "blacklisted, insulted and harassed for years." Pro-Palestinian advocates are frequently threatened online with being reported to Canary Mission, a secretive website that names and shames students and professors whom it accuses of spreading hatred of Israel...
>
> Another fearsome opponent is the online platform Act.IL, an app that exists to "fight back against the demonization and delegitimization of the Jewish state". Launched in 2017 by a former Israeli intelligence officer with partial funding by the Israeli government, Act.IL rallies American supporters of Israel and sends them on "missions" to combat criticism of the country often emanating from campuses. People joining a "mission" are given pre-prepared letters of complaint targeting Palestinian advocates which they are then encouraged to send to university administrators or legislators. Once the

"mission" is completed, participants are rewarded with badges and points.

One of Act.IL's "missions" was directed against a Palestinian-American student at Florida State University after he was elected president of the student senate. Ahmad Daraldik, who spent much of his childhood growing up in the West Bank, came under a concerted barrage of attack not only from the mobile app, but from Republican legislators who threatened to cut off funding from the school if action wasn't taken to demote him. He also faced opposition from city council members and fellow students who orchestrated three petitions against him. Daraldik was eventually ousted from the student leadership position...[32]

University professors are similarly subject to intimidation campaigns if they do not toe the mainstream (i.e., Islamophobic) line in their teachings and academic research. In 2000, after visiting the notorious El-Khiam prison where members of the Lebanese resistance had been "tortured and incarcerated in appalling conditions," the late Columbia University Professor Edward Said threw a symbolic "pebble"[33] towards an Israeli watchtower on the border. *Columbia Spectator* ran the front page headline, "Edward Said Accused of Stoning in South Lebanon," as if he had stoned someone to death.[34] In 2002, Daniel Pipes launched Campus Watch, which called for students to report professors who taught anything sympathetic to Islam. They would publish dossiers on these professors in order to single them out for intimidation. The effective goal was to silence their academic freedom and exercise of free speech.

When Barbara Bush died in 2018, Randa Jarrar, a tenured creative writing professor at California State University at Fresno tweeted, "Barbara Bush was a generous and smart and amazing racist who, along with her husband, raised a war criminal." In the wake of calls to fire her, the university's president said that, "This was beyond free speech. This was disrespectful." Pouring cold water on the concept of academic freedom or even the basic freedom of political speech, he added, "A professor with tenure does not have blanket protection to say and do what they wish." An investigation was launched but thanks to concerted efforts by civil liberty groups, the university did not take any formal action against her other than to condemn what she had said.[35,36] The lesson is nevertheless clear: Muslims disrespecting white political icons is not to be fully tolerated.

More recently, on Cornell University's campus, a Uyghur student and a member of the US House of Representatives were subject to a walkout for discussing the genocide targeting China's Uyghur population.[37] By creating friction and raining down controversy, such disruptive actions silence students by making it uncomfortable for anyone to raise human rights issues pertaining to Muslim populations.

College should be a welcoming environment for students and professors from diverse ethnic, religious, cultural, and national backgrounds who approach a variety of subjects from different perspectives. Nevertheless, it is hardly surprising that the same political and financial forces at work in society at large are found encroaching on university campuses.

Chapter 10

The War on Halal Food

Racist narratives even permeate the culinary world. Western diets are seen as constituting the norm, whereas non-western ingredients and forms of animal slaughter are seen as innately disgusting or barbaric. Xenophobia in the food industry became especially evident in the wake of the coronavirus pandemic, which the media was quick to blame on Chinese markets selling exotic meats not found in western cuisine. Yet, that kind of culinary rhetoric is not used against pork and chicken meat during outbreaks of swine flu and avian influenza, respectively. In Europe, the battle against kosher and halal meat has been raging, with the basic charge that these forms of animal slaughter divide citizens, violate animal welfare norms, and stealthily intrude religion into western societies.[1]

Halal and kosher slaughter are similar in that the main vessels of an animal's neck are severed by a sharp blade and the animal is allowed to bleed out. Halal slaughter also requires that the name of God be mentioned at the time of slaughter. The animals must be alive at the time of slaughter, otherwise the meat would be classified as carrion, which is forbidden. Whereas Jews following a kosher diet tend to believe that an animal must be conscious at the time of slaughter, Muslims are divided regarding the issue of consciousness as a criterion for halal slaughter. A requirement for consciousness equates to a prohibition on pre-slaughter stunning. A combination of Islamophobes, antisemites, and animal welfare activists have aggressively pushed for outlawing animal slaughter that is not preceded by stunning, and currently at least eleven European countries have such restrictions in place.[2] The European Court of Justice, Europe's highest court, has endorsed such legislation, ruling that EU law does not prevent countries from requiring that animals be stunned prior to slaughter.[3]

Historically, kosher and halal slaughter practices were portrayed as evidence of the bloodlust of Jews and Muslims and served as rationales for the persecution and expulsion of religious minorities from Europe. In modern times, the language has shifted to "animal welfare" but the basic concepts remain the same—there is no place for barbaric Jewish and Islamic practices in "civilized" Europe.[4]

"Animal welfare" serves as a thinly veiled cover for bigotry. As such, stereotypical hobbies of white men such as hunting with dogs, bows and arrows, and guns are not banned. Maceration, the wholesale grinding up of millions of un-stunned male chicks in the egg industry, continues unchecked. Pigs and calves are boiled and skinned alive in slaughterhouses; millions of farmed minks are subjected to carbon monoxide gassing, which is a particularly painful and prolonged form of death for these semi-aquatic animals; pigs, chickens, and turkeys are mass-culled by "ventilation shutdowns," the process of shutting off air and letting the animals die from suffocation and heat; and countless animals are tormented with electrocutions, carbon dioxide chambers, and repeated attempts at stunning.[4] To anyone who has seen halal slaughter in person, it is far more humane than what typifies mainstream practices in industrial food production.

Furthermore, this rigid concentration on the mode of slaughter overlooks the cruelty of life for most animals in western meat, egg, and dairy industries. Egg-laying hens living out their entire lifetimes in spaces so confined that they cannot even spread their wings, breeding pigs not having enough space to be able to turn around and see their own offspring, and the mass debeaking of chickens and tail-docking of cows are among the many forms of animal cruelty routinely carried out to maximize profits.[5] This has led to a push among some halal advocates to espouse halal as constituting an entire system of animal welfare that requires humane treatment of animals not only at the time of slaughter but also during the animal's lifetime.[6] Nevertheless, the cruelty inherent in western industrialized food production is widely accepted as innately necessary or even humane, while people obsessively focus on Muslim and Jewish practices that, in comparison, are relatively humane.

Politically, much of the conversation over halal has centered on the surreptitious encroachment of Islam into the lives of unsuspecting Europeans. Marine Le Pen, the far-right French presidential candidate, generated controversy by asserting that ninety percent of abattoirs in the Paris region serve halal meat and that there was an active cover-up of that fact. She continues to exploit the narrative that the French government is too weak to resist the encroachment of foreign cultures as an effective means to gain support from the electorate. French Chief Rabbi Haim Korsia called out Le Pen for "fomenting hatred and war between the government and religions, as well as interreligious animosity."[7]

The cultural war against halal food has spilled over into the push for "pork-or-nothing" school lunches and the elimination of any non-pork options in the name of secularism or *laïcité*.[8] Secularism is no longer the respect of people's divergent religious beliefs but rather the imposition of a dominant group's religio-cultural practices on religious minorities. The fear of being imposed upon is used to justify a mandate to impose on others. Indeed, the call for sameness undermines the concept of secularism, which requires tolerance of those with different beliefs. This desire for sameness is highlighted by memes such as, "England: We eat pork, drink beer, & speak English."[9]

The insistence on pork-only meals is particularly problematic because many Muslim children in European schools come from poor families where food insecurity can be an issue. Furthermore, pork-only meals marginalize Muslim and Jewish students who are made to stand out at school based on their diet, without any compensatory social benefit. Pressuring people to eat something they find innately repugnant is simply immoral. No white person would want to be forced to choose between eating dog meat or going hungry when plenty of other sensible options abound. Considering European historical contexts, pork-

or-nothing is just one step above the eat-pork-or-die mindset of the Spanish Inquisition.

The battle over food has exposed the intolerance of right-wing Europeans for any vestige of Muslim culture. Slovak member of parliament Andrej Danko said, "Islamisation (sic) begins with kebab and in Bratislava it has already begun. So understand what it could be like in 5-10 years."[10] In this mindset, a kebab shop is just the beginning; soon there will be women in niqab and minarets going up, Slovakia will be taken over by Muslims, and they will have no one to blame but themselves for having allowed the kebab shop to open in the first place. With this mindset, it is hardly surprising that Slovakia will not allow a single mosque to be built in the country.[11] The perceived delicacy and fragility of these societies in the face of ethnic diversity must be contrasted with the multi-ethnic and multi-confessional Islamic empires that embraced a diversity of cultures, religions, foods, languages, and technologies.

The halal and kosher food debate is just another iteration of the long and sordid history of the colonial discourse on food. Christopher Columbus, in his first voyage to the Americas, concluded that the avocados, beans, berries, cassava, chilies, corn, guavas, papayas, pumpkins, and tomatoes that the indigenous people consumed were inferior to the bread, olive oil, meat, and wine that the Spanish were accustomed to. As such, in his second voyage, he introduced European livestock, which soon ravaged indigenous croplands, contributing to mass starvation among native populations.[12] The war on native food supplies culminated in the systematic hunting of American bison to near extinction. In the 1800s, wild buffalo, which once numbered over 30 million, were systematically gunned down, leaving only a few hundred remaining in the wild. President Ulysses Grant saw the mass-hunting of buffalo as the solution to the country's "Indian problem," and the nation succumbed to a philosophy of, "Kill every buffalo you can! Every buffalo dead is an Indian gone."[13] In this context, controlling the food of Muslim and Jewish populations is hardly different, except that the language has shifted from one of calling for genocide to one of hiding the desire to ethnically cleanse society of a minority community under the guise of concern for animal welfare and universal liberal values. There is no better way to be rid of an unwanted ethnic group than to curtail its food.

The Christopher Columbus story highlights another reality—that even though there can be initial nativist resistance to culturally alien foods, over time, such foods can become dietary staples. After all, what would Italian food be like without noodles imported from China and tomatoes brought in from the New World?

Chapter 11

Muslim Intolerance vs Intolerance of Muslims

Among the most stereotyped portrayals of Islam and Muslims is that they are innately intolerant and therefore not compatible with western liberal and democratic values. Critical discourse analysis helps expose how such stereotypes are constructed, legitimized, and perpetuated through "us versus them" binaries. While the in-group's positives are emphasized and its negatives are de-emphasized, the out-group is subjected to the converse. It overemphasizes the humane qualities of one's own group while dehumanizing the perceived other, creating us-versus-them, good-versus-evil, and light-versus-darkness contrasts. Such dichotomies become transcendent as their underlying assumptions constitute the basis of common speech, media representations, academic inquiries, social policies, and political decision making.[1]

These dichotomies are also easily exploited for political gains. The free us versus the tyrannical them, the enlightened us versus the backward them, the feminist us versus the patriarchal them, the peaceful us versus the violent them, and the tolerant us versus the intolerant them all feature prominently in western conceptualization of Muslims. The most blatant examples of such simplistic contrasts are encountered in the context of aggression against Muslim states as well as in political speech in the run-up to democratic elections. George W. Bush's repeated good-versus-evil and light-versus-darkness quotes were examples of this, as were Donald Trump's innumerable racist comments. The "bad *hombres*" of Mexico are to be contrasted with the "fine" men of America, the "hatred" of Muslims with the love of

Christians, and the "sickness" of Muslims with the healthy minds of westerners.[2]

Such stark pronouncements only resonate because the content is widely accepted as factual given the pervasive acceptance of racist stereotypes. In a society where openly voicing such stereotypes is seen as distasteful, someone like Trump comes to be perceived as someone who "tells it like it is" because he bluntly asserts the stereotypes as facts. He is the one brave enough to say out loud what everyone *knows* to be true. The politicians who don't are merely seen as just "playing politics" or as trying to be "politically correct."

The prevalence of these beliefs gives rise to the types of microaggression commonly encountered by Muslims and other minority groups. Ibtihaj Muhammad, a hijabi African American Muslim woman from New Jersey who won an Olympic medal in fencing, describes her attempt at finding a job after graduating from Duke University. In one interview, the interviewer repeatedly questioned her about whether she would be comfortable working with people who were not of her faith.[3] The implication, of course, was that she would be intolerant of others because she was Muslim. Yet, the reality was that she had no problem working with others because of their faiths; it was others who had a problem working with her because of her faith. Her alleged intolerance was imagined; their intolerance was real. The intolerance for Muslims based on the false narrative that Muslims are intolerant meant that she struggled to find a job despite having graduated from a top university.

I once spoke with a hijabi Syrian American woman who had graduated from the Johns Hopkins University School of Medicine. When she interviewed for an obstetrics and gynecology residency in New York, the interviewer asked her if she would feel comfortable treating patients who are not of her faith. The fact that it would even be considered rational that a Muslim who grew up in America and who had attended college and medical school at diverse institutions in which Muslims constitute a miniscule minority would have a problem with others reveals the type of stereotypes that predominate. In her case, she withdrew her application from the program, but she was in a unique position to have many great opportunities. For marginalized, low-pay workers, these bigoted assumptions are the difference between employment on the one hand or starvation or the welfare office on the other.

Stereotypes help reverse reality in the popular imagination. When Donald Trump says that Muslims hate America, what this really means is that many Americans hate Muslims and hence this reality-inverting assertion constitutes a potential source of votes. Similarly, when Muslims are portrayed as intolerant, it merely masks the intolerance for Islam and Muslims. Furthermore, Muslims are seen as violent and warlike, even though it is the United States that has been at virtually perpetual war since its inception and Muslim nations serve far more as the victims of war than its perpetrators. Iran is perceived as a particularly belligerent state, even though it has not started a war against another country for nearly two centuries; the peace-loving United States, meanwhile, has engaged in over a hundred wars during its short two-hundred-year history. This is merely a continuation of the portrayal of colonial subjects as brutes, even though the colonial populations were in reality the victims of European brutality.

This racialized inversion of reality is hardly limited to Muslims. Native Americans were thought of as "savages" even as they were savagely annihilated to near extinction. Black men have been seen as rapists with an insatiable appetite for white women, even though the true rapists were the white slave masters who routinely raped black women and children. George H. W. Bush exploited this stereotype of black men by running ads linking his opponent, Massachusetts Governor Michael Dukakis, to Willie Horton, an African American murderer who raped a white woman while on furlough from a Massachusetts prison. Reverend Jesse Jackson, condemning the ads as offensive, said, "The use of the Willie Horton example is designed to create the most horrible psycho-sexual fears."[4] The racist ads were quite successful in ensuring Bush's electoral victory in the 1988 elections, highlighting how easy it is for politicians to exploit racist stereotypes to manipulate the electorate.

Can a Muslim Be President?

The prevalence of Islamophobic stereotypes creates seemingly rational discourses that otherwise would be nonsensical. For example, Ben Carson, a former Republican presidential candidate, insisted that Islam is not compatible with the US Constitution and that he would not advocate for a Muslim president. John Kasich, former Republican governor of Ohio and presidential candidate, when asked whether he would support a Muslim for president of the US, replied, "That's such a hypothetical question," then went on to add, "The most important thing about being president is you have leadership skills, you know what you're doing, and you can help fix this country and raise this country. Those are the qualifications that matter to me."[5] In a racialized context, Ben Carson is merely saying it as it is, whereas Kasich is being politically correct by dodging the question and sugar-coating the answer.

The answer each individual gives to the question, "Can a Muslim be president of the United States?" matters less than the fact that such a question can be posed in seemingly rational terms in the first place and not be dismissed as inherently nonsensical. No one goes around asking whether Bush can be president given his Christian faith. Such a question would be considered senseless. Considering that a Zogby poll found that 42% of Americans believe that Islam would influence the ability of a Muslim American to serve in a government post,[6] debating whether a Muslim is fit for political office can have seemingly rational traction.

Similar questions have historically been asked about Catholics in the US, where only two Catholics have ever been elected to nationwide office—John Kennedy and Joe Biden. Prior to the twentieth century, anti-Catholic prejudice made it impossible for a Catholic to run. In the mid nineteenth century, the Know Nothing Party was formed to oppose Irish immigration and a feared clandestine takeover of the United States by Roman Catholics determined to subjugate Washington to the Vatican. Their star and stripe flag carried the motto, "Native Americans beware of foreign influence,"[7] with "Native Americans" of course referring to white Protestants. In 1928, Al Smith became the first Catholic to run for president as candidate of a major political party; he lost to Herbert Hoover 444-87 in the electoral college. Anti-Catholic resentment spearheaded by the Ku Klux Klan helped ensure that he and other Catholics would be widely perceived as unfit for office.

Later, when John F. Kennedy ran for president, there was grave concern that if elected, he would be taking his orders from the Pope. He flew to Houston to reassure Protestant ministers that, "I believe in an America where the separation of church and state is absolute, where no Catholic prelate would tell the president how to act."[8] Considering white European Catholics went from a banned religious minority in the colonial era to an ostracized religious community through much of American history to being more widely accepted as fully American shows the painstakingly long process of minority acceptance and integration, while highlighting that only the whitest of Catholics—i.e., ones whose ancestors migrated from places like Ireland and Italy—have been more fully integrated. The integration of European Catholics was facilitated by increased Hispanic, Asian, and Muslim immigration providing new alternatives for xenophobic ire to be focused on. As pointed out by Falguni Sheth, liberal societies are inherently unable to exist without an "outcaste" group: "There is an inherent subtext to liberalism that systematically engenders 'exceptions' to the ideal framework of equal rights and protections."[9] There is always an ostracized group that is seen as fundamentally different and unassimilable. The question of whether a Muslim or woman or African American can serve as president presupposes fundamental flaws in those groups that are absent in white Christian men.

Muslim Tolerance

As to whether Muslims are tolerant, the answer is the same as whether Protestants and Catholics and Jews are tolerant. Some members of each group are more tolerant than others, but members of all these religious groups manage to live peacefully in multiethnic and multiconfessional states, to fulfill their civic duties, and to pay taxes and vote. We will address Muslim intolerance in terms of the rise of *takfiri* ideology in chapter 14.

Considering how commonplace bigoted vilification of Islam and Muslims are in western media, it is evident that Muslims tolerate criticism and insult quite well. All you have to do is walk into a bookstore, turn on Fox News, watch a movie, or get on social media to see pervasive demonization of Islam and Muslims. People routinely insult the Prophet (S), calling him a terrorist, a pedophile, a philanderer, a bandit, a madman, or a cult leader. Yet, one does not see Muslim book-burning ceremonies and those who make lucrative careers out of insulting Islam, with rare exceptions, go about quite fine. As a badge of honor, they constantly bemoan the occasional empty threat someone makes in a YouTube comment or the like; a young, attractive woman promoting makeup on social media is subject to more gruesome threats than they are.

As to whether Islam is tolerant of other faiths, the short answer is yes. Muslim empires have brought forth some of the most diverse, multiethnic, and multiconfessional societies ever seen. The Abbasid Caliphate inspired scholars from Arabia, the Near East, Persia, North Africa, China, the Indian subcontinent, and elsewhere to move to their imperial capital of Baghdad to promote philosophical, literary, and scientific inquiry. At its peak, the Ottoman Caliphate was comprised of a minority Muslim population, and religious groups were granted significant autonomy under the *millet* system. The Muslim Mughals ruled over an ethnically and religiously diverse society in the Indian subcontinent. The fact that most Balkans and Indians remain non-Muslim is living proof of the religious tolerance of Muslims.

In contrast, the historical religious tolerance of Europe is reflected in how many native Muslims remain in the Iberian Peninsula and in the fate of European Jewry in the 20th Century. Religious minorities have persisted for over a millennium in the heart of Islamic lands—in countries like Lebanon, Syria, Iraq, and Iran—showcasing the relative tolerance for religious minorities. Furthermore, Muslims have lived peacefully as minority communities in many lands from the dawn of Islam until now. This is not to say that Muslims have been immune to religious or ethnic strife. The early Abbasids, after all, were vicious in their repression of the Shia minority until the Shia Buyids rose to political prominence and effectively controlled puppet caliphs. The point is that Muslims are not as innately or distinctly intolerant as they are stereotyped to be. A mid-nineteenth century description of the tolerance of Muslims in the Ottoman Empire reads,

> What traveler has not observed the fanaticism, the antipathy of all these [Christian] sects—their hostility to each other? Who has traced their actual repose to the *toleration* of Islamism? Islamism, calm, absorbed, without spirit of dogma, or views of proselytism, imposes at present on the other creeds the reserve and silence which characterize itself.[10]

The importance of critical discourse analysis cannot be highlighted enough. It is easy to lull ourselves into being incredibly off-base in terms of important societal and global realities. Instead of seeing Soviet and American military intervention in Afghanistan as the cause of extremism, the cause is seen as flaws within Muslim communities or Islam, and the erroneous solutions sought are military in nature. Increased militancy and extremism in response to the deployment of foreign military force only validate the essentially flawed initial assumptions that Islam is fundamentally a militant religion and that Muslims are intolerant extremists. In the meanwhile, right-wing extremist groups are left unchecked to carry out deadly

...tacks because they are seen as "very fine people" by the likes of Donald Trump.[11] In a country like Iraq, Sunnis and Shias shared neighborhoods until the Americans came in, sowing anarchy, and leaving people vying for the protection of sectarian and ethnic militias. Within a few years, entire neighborhoods and towns became segregated. This was seen as a reflection of how Muslims are always at each others' throats and how Sunnis and Shias have been fighting it out for centuries. Yet, the real issue was western military occupation, not the imagined perpetual state of war among Muslims in general or Shias and Sunnis in particular. As stated by Ali-Karamali,

> My family is Sunni, but we currently attend a Shi'i Islamic center. Quite a few Muslims identify as neither Sunni nor Shi'a but simply as "Muslim" or even sometimes "Sushi," the latter term indicating disregard of or impatience with the negligible differences between Sunni and Shi'a... Sunnis and Shi'a have historically never engaged in campaigns of violence on the scale of, say, the Catholic-Protestant conflicts throughout history. They have never had a program of forced conversions at the level of, say, the Spanish Inquisition. Sunni and Shi'a have always recognized each other as valid Muslims. It's only rare extremists (a fraction of a fraction of the Muslim world) who do not accept the Shi'a as Muslims.[12]

Another problem with rhetoric that paints Muslims as inherently violent is that it leads to the conclusion that keeping Muslims out—e.g., Trump's "Muslim ban"—would make the country more secure. Yet, between 2008 and 2015, the chance of an American being killed by a foreign-born terrorist was 1 in 104.2 million per year. The chance of being killed by an animal was nearly one hundred times higher, at 1 in 1.6 million per year; thirty percent of such fatalities were due to stings by bees, hornets, and wasps.[13] Also, an irrational fear of Muslims led to travel bans against people from countries like Iran, Libya,

Somalia, and Yemen whose nationals have carried out zero lethal terrorist attacks in the United States in the last two decades.[14] As for the nineteen 9/11 hijackers, there were fifteen from Saudi Arabia, two from the United Arab Emirates, one from Lebanon, and one from Egypt, none of which were included in the list of countries on Trump's "Muslim ban." Irrational fears result in even less rational solutions that contribute nothing to national security and, if anything, exacerbate tensions that lead to further extremism on both sides.

The discourse surrounding Muslim intolerance covers up the reality of intolerance as an unfortunate phenomenon in many human societies, including quite notably among western populations. It is socially acceptable to question whether Muslims grasp the concept of freedom of speech, while overlooking whether conservative white Americans grasp its concept. When one looks at their reaction when the Dixie Chicks expressed shame that President George W. Bush was from their home state of Texas, their outrage when Colin Kaepernick took a knee to protest persistent racial discrimination, and their repeated enactment of anti-shariah and anti-BDS (Boycott, Divest, Sanction) legislation, it is hard to see how they are any more the champions of the core value of free speech than allegedly intolerant Muslims.

Perhaps tolerance is just an empty word with its meaning hinging on what it is that we choose to tolerate and how we display our intolerance. Calls for boycotts of Israel in international sporting venues because of its occupation of Arab lands are met with derision and proclamations that there should be no politics in sports. Sports federations, athletic teams, and individual athletes from Iran and other Muslim countries are routinely condemned and sanctioned for their refusal to engage with Israeli athletes in international venues. The freedom of these athletes to express their distaste for Israeli policies is not tolerated. When the International Olympic Committee (IOC) was urged to cancel the 2022 Beijing Winter Olympics in light of China's genocide against its Muslim Uyghur population, IOC president Thomas Bach declared, "With regards to the Uyghur

, ɔpulation, the position of the IOC must be to give political neutrality." Hence, the IOC can tolerate Chinese ethnic genocide but not the politicization of sports. Yet, when Russia invaded Ukraine, within days the IOC executive board declared that "Russian and Belarusian athletes should be excluded from international competition."[15] Such bans were not enacted following American military assaults on countries such as Afghanistan, Grenada, Haiti, Iraq, Panama, Somalia, Vietnam, etc. International sporting events are to be politically neutral and hence tolerate invasion, occupation, and genocide targeting the Global South, including predominantly Muslim populations, while they are to show a zero-tolerance policy towards military incursions into white Christian nations. In essence, international sports federations perpetuate the premise that only white lives matter, while maintaining a zero-tolerance policy towards dissenting voices among competing teams and athletes.

Chapter 12

Islamophobia without Muslims

As the civil war in Syria unfolded, millions of refugees fled conflict zones, especially those subject to the atrocities of Al-Qaeda (Al-Nusra Front), Daesh (ISIS), and other extremist organizations. The image that became emblazoned on the world's mind was that of Aylan, a 3-year-old Kurdish refugee who drowned on a beach in Turkey on his journey to seek refuge in Europe. Coverage of his death in the media helped humanize the unfolding catastrophe. The refugees came from a variety of faiths, as Syria's population is comprised of Sunnis, Alawites, Christians, Druze, and followers of other faiths.

The plight of these refugees became a tool of media figures, pundits, and politicians eager to exploit their misery to gain notoriety, generate profits, win elections, or cling on to power. In that vein, *Charlie Hebdo* published a cartoon with the caption, "What would little Aylan have become if he had grown up?" The cartoon portrayed ape-like humans chasing down women to grab their bottoms,[1] feeding into the stereotype of Muslim men as sexually compulsive subhuman beings who are a constant menace to helpless European women.

Syrian refugees provided a source of anxiety for xenophobes who saw them as Trojan horses, using the refugee crisis as a pretext to infiltrate and subvert western nations. Donald Trump, who was running for president as the crisis unfolded, said, "Two hundred thousand is the new number" of Syrians seeking refuge in the United States; that number includes "very strong men, young men" who "could be the ultimate Trojan horse."[2] In response to claims that most of the refugees were families fleeing violence, not terrorists, Donald Trump Jr.

veeted, "If I had a bowl of skittles and I told you just three would kill you. Would you take a handful? That's our Syrian refugee problem." Donald Trump tweeted in approval, "This image says it all. Let's end the politically correct agenda that doesn't put America first." Skittles' parent company tried to sidestep the controversy by declaring, "Skittles are candy. Refugees are people. We don't think it's an appropriate analogy."[3] Nevertheless, the ill-logic is simple—Syrian refugees include many Muslims; some Muslims are terrorists who will kill you; therefore, some Syrian refugees will kill you; hence, to protect America, we should bar all Syrian refugees.

What is lost in the conversation is the magnitude of the risk. It is not impossible for one of the refugees to come and kill Americans; it is just exceedingly unlikely. The Cato Institute examined the over three million refugees who have entered the United States since 1975 and found the odds of being killed by a refugee-turned-terrorist to be 1 in 3.6 billion.[3] This type of probability should not even register as a concern, especially since this probability is considerably lower than the chance of being killed by a white supremacist. In fact, the one terrorist caught hiding among Syrian refugees in Europe was Franco Albrecht, a half-German, half-Italian neo-Nazi who darkened his skin with makeup to pose as a Syrian seeking refuge in Germany. Having gathered a cache of weapons he had stolen from the German army, he was plotting a terrorist attack that would target Germany's political elite, hoping that it would get blamed on Syrian refugees. His plot was foiled when he was caught at Vienna's International Airport with a Nazi-era pistol; his fingerprints gave away his double identity.[4]

The type of racist ill-logic used in the Skittles meme is nothing new. In 1938, the publishers of the antisemitic Nazi newspaper *Der Stürmer* published a children's book entitled *Der Giftpilz* (*The Poisonous Mushroom*). The book compared Jews to poisonous mushrooms that are hidden among other mushrooms that may look the same on the surface, but that must be avoided lest they kill you. The book sold some 40,000 copies. Large murals were exhibited in public spaces to depict the "morals" of the book.[5] That Islamophobes reuse old antisemitic strategies is hardly shocking given the fact that racist tropes are generally not very imaginative and tend to recycle the same tired stereotypes and ill-logic.

The fear of Muslim refugees in the United States parallels previous historical examples. In the 1930s, Jewish refugees to the US were eyed with suspicion as harbingers of dangerous ideologies like communism and anarchism; they were alleged to be serving as agents or spies beholden to foreign organizations or nations; and they were accused of being part of a secret plan to infiltrate the nation and subvert it. Many were refused entry and sent back to die in the Holocaust. This same language was later used against Syrian refugees—that they harbor dangerous views, that they are potential agents of shadowy foreign organizations, that they are bent on sewing chaos in the west. Both during the Third Reich and the Syrian Civil War, civilians were fleeing the grip of an extremist fringe. The fact is that not a single Syrian refugee in the United States has been found to have terrorist ties by the State Department.[6] Nevertheless, too many fall for the fearmongering of the likes of Texas Senator Ted Cruz, who said, "It is the height of lunacy for a government official to welcome in tens of thousands of refugees when we know that among them will be ISIS terrorists." In light of such rhetoric, it is not surprising that 53% of Americans wanted the Syrian refugee program halted entirely compared to 28% who wanted it to remain in place. A further 11% wanted the US to welcome Syrian refugees, just not any Muslim ones.[7]

According to the 2020 US Census, approximately 1% of the US population is Muslim.[8] They live peacefully as citizens, permanent residents, and students. They serve as doctors, lawyers, teachers, plumbers, and police officers. Nearly two-thirds have attended college.[9] The "Muslim problem" that is featured prominently in American political discourse cannot be explained by actual problems American Muslims are causing but rather by widely held racist assumptions that create an anticipation of problems that do not exist.

In fact, Muslims are not even needed for Islamophobia to flourish. This phenomenon has been referred to as "Islamophobia without Muslims."[10] As highlighted by a Brookings Institution study, Poland serves as a prime example of this phenomenon. Poland is a country of approximately 38 million, the majority of whom are Roman Catholic. It is home to a small native population of ethnic Muslim Lipka Tatars, who number approximately 2,000-5,000 and who have peacefully coexisted there for some 700 years. There is also a small community of Muslims who have settled there in the past half century after attending Polish universities; they are typically highly educated and serve in fields like medicine and engineering. Muslims today comprise approximately 0.1% of the Polish population and have no notable presence in the country. Only 12% of Poles have ever met a Muslim; these are typically the wealthy, educated elite who have met Muslims during trips abroad. This, however, has not stopped the country from succumbing to an irrational fear of a Muslim takeover that has had significant political ramifications, essentially enticing Poles to trade in their political and civil liberties in return for being kept safe from the imagined threat posed by Muslim immigration.

Historically, Poland was a welcoming country for Jews, Muslims, and Protestant refugees. By World War II, 10% of its population was composed of Jews, only 10% of whom are estimated to have survived the Nazi occupation. The vast majority of survivors emigrated to Israel and the United States. A westward redrawing of Poland's post-war borders culminated in the expulsion of its German-speaking population and an influx of ethnic Poles from eastern territories that were ceded to the Soviet Union. This resulted in an ethnically homogeneous Polish state.

In 2015, as Europe struggled with the refugee crisis, Poland was generally spared because it was neither a transit nor a destination country for refugees. In accordance with EU refugee distribution plans, Poland was asked to admit 2,000 refugees. This number was subsequently raised to 9,000. The Law and Justice Party ran on a nativist and Islamophobic platform, promising to keep all Muslim refugees out of Poland. This rhetoric has helped them win election after election since 2015.[11] Since taking office, Law and Justice politicians have fanned the flames of Islamophobia to tighten and perpetuate their grip on power.

The reality is that Poland has an aging population and a substantial labor shortage, which is exacerbated by young and ambitious Poles seeking better wages in Western European economies. This has forced the importation of Ukrainian migrant workers, some two million of whom were estimated to be laboring in Poland in 2019.[12] In 2022, Poland opened its doors to two million Ukrainian refugees, 1.2 million of whom have formally registered for asylum.[13] It is not so much that foreigners are unwelcome, just not Muslim ones. Dominik Tarczynski, an ultraconservative Law and Justice parliamentarian who is currently serving as a member of the European Parliament, explains this as follows: "It has nothing to do with Islamophobia. It's all about safety... This is why our government was elected, and not even one Muslim illegal migrant will come to Poland ever." As for what he means by safety, he cites the Islamophobic myth that Muslim men are rapists.[14]

Whereas not a single Muslim refugee is to be admitted, Poland scrambled to accommodate countless Ukrainian refugees in light of the Russian military assault.[15] African, South Asian, and Middle Eastern students attending universities in Ukraine who were trying to flee the Russian onslaught were prevented from reaching the border by Ukrainian forces who pulled them off buses at gunpoint, hurled vulgar racial slurs at them, and then dumped them in the middle of nowhere to freeze to death.[16] The ones who made it across the border were subjected to vigilante white supremacist mobs in Poland who freely roam around attacking dark-skinned refugees.[17]

There is a stark contrast between how Ukrainian war victims are perceived in the west in comparison to those from Muslim majority countries. CBS News senior correspondent Charlie D'Agata said in regard to Ukraine, "This isn't a place, with all due respect, like Iraq or Afghanistan that has seen conflict raging for decades. This is a relatively civilised, relatively European—I have to choose those words carefully, too—city where you wouldn't expect that, or hope that it's going to happen." His assumption is that Afghanistan is innately uncivilized and conflict-ridden, whereas it was quite peaceful and civilized until the 1979 Soviet invasion. Meanwhile, Ukrainians played up their whiteness in a quest for sympathy. David Sakvarelidze, Ukraine's former deputy prosecutor general, said on BBC, "It's very emotional for me because I see European people with blonde hair and blue eyes being killed every day with Putin's missiles and his helicopters and his rockets." On Al Jazeera English, it was proclaimed that Ukrainian refugees are "prosperous, middle class people" who "are not obviously refugees trying to get away from areas in the Middle East that are still in a big state of war; these are not people trying to get away from areas in North Africa, they look like any European family that you would live next door to."[18] Indeed, it is hard to watch any coverage of the Russian invasion of Ukraine without seeing the heightened concern about civilian well-being. This contrasts with the reporting on wars the United States inflicted on countries like Iraq and Afghanistan where bombs and missile strikes killing countless civilians were widely ignored across the American media, dismissed merely as "collateral damage."

It is worth noting that Islamophobic Poles cite nationalist legends surrounding King John III Sobieski's victory over the Ottoman Empire during its 1683 siege of Vienna. To use this to justify hatred of Muslims is to forget about how neighboring Christian powers made Poland cease to exist in the eighteenth century and repeatedly redrew its borders at will during the twentieth century. Poles have suffered far worse atrocities from Germans than from Turks. After World War II, Poland became a satellite state that was militarily occupied and politically controlled by the Soviet Union. For Poles to imagine that the main problem facing their country today is Muslim immigration highlights the delusional basis of Islamophobia.

Today, Poles often serve as a stigmatized minority in Western European states. In an Al Jazeera English interview, Mehdi Hassan pointed out to Dominik Tarczynski,

> Many would say it's hypocritical that you say you don't want Muslim immigrants in your country because they commit crimes, there's a security threat, and yet you hear exactly the same rhetoric about Polish immigrants in the UK from right-wing politicians in the media there. They say the Poles are groping women, they're feckless, they're criminals, they won't integrate. Don't you see the irony or the hypocrisy of treating Muslim immigrants to Poland in the same way that some British treat Polish immigrants?[19]

Tarczynski had no real answer to give, other than to stress that these situations are not the same; Muslims cannot be compared to Poles. The unfortunate reality is that Tarczynski's white supremacist ill-logic is one that resonates widely: white people are innately not a problem in the way Muslims are.

Hungary provides another notable example of Islamophobia without Muslims. The country, under the leadership of Viktor Orban and his Fidesz Party, has descended into an abyss of xenophobia, Islamophobia, and antisemitic conspiracy theories often featuring the liberal Hungarian American philanthropist George Soros. According to the Brookings Institution,

> Traditionally, the Roma and the Jews have been the most important targets of the Hungarian far-right. However, since 2015, xenophobia mainly related to immigration has become the primary layer for the presence of the ideology of both the far-right and the populist right in Hungary. While objection against the Roma was always the strongest, opposition to refugees/migrants, Arabs and Muslims has caught up with or even eclipsed it. Anti-immigration, anti-Arab

and anti-Muslim sentiments, which hardly existed in
Hungary before, are mainly based on the perceived
cultural differences, and explained in the context of a war
between cultures and civilizations. Mainstreaming and
legitimizing hatred against refugees and migrants by the
government's messaging has led to increasing rejection of
other minority groups and nationalities too (e.g.,
LGBTQ people, Romanians)... Due to the lack of a
visible Muslim community, hardly any Hungarians
encounter Islam in their daily lives and have any
knowledge on it. Therefore, Islam was not present in the
public discourse before 2015... The anti-Muslim
narratives that now dominate political discourse were
essentially imported from Western European far-right
discourse in which Islam is framed in the context of a
cultural war between the Christian West and the Muslim
world.[20]

The rapidity with which racist and Islamophobic
concepts can spread is quite notable. It appears that social media
plays a significant role in this regard, as it allows fringe concepts
to quickly reach wide audiences who otherwise might remain on
the sidelines of such issues.

Chapter 13

How Social Media Fuels Islamophobia

As a hijabi Somali American representative from Minnesota, perhaps no one in the United States has been subject to as many Islamophobic tweets and memes as Ilhan Omar. According to a study by Lawrence Pintak and colleagues, during her 2018 campaign, half the tweets that mentioned her included overtly Islamophobic or xenophobic language. Notably, the majority of the offensive posts came from a small number of provocateurs that seed such posts into Twitter. However, these accounts do not constitute the main source of the ensuing Twitter traffic. Rather, this is carried out by what are termed as "amplifiers," accounts that collect and mass-circulate retweets and create replies to generate a megaphone effect that makes such tweets trend on Twitter. Of the top 20 amplifiers, 16 were not authentic accounts but rather computerized bots or "sockpuppets," which are accounts that use fake identities to deceive other users.[1,2]

Another strategy is the use of "cloaked" websites, which are basically false-flag operations in which Islamophobes pose as radical Islamists who disparage Europeans and promise an Islamist takeover of European nations. This type of content is guaranteed to generate Islamophobic comments and helps promote antipathy towards Muslims and refugees within the wider community.[1,3] The following quote from a fake Danish Islamist Facebook page created by far-right Danes typifies how such cloaked websites can help spread Islamophobic fears:

> Alhamdulillah. We take over Denmark and you kuffars [infidels] can't even stop us. We transform s--tty Denmark into an Islamic state and this will happen

before your eyes, and you can't do a thing about it. Your
churches will be turned into mosques, your wh-re
women will be f--ked and used by us Muslims to make
our babies, we take your money that you work 7 to 5 to
earn while we Muslims live in luxury, your food will
become halal and your laws will be sharia and what are
you going to do about it? NOTHING![3]

Fake news stories targeting Muslims feature prominently
on social media. Examples include fictitious accounts of refugees
urinating on local supermarket shelves, made-up reports of stores
being forced to close because too many refugees shoplift from
them, and false accusations of rape. Karolin Schwarz and Lutz
Helm set up a website called Hoaxmap that highlights how many
of these stories have no factual basis.[4] One would be tempted to
conclude that Muslims must be extremely law-abiding,
otherwise there would be enough real crimes to report and no
need for Islamophobes to have to resort to forgeries to disparage
Muslims.

Social media platforms, along with right-wing media
outlets, give voice to a lineup of "ex-Muslims" who are portrayed
as exposing the true depravities of Islam. A prominent example is
Ayaan Hirsi Ali, who claimed asylum in the Netherlands based
on a fictitious account of being a Somali woman who had been
forced against her will into an arranged marriage. It later turned
out that she had been living a comfortable life in a posh Kenyan
suburb and had in no way been forced to marry. Even the name
she used on her asylum application was fake. In the Netherlands,
she gained prominence through her outspoken Islamophobia and
was elected to the Dutch parliament in 2003.[5] She has continued
to make a living out of her rabid Islamophobia. It is worth noting
that pretending to leave Islam is one way to obtain asylum in
European Union countries, since it is automatically assumed that
it would be too dangerous for an apostate to return to a country
like Iran, Afghanistan, or Somalia.[6] Given the financial and legal
benefits of publicly leaving Islam, the proliferation of highly vocal
ex-Muslims in the west is hardly surprising.

The spread of fake news on social media is merely the modern corollary of fictitious race-baiting books that proliferated in the past. *The Protocols of the Elders of Zion*, which purported to be a text revealing a Jewish plot for world domination, featured heavily in European antisemitism. In the anti-Catholic context, the 1836 book entitled *Awful Disclosures of Maria Monk*, also known as *The Hidden Secrets of a Nun's Life*, portrayed convent life as one involving lurid sexual depravities and widespread infanticide of babies allegedly born to nuns and fathered by priests. Official investigations found no evidence to corroborate these allegations, but such findings were dismissed as cover-ups, and the book continued to inflame anti-Catholic sentiment for decades.[7] Instead of dismissing the work for the fraud that it was when none of its allegations could be corroborated, many Protestants saw the book as providing a courageous account of what really goes on in a convent. Today, a long list of books raise the alarm regarding the threat of Islam and promise to expose what really goes on in the Islamic world or in the perverted minds of Muslims. However, in contrast to a book that requires hours to read, a bigoted meme can reach millions of people within seconds.

Social media is often seen as an a democracy of ideas, an impartial platform that provides an equal opportunity for all beliefs to proliferate, including hate speech ranging from rhetoric calling for the ethnic cleansing of Muslims to the teachings of extremist *takfiri* groups. This is not the case. Executives from YouTube, Facebook, and Twitter testified to the US Senate that they make aggressive use of artificial intelligence to detect and delete content from groups like Daesh and Al-Qaeda. Yet, they made virtually no mention of any attempts to remove white supremacist and Islamophobic content. This is due to the basic assumption about who the terrorists are, who actually poses a threat, and where the security risks lie. They see little reputational or economic risk to magnifying extremist right-wing content that is effectively accepted as normative in western societies. As such, Muslim groups are selectively targeted for enforcement of these platforms' terms of service, whereas white cyber hatemongers are allowed to flourish.[8] This is typical of racially discriminatory law enforcement, in which the dominant group enjoys the protections of the law (i.e., the right to free speech on social media), whereas racialized communities are subject only to the restrictions imposed by the law (i.e., being banned for violating the terms of service). That "law enforcement" in the case of social media is not directly governmental but rather corporate only highlights widespread racialized disparities when it comes to free speech. It is not surprising that Facebook complies with 95% of Israeli requests to remove unfavorable content,[9] even when such content is not antisemitic but rather documents Israeli aggression against Palestinian civilians, criticizes Zionist racism, or even simply portrays the Al-Aqsa Mosque in Jerusalem.[10]

Islamophobia is hardly the only milieu in which social media companies profit from hate speech, conspiracy theories, and misinformation campaigns. The coronavirus pandemic has seen an oversized amplification of unscientific and overtly absurd anti-vaccination narratives across social media platforms, resulting in the needless death of tens, if not hundreds, of thousands of unvaccinated people. That social media companies are allowed to profit generously from objectively harmful hate speech and conspiracy theories is an unfortunate byproduct of the current legal framework that absolves them of liability for the content that they spread. Hence, Facebook, Instagram, Twitter, YouTube, and others are free to implement an arbitrary regime of censoring certain content while allowing other even more harmful content to flourish.

WhatsApp has played a central role in the rise of "cow vigilantes" in India. These Hindu extremists, in the name of "cow protection," spread misinformation campaigns targeting minority Muslim and Dalit ("untouchable") communities, resulting in repeat acts of mob violence.[11] Such lynchings became more commonplace after the election of the Islamophobic BJP leader Narendra Modi in 2014, highlighting the reciprocal role of right-wing politicians and online hatemongering.[12] In one instance, five Muslims with a permit to legally transport dairy cows were dragged out of their truck, accused of transporting cows for slaughter, and lynched by a mob of 200 Hindus. One of the Muslim men died. When the police arrived, they arrested the men transporting the cattle but not the members of the mob.[13]

Islamophobia's spread on social media has real consequences. In one study published in *Communication Research*, exposure of experimental subjects to negative media footage of Muslims results in "increased perceptions of Muslims as aggressive, increased support for harsh civil restrictions of Muslim Americans, and increased support for military action in Muslim countries."[14] This is not a purely theoretical issue when one considers that the ethnic cleansing of Rohingya in Myanmar's Rakhine State was fueled through Facebook. Social media can have an even more oversized effect in developing nations, where a significant portion of the population is illiterate and therefore particularly susceptible to racist clickbait. The rampant spread of Islamophobic content on social media contributes to the cultural normalization of Islamophobia and to the creation of racialized stereotypes that depict an ethnically, culturally, and intellectually homogeneous Muslim mass that poses a dire threat to social cohesion and safety. The benefit of this type of speech is hard to fathom. Furthermore, the anonymity provided by the internet only promotes hate speech by people who would censor themselves if their identities were linked to what they say.

That fake Islamophobic content is a cash cow for social media companies is highlighted by a network of seventy Macedonian websites that publish disinformation and fake news for profit. Eight of their top ten most viral stories featured the word "Muslim" in the headline. According to Whitney Phillips, an assistant professor at Syracuse University who researches online harassment, "Islamophobia happens to be something that [has] made these companies lots and lots of money."[15] The unfortunate truth is that hate sells. Maria Monk's fictitious account of life in the convent remained the number one bestseller in the United States after the Bible for many years, generating significant monetary and political windfalls for anti-Catholic bigots.[16] Today, Alex Jones, an American far-right radio show host and rabid conspiracy theorist has a net worth estimated to be as high as $270 million.[17]

This is not a call for strict government censorship of content posted on the internet. Rather, it is a call to stop amplifying and promoting ideas that are hateful, that incite violence and war, that promote intercommunal strife, that are destructive to public health, and that are racing the planet towards catastrophe, while still allowing ample space for openly airing contrarian opinions. Though a perfect balance may be hard to attain, the current status quo is far from ideal.

Chapter 14

The Place of Non-Muslims in a Muslim State

Islamophobes lean heavily on stoking fears of an Islamic demographic or military takeover followed by the imposition of shariah law and either forced conversions to Islam or the horrors of living under an Islamic state. Maps showing the rapid early expansion of the "Islamic" empire are often used to drive home the point that, unless the spread of Islam is checked, everyone will be forced to convert to Islam.

It is historically true that, over the span of a few decades, the first three caliphs followed by the Umayyad Caliphate defeated the Zoroastrian Persian and Christian Byzantine forces, creating an empire that spanned from Central and South Asia across the Middle East and North Africa to the Iberian Peninsula in Europe. During the Abbasid Caliphate, the open embrace of racial and ethnic diversity as well as increased fascination with the arts, sciences, and literature of other cultures ushered in what was known as the Golden Age of Islam.

Despite the rapid geographic expansion of the "Islamic" realm, the spread of Islam as a religion occurred rather slowly, as the initial Arab conquerors were not particularly keen on converting the conquered populations. Nevertheless, over the span of centuries, Islam gradually became the predominant religion throughout a vast geographic range, including countries as far as Indonesia and Malaysia that were never militarily conquered. The Ottoman Turks later established what they declared to be a caliphate that, at its peak, controlled much of the Middle East, the Mediterranean coast of Africa, the Nile Valley, and Eastern Europe. Their general tolerance of religious diversity is easily seen in how Christianity has survived and thrived in

Eastern Europe and the Balkans despite centuries of nominal Muslim rule. To this day, the seat of the Orthodox Church remains in Istanbul.

Nevertheless, in Islamophobic fearmongering, Muslim domination is portrayed either in terms of forced conversions (i.e., the Quran or the sword) or in the context of subjugation (i.e., accepting *dhimmi* status and paying *jizya*). Forced conversions have no real basis in Islam, as the Quran clearly states, "There is no compulsion in religion,"[1] and it is evident that someone cannot be forced to meaningfully believe in something with a sword held to the throat. This is not to say that isolated historical incidents of what could be seen as forced conversions have not occurred. Rather, they constituted isolated exceptions rather than the norm. The concepts of *dhimmi* status and *jizya* taxes draw their origins in the following verse of the Quran:

> Fight those who do not believe in God and the Last Day and who do not forbid what God and His Messenger have forbidden and who do not profess the Religion of Truth from among the People of the Book until they willingly pay *jizya* and are subdued.[2]

This verse lays out the foundations for the status of non-Muslims living in a Muslim state, referred to as *dhimmis*. People of the Book in the context of the time this verse was revealed specifically referred to Christians, Jews, and perhaps Zoroastrians and Sabians, but *dhimmi* status has historically been extended to followers of many other faiths. What this verse does not entail is their forced conversion, but rather the terms upon which they can live peacefully in a Muslim state. The two basic tenets are simple—pay your taxes and submit to the authority of the state. This is hardly different than what is expected of a citizen or resident of any state. As long as you do so, you are free to practice your religion, to raise pigs and eat pork, to cultivate vineyards and make wine, and marry and divorce and be buried according to your own traditions within your own community.

Jizya was a poll tax paid by non-Muslims in return for military protection, a guarantee of safety and security by the state, and an exemption from military service. Poll taxes were an extremely common form of taxation at the time and remained so for centuries thereafter. Muslims, to this day, pay an obligatory poll tax in the form of *zakat al-fitra*. It appears, based on historical examples, that *dhimmis* who agreed to join Muslim armies were exempted from *jizya*. There is conflicting evidence as to whether the *jizya* taxes were higher than the *zakat* taxes paid by Muslims. Regardless, disparities in taxation served as disincentives for conversion. If the *jizya* tax levied on non-Muslims was higher than the *zakat* tax levied on Muslims, the state had a financial interest in having the population not convert. Conversely, if the *zakat* tax was higher, there would be no financial incentive for a *dhimmi* individual to convert to Islam. Indeed, the rate of conversion to Islam outside the Arabian Peninsula in the first century of Islam was dismally low, estimated at well below ten percent.[3]

Meanwhile, *dhimmis* were allowed to freely practice their religion and to establish courts for the settling of disputes within their own communities. The state's court system would be available for inter-communal disputes or for cases in which the state's court system is sought out by the complainants. Islamophobes who present Islam as a religion that, in contrast to Christianity, was spread by the sword, overlook how Christianity was often forced upon Europeans on threat of death and how Indonesia, the world's most populous Muslim-majority nation, was never conquered by foreign Muslim armies.

Currently, I am not aware of any Muslim state collecting *jizya*, as religious minorities are typically well integrated and are expected to provide military service at times of war. At the same time, non-Muslims are not obligated to pay Islamic taxes such as *zakat* and *khums*. Nevertheless, there is persistent fearmongering by Islamophobes that unless Muslim encroachment is aggressively combatted, Europeans and Americans will eventually have to submit to *dhimmi* status and pay *jizya*.

The Rise of Daesh (ISIS)

The reality is that *jizya* was a tax that was intended for very specific (*khass*) circumstances. Even though books of jurisprudence discuss *jizya*, it is not applied in modern Muslim states. This is not contrary to Islamic teachings, as Muslim scholars, rulers, and societies are free to determine whether the conditions for this form of poll tax are met and what the amount of the tax would be. Yet, headlines such as, "Islamic State Warns Christians: Convert, Pay Tax, Leave Or Die,"[4] cement a stereotyped view of Muslims irrespective of the reality that Daesh's terrorist pseudostate is hardly emblematic of Islam.

The Islamic State in Iraq and Syria (ISIS) refers to an extremist militant *takfiri* quasi-state that was created in parts of war-torn Iraq and Syria where there was a loss of central authority in the aftermath of the US invasion of Iraq and the western-backed civil war in Syria. They claimed to have established a worldwide caliphate and called on Muslims from across the globe to join them. An estimated 30,000 fighters joined their cause.[5] This comes to approximately 0.0017% of the worldwide Muslim population, or 1 in 60,000 Muslims. In line with western geopolitical interests at the time, NATO member Turkey initially turned a blind eye to ISIS recruitment and allowed its border with Syria to be used to transport recruits to fight against Bashar al-Assad's government in Damascus. Once ISIS started carrying out terrorist attacks in Turkey, Erdogan changed course and cracked down on the free movement of ISIS fighters along the border.[6] Meanwhile, the United States, whose forces were stationed in Iraq at the time, stood idly by as ISIS captured city after city in Iraq, culminating in the fall of Mosul, Iraq's second largest city. A mere two days later, Iran deployed forces to help bolster Iraqi combat troops and to help retake cities like Tikrit.[7] The Obama administration, meanwhile, wasted precious time splitting hairs over whether these terrorists should be called "ISIS" or "ISIL," which merely replaces "Syria" with

"Levant."[8] It took the US two months after the fall of Mosul to commence airstrikes targeting the group.[7]

Considering that mainstream Muslims consider the "Islamic State" to be neither Islamic nor a state, they typically refer to ISIS as Daesh, a pejorative acronym based on ISIS' Arabic name *al-Dawlah al-Islamiyyah fil-'Iraq wash-Sham*. Daesh, in Arabic, roughly translates to "bigot" or "thug." To combat the widespread use of the word "Daesh," The group threatened to cut off the tongues of anyone who referred to them as such.[9] It's not surprising that "Islamic State" as a description for this entity has had more traction in the west than in the Muslim world. Most Muslims find it hard to refer to Daesh as "Islamic State," since their rule did not in any way resemble the way most Muslims imagine an Islamic state would be. The Islamic State is about as Islamic as the Democratic People's Republic of Korea (i.e., North Korea) is democratic. Nevertheless, many westerners might be inclined to imagine that living in an Islamic state or a Muslim-majority nation would be quite similar to living under Daesh.

The self-proclaimed name "Islamic State" promotes the impression that Islam calls for sectarian ethnic cleansing, beheading of prisoners, and sexual enslavement of minority communities. Indeed, ISIS almost epitomizes western Islamophobic views. It is hardly surprising that ISIS' highest per-Muslim-capita recruitment rates have been from European countries,[5] where impressionable and marginalized Muslim youth develop their understanding of Islam through the lens of western media without exposure to effective counter-narratives. In fact, the top risk factor for someone becoming a jihadist is being from a French-speaking country.[10] The typical low level of religiosity and lack of meaningful Islamic education noted among ISIS recruits is hardly surprising. According to Musa al-Gharbi, an instructor in the School of Government and Public Service at the University of Arizona,

> While ISIS' membership is exclusively Sunni, it is important to note that, within the Iraqi context, "Sunni"

and "Shia" represent sociopolitical identities more than religious ones. The Sunni grievances against the government are not that it imposes Shia interpretations of sharia law, or otherwise interferes with Sunni religious practices. Instead, the Sunni are outraged by their political and economic disenfranchisement in Iraq's confessional political system (put in place by the United States)... Rather than joining out of religious conviction, many recruits are driven to the organization for financial reasons. The economy of Syria has been decimated by the war... Many in the rural areas of Iraq are also in economic crisis... ISIS exploits this desperation, offering superior wages for those who join, whether on a freelance or regular basis. In short, a good many ISIS fighters are essentially mercenaries rather than zealots...

Exogenous ISIS recruits tend to be more fanatical than the indigenous ones and more focused on waging war, but even most of these are not driven primarily by religion. For those hailing from other parts of the Greater Middle East, they generally take up arms to fight against dictators, occupiers and their proxies. They have political goals in mind. Others are in it for the money: ISIS pays foreign fighters $1,000 per month, a fortune for many from Africa or parts of the Mideast.

Western ISIS recruits are driven by a host of psycho-sociological factors, but religion does not seem to be the major one. Many join to be part of a group, to participate in some larger and successful cause, to make a difference and do something important. Others, because they seek "cognitive closure" and are thereby drawn to the straightforward ISIS "good v. evil" narrative. Many of them want to "fight the system" rather than purge infidels or pursue the political goals local Sunni are striving for. Still others are just thrill seekers, nihilists or psychopaths looking to dive into a bit of carnage. Many of these are not Muslims, nor do they or their families hail from [the] Middle East. Others are recent converts who adopted Islam as an expression of their pre-existing support for ISIS, rather than supporting ISIS as a result of their religious beliefs.[11]

The Origins of Takfiri Ideology

Takfiri, which roughly translates to "excommunicational," refers to Muslims who consider other Muslims who dispute their beliefs to be disbelievers. In general, Muslim societies have been rather tolerant of a wide set of cross-sectarian and intra-sectarian beliefs, juristic rulings, and practices. The first *takfiri* group, known as the Kharijites, formed in 657 CE, denouncing as apostates both Ali (AS), who was the fourth Sunni caliph and first Shia Imam, and Muawiya, the rebellious governor of Syria who subsequently ascended to the caliphate. The Kharijites led a series of uprisings that were quelled over the ensuing decades; they soon ceased to be a significant threat in the Islamic heartland. The small Ibadi communities in Oman and parts of North Africa represents the only Kharijite offshoots that remain to this day.

A historically significant revival of *takfiri* ideology emerged centuries later in the writings of Ibn Taymiyyah (1263-1328 CE), a Sunni Hanbali scholar who lived in the era succeeding the Mongol defeat of the Abbasid Caliphate and the sacking of Baghdad. The Hanbali school of Sunni jurisprudence (*madhhab*) is generally considered the most literal of the four Sunni schools (Hanafi, Shafi'i, Maliki, and Hanbali), as it calls for a strict literal following of the Quran and hadith in contrast to the more rational approaches to jurisprudence advocated by the other *madhhabs*. His school has remained the smallest of the four Sunni *madhhabs*, with its followers generally confined to portions of the Arabian Peninsula.

The Mongol army attacking the Mamluk Sultanate in Syria was headed by Ghazan Khan, a Sunni Muslim, and included an ethnically and religiously diverse military force. Ibn Taymiyyah issued a fatwa dismissing Ghazan Khan, a Sunni Muslim, as an ideologically flawed apostate because he did not rule in accordance with shariah but rather in accordance with Mongol *yasa* principles. He thus made it obligatory to fight Ghazan's forces. A subsequent fatwa condemned Oljeitu Khan, Ghazan's successor and a convert to Shiism, as a heretic.[12] His fatwas generally stood out for denouncing Shias and Sufis as heretics and for banning the seeking of intercession from saints. He railed against rationalist Sunnis like Fakhr al-Din al-Razi who believed that scriptural sources are subject to rational interpretation. In a clear break from precedence in which Muslim scholars agreed to disagree with one another, he declared his intellectual opponents as outside the pale of Islam. He was imprisoned multiple times for his controversial edicts and finally died in prison. Even though he was popular among the masses, his theological writings were generally dismissed by the scholarly class of the time. To a great extent, his views cannot be seen outside the context of the military and intellectual conflicts that raged during his lifetime. Indeed, towards the end of his life, he recanted his previous *takfiri* ideology, saying that he would no longer consider someone a non-Muslim as long as the person performed the ablution (*wudu*) needed for prayers.[13] Even this standard is highly problematic, as ritual dereliction is not the same as apostasy and indeed there is no specific worldly punishment imposed on someone who doesn't offer daily prayers. Furthermore, the standard for determining whether someone is Muslim is spelled out in the Quran: "Do not tell someone who offers you [the salutation] 'peace [be upon you],' 'You are not a believer.'"[14] Simply put, anyone who feels part of the Muslim community is a Muslim.

In the eighteenth century, Muhammad ibn Abd al-Wahhab revived Ibn Taymiyyah's ideology and spearheaded a *takfiri* movement in Najd, in what is now Saudi Arabia. He classified as *shirk* (polytheism) common Muslim practices such as the veneration of saints. His followers desecrated and destroyed ancient Islamic holy sites such as the Baqi Cemetery in Medina, where many of the Prophet's (S) family members and companions are buried. Anyone comparing what one finds in Mecca and Medina today with Ottoman-era photographs of the cities[15] would be outraged by the razed holy sites that serve as a permanent reminder of the erasure of Islamic cultural and religious heritage at the hand of Wahhabi fanatics. Countless Muslim civilians were massacred by Wahhabis in cold blood, including women, children, and captives who were beheaded in manners completely foreign to the Islamic tradition. According to Sumbul Ali-Karamali,

> Were it not for two historical factors, Wahhabism would likely have dwindled, as extremist movements usually do. First, the British in the late eighteenth century encouraged the Wahhabis (along with other local ethnic and religious groups) in their campaign to foment rebellion against the Ottoman Empire. Second, the al-Saud family, contending to gain control of the Arabian Peninsula, offered the Wahhabis a partnership: we'll adopt you religion, said the al-Saud, if you fight for us. The Wahhabis accepted. Thus, when Saudi Arabia was founded, in the early twentieth century, Wahhabism became its official religion.[16]

The subsequent use of Saudi oil money to disseminate Wahhabi doctrines across Muslim lands culminated in further spread of *takfiri* ideology. This spread occurred with the consent, and at times open enthusiasm, of western governments who saw Wahhabism as an antidote to all of their problems—pan-Arab Nasserite nationalism, Soviet communism, and the Iranian Revolution.[17] Various offshoots, who collectively call themselves Salafis, have emerged, all with similarly narrow, intolerant, sectarian views.

Modern-day *takfiris* generally reserve most of their ire for Shias, but they do not spare the many Sunnis who disagree with their views. The western media has had a significant role in advertising Wahhabi ideology by promoting the concept that they best represent Islam and Muslims, even though their core beliefs constitute relatively modern innovations at best. It would be more accurate to imagine such groups as a sect within a sect within a sect within a sect of Islam (i.e., the Wahhabi offshoot of the Ibn Taymiyyah branch of the Hanbali school of the Sunni sect of Islam), as opposed to representative of historical or contemporary mainstream Muslim ideology.

It must be said that the vast majority of *takfiris* are not violently intolerant. They just lament on occasion why so many people, including most of the Muslims they see, are misguided. They see the unenviable state of Muslim lands and imagine, rightly or wrongly, that implementing their understanding of Islamic principles and laws would be the solution to the social and political ills that they witness. They neither have the desire to coerce anyone to change nor the impulse to carry out any acts of violence. They are no different than conservative Christians who believe that most of humanity is deprived of the grace of God and hence headed to hell and that the solutions to all social problems are to be found within their understanding of Scripture.

The presence of intolerance among some Muslims is neither sociologically not psychologically distinct from intolerance seen in other societies and is equally lamentable. It is painful to watch people in any population succumb to bigotry and hatred. Governments, the media, intellectuals, and ordinary citizens all have active roles to play in combating intolerance among all populations. A free media must widely expose intolerance without falsely scapegoating entire religions. Instead of holding up Saudi Wahhabism as the epitome of Islam, it should be portrayed as but one recent fanatical offshoot emanating from what historically constituted the outer fringes of the Muslim community.

Part III

Fear of Toxic Muslim Masculinity

by

Leila K. Asadi

Chapter 15

The Rapefugee Crisis

In 2016, wSIECI, a Polish magazine, published a highly inflammatory cover depicting a blonde woman draped in the European Union flag being attacked by three hairy-armed brown men. Just in case further clarification was needed, the cover exclaimed, "Islamic Rape of Europe."[1] This is merely a new chapter in the sordid history of European fear of ethnic minorities raping white women. After World War I, there was outrage that French troops occupying the German Rhineland included African soldiers. The British author E. D. Morel, writing in *The Nation*, condemned "thrusting barbarians—barbarians belonging to a race inspired by Nature... with tremendous sexual instincts—into the heart of Europe." German society went into a frenzy, fearing how mixed-race *mischlings* would destroy the purity of the German race. Hitler ranted in *Mein Kampf*, "It was and is the Jews who bring the Negro into the Rhineland, always with the same secret thought and clear aim of ruining the hated white race by the necessarily resulting bastardization, throwing it down from its cultural and political height, and himself rising to be its master."[2] Nazi propaganda used images depicting Jews as sexual predators posing a vital threat to German women and the "purity" of the Aryan nation. Such images played a central role in dehumanizing Jews and fanning the flames of antisemitism.[3]

The fear of darker-skinned individuals being brought into the heart of Europe—then by the French or Jews and now by Angela Merkel or George Soros—creates angst among nativist populations. In Poland, the thought of accepting a few thousand refugees created a furor. A mob of Polish nationalists chanted against Islam and migrants in the name of "God, Honor, and Fatherland," while burning an effigy of a Hasidic Jew wrapped in a European Union flag.[4]

In the United States, the fear of black men raping white women has been central to the post-slavery racial narrative. Throughout slavery, white men raped black women with impunity. After emancipation, the innocent and gullible white woman was seen as vulnerable to the insatiable sexual appetite black men have for white women. The 1915 silent movie *The Birth of a Nation* helped solidify the image of the unintelligent and sexually aggressive "Negro." This movie led to the rebirth of the white supremacist Ku Klux Klan, highlighting the significant role the media plays in creating and perpetuating racial stereotypes and myths.[5]

Throughout the Jim Crow era, black men would be lynched based on mere rumors that they had perpetrated sexual offenses against white women. Emmett Till became the glaring face of this type of atrocity when, at the age of 14, he allegedly whistled at 21-year-old Carolyn Bryant Donham. Her husband and his half-brother kidnapped Emmett, bludgeoned him, and subsequently shot him to death. The two brothers were arrested and tried, but an all-white, all-male jury acquitted them of the charges after the woman testified in court that she had heard Emmett say that he had done things "with white women before." The killers openly admitted to carrying out the murder and even sold their story for $3,000 to *Look* magazine. In 2007, at the age of 72, Donham confessed that the story was fabricated, that her testimony was perjurious, and that Emmett Till had not made any verbal or physical advances on her.[6] The sexually fetishized image of a black man with an insatiable desire for raping white women has persisted, and served as a central theme in the Willie Horton ads repeatedly aired by George H. W. Bush's 1988 presidential campaign. This is despite the reality that actual black rapists show no preference for raping white women.[7] Post-emancipation stereotypes have also developed for minority women. These have included the conceptualization of black and Latina women as inherently promiscuous and of Asian and

Native American women as innately submissive. Both stereotypes effectively serve to justify their rape by white men.[8]

That rape is seen as a colored problem is illustrated by *Time* magazine's March 21, 2016 front cover that shows a naked, very dark-skinned, and very pregnant black woman with the caption, "The Secret War Crime: Ending the scourge of conflict rape."[9] It insinuates that rape is a problem when it comes to conflicts in Africa where black men rape at will. *Time* had a choice: it could have published this image or it could have published the image of one of the 4,000 Bosnian women who had been impregnated by their white, European, Christian, Serbian rapists. In that war, more than 50,000 Bosnian women were held in what became known as "rape camps," where they were repeatedly gang raped.[10] Unsurprisingly, this atrocity did not make it to the cover of western magazines with the headline, "The Rape of Europe," as such an image would not fit the stereotype of a rapist as someone with darker skin. That *Time* thought it wise to exploit the unclothed image of a raped pregnant woman to boost sales is a whole other subject.

New Year's Eve Attacks in Cologne

Fears of Muslim men raping European women was aggravated by the outbreak of reported sexual assaults in Cologne, Germany during its 2015-2016 New Year's Eve celebrations. Groups of drunk men allegedly groped hundreds of women, with some of the sexual assaults apparently used as a ruse for robbing them of their cell phones and wallets.[11,12] The German media, at the time banned from reporting an alleged perpetrators' ethnicity, was accused of a cover-up. Quickly, the issue was blamed on refugees, with "Frau Merkel invited me," a phrase allegedly uttered by one of perpetrators, trending on social media. This incident was hijacked by anti-immigrant groups to fan the flames of xenophobia. Geert Wilders, leader of the far-right Dutch Freedom Party, used rhetoric like "sexual terrorism" and "testosterone bombs" to describe the Muslim presence. He proposed a Muslim immigration ban and the mass detention of all male Muslim asylum seekers. Within weeks, violence targeting refugees surged.[3] Shots were fired at refugee housing in Gräfenhainichen. A refugee shelter in the town of Bautzen was burned down; as the building went up in flames, local residents cheered. The entire nation's attitude towards refugees soured.[13] According to an article by Saskia Bonjour and Sarah Bracke,

> Much has been written about the events, with many conflicting accounts of what happened—notably about the numbers of perpetrators and victims involved—or about the organized or spontaneous character of the mob. But a few things are consistent: many women were sexually assaulted that night, the perpetrators were described as North African or Arab, and moral panic surrounded the event. The moral panic, however, was not so much about the vexed question of sexual violence at large, but rather, about the presence of racialized men in the cities of Europe.[3]

The unfortunate reality is that being groped in crowded public spaces like nightclubs and bars is part and parcel of a night out for western women. In a survey of 14,000 students in the UK, 91% of women reported being groped in a nightclub, an act that "happens on such a casual basis that often you don't really know who did it or why."[14] In Brazil, which has a negligible Muslim population, 86% of women reported being groped in a nightclub. To study the phenomenon, three women were outfitted with a smart dress that "recorded each nonconsensual touch they experienced, not including general touches from passers by or accidental bumps. Over a 3 hour and 47 minute period, the women were touched a combined 157 times without their consent by men. This averaged out at over 40 times per hour."[15] As Lisa Clarke, a British social activist put it, "There's a culture in club life that accepts it as the norm and if you're not ready to accept that then... you're not welcome."[16]

Given such realities, several hundred women getting groped in crowded New Year's Eve festivities in a city of one million people is not surprising. What changed in Cologne was not that western women suddenly found themselves getting groped, but rather that it was allegedly Muslim men who were doing the groping. In response to social media frenzy accusing Muslim men of carrying out mass sexual assaults, reporting every incident became a patriotic duty. German women came out by the hundreds to report having been assaulted, even though most could not readily identify the assailant given the dark and crowded conditions at the time. Without the charged racial milieu, these incidents would have gone unreported, otherwise local police precincts would be inundated every Friday night with thousands of sexual assault allegations being filed by clubgoers and bar hoppers.

France 24 analyzed the images and videos that accompanied the social media posts expressing outrage at the Cologne attacks. It found that "although the women in the photos have bloodied faces, bruised bodies and petrified expressions... many of these pictures are actually fakes." An image of a woman with "blond hair, blue eyes, and [an] angelic face splattered with blood" turned out to be a recycled photo that had been used as far back as 2007 by xenophobes trying to link "foreigners" with "sexual violence." Another picture alleged to be that of a German woman being "sexually assaulted by more than 1,000 Arabs" had been used previously in an article on rape published by an Indian news site in 2014. A photograph of a "young blue-eyed woman whose mouth is covered with blood" was actually that of a British woman "attacked by another woman in a Manchester bar in 2013."[17] It was exactly these sorts of fake images that led to the outpouring of sexual assault allegations and public outrage targeting refugees.

The moral panic led to traditional media outlets reporting fake news stories of sexual assaults carried out by Muslim men. A year after what unfolded in Cologne, *Bild*, Germany's most widely circulated newspaper, reported that fifty "Arab-looking" men assaulted women on New Year's Eve in

Frankfurt. The news spread far and wide on social media and through reprinting and rebroadcasting on other news outlets. By February, it had become apparent that there was no factual basis to the story and *Bild* issued an apology.[18] The apology was too little too late when one considers that the fake news had already had its effect and that a belated apology comes across, in a racially charged context, as either a cover-up or a sugar-coating of what really is happening. Somehow the police and the media are always alleged to be colluding to cover up evidence of Muslim crimes.

Even though the events led to massive outrage targeting the newly arrived Syrian refugees, the men who were arrested for these assaults were predominantly "illegal" economic migrants who had been denied work permits and who were basically awaiting deportation.[37] Considering the technical difficulties in repatriating migrants to their countries of origin,[19] they become trapped in a vicious cycle of unemployment, dispossession, poverty, marginalization, and desperation. Since only 1-2 percent of North Africans in Germany had been granted legal asylum as of 2017, it is unfortunate though not surprising that they would be at increased risk of joining organized crime or of being drawn to extremist organizations.[20]

The main social risk to the moral panic that surrounds these types of incidents is that they lead to incorrect diagnoses of the problems, scapegoat the wrong groups of people and types of beliefs, and promote misguided policies that worsen rather than improve the situation. Hence, the problem is diagnosed as being welcoming to refugees, Islam is denounced as misogynistic, Muslim men are labeled as rapists, and the policies proposed are to increase the marginalization of immigrant communities.

In a Freedom of Information request, the British Ministry of Justice was asked what percent of men in prison on rape convictions were Muslim, given the prevailing rumor that 60% of convicted rapists in Britain were Muslim. The answer was 12%.[21] Similarly, a *Der Spiegel* report found that 9.1% of sexual assault cases in Germany involved suspects who were immigrants.[22] When one considers that 13% of Germany's population consists of first-generation immigrants,[23] the "rapefugee" problem appears to be rather exaggerated. It is also noteworthy that the Muslim population in Europe tends to skew young; over half of Muslims in England and Wales are under the age of 25.[24] Considering that sexual assaults are more prevalent among adolescents and young adults and taking into account the higher conviction rates for perpetrators from minority communities when the victim is a white woman,[25] it becomes difficult to assert an association between Muslim religion and criminal sexual assault. Moreover, it is presumptuous to assume that all immigrants committing crimes are Muslim, as there are plenty of Christian, Hindu, and Buddhist immigrants in Europe. The contention that immigrants generally increase crime is hardly credible when violent crime rates in countries like Germany and the United States have progressively dropped as the nonwhite proportions of their populations have increased. In 1992, Germany had a homicide rate of 1.74 per 100,000; in 2018, this value was 0.95.[26] In the United States, these values were 9.25 and 4.96, respectively.[27] Meanwhile, during that quarter century, both countries experienced staggering growths in their minority immigrant populations.

The racialized stereotype of Muslim rapists is hardly limited to Europe. In India, Mahesh Hegde, a co-founder of the right-wing Indian propaganda portal Postcard News, claimed on Twitter, "From 2016-2018, total 84,374 rapes happened in the country, 81000 rapists were Musl*ms, 96% of the women and the children targeted by the rapists were Hindus."[28] Needless to say, there is no data to back up such absurd claims.

The case of Sabbar Kashur highlights how courts can determine the presence or absence of consent (i.e., consensual intercourse versus rape) based on whether the accused perpetrator is Muslim. Kashur, a Palestinian man, had intercourse with a Jewish woman whom he had just met. Two weeks later, she found out that he was Arab and pressed charges. An Israeli court convicted him of "rape by deception" and sent him to prison. He had never told the woman that he was Jewish; she had simply assumed that he was because his nickname was

Dudu, which is a common nickname for Israeli Jews named David.[29] Clearly, the court considered the act to have constituted rape only because he was Arab, not because he had committed rape.

The perception of Muslim men as sexually menacing has led Norway to coerce immigrants to attend formal classes on sexual violence. It is worth noting that while immigrants compose over 16% of Norway's population, 87% of the 1,266 sexual crime charges filed in 2014 were against native Norwegians.[30] Nevertheless, immigrant men are perceived as being disproportionately prone to sexual predation. One should contrast patronizing descriptions of how Muslim men stare at Norwegian women[31] with almost flirtatious everyday descriptions of white men "checking women out." The former is claimed to contribute to a threatening environment in which women feel uncomfortable; the latter merely makes a woman blush. Setting up classes specifically targeting immigrant men showcases how policymakers enact social policies based more on stereotypes than facts, while completely ignoring the pernicious threat posed by white men staring at and verbally abusing hijabi women in the west.

Such allegations are reminiscent of the racialized crime of "reckless eyeballing." During slavery, this constituted a black person not showing proper racial deference by making eye contact with a white person. Under Jim Crow, this morphed into the prosecutable crime of a black man looking at a white woman, which was equated with an intent to rape.[32] In a racialized context, something as banal as making eye contact can take on criminal dimensions.

Instances in which Muslim men catcall or insult a white woman are seen as inherently worrisome, as if catcalling is limited to Muslim men. Any young woman walking down the streets of Rome or Florence knows how common it is to be catcalled by white Italian men. Freedom of speech being equated with the freedom to offend is forgotten when the catcaller is Muslim; rather, re-education and a need for cultural sensitivity training are demanded. Much is made of Muslim men calling German women "wh-res,"[33] when in reality slut-shaming is more a reflection of near-universal patriarchy than of a specific problem with Muslim men. Lotta Brännström and colleagues, in an article entitled, "'You Are so Ugly, You Wh-re'—Girls in Rural Sweden Discuss and Address Gendered Violence," discuss how pervasive gendered violence in rural Sweden causes marginalization of young women by hegemonic masculinity.[34] Though this is an unfortunate problem, it is hardly one that is limited to Muslim men.

It is invariably assumed that these young immigrant men need western cultural education, not an Islamic one, when they should perhaps be reminded of the Quranic verse, "Tell the believing men to lower their gaze and to guard their modesty."[35] In case it is alleged that this verse is sexist in that it only tells men not to gaze at women, the very next verse reads, "Tell the believing women to lower their gaze and to guard their modesty."[36]

That some women in Cologne were groped, attacked, or robbed on New Year's Eve is beyond question. However, these reprehensible acts carried out by a handful of thieves and drunks cannot be blamed on Islam by the same Islamophobes who claim that Islam is the religion of cutting-off the hands of thieves, the religion of lashing people who drink, and the religion that has zero tolerance for any form of extramarital sexuality. If anything, this would not be the result of Islam, but of the lack of religiosity in some of its adherents. Hence, the narrative forwarded was that this incident was a form of social control by men who had completely subjugated women in their own countries and who were now trying to do the same to European women.[37] If that were the case, the events of Cologne should be commonplace in other western cities with sizeable Muslim populations.

The exact details of the events that unfolded in Cologne may never be known, but the racialized backlash parallels similar events in American history, such as the 1906 Atlanta race riot. According to Carol Anderson,

In Atlanta in the fall of 1906, local newspapers, law enforcement, and politicians' toxic anti-Blackness stoked that fear, fed that rage, and turned the city into a war zone. Four major papers in the city ran months of front-page stories with ghastly details of African American men harassing, sexually assaulting, and raping white women. No city street was safe. No park was carefree. No home secure. All were made unsafe by the presence of Blackness. Although the stories of Black men gone wild... were false or overdramatized for shock effect, the stories sold papers. Circulation doubled at the *Atlanta Evening News.* Tensions in the city kept rising with each new tale of African American debauchery, sadism, rape, and defilement of white virginal purity. The *Georgian* editorial page made it clear: "If the negro were no longer a part of our population, the women of the South would be freed from their state of siege..." Gubernatorial candidates and rival newspapermen... "did everything in their power to fan the flames of racial hatred." They vowed to cleanse the state of "Negro domination." ... There were more and more claims of rape and sexual assault... Many of those appeared to be that an African American man looked at a white woman. Glanced her way. Peered at her salaciously. Two of the charges, however, were true. Painfully true. Each, nonetheless, was reported with... lewd, rage-inducing details conjuring up the imagery [of] Black barbarism... By September 22, 1906, white men had had enough... The angry crowd quickly turned into a lynch mob. It was the new "nigger-hunt." ... In a frenzied crime spree, Black businesses were trashed, looted, and destroyed. Black people were pulled off trolley cars and pummeled, shot, and stabbed... There was going to be a world-class bonfire as the Black working-class community, known as Darktown... was [to be] burnt to the ground...[38]

The Tulsa race massacre of 1921 also started over a false racialized rape allegation. A 19-year-old black man tripped as he entered an elevator. Losing his balance, he accidentally stepped on the foot of the elevator operator, a 17-year-old white woman. Hearing her shriek, a clerk in a nearby store assumed that an attempted rape had occurred, so the black man was arrested and held in the Tulsa County Courthouse. In response to media frenzy over the incident, a mob of two thousand angry whites formed to lynch the man. When local blacks came out to prevent the lynching, events spiraled out of control and the mob proceeded to burn down 1,256 homes and virtually every church, school, and business in the Greenwood District, a rather prosperous African American neighborhood. Even the local hospital was not spared. Between 100 and 300 people were killed. Not a single white perpetrator was ever prosecuted or punished. Instead, thousands of blacks were detained and only released when a white person would take responsibility for their subsequent behavior.[39]

Finally, it is worth pointing out that fringe extremist groups like Daesh enshrine a theology of rape, believing that Islam allows them to rape the Yazidi women and children unfortunate enough to end up under their dominion.[40] Their acts are well-orchestrated to cause outrage and to raise intolerance towards and hence to marginalize Muslims in the west in order to help increase their own recruitment. Western Islamophobes like Sam Harris give their extremist ideology further credence by claiming that their understanding of Islam is the literal and hence essentially correct one,[41] when a literal reading of Islamic precepts would prove the exact opposite. More than 120 Muslim scholars from around the world wrote an open letter to the followers of Daesh, denouncing in Islamic terms their perversion of Islamic principles and laws.[42] Daesh's far-right intolerance is a novelty in countries like Iraq and Syria, and in no way can be seen as the Muslim norm. Suffice it to say that had the massacre of Yazidi men and mass-rape of their women been historically considered Islamic, Yazidis would not still be found in Iraq.

Fear of Miscegenation

Aside from the irrational fear that men from minority groups rape white women, there is also a fear of consensual interracial intercourse leading to miscegenation, which is of particular concern when a couple includes a colored man and a white woman. Considering that miscegenation would become more prevalent if minority populations are accepted as equally and fully human, dehumanizing minorities becomes crucial to maintaining racial purity. After suffering a mob attack for being in the company of two white women, Frederick Douglass, the mixed-race American civil rights activist, said,

> Polished American gentlemen would applaud a deed of ruffianism like the one in question, although they might shrink from the performance of the deed itself. My offence is alleged to be that of walking down Broadway in company of "two white women." This, however, is not a fair statement of that offence. My offence was that I walked down Broadway, in company with white persons, on terms of equality. Had I been with those persons simply as a servant, and not as a friend, I should have been regarded with complacency by the refined and with respect by the vulgar class of white persons who throng that great thoroughfare. The clamour here about human equality is meaningless. We have here an aristocracy of skin, with which if a man be covered, and can keep out of the state prisons, he possesses the high privilege of insulting a coloured man with the most perfect impunity. This class of aristocrats are never more displeased than when they meet with an intelligent coloured man. They recognize in him a contradiction to their ungenerous and unsound theories respecting the negro race, and, not being able to reason with him down to a level with the brute, they use brute force to knock him down to the desired level.[43]

Avoiding miscegenation is not a universal human value. Miscegenation was the norm in Islamic societies, with Arab and Persian populations mixing rather freely with Turkic and Mongol invaders as well as slaves brought in from Europe, Africa, and Central Asia. In contrast to countries such as the United States, South Africa, and Australia, racial lines are virtually impossible to discern in the Middle East. The white populations of North America, Southern Africa, and Australasia remain virtually undiscernible from European native populations despite centuries of separation. In the United States, this was accomplished by virtual elimination of the native population followed by racialization and segregation of the portion of the population that had African descent. Historically and even today, mixed-race children have been classified as black and thereby enslaved or otherwise segregated and discriminated against as part of the "colored" caste, further maintaining white racial purity. Cultural prohibitions on interracial marriage persist, to the point that even now less than 3% of American white women are married to non-whites.[44]

This can be contrasted with countries like Mexico, where, in a manner similar to Middle Eastern Muslim nations, widespread miscegenation has blurred racial lines. *Mestizaje*, racial and cultural amalgamation, has been an integral part of Mexico's ethnic identity. It is perhaps not surprising that Islamophobia has never taken root in countries like Mexico. This is not necessarily due to the small number of Muslims in Mexico, as countries like Poland and Hungary have been in the grip of virulent Islamophobia despite similarly negligible Muslim populations. Rather, this is due to white supremacist and social Darwinist ideologies that predominate in developed western societies that create a cultural aversion to interracial mixing.

Chapter 16

Economic Gender Inequality in Islam

A common Islamophobic stereotype is that in Islam, women are effectively men's property and that they have no property rights of their own, akin to the way it was in Europe in premodern times. Quite to the contrary, in Islam, a woman is not the property of her father or husband, and she cannot be married off without her consent. According to the Quran, both men and women are entitled to private ownership rights over their personal property, whether acquired through personal earnings[1] or inheritance.[2] A wife has no ownership rights vis-à-vis her husband's private property, but she does have a legal economic right to be provided food, shelter, and clothing appropriate for her social status. Her husband has a financial obligation to provide these and if he does not, an Islamic judge can order his assets seized to adequately provide for his wife and children.[3]

Conversely, the husband has no rights over the personal property of his wife. She does not have any obligation to provide for any living expenses and she can trade, spend, or donate from her own property freely without her husband's interference. If she chooses to contribute financially to the family, she can, but she cannot be compelled to do so. She can lend her husband money and complete repayment of the loan would be obligatory. Furthermore, the woman is entitled to full control of her dower (*mahr*, *sadaq*), which is tangible property that is statutorily bestowed upon her by her husband at the time of marriage. The dower does not go to the bride's father, as might be assumed, but rather becomes her personal property. In fact, a bride's family cannot demand financial compensation from the groom in return for consenting to the marriage,[4] and any portion of the dower promised to the bride's father is legally void.[5] A dower must be contrasted with a dowry, which is property given to a groom by the bride's family, as is customary in Hindu marriages.[6]

The financial independence of Muslim women is not merely hypothetical; it was one of the founding principles of Islam. The Prophet's (S) first wife, Khadija, was a wealthy trader who retained control of her property throughout her 25-year marriage to the Prophet (S). Indeed, before they were married, she was the Prophet's (S) employer who had tasked him with managing a caravan to Syria. At the time of their marriage, she was 40 years old and had children from previous marriages, whereas Muhammad (S) was 25 and previously unmarried. Her voluntary charitable financial support was the lifeblood of the early Islamic community and her death constituted a massive setback that contributed to the exodus of the Muslims from Mecca to Medina. Given her unwavering devotion to the Islamic cause, she is universally revered by Muslims of all denominations.

Islam's granting of property rights to women contrasts sharply with traditional premodern western norms in which women did not have the right to own and control property. The New York legislature passed the Married Women's Property Act of 1848, which is considered to be the first western law that provided women with a semblance of meaningful control over their own personal property.[7] Similar legislation was not passed in England until 1882.[8] It was not until the 1970s that a woman could open a bank account or apply for a credit card without her husband's permission.[9]

In my experience, westerners unfamiliar with Islam often dismiss these issues as merely academic. Even if Muslim women have a de jure right to private property, surely they must de facto be deprived of such rights in favor of their husbands. This is, however, simply inaccurate. My paternal great-grandmother lived in Sabzevar, a town in northeastern Iran. She was rather wealthy, having received a substantial inheritance. Her husband, in comparison, was considered relatively poor. He never felt any entitlement to her wealth and never exerted any control over her property.

Proposed Bans on Muslim Dowers

In 2020, Mattias Tesfaye, Denmark's integration minister, proposed banning the dower (*mahr*), an obligatory financial commitment a Muslim man makes when he marries a woman.[10] The amount is up to the couple to decide, and can range from something trivial like a ring or dress to quite substantial quantities of cash, jewelry, or gold. The dower becomes an immediate financial obligation towards the wife which she can demand at any time. In some Islamic cultures, it is customary for the dower not to be demanded unless the husband divorces the woman. Regardless, the dower is one form of economic empowerment for women and provides financial security in the form of tangible property that the woman exercises full economic control over and that cannot be taken from her. The Quran clearly states, "[If] you have given [your wife] a great treasure [as dower], do not take any of it back. Would you take it through calumny and manifest sin?"[11]

Anti-shariah legislation in the United States has infringed on the ability of Muslim women to legally demand their dowers. As a result, Muslim women end up financially victimized by the Islamophobes who claim they are trying to "save" them. According to Ali-Karamali,

> In states that have enacted anti-shariah laws... a court would be allowed—perhaps even be required—to invalidate a contract simply because it's based on shariah... This has real-world, often unjust consequences. One such unjust result occurred in Kansas... In *Soleimani v. Soleimani*, after her divorce, a wife sought enforcement of the mahr provision in her marriage contract, which required her husband (whose assets had amounted to $7 million before his marriage) to pay her a mahr of $677,000... Because of the Kansas anti-shariah law, the trial court could neither interpret

the contract by applying Islamic law nor honor the mahr provision... The result? Instead of receiving her $677,000, the wife received $692 per month for two years.[12]

It should be noted that Mattias Tesfaye is the same minister who asked Danish imams to tell Muslim women to have "sex before marriage like all other women."[10] His comments betray his stereotyped assumptions that young Muslim women lack agency, are completely under the control of Muslim religious leaders, and need to be told by older men whether or not to engage in premarital sex. He wouldn't deem it sensible to ask Catholic priests to command Catholic women to fornicate. He also seems to overlook the fact that a quarter of Danes aged 18 and 19 have not had intercourse and that 88% of this group plans on waiting until marriage.[13] Such decisions are highly intimate ones that involve personal, family, and religious values, physical and mental health considerations, and individual variations in desire to prioritize academic or other achievements over sexual experiences. It appears that human societies generally suffer more ill effects—sexually transmitted infections, unwanted teenage pregnancies, and mental health consequences—from the hookup culture than from premarital abstinence.

Gender Inequality in Islamic Inheritance Laws

The assumption that Islam is a backward religion when it comes to women's economic rights falls flat especially when one considers historical and societal contexts. As a result, some Islamophobes and critics of Islam concentrate on the one specific area in which they can objectively point to economic gender discrepancy—inheritance.

Islamic inheritance laws are exceedingly complex. However, in some of the most common inheritance situations, men inherit twice the share of women. For example, if someone dies and has children, the Quran dictates that each son inherits twice the share of each daughter.[14] Similarly, if there are no children but both parents are living, the father inherits two-thirds while the mother inherits one-third of the estate.[15] A husband will inherit one-fourth of his wife's estate if she has children and one-half if she does not; conversely, a wife will inherit one-eighth of the husband's estate if he has children and one-quarter if he does not.[16] In the absence of children, spouses, and parents, "if there are both brothers and sisters [remaining], the male will [receive] the share of two females."[17]

In some instances, however, there is no difference between the sexes, such as when "the parents [of the diseased] are each entitled to one sixth if he has offspring."[18] Considering different permutations of consanguinity and gender among heirs, it has been asserted that women inherit less than men in four situations, more than men in sixteen situations, and equal to men in ten situations.[19]

Typically, the discrepancy in inheritance among close family members has been explained by differences in financial responsibility. A woman who inherits would be entitled to complete control over her inheritance while also having a right to sustenance from her father or husband, a right to the marital dower promised by her husband, and freedom from any claim against her property by other family members. In contrast, when a man inherits, his wife, children, and other family members retain a claim of support against his property.[20] As such, the added financial responsibilities are offset by an increased share of inheritance in some situations. This can be seen in terms of establishing equity in the absence of complete equality.

If someone has not made a will, Islamic inheritance laws will be applied to entirety of the estate. However, Islamic law allows for a will or bequest (*wasiyyah*) to be made to dictate division of up to one-third of the estate in accordance with the wishes of the deceased. As such, Islamic law provides leeway for individuals to set right any perceived injustices that formulaic division would create for their specific situation.

Suppose an unmarried woman has two heirs, a son and a daughter, and they are both unmarried and living independently, with the daughter having a lower-paying job than the son. She may decide to give her daughter the entirety of the one-third of her property that she is entitled to bequest. In this situation, supposing she dies with a $180,000 estate, the daughter would be given $60,000 (one-third from the bequest) plus $40,000 (one-third from inheritance) for a total of $100,000. The son would receive $80,000 as inheritance. That formulaic division of the estate is carried out only after bequests have been bequeathed is clearly enshrined in the Quran.[21] Furthermore, Muslims are exhorted to specify their bequests prior to death: "It is prescribed for you, when death approaches any one of you, if he is to leave any wealth, that he bequeaths reasonably unto parents and near relatives. [This is] a duty for the pious."[22]

The complexity of Islamic inheritance law is typically overlooked in favor of simplistic assumptions that Islam inherently deprives women of financial autonomy and inheritance rights. *The New York Times*, in a 2018 article, claimed, "In Muslim countries, laws governing inheritance are derived from verses in the Quran... Distant male relatives can supersede wives, sisters and daughters, leaving women not just bereaved but also destitute."[23] In reality, there is no Islamic shariah situation that allows for distant male relatives to supersede Muslim wives, sisters, and daughters in inheritance. That such a presumption is made and is not editorially corrected is because it seems so believable that it hardly needs fact-checking even though it is patently false.

The reason it is so easy to presume that Muslim women are superseded by distant male relatives is that western societies are seen as more socially developed and hence evolutionarily more evolved; every other society, in contrast, is seen as developmentally delayed, caught behind somewhere along the European evolutionary timeline. As Edward Said put it, "the Oriental was always *like* some aspect of the West."[24] As such, the status of women in Islamic law must be similar to that of European women at some point in the past. This is how Islamic law is conflated with the premodern English concept of entailment seen in popular works of fiction like Jane Austen's

Pride and Prejudice, in which the estate of Mr. Bennett would go to a cousin, leaving his wife and three daughters penniless, unless one of the daughters were to marry the cousin. This situation would simply never arise under a shariah legal system, as the wife would receive one-eighth of the estate and the daughters would share the rest equally.[25] The cousin would receive nothing unless a specific bequest were to be made, in which case his share would, at most, comprise one-third of the estate.

The issue of gender differences in inheritance is also used to categorize Muslims as innately backward people who blindly follow an outdated and archaic holy book and hence constitute a population that cannot truly be integrated within a liberal society in which more enlightened Judeo-Christians thrive. The Quran is quite simply seen as posing a societal challenge in a way that the Bible is not. Such claims overlook the fact that the Bible also addresses not only how women inherit but also how they are themselves inherited. Simply put, if a man dies, the Old Testament stipulates that his daughter would inherit nothing if he has a son: "Say to the Israelites, 'If a man dies and leaves no son, give his inheritance to his daughter.'"[26] As for the wife, not only does she not inherit at all, she stands to be inherited herself: "If brothers are living together and one of them dies without a son, his widow must not marry outside the family. Her husband's brother shall take her and marry her."[27] In contrast, the Quran says, "It is not lawful for you to inherit women against their will."[28] The issue is not to pick on biblical laws, but to highlight the hypocrisy inherent in accepting Judeo-Christian texts as compatible with western liberal values, while assuming that Islam and the Quran are somehow antithetical to modernity. This is a particularly salient point when one considers that the loudest Islamophobic voices are often heard from the religious right in countries like the United States, Hungary, and Poland.

Chapter 17

Gender Inequality in Legal Affairs

A common allegation is that Muslims are not compatible with a liberal democratic society because of the status of women in Islam. The Quran allegedly enshrines a sexist system that sees women as less than fully human. Hence, in contrast to people hailing from the Judeo-Christian tradition, Muslims cannot be properly integrated into western societies. For example, a woman's testimony is said to count as half that of a man's, her blood money is half that of a man's, and women lack equal rights when it comes to issues such as divorce and child custody. The ill-logical conclusion is that since Muslims believe in the Quran, they cannot really conform with a system of legal gender equality the way Christians and Jews can.

In this discussion, my goal is neither to go into exhaustive details of *fiqh* nor to deliver apologetics for traditional Islamic jurisprudence but rather to show the nuances involved in many of these issues and that, within a traditional shariah context, civil contracts (*'uqud*) including marriage and divorce can be modified through mutual agreement to provide greater gender equity. Furthermore, showing that similar issues exist in the Old and New Testaments demonstrates that Muslims are no less compatible with a liberal state than religious Christians and Jews who believe in their holy texts yet serve as integral members of liberal democratic societies. Within a racialized context, nitpicking specific Islamic jurisprudential precepts invariably amounts to confirmation bias—seeking out only the type of evidence that supports a preconceived notion (e.g., Islam is violent, Islam is sexist, etc.). The same exact type of evidence, when pertaining to other religions, is simply ignored.

It is also worth noting that peculiarities of specific Muslim nations are often taken to be indicative of Islam itself. For example, for decades Saudi Arabia was the world's only country that banned women from driving. This fed into the stereotype of Islamic misogyny and sexist discrimination through two assumptions: first, that Islam had something to do with the ban, and second, that any truly devout Muslim society would adopt such a policy. It is simply overlooked that there is no Islamic law that prohibits women from driving, that Saudi Arabia is the only Muslim country to have enacted such a driving ban, that women drive in other Arab nations, and that the Quran explicitly bans prohibitions on things that are permissible (halal).[1] A peculiarity of Saudi Arabia's pseudo-Islamic Wahhabi state became equated with Islam itself. Similarly, horrific restrictions on women under Taliban rule in Afghanistan has fed into stereotypes of what life would be like for women under Islam. In reality, Taliban rule is not traditionally Islamic per se, but rather a modern symbiosis of Pashtun tribal nationalism and reactionary Deobandi Salafi ideology. To consider peculiar regional practices as reflective of the wider Islamic world would be like imagining that all Christians pass around venomous snakes in church just because some fringe denominations do.[2]

Women as Witnesses in Legal Disputes

Financial transactions can involve the exchange of present goods such as paying for a pair of shoes and walking off with them, or they can involve the creation of a debt obligation, such as with loans or with the sale of an item that will be delivered in the future. The latter instances create a higher likelihood for disputes to arise if there are discrepancies in how the terms of the agreement are recalled. To reduce this risk, the Quran spells out recommendations, including having the agreement recorded in writing as well as employing witnesses:

O you who believe! When you contract a debt that
creates future obligations at a specified time, record it in
writing... And call to witness, from among your men, two
witnesses. And if two men are not present, then a man
and two women whom you approve of as witnesses, so
that if the one errs [in recalling the details of the
transaction], the other can remind her...[3]

The issue taken with this verse is that it calls for two male
witnesses or one male and two female witnesses if two men
cannot be found. As such, Islam is accused of counting the
testimony of women as half that of men. The basic issue here is
that a mountain is made out of a molehill. The verse is not
creating an obligation in terms of having to have witnesses for
financial agreements, but rather recommending that agreements
be put in writing and that scribes and witnesses be involved.
Having more than one witness is recommended regardless of
whether there are men or women, but in no way mandated. As
Ayatollah Khomeini put it, "Other than with divorce and *zihar*[1],
there is no contract or personal act (*iqa'*) that requires two just
witnesses. It is not as if anyone who wants to buy or sell
something or to enter another contract must have two just
witnesses present."[4] In fact, Sunni schools of jurisprudence don't
even require witnesses for divorce. Furthermore, in civil matters,
a judge is free to admit many kinds of evidence. It should be
noted that to the extent I quote fatwas from Ayatollah Khomeini,
it is not to promote any one scholar or jurisprudential school;
rather, it is because his rulings constitute the hallmark of fatwas
in the popular western imagination and because he can hardly be
accused of promoting apologetical or modernist interpretations
that don't reflect traditional jurisprudence.

As the verse is phrased, it appears to be more for the
comfort of the woman than for her diminution. A woman brought
in to testify in a civil matter could feel intimidated if the two

---

[1] *Zihar* is an Islamically outlawed form of pre-Islamic divorce in which
a man tells his wife, "You are like my mother's back."

claimants are men, the other witness is a man, the judge is a man, etc. Having another woman there would ensure her comfort during the court proceedings, so that if one woman does not recall the details accurately, she does not have to feel bullied by litigious men but rather can confer with another woman. Instead of excluding women, having two women testify actually includes more women in the process. The issue of women feeling harangued by mobs of aggressive men in judicial and legislative proceedings has come under increased scrutiny in recent years. Activists point out to how insensitively Anita Hill was treated by the US Senate during its confirmation hearings for Supreme Court nominee Clarence Thomas, whom she accused of sexual harassment. According to *The New York Times*, "The 1991 hearings were a surreal spectacle, as senators prodded an obviously uncomfortable Ms. Hill through awkward testimony about penis size, pubic hair and a pornographic film star known as Long Dong Silver." The Senate judiciary committee at the time was headed by Delaware Senator Joe Biden, who during his 2020 presidential campaign expressed "regret for what she endured" during her grueling Senate hearing.[5]

In Islamic jurisprudence, there are instances, indeed, when the testimony of a man is not accepted no matter how many men testify. The prime example is in determining whether a child who died after birth was born alive and hence would be entitled to inheritance in certain circumstances. Only the testimony of women who heard the child's cry is admissible; the testimony of men is not.[6] Furthermore, if a dispute arises in regard to the amount of a woman's dower and no other witnesses exist, the sworn testimony of the wife is granted precedence over that of the husband.[7]

In contrast to civil law, *hudud* pertains to crimes against God and include a relatively small number of offenses such as specific types of theft, highway banditry, illicit sexual intercourse, false sexual accusation, and the consumption of intoxicating beverages. For *hudud* punishments, there are disagreements over whether the testimony of women is admissible and how female witnessed count towards meeting the

202The ill-Logic of Islamophobia

required number of witnesses. Regardless, when one considers the exceedingly high evidentiary bar in place for and the general antipathy towards doling out *hudud* punishments in Islamic jurisprudence, any additional burden of proof would be neither surprising nor unwelcome.

It is worth nothing that in traditional Jewish law, the testimony of women was excluded. According to the Jewish Virtual Library,

> It is derived from Scripture that only men can be competent witnesses. Maimonides gives as the reason for the disqualification of women the fact that the bible uses the masculine form when speaking of witnesses (Sif. Deut. 190; Shev. 30a; Sh. Ar., ḤM 35:14; Yad, Edut 9:2)... Another reason was suggested in the Talmud: that the place of a woman was in her home and not in court (Shev. 30a; cf. Git. 46a)... Women are admitted as competent witnesses in matters within their particular knowledge, for example, on customs or events in places frequented only by women (Rema ḤM 35:14; Darkhei Moshe ḤM 35, n. 3; Beit Yosef, ibid., n. 15; Terumat ha-Deshen Resp. no. 353); in matters of their own and other women's purity (Ket. 72a; Ket 2:6); for purposes of identification, especially of other women (Yev. 39b); or in matters outside the realm of strict law (BK 114b). In post-talmudic times, the evidence of women was often admitted where there were no other witnesses available (cf. e.g., Resp. Maharam of Rothenburg, ed. Prague, no. 920; Resp. Maharik no. 179), or in matters not considered important enough to bother male witnesses (Resp. Maharik no. 190; Sefer Kol Bo no. 116). In Israel, the disqualification of women as witnesses was abolished by the Equality of Women's Rights Act, 5711–1951.[8]

In accordance with prevailing Jewish law, the New Testament claims that when Mary Magdalene purportedly witnessed the resurrection of Jesus (AS), her testimony was rejected.[9] Furthermore, the role of women in public and church life was limited by concepts such as, "I do not permit a woman to teach or to assume authority over a man; she must be quiet,"[10] and "women should be silent in the churches, for they are not permitted to speak."[11] As such, use of textual sources to support the stereotype of Islam as a particularly sexist religion is disingenuous at best.

Inequalities in Retributive Punishments (Qisas)

Aside from *hudud*, there is the category of criminal punishments are known as *qisas*, which refers to retributive punishment for death and injuries, commonly thought of as "an eye for an eye." The Quranic basis for *qisas* is reflected in the following verse:

> We prescribed for them therein: A life for a life, an eye for an eye, a nose for a nose, an ear for an ear, and a tooth for a tooth; and for wounds, an equitable retaliation. But if anyone charitably forgoes [retaliation], that shall be an expiation for him.[12]

A victim or victim's family has three choices—to demand physical retribution (*qisas*), to forgo retribution in return for financial recompense (*diya*), or most preferably to forgive the perpetrator in return for God forgiving his or her own sins. The preference for lenience even when one has a legal right to claim is a general Quranic principle. The Quran says, "to forgo [your rights] is more befitting of piety, so do not neglect being generous to one another."[13] Similarly, with respect to loans, "if the debtor is in [financial] distress, then let there be a postponement until [a time of] ease, but to remit the debt as an act of charity is even better for you."[14]

The basis for the second option (*diya*) is set forth in a verse that addresses involuntary manslaughter[15] as well as in the following verse:

O you who believe! Equitable retaliation (*qisas*) is
prescribed to you in cases of murder: a free man for a free
man, a slave for a slave, and a woman for a woman. But
whoever is forgiven by his [injured] brother for [having
committed] something, then follow it up with suitable
recompense that is granted graciously. This is an easing
and a mercy from your Lord. After this, whoever
exceeds the limits shall have a painful punishment.[16]

That retaliation (*qisas*) and recompense (*diya*) are seen
as an easing or a mercy is because they set strict limits to
retribution and prevent needless escalation and unjust demands
for retaliation. Nevertheless, controversies arise from the fact that
in traditional jurisprudence, the *diya* for a *dhimmi* non-Muslim is
lower than that of a Muslim man and the *diya* for a woman is half
that of a man in the case of death of certain injuries. It is
noteworthy that in 1991, Article 297 of the 1991 Islamic
Punishments Act in the Islamic Republic of Iran equalized the
diya for Muslims and non-Muslims.[17] This highlights the
flexibility of shariah implementation in a modern context.

The apparent gender inequality is likely due to different
economic values granted to women in society. This is hardly
surprising when one considers that in American courts, white
men, on average, receive up to 74% higher economic damage
payouts as compared to white women. This has to do with actual
or perceived differences in lifetime economic earning potential,
as well as consideration of the possible effects of marriage and
childbirth on a woman's future earnings.[18] Indeed, there has been
a gender pay gap in western countries such as the United States
that, due to a variety of reasons, has proved impossible to
eradicate.[19]

The case of Ameneh Bahrami brought the issue of "an
eye for an eye" to international prominence. She was an Iranian
university student who spurned the marital request of Majid
Movahedi. In 2004, he splashed her face with acid, leaving her
disfigured and blind in both eyes. She insisted on *qisas*—i.e., he
would be blinded in return. Iranian courts ruled in her favor,

allowing her to proceed with putting acid in his eye to blind him in retaliation for his crime. There was an outcry from international human rights organizations that considered the punishment "cruel and inhuman," presumably advocating for the lengthy prison sentences that epitomize western and more particularly American criminal justice systems. At the last minute, the victim forgave the perpetrator and spared his vision.[20] Islamophobes were critical of this incident from beginning to end, blaming the acid attack, the eye for an eye punishment, and the forgiveness all on Islam. How Islam justifies an acid attack is never explained, but as will be discussed in the chapter on honor killings, the violence Muslim men inflict on Muslim women is often posed in the framework of racialized or religious causation, whereas the violence perpetrated by white men on white women is generally blamed on individual factors. According to an article published in South Africa's *News24*, "Muslims are using the book to justify throwing acid over women if they dare step out of line. I don't think this is a religion worth following, and if you happen to be female, the quicker you reject this the better."[21] That such an absurd set of claims can be made and published by leading news sources highlights the pervasiveness of unchecked racialized assumptions about Muslims and their sacred texts.

Acid attacks hardly constitute a Muslim cultural crime, with London having become the acid attack capital of the west, if not the world. There was a sharp rise in acid attack in London, with the number of such offenses surging from 66 in 2012 to 752 in 2018. Seventeen of the victims were under the age of ten, including a two-year-old.[22] Acid attacks have featured prominently in attacks on innocent Muslim civilians. In 2017, John Tomlin doused acid on Jameel Mukhtar and Resham Khan, cousins who were out celebrating the latter's twenty-first birthday. The victims, permanently scarred from third degree burns, now endure constant pain and suffer from eye and ear injuries.[23] Khan's dreams of becoming a model were dashed. Acid attacks primarily targeting Muslims became so common by 2017 that Muslim women in Britain were afraid to leave their homes.[24] Nevertheless, acid attacks continue to be perceived as a Muslim cultural crime.

Inequalities in Divorce

Another civil matter that has been cited as discriminatory is how easy it is for a Muslim man to divorce his wife, as opposed to the converse. Muslim women have a number of jurisprudential recourses for Islamic divorce, but the easiest solution to this problem is to stipulate as a condition of the marriage contract that the woman have the right to divorce herself on the husband's behalf if she so chooses.[25]

In the Islamophobic context, it is made to appear that only Muslim women are trapped in religious marriages that they have no easy way out of. Yet, in Jewish law, divorce is the exclusive right of the husband, and neither the Roman Catholic nor the Coptic church recognizes any type of divorce. The Catholic Church can grant an annulment, but this is not a divorce; rather, it is a determination that the conditions for a valid marriage never existed in the first place. Hence, annulments are not particularly easy to obtain.

It is noteworthy that a significant source of Muslim-Coptic tension in Egypt is that, in many cases, the only way for a Coptic woman to escape being trapped in perpetual misery in an unhappy marriage is through conversion to Islam. This is because conversion would annul the marriage unless the husband were to convert at the same time. In one example, Wafaa Constantine, 53, and Camilla Shehata, 25, tried to leave their marriages to conservative Coptic priests. After hitting dead-ends through ecclesiastical channels—the Coptic Church forbids divorce—they converted to Islam. Egyptian police apprehended the women and handed them back to their husbands. Egyptian Christians, embarrassed by the situation, protested, claiming that Muslims had abducted the women and forced them to convert in the first place. "Islamists," in return, accused the church of holding the women against their will and forcing them to convert back to Christianity. The suffering of these two women turned into an international incident when Al-Qaeda exploited this controversy as a pretext to lay siege to a church in Iraq.[26] Whereas Hamas was quick to denounce attacks on churches,[27] it is not clear if anyone other than some Salafis have denounced the forced entrapment of Coptic women in abusive marriages and their being deprived of the freedom to choose their faith.

The west nonetheless continues to be plagued by stereotypes concerning Muslim marriages—that Muslim husbands hold a monopoly on abuse, that Muslim wives are universally trapped in intolerable marriages with ultra-misogynist men, and that Christians and liberals must intercede religiously, culturally, or militarily to save these women. That Muslim women are the ones most in need of saving is a racist myth. This is not to deny that some Muslim women have awful marriages; people of all faiths do. This is to assert that there are countless Muslim women who are blessed to have loving, kind, and loyal husbands with whom they live "till death do them part" in mutually respectful unions. Married Muslim women are in no more need of being saved than any other married woman.

Chapter 18

The Polygynous Muslim Man

In popular imagination and Hollywood portrayals, Muslim men are polygynous, with large harems of exotic women at their disposal. Numerous memes show Muslim men with four wives and innumerable children milking the western welfare state. A video went viral on YouTube claiming that in Michigan a Muslim man can register his second, third, and fourth wives as extended family and receive welfare benefits for all of them. The instructions for how to apply for all four wives are supposedly disclosed when one presses "3" for Arabic when calling the welfare office. The video exclaims, "It's official. The camel's nose is in the governmental bureaucratic tent in Michigan, feeding on our hard-earned money we pay in taxes!"[1,2] This type of fake news thrives off of the fear that parts of Michigan like Dearborn have a significant Muslim population, the myth that the welfare state takes from whites and gives to minorities, and anxiety surrounding population replacement.

Polygyny finds its basis in the one verse of the Quran that allows a man to take up to four wives. While polygyny is allowed in traditional jurisprudence, it is neither mandated nor particularly recommended. It became necessary after numerous Muslim casualties in the Battle of Uhud, when the issue of caring for orphans and widows came to the fore. The Quran says,

> If you fear that you will not deal fairly with the orphans, you may marry whichever women that suit you—two, three, or four. If you fear that you cannot be equitable [to them], then marry only one or what your right hands may possess; that will be closer to avoiding injustice.[3]

In this verse, it is evident that being able to treat wives equitably is of prime concern. In another verse, the Quran says, "You will never be able to treat [your] wives equally, no matter how hard you strive. But do not turn altogether away [from one], leaving her hanging (i.e., neither meaningfully married nor actually divorced)."[4] This verse stresses the fact that meeting the Islamic requirements for polygyny does have its challenges.

Even though many Muslim nations allow polygamy, it is currently most prevalent in countries in Western and Central Africa, where it is culturally acceptable. According to Pew,

> In Burkina Faso, 45% of people who practice folk religions, 40% of Muslims and 24% of Christians live in polygamous households... [In] Chad... Christians (21%) are more likely than Muslims (10%) to live in this type of arrangement... Fewer than 1% of Muslim men live with more than one spouse in Afghanistan, Pakistan, Bangladesh, Iran and Egypt—all countries where the practice is legal."[5]

In fact, polygyny is not a specifically Islamic custom. The Old Testament allows polygyny as long as the first wife continues to be provided for financially: "If he takes an additional wife, he must not reduce the food, clothing, or marital rights of the first wife."[6] Solomon (AS) is said to have "had seven hundred wives of royal birth and three hundred concubines."[7] Polygyny was eventually abandoned by Jews living in the Roman Empire, as Roman law only recognized one legal wife. It is noteworthy that Martin Luther, the founder of the Protestant Reformation, believed in polygyny. As stated in Reverend Patrick O'Hare's book *The Facts About Luther*,

> Luther was an out-and-out believer in polygamy. To say that he did not "counsel" polygamy, or that he advised that it should be kept secret as a sort of matter of "conscience," is utterly beside the facts. When Brück,

the Chancellor of the Duke of Saxe-Weimer, heard that
Carsltadt in 1524 advocated polygamy he consulted
Luther on the new and pernicious teaching. The
Reformer, not in the least abashed, openly and distinctly
stated: "I confess that I cannot forbid a person to marry
several wives, for it does not contradict the Scripture. If
a man wishes to marry more than one wife he should be
asked whether he is satisfied in his conscience that he
may do so in accordance with the word of God. In such
a case the civil authority has nothing to do in the matter."
... Many other clear statements wherein Luther sanctions
polygamy might be reproduced here, but the one given
above will suffice for the present... He dared not
repudiate the principle of the polygamy he had adopted
from the very commencement of his reformation and yet
he feared to sanction the promulgation of a general law
allowing polygamy to all on account of the scandal and
difficulties it would occasion.[8]

In Islamophobic polemics, polygyny is typically brought
up in the context of making Muslim culture seem completely
antithetical to western values, as part of a feminist attack on
Islam, or as a way to denigrate the Prophet (S) for having had
multiple wives. Considering the rarity of polygyny in the vast
majority of Muslim countries today, the racialized attacks
amount to nothing but perpetuating inaccurate stereotypes.

Within the context of women's rights, it is true that
women do not have the right to polyandry (having multiple
husbands) in Islam, presumably due to the importance placed on
determining paternity in Islamic jurisprudence. However,
polygyny does not specifically benefit men as a group. If the rate
of polygyny outstrips the gender population gap, it will become
difficult for some men to find spouses, which can be detrimental
to these men. Whether polygyny is beneficial or harmful to
women depends on social context. In one way, it creates added
choice—a woman might prefer a married man of means to a
monogamous relationship with one who would struggle to

provide for her and her offspring. In poverty-ridden societies, this option may spell the difference between survival and starvation.

Furthermore, outlawing polygyny does not solve the social issues that drive some women into the arms of married men in return for emotional and/or financial support. In the west, this is seen in the form of mistresses and sugar babies. The fact that polygyny is outlawed simply leaves them stripped of any legal standing and completely at the mercy of fickle partners whose wives may find out about the affair at any time. The outlawing of polygamy in many Muslim countries, such as Turkey, has not exactly helped the plight of women. Some Turkish men have "illegally" married Syrian refugees, taking them as second or third wives. These women enjoy no civil legal protections.[9] As such, banning polygyny does not necessarily benefit women. It could be argued that it would benefit the first wife, but that is not necessarily the case if the husband simply takes mistresses, squanders the family's money at strip clubs, or consorts with escorts. Hence, outlawing polygyny doesn't exactly rid society of its purported ills; it merely creates new and possibly even more detrimental ones. This is a perfect example of how any set of rules one imagines would invariably advantage one group and disadvantage another. As Stanley Fish put it, "You can only fight discrimination—practices that disadvantage some groups—with discrimination—practices that disadvantage some other groups."[10]

The fact that criticism of polygyny in Islam is disingenuous at best is highlighted by the example of Ayan Hirsi Ali. As a prominent Islamophobe, she repeatedly rails about how wrong it is for Muslim men to take more than one wife. In the meanwhile, she carried on an affair with Niall Ferguson, a married father of three[11] and a proud, self-proclaimed "neo-imperialist."[12]

In any case, obsessing over the types of non-monogamous relationships that work for people in other cultures is disingenuous considering how Tinder, Bumble, Hinge, Grindr, and endless other apps and websites allow for numerous sequential or concurrent short- and/or long-term relationships.

As such, the disdain for Muslim polygamy emanates more from cultural imperialism and bigotry than from strict sexual mores.

To the extent that polygyny is a problem, the solution is better educational and economic empowerment of women, improved global equity that reduces dire poverty, and energized efforts to promote peace and security worldwide. This would do more than complaining about Islam or outlawing polygyny would do to help ensure that girls and women are not forced to marry out of desperation or fear of starvation. Islam saw polygyny as one method to address dire social issues, and it is clearly not intended to be practiced universally, if only because no society has the gender population gap to provide every man with up to four wives.

On the topic of polygyny, one cannot forgo mention of the diatribes against the Prophet (S) on the basis that he took several wives during his lifetime. His marriage at age 25 to Khadija (AS) who was 40 years old at the time was monogamous. Her death resulted in the loss of a great source of financial and spiritual support for the Muslim community. Around the same time, the Prophet's (S) uncle Abu Talib passed away also. He had provided Muhammad (S) and his followers with immunity from execution during their time in Mecca. After that, the Muslim community found itself in a dire situation with its survival threatened. This led to the exodus to the city of Yathrib, which was then renamed Madinah al-Nabi (City of the Prophet), more commonly known as Medina.

Under these circumstances, cementing tribal ties to provide protection to the Prophet (S) and his followers became of paramount importance. This explains many of the Prophet's (S) marriages around that time. After the Battle of Khaybar, he married Safiyya, a Jewish noblewoman, thereby cementing ties of kinship with the Jewish tribes of Arabia. He similarly married Umm Habiba, the daughter of Abu Sufyan, who was the leader of the pagans of Quraysh, the tribe in Mecca that constituted Islam's main military adversary through almost the entire prophetic mission. Maria al-Qibtiyya was an Egyptian Coptic Christian woman sent to the Prophet (S) by the Byzantines. She bore him his only son, who died in infancy. He also married Maymuna bint al-Harith, thereby establishing kinship ties with Arabian and Yemenite tribes that had previously opposed him. Aside from realpolitik, some of his marriages served social purposes. After the Battle of Uhud, he married Umm Salama, who was older, had multiple children who needed support, and who had been left widowed by the war.

The Prophet's (S) marriage to his cousin Zaynab features prominently in anti-Islamic propaganda. Zaynab was married to Zayd, who was the Prophet's (S) freedman and adopted son. As the marriage frayed and finally ended, the Quran proclaimed that adopted children are not the same as biological children;[13] hence, the prohibition on marrying's one's daughter-in-law would not apply to the spouses of adoptive children. Islamophobic pundits set aside the entirety of the detailed hadith literature on the event in favor of a single dubious historical narrative lacking a viable chain of transmission (*isnad*). In this account, Muhammad (S) accidentally saw Zaynab and was so mesmerized by her beauty that Zayd divorced her so that the Prophet (S) could marry her instead. How the Prophet (S) would have been unaware of what his cousin looked like his entire life is hard to explain, particularly considering that hijab was not enacted till later in the prophetic mission. Nevertheless, this account serves well for the purpose of salacious storytelling.[14]

If anything, the Prophet's (S) example shows that there is a place for monogamy as well as situations where taking multiple wives can be beneficial. Whereas political benefits include the establishment of tribal ties that promote peace and stability, social benefits include providing additional options to unmarried, divorced, and widowed women so that they may seek emotional, physical, and financial support through legally sanctioned matrimony. This is far from the portrayal of Muslims as uniquely compelled by their insatiable sexual appetites and need for ever-enlarging harems.

Chapter 19

Portraying Muslims as Pedophiles

As despair set in for Donald Trump and his followers in the run-up to the 2020 US presidential election, they started insinuating that Hunter Biden and perhaps Joe Biden himself were pedophiles.[1] Four years earlier, with desperation taking hold in the face of dire polling numbers, Trump supporters pushed the conspiracy that Hillary Clinton was running a child sex trafficking ring out of the basement of a Washington, DC pizzeria. On December 1, 2016, Edgar Maddison Welch, armed with an AR-15 semiautomatic rifle and intent on saving trafficked children, raided the restaurant only to find that it did not even have a basement.[2] It might be assumed that the conspiracy theory would end there, but it actually morphed into the QAnon theory, according to which a "cabal of Satan-worshiping Democrats, Hollywood celebrities and billionaires runs the world while engaging in pedophilia, human trafficking and the harvesting of a supposedly life-extending chemical from the blood of abused children." Donald Trump is claimed to be waging a desperate a battle to save us from their machinations.[3]

Given this cultural tendency to deride anyone whom one doesn't like as a pedophile, it cannot come as a surprise that Islamophobes commonly fall back on the trope that Islam is a depraved religion because its prophet is a pedophile. The argument is based on a highly disputed tradition in *Sahih Bukhari* suggesting that Aishah was six when she betrothed the Prophet (S) and was nine when the marriage was consummated.

Their argument falls flat for a multitude of reasons. First, considering birth certificates with accurate dates of birth weren't exactly commonplace in the seventh century, it is not clear based on historical evidence that Aishah was as young as alleged. Indeed, a multitude of historical evidence suggests that she was much older at the time.[4] Anyone studying Islamic history knows that substantial disagreements exist over the years of births. Even the exact date of the Prophet's (S) passing is a matter of dispute, despite the fact that he was a prominent figure with an immense following by the time of his death. Accurate recordings of the dates of birth of people who only later became prominent were nearly universally absent. This is hardly a historical thing, as even today, only 33.6% of birth certificates in rural Pakistan are considered to be accurate,[5] which creates confusion as to whether someone has attained the legal age of marriage. This issue is hardly limited to distant lands and ancient times. According to Scott Allen, in the west today, "age fabrication is prevalent in sports, whether the motive is to make an athlete old enough to sign a contract, young enough to be considered an elite prospect, or to meet a minimum or maximum age requirement for competing in an event."[6]

Second, such allegations being specifically aimed at Muslims is clearly discriminatory since parallels exist in other faiths. Eastern churches believe that Joseph the Carpenter was 90 years old when he married Mary (AS), who was 12 at the time.[7] The Bible ordains killing all men, women, boys, and non-virgin girls, while keeping the virgin girls as sex slaves: "Kill every male and every woman who is not a virgin."[8] Similarly, the Israelites were told, "Kill every male among the little ones, and kill every woman that hath known man by lying with him. But all the women children, that have not known a man by lying with him, keep alive for yourselves."[9] Considering the young age of marriage at the time, this edict primarily spared prepubescent girls from massacre. And just for clarification, this was not one or two virgins, but some "32,000 women who had not had sexual relations with a man."[10] Furthermore, when the Benjaminites needed wives, they were told to hide in the vineyards and kidnap young girls from Shiloh when they would come out to dance.[11] A man was even allowed to sell his young daughter into sex slavery.[12] According to the Talmud, "The Sages taught in a *baraita*: A girl who is three years old is betrothed through intercourse; this is the statement of Rabbi Meir. And the Rabbis say: She must be three years and one day old... A girl who is three years old, and even one who is two years and one day old, is betrothed through intercourse... [as] a girl two years and one day old is considered like a three-year-old."[13] The point of citing these quotes is not to suggest that Christians and Jews are pedophiles or that Jews marry two-year-olds; the idea is simply absurd. To the contrary, it is to show that the Islamophobic obsession with pedophilia in Islam is similarly absurd and arises from an Orientalist fixation on Muslim lasciviousness.

Third, historically, getting married at what today seems like a very young age was not unusual. In medieval times, getting married between the ages of 5 and 10 was common and many teenagers were already widowed. Such marriages were typically not consummated until puberty. Prior to the twentieth century, Scottish law held that the age of marriage under the Law of Scotland was seven years, but that under common law people could marry at any age. The age of consent in England was set to 12 in 1275 but was subsequently lowered to 10 in 1576, an age restriction that was generally adopted in American colonies. Notwithstanding these statutes, it was accepted that people would commonly marry at younger ages. As such, under British common law, the age of consent was considered to be 7; accordingly, the age at which a married girl was eligible for a dower from her husband's estate was 9. In Delaware, the legal age of consent remained 7 until the mid-1960s.[14] Women getting married at young ages was neither uncommon nor particularly controversial. This, of course, specifically pertained to free white women, as slaves were sexually abused by their owners at any age with no legal repercussions.

Fourth, the modern legal age of consent, which in the west typically ranges from 14-18, usually applies only to sex outside of marriage. For example, in Texas, statutory rape laws do not pertain if "that the actor was the spouse of the child at the time of the offense."[15] In fact, as of 2019, there were twelve US states with no minimum age of marriage: California, Idaho,

Maine, Massachusetts, Michigan, Mississippi, New Mexico, Oklahoma, Rhode Island, Washington, West Virginia, and Wyoming.[16] Unlike modern western legal codes and cultural norms which openly allow underage extramarital sexual experimentation, Islam only allows sex within a system of marriage. As such, out-of-wedlock teenage pregnancies tend to be a much more significant social burden in the west than in Muslim societies, drastically curtailing the educational and occupational opportunities of countless women, contributing to child neglect and abuse, and straining welfare budgets.

Fifth, defining the current western standard for marital age as the standard for all places and for all times constitutes cultural imperialism. The concept of adolescence as an extension of childhood is a modern concept that can hardly be considered universal. My own great grandmother was married at ten and had her first child at fourteen. Her marriage was, by all accounts, a success. I know a man from Mexico whose grandmother married at ten also. His mother, in turn, was set to be engaged at the age of eleven, but instead fell in love with another man, got pregnant, and moved to the United States, where she gave birth to him at the age of thirteen. I have also met an American-born woman who was pregnant out-of-wedlock at the age of twelve, became an emancipated minor, and at the age of fourteen ran off with a married man who was twenty-four; they're still together twenty years later and have had six children together. To dismiss these sorts of partnerships that do not fit into the upper-middle-class white western ideal as pedophilic would insinuate that the vast majority of human societies throughout history were perverted while only modern westerners have a sense of morality and humanity and the right to force everyone else to accept their exact cultural norms.

Sixth, current western norms for marriage age are absurdly high considering that life expectancy was a mere 29 years globally in 1800.[17] For humans to postpone marriage until after completing their PhD was simply not realistic. To the extent humans exist today, it is because they did not delay marriage until an age in which they would need *in vitro* fertilization to get pregnant. As a religion that purports to be for all people, for all places, and for all times, Islam has to allow for wide cultural variations in marriage age in a way that modern western legal and cultural norms are simply incapable of given their limited temporal and geographical scopes. Indeed, the open embrace of cultural diversity sets Islam and colonial and neocolonial modernism apart. Furthermore, marrying at a young age is not an Islamic obligation and delaying marriage until one has attained the requisite emotional and physical maturity is considered ideal.

Seventh, it is hard to overlook the endless stories filling western newspapers about child brides in Yemen,[18] Iran,[19] Syria,[20] and elsewhere.[21] These stories feed the narrative that Muslim women need to be saved by western intervention from pedophilic Muslim men who sexually exploit them. A 12-year-old in Yemen having a bad marriage would not be considered worthy of international news headlines if there was not a constant need to feed colonial and Islamophobic narratives. In a free, capitalist press, the news reports what sells; anything that corroborates the culturally dominant narrative is good for business. Yet, it barely makes the news, never mind receiving national or international attention, when Americans prostitute out their children to support their substance abuse habits, such as when a 3-year-old in Oklahoma was prostituted out to support his parents' methamphetamine addiction.[22] At the age of 15, Hollywood actress Demi Moore was "wh-red out" by her own mother to a much older man for $500 that she needed to feed her addiction to alcohol.[23] There is more coverage dedicated to outlandish stories from far-off lands than there is to address the ills of consuming alcohol, which according to the Centers for Disease Control and Prevention causes 95,000 deaths annually in the United States alone.[24] Alcohol's victims are not only the alcoholics and drunks but also the ones they kill and maim while driving as well as the wives and children they beat and kill.

Eighth, an estimated 84% of the world's twelve million child marriages, defined as marriage while under the age of ten, occur in Hindu communities.[25] According to Hindu narrations,

Rama married Sita when she was 6;[26] Krishna abducted and married 8-year-old Rukmini who was already betrothed to Sisupala;[27] and the gods were trying to marry girls under the age of 6 to Shiva.[28] As pointed out by anti-Hindu polemicists, Hindu religious texts—not unlike their traditional Islamic counterparts—repeatedly stress than a man ought to marry off his daughter before she reaches puberty.[29] Considering the cultural and historical contexts, this was not unusual, nor is this a reason to fuel anti-Hindu, anti-Muslim, or any other type of bigoted sentiment.

Notwithstanding such facts, in the west, Islam is often conflated with pedophilia. Perhaps mentally shaken up by the events of September 11, 2001, Reverend Jerry Vines, former president of the Southern Baptist Convention, the largest Protestant denomination in the United States, called the Prophet (S) a "demon-possessed pedophile." Jack Graham, who has also served in that role, called Vines' comments "strong but accurate." Jerry Falwell, a prominent Southern Baptist televangelist, backed away from the "demon-possessed" part of the comments, only to confirm the "pedophile" part.[30]

Numerous social media memes capitalize on the pedophile stereotype. In one, a man with a big beard and a stereotypically Arab garb says, "My wife called me a paedophile. Thats (sic) a big word for a 9 year old."[31] In another, a Muslim-appearing man is holding a newborn to his face; the caption reads, "Hmmm, that new wife smell."[32] Such memes enable a stereotype to travel far and wide without allowance for meaningful nuance, discussion, or recourse.

Accusations of pedophilia provide a cheap and easy shot and place the victim in the uncomfortable position of having to explain either why "pedophilia" is okay or to get into tedious nuances of Islamic law or human history that appear apologetic. The word "pedophile" in this context is a thought-terminating cliché, lacks any cultural context, and forces a very narrow norm for acceptance of intra- and extra-marital sexual relationships. If anything, "pedophile" in this context is used as a highly emotionally-charged and indeed inaccurate word, considering that it describes one who is attracted to prepubescent children, whereas in Islamic marriages, consummation must be delayed until maturity is attained.[33]

Chapter 20

Honor Killings and Wife Beatings

According to Human Rights Watch (HRW), "Honor crimes are acts of violence, usually murder, committed by male family members against female family members who are perceived to have brought dishonor upon the family." Even though it goes on to specify that "honor crimes are not specific to any religion, nor are they limited to any one region of the world," [1] in the popular imagination, Muslim men hold a monopoly on honor killings. As Rafia Zakaria said in *Against White Feminism*,

> The HRW definition does not prescribe that honor killing is specific to people of color. That is an implicit white assumption. A label of honor killing would never be attached to any of the thousands of white-on-white cases of intimate partner violence. It is the presence of a Black or Brown male perpetrator that fosters the idea that a crime is determined by the cultural or religious identity of those involved. [2]

Much like how terrorism is defined as an act of violence carried out by a Muslim, the homicide of a woman becomes an "honor killing" when carried out by a Muslim man. As Zakaria points out,

> Muslim honor killings must be seen as uniquely evil in the eyes of the West. Yet not only does this characterization demote feminists of color as passive, unable to curtail their uniquely violent men, it also does a tremendous disservice to white women, obscuring the

true extent of the poison of gender-based violence and its tacit acceptance by the legal systems rooted in English Common Law and the Napoleonic Code. Certain "cultural crimes" (honor killings, female genital cutting, child marriage, and so on) are now set apart from universal, "normal" crimes... Yet given that the moral architecture of colonialism depends on the casting of the native as morally inferior, it is essential to question those assumptions. The very idea of cultural crimes specific to native peoples, and laden with a specifically heightened moral disgust, allowed colonists to paint local populations as inherently morally abject. Thus coercive and exploitative colonial intervention could be recast as a benevolent and necessary civilizing presence.[3]

As pointed out by Zakaria, an instance of spousal violence in a faraway land, as unfortunate as it might be, is hardly worthy of international news, but western journalists can promote their own careers by reporting on such events.[4] It is culturally reassuring for western readers to know that postcolonial societies are still reeling from the barbarities of their underdeveloped societies and comforting for them to know that westerner reporters, activists, and missionaries are engaged in saving these people from their depraved cultures and religions.[5] These journalists are effectively "promoting the narrative that violent military incursions are designed to liberate women." It is assumed that the wishes of Muslim women "always align with what white feminists think they should want, rather than as people with independent political positions and perspectives."[6]

While American soldiers and feminists are busy "liberating" Muslim women, an unfortunately high number of western women within a few miles' radius of the reader are black and blue or in casts, recovering from injuries inflicted by their partners. Those may be the lucky ones when compared to the over 5,000 American women who are killed each year by intimate partners.[7] Indeed, statistics reveal how widespread domestic violence is. According to the National Coalition

Against Domestic Violence, in the US, over 10 million adults experience domestic violence annually, with 1 in 4 women and 1 in 10 men experiencing intimate partner violence.[8]

To highlight the reality that "honor killings" are an exaggerated problem whose imagined pervasiveness is conjured up by racist stereotypes, one must consider that the female homicide rate in the United States is the same as that in Yemen, at 1 per 100,000 per year, which is higher than the rates seen in Afghanistan, Iran, or Saudi Arabia. Countries like Algeria, Bahrain, and Kuwait have female homicide rates closer to 1 per million.[9] As such, the concept of "honor killings" not only serves to stigmatize Muslims but also to whitewash analogous if not identical crimes carried out by western men.

Pinning a social problem or type of crime on an individual's race, ethnicity, or religion is a common component of racist discourse. A black man who is a drug addict and commits crimes to support his habit is perceived to be in this unfortunate situation because he is black. In contrast, a young, stereotypically attractive white girl who dies of a heroin overdose is seen as the victim of mental illness, drug addiction, peer pressure from bad friends, or some flaw of the medical system. Her whiteness never has anything to do with her addiction. Similarly, a wife's murder in Pakistan is reflective of a fundamental flaw of Pakistani culture or religion; the same crime committed by a white man in the United States is just due to a marital dispute that got out of hand. The crimes are not even given the same name; "honor killing" elicits far more moral outrage than the more sterile "partner-on-partner violence" or the more romanticized "crime of passion" carried out by western men.

There is a racialized concept that the most grotesque forms of domestic violence are a problem foreign to western societies. Accordingly, Canada has updated its citizenship guide to stress that such acts of violence are purely "cultural"—i.e., alien to Canadian society. It states, "Canada's openness and generosity do not extend to barbaric cultural practices that tolerate spousal abuse, 'honour killings,' female genital mutilation, forced marriage or other gender-based violence."[10] In essence, the crime of domestic violence is a "cultural" crime when committed by minorities and an "individual" crime when committed by whites. That patriarchal white culture enables wife-beating just as much as any other culture seems preposterous. Similarly, "forced" marriages are seen as endemic to non-western cultures, even though plenty of Americans are forced to get or stay married for reasons as mundane as being able to obtain or keep health insurance.[11] This uniquely American type of marry-or-die dichotomy does not elicit the type of moral outrage that accompanies "forced" marriages in the Muslim world.

Take the case of Stephanie Kirkpatrick, a 29-year-old special needs teacher in a Houston suburb who was shot in the head by her husband, Daniel Polittle, an unemployed philanderer. I bring up her example not because it is horribly unique but because I know one of the victim's friends. The reality is that had she not married this white Christian man, she would still be living today. Yet, no matter how many horrific incidents like this occur, western society is seen as innately enlightened and feminist, while no matter how small the number of stereotypical "honor killings" carried out by Muslim men, Muslims are seen as beset by a depraved culture of "honor killings." This is partly because western media is overeager to report on any instance of intimate partner violence committed by Muslim men. According to the Violence Policy Center, "about a dozen murder-suicides take place in the US every week, about two-thirds of which involve intimate partners." Yet, when a mentally ill Muslim American man killed his wife and then committed suicide, the event was considered worthy of international news.[12] This is not to excuse even a single incident of domestic violence in any society; rather it is to point out the moral panic that specifically surrounds crimes committed by racialized men. Even with cultural crimes that lack any easy comparison in other societies, such as school shootings in the United States, the problem is hardly seen as a shortcoming of American culture or faith.

It should be stated that "honor killing" is a western concept, as such a phrase does not exist in Islamic jurisprudence, and "besmirched honor" does not provide immunity from retributive or compensatory punishment. That such crimes occur is abhorrent but not a sign of something uniquely problematic with either Islam or Muslims. Nevertheless, being innately prone to committing honor crimes has become an essential part of the western stereotype of Muslim men. When Hae Min Lee, a Korean American magnet student was found murdered, Baltimore police were quick to fixate on her Pakistani American classmate and ex-boyfriend, Adnan Syed, who they assumed carried out the murder as an act of "honor killing." He was convicted based on a story spun around this concept, despite the flimsiness of any evidence linking him to the murder and despite alibis that made it practically impossible for him to have carried out the crime. The police even skipped performing DNA testing on the human tissue under the victim's nails, while foolheartedly pursuing the honor killing theory. To them, an honor killing Pakistani American seemed a more likely culprit than the drug-dealer who actually knew where the victim's body had been buried.[13] As Rabia Chaudry, an activist who published a book on Syed's conviction, put it, "the state framed an argument based on absolutely no evidence that Adnan's honor had been besmirched."[14] The pervasiveness of such racist stereotypes is what enable gross miscarriages of justice to plague the American criminal justice system.

The racist "honor killing" stigma is also employed to justify the use of force against Muslim civilian populations, with western military occupation applauded as emancipatory, civilizing, and beneficial to "third world" citizens, particularly Muslim women. The August 9, 2010 cover of *Time* magazine featured the heart-wrenching image of an Afghan woman with an amputated nose and the caption, "What Happens if We Leave Afghanistan." Nasal amputations simply do not exist in Islamic law, but that is beside the point. The implication is that the US is in Afghanistan to save its women from being brutalized by Muslim men. The fact that this amputation occurred under

American military occupation is somehow completely
overlooked. Nor does *Time* ever decide to grace its cover with
the mutilated bodies of white women brutalized or murdered by
their abusive boyfriends and husbands, even though that is
undoubtedly a far more common occurrence than nasal
amputations in Afghanistan.

Domestic Violence in Islam

Even if honor killings are not permitted in Islam, critics of Islam
say that surely beating your wife and expecting her complete
subservience are, since the Quran says,

> Men are guardians over women because of how God has
> blessed some over the others and because of what they
> spend from their wealth [to support the family]. So the
> virtuous women are those who humbly submit [to God]
> and who guard, in their husband's absence, what God
> would have them guard. As for those whose ill-conduct
> (*nushuz*) you fear, advise them, avoid sharing a bed with
> them, and strike them. Then, if they obey you, seek
> nothing against them. Surely, God is High, Great.[15]

To take this verse as blanket permission to beat one's
wife is rather problematic, as the verse spells out gradations of a
concept in Islamic jurisprudence known as conjoining the good
and forbidding the evil (*al-amr bil-ma'ruf wa an-nahy 'anil-
munkar*). Suppose someone is about to commit a crime. You are
to advise the person not to do so, make your displeasure with the
plan evident, hide the guy's car keys and gun to foil his plans, and
if all else fails you can actually physically force the person to
desist if it is a matter of utter importance. Islamic law books have
long chapters dedicated to the conditions for enjoining the good
and forbidding the evil and what steps can be taken depending
on the context.[16] Not every issue needs a call to the police and

the involvement of the state's apparatus for violence, which seems to be the preferred solution in western societies.

The Quran is adamant that harming one's wife either physically or emotionally is impermissible: "Keep them honorably or divorce them honorably; do not keep them, intending to inflict harm and to transgress."[17] As such, Islam does not allow keeping one's wife to inflict emotional and physical torment. Furthermore, Muslims draw their inspirations from the example of the Prophet (S) who according to hadith, "never ever hit anything, any woman, or any servant."[18] He also ordered his companions not to beat their wives.[19] This is not to deny that there are Muslim men who beat their wives; there are also Muslims who drink alcohol and eat pork chops. The Islamophobic image of a wife-beating, honor-killing Muslim man is nothing but an inaccurate, racist stereotype that distorts reality.

As for the Quranic verse referring to men being guardians over women, this appears to be a sociological statement of how things are rather than a command for how things ought to be. "Allah has blessed some over the others" refers to physical strength, financial means, or in some instances level of education or faith; "because of what they spend of their sustenance" refers to the financial duty a man has to provide for his wife. A wife who is provided for by her husband has obligations in return; marriage is not a one-way street.

Even if the verse is taken at face value as condoning patriarchy, to use this to specifically demonize Muslims is hypocritical, especially when the criticism comes from Bible-thumping Christians. The New Testament is quite explicit in telling women, "Submit yourself to your own husbands."[20] It reiterates this concept when it says, "Wives, submit yourselves to your own husbands as you do to the Lord. For the husband is the head of the wife as Christ is the head of the church... Now as the church submits to Christ, so also wives should submit to their husbands in everything."[21] It also says, "I want you to understand that Christ is the head of every man, and the husband is the head of his wife, and God is the head of Christ."[22] As for men serving as guardians over women, it says, "Women should remain silent in the churches. They are not allowed to speak, but must be in submission, as the law says. If they want to inquire about something, they should ask their own husbands at home; for it is disgraceful for a woman to speak in the church."[23] Furthermore, the Bible appears to condone domestic violence where it calls for beating people with "a rod" if they are "devoid of understanding"[24] or a "fool,"[25] and asserts that "blows that hurt cleanse away evil."[26]

The simplistic logic that Muslims are wife-beaters because the Quran allows wife-beating falls apart when one considers that similar textual quotes can be found in other scriptures. This is not to claim that Christian women are submissive or that Christian men are wife-beaters. It just goes to demonstrate that picking scriptural verses out of context does not say much about how any one individual or society behaves. If pointing out a single Quranic word out of context can prove than Muslim men are wife-beaters, why not conclude by the same logic that Muslims are "the best nation that has ever arisen for humanity,"[27] simply because the Quran says so? Hence, explaining Muslim misogyny by alluding to Quranic verses or to hadith constitutes racist ill-logic, as the reasoning is applied only to confirm pre-existing stereotypes.

The concept that a verse or tradition reflects on Muslims at large is hardly logical. The Quran forbids alcohol, gossiping, and fornication. Yet, it would be foolish to conclude that no Muslim drinks, gossips, or fornicates. In an Islamophobic context, Muslims epitomize any obscure negative thing that can be dug up out of context, but mysteriously never enjoy any of the positive qualities that are consistently enjoined in the Quran and hadith, like being charitable and merciful, contemplating deeply and pursuing knowledge, being kind and honest, and making peace and contributing to social and economic prosperity. As such, Muslims and Islam are collectively painted with a brush of terrorism and misogyny based on the actions of a select few and a small number of verses and traditions taken out of the greater political, historical, social, theological, and textual contexts, while completely ignoring any positive qualities or messages the faith enjoins.

If one were to hold the west to the standards by which Muslims are judged, western justice would be nothing but waterboarding of detainees, illegal renditions, and holding suspects for decades without trial; western culture would be nothing but racism, misogyny, and pornography; and western cuisine would be nothing but McDonald's and junk food you'd get out of a vending machine. This is perhaps how some Muslim extremists do see western civilization, but it is hardly an accurate portrayal. It is only reasonable to expect that all cultures and societies be seen for the totality of what they are.

If one were to employ the ill-logic used in Islamophobic discourse onto western societies, one could easily say that the Bible tells women not to talk in church, hence women are not to speak in public, which explains why women are such a minority in corporate boardrooms[28] and why, even when they become Supreme Court justices, they can barely speak without getting cut off by their fellow male justices.[29] Yet, this logic misses the point. The Bible didn't create misogyny; societal misogyny created our understanding of the Bible. The same is true of Islamic societies, where misogyny exists irrespective of Islamic principles. For instance, in an Islamic marriage, the books of jurisprudence are clear that a wife has no duties to cook for or clean up after her husband, as providing food and a suitable living space falls onto the husband.[30] Similarly, she has no obligation to breastfeed her child and can demand payment for providing nursing services,[31] as it is the husband's duty to provide the child's nourishment as well. Yet, there are plenty of Muslim women who cook, clean, and tend to their children, just as there are many non-Muslim women with identical gender roles. That this is seen as a traditional Islamic role is based purely on societal interpretation, not on a rigid implementation of Islamic jurisprudence. In this vein, in 1992, the Iranian legislature allowed women in divorce proceedings to claim financial compensation for household work performed voluntarily during the marriage, as these chores are not considered marital duties under Islamic law.[32]

One of the hallmarks of racism is ascribing a different set of motives for acts when these acts are performed by minority groups. This extends to the most banal of activities. For example, western journalists report with amazement their discovery that some people in Iran watch the HBO series *Game of Thrones*. To explain this apparently shocking finding, it is asserted that they are drawn to the series because it mirrors Persian epic stories of pre-Islamic times, reminds them of the power struggles after the death of the Prophet (S) that form the basis of the Shia creed, or because the Lord of Light reminds them of a Zoroastrian god they have not worshiped in well over a millennium.[33] Their motives for watching this show are assumed to be different than the motives that draw large western audiences. It is overlooked that perhaps some people in Iran are drawn to savage violence, endless intrigue, a stereotypically attractive cast, and a splattering of indecent scenes just like American and European viewers are. Similarly, when a Reuters correspondent decided to run a story on Iranian women who were learning the martial arts of ninjutsu, the athletes were labeled pejoratively as "ninja assassins" who "could be the West's worst enemy."[34] As the *Daily Mail* put it,

> As Israel steps up pressure on Iran, over fears the country is building nuclear weapons, these lethal ninjas could be called upon to represent their country if relations descend into military conflict. Iran has a mandatory Army conscription for men aged 18, but it is limited to 18 months service, so these kunoichi could prove very useful.[35]

That a rational person could write such a senseless paragraph, that an editor would read and approve of it, and that it would end up published in a widely-read periodical highlights the extent to which everything Muslims do is seen through a one-dimensional lens. It's not possible that these women simply enjoy the sport; they must have a more sinister motive or purpose. In contrast, the western military forces invading Muslim countries to the east and west of Iran are only bringing peace, freedom, democracy, and modernity; the possibility that they might have anything but the most honorable of motives is hardly entertained.

To conclude, the concept that Muslim men constitute the pinnacle of misogyny, are habitual wife-beaters, and uphold their "honor" through murdering women is part of the colonial and neocolonial narrative on Islam. According to this narrative, Muslims subscribe to fundamentally backward and brutal religious and cultural norms; people in Muslim societies are so brainwashed or otherwise subjugated that they cannot save themselves; and it remains the burden of the ever-beneficent west to free them from their religio-cultural flaws, whether through activism or through force.

Chapter 21

Love Jihad

Love jihad is an Islamophobic conspiracy theory that claims that Muslim men use love, seduction, and marriage as part of a conspiracy to convert women to Islam and thereby take over society. This concept has particularly taken root in India, where any instance of a Hindu woman forming a romantic bond with a Muslim man is seen as part of an organized conspiracy, sometimes with international backing. According to Dibyesh Anand,

> Hinduvta ("Hindu-ness," shorthand for Hindu nationalism) in India is a chauvinist and majoritarian nationalism that conjures up the image of a peaceful Hindu Self vis-à-vis the threatening minority Other. Hindu nationalism normalizes a politics of fear and hatred by representing it as a defensive reaction to the threats supposedly posed by Muslims... Hinduvta is porno-nationalism in its obsessive preoccupation with the predatory sexuality of the putative Muslim figure. The proponents of Hinduvta mobilize and generate negative stereotypes of Islam and Muslims to legitimize violence against actual Muslims living in India.[1]

According to the theory of love jihad, a Muslim man might feign love to trick a Hindu girl into converting to Islam; he might conceal his faith and the unsuspecting Hindu girl only finds out that she married a Muslim man after the marriage has already been consummated; or the seduction of Hindu girls might be masterminded by international terrorist organizations.

Conspiracy theorists, such as BJP Member of Parliament Sakshi
Maharaj, even allege that Muslim boys are offered cash rewards
by jihadist *madrasas* for seducing Hindu, Sikh, and Jain girls.[2]
The frenzy has reached the point that state governments
have ordered official inquiries into love jihad.[3] In 2020, Uttar
Pradesh outlawed conversion for the sake of marriage, making it
a crime punishable by up to ten years in prison in addition to
hefty fines.[4] Karnataka has drafted a similar bill.[5] Considering
that the majority of both Muslims and Hindus oppose interfaith
marriage, it is hardly surprising that politicians would find this an
easy way to drum up electoral support. In a country where nearly
two-thirds of Hindus believe that it is very important to be Hindu
to be "truly Indian,"[6] continually portraying Muslims as a
subversive foreign element in society parallels the Islamophobic
discourse seen in western societies.

The stereotypes that fall under love jihad are varied, as
they portray Muslim men as both brutish and hypersexual on the
one hand and irresistibly charming and calculated on the other.
In contrast, Hindu women are invariably portrayed as gullible
and naïve and hence in need of protection by Hindu men, be it
through the power of law or through mob violence. As a form of
moral panic, this fear is not limited to Hindus; Catholics in Kerala
have similarly succumbed to a fear of love jihad targeting
Christian women.[7] Nor is it limited to India, as Sikh
organizations in the United Kingdom claim that Sikh women are
seduced by well-dressed Pakistani men driving expensive cars;
alleged cases invariably end in rape and forced prostitution that
go unpunished because of police apathy.[8] That any woman might
be seduced by a handsome, impeccably-dressed, and wealthy
Pakistani man driving a flashy car would hardly be shocking; the
bigotry lies in assuming that the Muslim man invariably has
sinister or even criminal motives.

Patriarchal misogyny is an inherent component of the
fear of love jihad. As such, any type of social control over women
to prevent them from falling victim to the irresistible charms of
Muslim men is seen as justified. Some towns in Uttar Pradesh
have resorted to restricting the use of cell phones by adolescent

girls to prevent them from falling prey to Muslim men waging love jihad.[9] In a number of instances, vigilante mobs, often with the assistance of the police, kidnap women and forcibly return them to their parents or coerce them to marry right-wing Hindu nationalists to prevent them from converting to Islam or marrying a Muslim man.[10]

The discourse has, unsurprisingly, been shrouded in fears of population replacement and terrorism. Rajesh Awasthi, a leader of the right-wing Hindu VHP organization explained his concerns: "If one daughter from our community goes to their community, that means there will be 10 terrorists in their community. If she has 10 children, they will be terrorists... We will lose out on one family, and they will gain 10 families."[10] That being Muslim is the equivalent of a being a terrorist is an unassailable assumption among his followers.

The Indian love jihad narrative parallels the sexual fetishization of black men in the US and the belief that dainty and gullible white women must be protected from the insatiable sexual appetites of black men. Both instances carry the inherent risk of violence targeting men belonging to the stereotyped minority groups. I see this phenomenon as "when a white woman cries, a black man dies,"[11] as was highlighted in the case of Emmett Till, who was brutally murdered in Mississippi under the false pretext that he catcalled a white woman. In India, vigilante violence targeting Muslim men in the name of combating love jihad has led to horrific crimes such as the following:

> A Muslim laborer, later identified as Mohammad Afrazul, apparently unaware that he is being filmed, strolls under a tree, while another man, holding a pickaxe, jogs up behind him, takes aim, and lodges it in his upper back. Afrazul turns around, uncomprehending. "What did I do, sir?" he manages to shout. His attacker, later identified as Shambhulal Regar, from a town north of Udaipur, stumbles between blows, preparing to strike again. The camera follows, at a distance. "I am dead, I am dead," Afrazul cries. Finally, he lies motionless where

he has fallen. Regar speaks to the camera. "Jihadis," he says, breathing deeply. "This is what will happen to you if you spread love jihad in our country." Then he sets Afrazul on fire.[12]

The basic love jihad narrative is not limited to the milieu of people from the Indian subcontinent, as similar echoes can be heard in western narratives. According to Edward Said,

I give the example of Dodi Fayed, you know, the erstwhile suitor of Princess Diana. Well a few days before he died I read through the English press and it was full of the racist clichés of Orientalist discourse... *The Sunday Times*, one of the leading newspapers in England, had a headline to a 15,000 word story entitled, *A Match Made in Mecca*. And the idea of Muslim conspiracy as trying to infect, you know, taking over this white woman by these dark people, with Mohammad, the prophet Mohammad who is a historical personage of the seventh century somehow stage-managing the whole thing. That's the power of the discourse you see, if you're thinking about people and Islam and about that part of the world those are the words you constantly have to use.[13]

Protecting women is used in other modern-day racialized contexts, such as when Donald Trump, referring to a "caravan" of Central American refugees coming to the United States, proclaimed, "Border security is very much a woman's issue... Women want security. They don't want that caravan."[14] As such, protecting the dainty white woman from the threats posed by brown men provides a pretext for the unleashing of violence targeting migrants at the southern US border. We must be proactive in calling out clichés in which one group of women need protection from brutish and hypersexual men from another ethnic group, as the victims of this form of racism include both the women from the dominant group who are subjugated and

236 The ill-Logic of Islamophobia

controlled in order to be saved as well as the men from the racialized group who become targets of violence.

Chapter 22

Portraying Muslims as Homophobes

It is commonly alleged that Muslims are homophobic and therefore intolerant and incompatible with western liberal values. In one meme tweeted by Allen West, who served both in the US House of Representatives and as chairman of the Republican Party of Texas, a man tells a woman, "I don't believe that women have any rights, and I think gays should be hanged," to which she retorts, "Wow, what a complete primitive a--hole you are! You must be a Republican." He responds, "No, actually, I'm a Muslim and those are my religious beliefs." She then says, "Oh! I'm sorry! I apologize! I hope you don't think I'm Islamophobic!"[1] This meme captures the conservative frustration with liberals who preach tolerance for both Muslims and homosexuals even though Muslims are assumed to be innately homophobic.

While it is true that traditional Islamic jurisprudence considers homosexual acts as sinful and constituting one of the *hudud* offenses, this cannot be seen as particularly different than punishments for heterosexual extramarital sexual relations. The bar for proof is exceedingly high—four just male witnesses must see the penetrative act, an evidentiary requirement that is virtually impossible to attain. As with adultery and fornication, if the witnesses fall short, each person making the allegation will be whipped eighty lashes.[2] This is clearly to dissuade people from coming forth with any type of salacious allegation. It must be admitted that the Islamic concept of sexuality is not particularly liberal in that it does not condone extramarital sexual experiences. However, that does not make Muslims particularly problematic in a liberal society, as the freedom to engage in extramarital sex hardly constitutes an obligation to do so.

That Islam leads to homophobia does not stand up to scientific scrutiny. A study of 9,000 Arab Muslims in nine Arab countries found that "religiosity does not singularly cause more negativity of homosexuals and homosexuality." Furthermore, a substantial group disapproved of homosexuality but not of homosexuals, in what can be termed as a "hate the sin but love the sinner" mentality.[3]

I would even argue that homophobia is antithetical to Islam, which does not equate a sinner with their sin. A sin is often seen as something extrinsic to an individual; the idea is often that "Satan got into so-and-so and tempted the person to do such-and-such." If it is argued that homosexuals are specifically targeted in Islam to be made to feel sinful, that hardly holds, considering that masturbation is also considered a sin by many jurists and hence it creates significant guilt among many Muslims. Anyone can go on the MuslimNoFap subreddit to see how some Muslims struggle to overcome this sin.

In the *History of Human Sexuality*, Michel Foucault, who was himself gay, asserted that in the late nineteenth century Europe, a scientific fascination developed with classifying people according to the sexual acts they engaged in. In this context, homosexuality went from constituting the sinful act of sodomy to either a disease or an essential human trait. The latter has allowed the homosexual to be seen as a distinct "species" and hence be subjected to the racialized prejudice that we now know as homophobia.[4] Considering that Islam does not condone this view, the concept of racialized hatred toward homosexuals is not a prominent part of societal discourse in Muslim countries in the way it has been in the west. It simply exists as one of many "sinful" habits—e.g., drinking, gambling, philandering—that Muslim societies often overlook. It takes a place similar to the use of marijuana and other drugs in western societies. Even if you don't approve of using drugs, you don't exactly call the cops because you find your college roommate smoking a joint. Similarly, Muslim societies are not beset by moral panic surrounding gays and lesbians in the way that western conservatives have been.

Furthermore, Islam respects an absolute right to privacy and prohibits snooping into the personal lives of others. The following anecdote provides an example of this Islamic principle:

> Umar (the third caliph) used to patrol [Medina] at night. [One night] he climbed a wall and saw a woman and a man with some wine. Umar said, "O enemy of God! Do you think that God would cover for you while you are sinning?" The man said, "O Commander of the Faithful, don't rush [to judge] me. If I disobeyed God in one matter, you disobeyed Him in three. God says, 'Do not spy,'[5] whereas you just spied. God says, 'Enter houses from their doors,'[6] whereas you climbed up the wall. And you entered without permission, [whereas] God says, 'Do not enter a house other than your own until you ask permission and salute its inhabitants.'[7]" ... So Umar forgave him and went away, leaving him be.[8]

This shows the extent to which respecting personal privacy is critical in Islam. Spying on others, inquiring about their "sinful" habits, and gossiping and backbiting are strictly forbidden.[9] Even if you find out about the potentially sinful sexual acts someone else commits, you can't tell anyone. If you do, you are subject to eighty lashes.[10] Islam does not condone embarrassing people or slut-shaming.

Are Islam's views on homosexuality super liberal? No. But the portrayal of Muslims as particularly homophobic is merely one part of the stereotyping of Muslims as innately intolerant and unwestern even though their attitudes are hardly different from that of conservative Christians. In fact, traditional Islamic laws are no more strict than the biblical rulings that say, "Do not have sexual relations with a man as one does with a woman; that is detestable,"[11] and "If a man has sexual relations with a man... they are to be put to death."[12] Indeed, verses of the Quran describing the divine destruction of Sodom and Gomorrah where homosexuality was prevalent mirror similar biblical accounts.[13]

The New Testament also takes a harsh attitude towards sodomy when it says, "Or do you not know that wrongdoers will not inherit the kingdom of God? Do not be deceived: Neither the sexually immoral nor idolaters nor adulterers nor men who have sex with men..."[14] Similarly, it stresses the sinfulness of homosexuality: "We also know that the law is made not for the righteous but for lawbreakers and rebels, the ungodly and sinful, the unholy and irreligious, for those who kill their fathers or mothers, for murderers, for the sexually immoral, for those practicing homosexuality."[15] The punishment for homosexuality in the New Testament is death: "Men committed shameful acts with other men... they know God's righteous decree that those who do such things deserve death."[16] Considering these biblical quotes, it might come as a surprise that the Quran does not enjoin any punishment for homosexual acts.

In terms of tolerance, according to a Pew survey, 52% of American Muslims believe that homosexuality should be accepted by society. This is considerably higher than the 34% of white evangelicals who hold the same view.[17] This goes against the stereotype of Muslims as distinctly intolerant of homosexuals. Yet, these findings are hardly surprising. Muslims living in western countries, as a group whose own freedom of religion is often in peril, generally advocate for a society in which the government does not dictate religious norms. Furthermore, Islam does not dictate or regulate the private sexual and marital lives of people of other faiths.

As for transgender rights, Muslim attitudes vary widely. In Iran, a fatwa by Ayatollah Khomeini allowing sex reassignment surgery[18] has turned the country into the world's second largest performer of such procedures after Thailand.[19] Contrary to subsequent western media insinuations that Iran was forcing its homosexuals to undergo sex change operations,[20] Zara Saeidzadeh found that "sex-change surgery is not obligatory" but allows trans people who want to complete their transition to do so.[21] It must be added that Khomeini's fatwa in this regards is by no means universally accepted among Muslim scholars, but it highlights the diversity of juristic opinions seen within traditional Islamic jurisprudence.

Chapter 23

Circumcision as Mutilation

Male circumcision involves removal of the foreskin, which is the part of the penile prepuce that covers the glans penis. It is an ancient religious rite, part of the Abrahamic covenant that has persisted within Jewish and Muslim societies for millennia. It is also practiced culturally in many other communities, particularly in Africa. There is some disagreement among Islamic schools of jurisprudence as to whether male circumcision is mandatory or highly recommended, with the Shia Ja'fari and the Sunni Shafi'i schools considering it mandatory, while other Sunni schools consider it highly recommended. Technical juristic nuances aside, male circumcision is almost universally adopted by Muslim communities worldwide.

According to the Mayo Clinic, the health benefits of male circumcision are manifold and include easier hygiene, decreased risk of urinary tract infections and resulting kidney problems, decreased risk of sexually transmitted infections including HIV, prevention of phimosis (painful strictures), and decreased risk of penile cancer as well as cervical cancer in the female partners of circumcised men.[1] The CDC has advised the use of male circumcision to reduce HIV transmission from both vaginal and anal intercourse. According to data from three clinical trials, male circumcision can reduce a man's risk of acquiring HIV by 50-60%, syphilis by 42%, genital ulcer disease by 48%, genital herpes by 28-45%, and carcinogenic strains of human papillomavirus by as much as 47%.[2] The World Health Organization (WHO), based on results from three randomized controlled trials, is now championing the global implementation of male circumcision as one of the most effective methods to curb the HIV epidemic.[3] The incidence of penile cancer in Israel, which has a high prevalence of male circumcision, is exceedingly low, at approximately 1 per million per year. This should be contrasted to Brazil, where the reported incidence is up to 68 times higher, due in great part to its low prevalence of male circumcision.[4] Perhaps a single hadith summarizes these health findings best: "Circumcise your children on [their] seventh day [of life], for it is more hygienic (*athar*)."[5]

Of course, for Muslims and Jews, medical evidence is hardly necessary; these are matters of religious obligation or custom, and hence scientific data is not required to justify male circumcision. In the United States, circumcision is fairly common; approximately 60% of male newborns are circumcised.[6] In contrast, in European countries, circumcision is not commonly practiced. The reason Europeans are not typically circumcised is based more on custom than science. Nevertheless, this religio-cultural difference creates fertile ground for xenophobic, anti-immigrant, Islamophobic, and antisemitic sentiments to play out in various European countries.

Restrictions on Male Circumcision

In 2012, a German court ruled that circumcising boys for religious reasons amounts to bodily harm and that circumcision contravenes a child's right to decide later in life on his personal religious beliefs.[7] This case stemmed from medical complications that arose when a 4-year-old Muslim boy underwent a circumcision. The physician performing the procedure was prosecuted because he was alleged to have "physically mistreated another person and injured that person's health by means of a dangerous instrument." Eventually, the courts cleared the physician based on the fact that the physician could not have been expected to know that circumcisions were illegal.[8]

In fact, there is no law in Germany barring circumcision so the physician could not have known that xenophobic judges might retroactively rule the procedure to have been illegal. The court decision forced the Jewish Hospital in Berlin to suspend circumcisions, which only pushed parents to pursue these procedures outside the medical system where the risk of complications would presumably be higher. A rabbi in Berlin called this decision "perhaps the most serious attack on Jewish life in Europe since the Holocaust." Lord Sacks, Britain's Chief Rabbi, pointed out that the ruling was primarily meant to target Muslims, with Jews only suffering as a result of "collateral damage."[8] He appears to be correct—in Denmark, amendments were proposed to ban male circumcision performed after the eighth days of life to protect "Danish Jews and their opportunity to practice their religion."[9] This is because Jewish circumcisions are customarily performed on the eighth day after birth, whereas Muslim circumcisions can be delayed.

The basic assumption underlying laws targeting Muslim religious practice is that Muslims are innately barbaric and hence their customs are heinous and have no place in modern society. Such sentiments are reflected in the inflammatory musings of the German national daily *Die Welt*: "The circumcision of Muslim boys is just as heinous as the archaic custom of the genital mutilation of little girls. It is an instrument of oppression and should be outlawed."[8]

After much outcry from Jewish, Muslim, and Christian groups against the encroachment on religious liberties, the Bundestag (German federal parliament) adopted a law permitting male circumcisions. However, the issue continues to pop its head up, buoyed by politicians eager to exploit minority stigmatization for votes. Considering that 67% of men and 56% of women in Switzerland believe that the practice should be banned,[10] circumcision proves too tempting for politicians to pass up in their quest to drum-up votes. As such, political parties across Europe have issued formal policy declarations regarding male circumcision. In Iceland, where an average of only one or two circumcisions are performed each year due to the small size of its Muslim and Jewish populations, a bill was proposed equating male circumcision with female genital mutilation, making it a crime punishable by a six-year prison sentence. In response to pressure from the United States, the legislation has been set aside for now, though not entirely shelved.[11]

Female Genital Cutting

The hysteria over male circumcision pales in comparison to the reaction to female genital cutting (FGC), which has become a hot-button issue. Over the past few decades, the terminology has shifted from "female circumcision" to "female genital mutilation" (FGM), an umbrella term that hampers any discussion of what specific practices are being addressed. Furthermore, the incorrect association of brutal forms of FGM with Islam only complicates the matter. Appropriately addressing FGC requires a more precise definition of the anatomy and procedures involved, followed by a discussion of Islam's stance on the subject.

The World Health Organization classifies FGM procedures into multiple subtypes. Type Ia procedures involve removal of the clitoral hood, which is the fold of skin that covers the clitoral glans. The clitoral hood is analogous to penile foreskin that is removed in male circumcision. The clitoris itself resembles a small penis, as the two organs represent divergent development of a single embryonic structure, and these organs provide a significant portion of sexual stimulation to women and men, respectively. The clitoral shaft is a midline internal structure attached to the undersurface of the pubic bone and is therefore not easy to access surgically. The clitoral glans is the external portion of the clitoris and is analogous to the glans penis.[12] Type Ib procedures involve removal of the clitoral hood along with removal of some portion of the clitoral glans.

Type II procedures involve removal of the labia minora (Type IIa), which can be accompanied with partial or total removal of the clitoral glans (Type IIb) or labia majora (Type IIc). Type III, also referred to as infibulation, involves narrowing of the vaginal opening by cutting and suturing the labial minora (Type IIIa) or labia majora (Type IIIb). Type IV involves other "harmful procedures" such as "pricking, piercing, incising, scraping and cauterization."[13]

Infibulation, also known as pharaonic female circumcision, is typically performed on younger women so that they are unable to have intercourse prior to marriage. Only a small opening is left for urine and menstrual blood to exit. At the time of marriage, a wider opening is created through either sexual intercourse or surgical incision. For childbirth, the vaginal orifice is opened but often sutured again in a process called defibulation or deinfibulation. There has been concern that women subject to infibulation are at increased risk of obstetrical, gynecological, and urological complications.

FGC appears to be an ancient, pre-Islamic custom that originated in the Nile Delta and spread from there. It is routinely performed in lands surrounding the Nile River and in an equatorial band across Africa. Communities with diasporic or religio-cultural ties to this region of Africa also practice FGC. An example is the Dawoodi Bohra community in India,[14] which traces its theological origins to the Fatimid Dynasty based in Egypt. FGC is generally not practiced in Northwestern or Southern Africa. The practice of FGC does not correlate specifically with Islamic faith, as it is practiced by Christians and followers of other faiths residing in these geographic regions.[15] In countries like Eritrea, FGC is commonly practiced by Muslims, Catholics, and Protestants alike.[16] Isolated instances of FGC has also been reported among conservative white Christians in the United States.[17] Nevertheless, discussions of FGC in the west often leave readers with the impression that Islam is the culprit.

There is no mention of either male or female circumcision in the Quran. Whereas numerous widely-accepted traditions exist regarding male circumcision, there is little direct discussion of FGC in Islamic sources. According to one tradition cited by Abu Dawud, the Prophet (S) advised a woman who was performing FGC in Medina, "Do not cut severely as that is better for a woman and more desirable for a husband."[18] Similar Shia traditions claim that the woman performing FGC had migrated to Medina from elsewhere. According to these accounts, when the Prophet (S) found out that she was performing FGC, he advised her to minimize the cutting and to keep it very superficial without explicitly forbidding her from doing so.[19] It should be noted that this entire story is dubious, as Abu Dawud explicitly dismisses the tradition he cites as "weak (*da'if*)," and FGC is not practiced by mainstream Twelver Shia communities.

There is absolutely no hadith in which the Prophet (S) advised a woman to be circumcised and no evidence that his wife Khadija or his daughter Fatima (AS) were subject to FGC. There are Shia and Sunni traditions that state that, "Circumcising boys is *sunnah* (Islamic tradition) but circumcising girls is not *sunnah*," and that "Circumcising girls [is considered] noble but is not from *sunnah* and is not something obligatory." [20,21] As pointed out by Bayhaqi, these traditions suffer from questionable chains of transmission.[20] Even if one were to accept these traditions at face value, one would conclude that FGC was not seen as having a specific Islamic basis, but rather as a cultural phenomenon that was practiced by some Muslim communities. It is noteworthy that FGC is not commonly practiced in countries that constitute the heartland of Islam, such as Saudi Arabia, Syria, Iran, and Turkey.

If the content of these traditions is accepted, it merely shows that the Prophet (S) did not explicitly ban a practice alien to Islam, highlighting the inherent tolerance of Islam for divergent cultural traditions. However, he did restrict FGC to ensure that harm is not done, thereby limiting the procedure to what the World Health Organization classifies as Type I procedures. Indeed, to the extent FGC is limited to Type Ia procedures, there is no specific medical harm and no decrease in female sexual pleasure. According to Dr. M. Ihsan Karaman, a urologist and medical ethicist,

> The hood (prepuce) is a fold of skin surrounding the glans penis in men and the clitoris in women. It is the part that is removed in male circumcision. In some girls, this fold of skin is redundant or overdevelops during puberty, thus covering the clitoris entirely and preventing

sufficient contact between the penis and the clitoris during sexual intercourse as well as causing discomfort for [the] woman because of squeezing under the pressure of male external genitalia. This results in a loss of stimulation, preventing the woman from having pleasure and orgasm. Removal of such redundant folds of skin through hoodectomy (clitoral hood reduction) increases pleasure during intercourse and facilitates orgasm. The presence of such redundant skin is a real medical indication for surgery, and its removal is beneficial to sexual health. Today, clitoral hood reduction and similar types of hoodplasties are among the most common aesthetic genital surgeries in the Western countries. In a 1979 report, WHO underlined the fact that this type of surgical intervention does not present any harm. "With regard to the type of FC which involves removal of the prepuce of the clitoris, which is similar to male circumcision, no harmful health effects have been noted." Thabet and Thabet have also showed that individuals who underwent type-1A FC (hoodectomy only) is (sic) not different from uncircumcised women in terms of sexual scores obtained from both groups.[22]

A variety of cosmetic surgical procedures targeting female genitalia have become increasingly commonplace in the West, particularly with the more recent proliferation of "V-selfies."[23] Surgical procedures akin to Type Ib FGC, involving removal of part of the clitoris, are performed in the west by surgeons for women with enlarged clitorides to make them more aesthetically pleasing. Clitoromegaly may be due to congenital anomalies, hormonal disorders (e.g., polycystic ovarian syndrome), abuse of anabolic steroids, and the use of testosterone in hormone replacement regimens.[24] In all these situations, women are vying for what would be considered "ideal" genitalia by prevailing western standards. It is therefore not the mere performance of surgical procedures targeting the female genitalia that leads to moral panic, but rather the non-western ideal that women from certain ethnic groups are trying to achieve.

It is alleged that FGC is different than cosmetic surgery performed in the west because the latter is performed by consenting adults who accept the risks of surgery, whereas the former is often performed on girls lacking the capacity to consent. Yet, girls in the west are almost universally subject to ear piercings.

Anyone spending time working in a dermatologist's office would be quite aware of how common it is for ear piercings to lead to infection, allergic contact dermatitis, earlobe lacerations, and keloid formation. The keloids, experienced more commonly by women of color, are often quite painful and can leave the ear permanently disfigured. Yet, virtually every girl born in the west is subject to this rite of passage, often at a very young age, and there is neither social outcry nor any concerted public health campaign to raise awareness of the ill effects of ear piercings. It is not the potential for harm but rather the foreignness of a custom that seems to underly societal reaction.

It is also alleged that FGC is forced upon women by men as a form of social control. In reality, anthropologists who are most intimately familiar with societies practicing FGC observe that the custom is mostly perpetuated by elder women who have undergone the procedure themselves. Moreover, many of the girls and women undergoing FGC are quite aware of the potential risks but eagerly seek the procedure nonetheless.[25] It is also worth noting that Muslim scholars and activists have been at the forefronts of the struggle to end FGC and numerous fatwas have been issued to curb this practice.[26] This reality goes against the prevailing view that FGC is a byproduct of strict Islamic observance.

Much is made of the health consequences of FGC, particularly in light of the World Health Organization study which found that obstetrical risks are higher in women who have undergone FGC. However, the magnitude of the elevated risk is not as impressive as one might expect. Perinatal infant mortality increased from approximately 4-6% in women without FGC to around 5-7% in those with FGC, with most of the excess risk seen in subpopulations that had a higher baseline risk to begin with. Furthermore, the study was hospital-based even though many of the FGM patients were rural. This means that there was significant selection bias, as rural women with complicated pregnancies were more likely to travel to the city to give birth in a hospital, while those with uncomplicated pregnancies would just give birth in their villages. The fact that the outcomes reflect confounding risk factors other than FGC is evident in that patients subject to types II and III FGC had higher blood loss after Cesarian sections, even though the procedure in no way involves the external genitalia. Even the study's authors admit that "the mechanism by which FGM might cause adverse obstetric outcomes is unclear."[27]

The outpouring of western concern for the health of African and Muslim women is quite welcome to the extent that it reflects genuine concern about their wellbeing as opposed to efforts to denigrate foreign customs. Yet, it is hard not to question how much genuine concern there is for the health of "third world" people. One might be tempted to argue that the Opium Wars that forced China to accept addictive British narcotics was a matter of "ancient history." However, today, western institutions such as the US Chamber of Commerce aggressively lobby for the worldwide interests of the western tobacco industry. Developing nations that try to curb cigarette smoking are hamstrung by treaty obligations with western countries, are subject to expensive litigation brought against them in international courts, and are victims of aggressive lobbying campaigns organized in Washington.[28] I imagine that the health benefits of curtailing American cigarette and weapons exports would outweigh any benefits to be gained from curtailing regional cultural practices.

Male circumcision as well as female genital cutting are issues imbued with cultural and religious significance that potentially carry medical and public health ramifications. Instead of turning these subjects into cultural battlefields that stigmatize minority groups and create moral panic, they should be addressed objectively in terms of what they entail, what benefits and risks accompany each specific procedure, what religious customs and laws actually say about the topic, and how risks can be mitigated while being culturally sensitive. We must avoid allowing male circumcision and FGC to become yet another racialized distinguishing feature that serves to marginalize men and women from minority communities whose genitalia do not conform to the western norm.

Part IV

Fear of Muslim Integration

Chapter 24

We Can't Take Any More Muslim Immigrants

In the United States, Islamophobia flourished after the September 11, 2001 attacks, with Muslims almost immediately cast into the archenemy position left open following the collapse of the Soviet Union in the early 1990s. In Europe, Islamophobia surged as the Arab Spring led to waves of refugees from countries across Northern Africa and Western Asia. Following the 2011 NATO military intervention in Libya that toppled Muammar Gaddafi, a sea route opened for people from Africa to cross the Mediterranean into Southern Europe. By 2015, refugees from the civil war in Syria, the American invasions of Afghanistan and Iraq, the Boko Haram insurgency in northern Nigeria, Al-Shabaab militancy in Somalia, and the brutal conscription regime in Eritrea were joined by Europeans from Kosovo, Albania, Serbia, Ukraine, and elsewhere in a large-scale migration towards Western Europe. Europe was soon "flooded" with refugees. Many of the Syrian refugees would cross from Turkey across the Aegean Sea into Greece, from where they would journey westward across various European land borders.

According to EU regulations, the country where a refugee first enters the union is responsible for handling the asylum claim. Since the refugees primarily arrived in Greece and Italy, they would either apply for asylum there and thereafter attempt the rest of their journey, or they would trek on land to apply for asylum at their destination country. Many of the latter would leave Greece and pass through the Balkans, only to re-enter the European Union in Hungary, where many were detained in squalid refugee camps. Efforts to repatriate refugees to the country of first entry became impractical given both the large number of refugees involved and the difficulties countries like Greece and Italy would face if they were required to process the asylum applications of all refugees arriving at their borders.

To ameliorate the situation, Germany and Sweden allowed refugees who made it to their countries to apply for asylum there without deporting them back to the country where they had first entered the European Union. Angela Merkel explained the policy as follows:

> The basic right to asylum for politically persecuted people knows no upper limit; this also applies to the refugees who come to us from the hell of a civil war. But people from safe countries, especially from the Balkans, come to us... [with an] understandable desire to lead a better life. But if there are no grounds for asylum, and this is the case with these people in almost all cases, then they have to return to their countries quickly. That is why we will speed up the asylum procedures. At the same time, however, we want to make legal immigration possible for a smaller number of people from the Balkans, for example if they can show that they have a job here.[1]

This declaration cemented the desire of refugees to make it to Germany. Feeling inundated by the large number of refugees, country after country in Europe adopted border controls to reduce the flow of migrants. Eventually, the EU and Turkey came to an agreement whereby Turkey would receive 6 billion euros in financial compensation in return for blocking refugees from crossing into Europe.[2] Similarly, Italy provided financial support to the Libyan coast guard to block ships carrying migrants from crossing the Mediterranean.[3] Though the flow of migrants was rapidly quelled, the sudden influx of foreigners helped fuel xenophobic resentment. Viktor Orban in Hungary and the Law and Justice Party in Poland solidified their grips on power by brandishing their anti-migrant credentials. Since most of the refugees were Muslim, Islamophobia became an even more prominent political force across the continent

While many valiant Europeans went out of their way to welcome refugees and to help ensure their humane treatment, others started complaining that there was insufficient housing for the refugees, that refugees would overwhelm social welfare programs, that refugee children would overcrowd schools, that refugees would raise crime rates and carry out terror attacks, and that the refugees were from alien cultures and religions and therefore would be unable to integrate into European societies.

An oft-repeated question was why should the refugees come to Europe and not be taken in by neighboring countries or other Muslim nations where the belong? As a member of Poland's far-right put it, why should Poland take Syrians? Why don't they go to Saudi Arabia instead?[4] The reality is that many have gone to Saudi Arabia, but instead of being categorized as refugees, they have been classified as foreign workers employed through the *kafala* system, which can be thought of as a form of sponsored work visa. As such, Saudi Arabia has become home to as many as 500,000 Rohingya, 400,000 Palestinians, and one million Syrians.[5] While Turkey accommodated millions of Syrian refugees, Poland allowed migrants at the Belarusian border to freeze to death rather than provide them asylum;[6] Croat security forces savagely attacked migrants, forcing them across the border into Bosnia-Herzegovina;[7] and Denmark stripped refugees of all their possessions, including family heirlooms.[8] The brutality unleashed across the European Union's borders has reached new heights, as reported in 2021 by *The Guardian*:

A company of men in dark uniforms and balaclavas, all carrying clubs. They are battering a group of people, repeatedly clubbing them on their arms, legs and backs. They push them into a river that marks the boundary of the European Union. "Go," they yell. "Go." It's not an incident on the border between Belarus and Poland, the latest migrant flashpoint on the EU border... It happened 1,000 miles to the south, between Croatia and Bosnia-Herzegovina. And it's been happening for months, but with much less publicity or scrutiny... The uniforms worn by the men in black on the Croatia-Bosnia border carried no insignias. An investigation... has exposed them as members of special Croatian and Greek police units. Their job? To use violence to force undocumented migrants out of the EU and into non-EU states. The operations are deemed "pushbacks," a euphemism for illegal, violent expulsion. They happen all along the EU's south-east border. Not just on land but at sea, too. Men from elite units in the Greek coastguard, again all dressed in black, wearing balaclavas and with no identity markings, regularly seize migrants, put them on orange life rafts, provided by the EU, push them out to sea towards Turkey and leave them to their fate.[9]

To many living in the west, the general sentiment is that the entire world's population is clamoring to make it to first world countries for economic reasons, neglecting the fact that countries like Iraq and Syria did not experience an exodus of refugees until they were ravaged by war. It should be noted that the vast majority of the world's estimated 84 million forcibly displaced people do not seek refuge in the west. Rather, most are internally displaced. The top five sources of refugees today are Syria with its protracted civil war, Venezuela with its economic collapse due to western sanctions, Afghanistan which has been reeling from repeat western invasions and intervening civil conflict, South Sudan which has not seen stability since the west agitated for its secession from Sudan, and Myanmar where Buddhist nationalists repeatedly ravage ethnic minority communities.

The top countries receiving refugees are not the United States, Denmark, France, or the United Kingdom, as one might suspect based on the amount of xenophobia emanating from them, nor does the list include countries like Poland or Hungary whose politicians' electoral lifeblood is xenophobia. Rather, the top three are Turkey, Colombia, and Uganda, followed by Pakistan. Furthermore, Turkey has a refugee population that is more than three times as large as Germany's, despite the two countries having nearly equal populations.[10] Germany is the only western nation that makes it on the list of the top ten countries that host refugees.[11] Looking at the number of refugees per capita, Lebanon tops the list at 209 per thousand, followed by Jordan at 90 per thousand. These numbers contrast to Sweden at 15 per thousand, Germany at 3 per thousand, the United Kingdom at 2 per thousand, and the United States at less than 1 per thousand.[12] These figures highlight how western countries are not quite as overwhelmed by refugees as one might imagine, particularly considering that these are the countries with the highest levels of financial, technological, and human capital.

Blocking the entry of asylum seekers into Europe because European countries cannot possibly handle any more refugees does not make these innocent civilians vanish into thin air. It just keeps them in countries closer to the conflict zones, where they are subject to dire humanitarian conditions. In many instances, refugees are forced back to the lands they so desperately fled.

It cannot be denied that refugees create burdens for host societies. That is, however, not a reason to deny asylum, as seeking refuge is a fundamental human right. Article 14 of the Universal Declaration of Human Rights reads, "Everyone has the right to seek and to enjoy in other countries asylum from persecution."[13]

Whether Islamophobia causes anti-refugee sentiment in Europe or vice versa is hard to discern; most likely they feed off each other. Regardless, the refugee crisis has contributed heavily to the electoral success of far-right political parties across Europe. The European far-right had already been energized in the aftermath of the 2007-8 Global Financial Crisis, which pitched Germany against Eastern European countries like Greece. Being forced to accept a status as second-class European whose Euro-denominated bonds would initially not be guaranteed and whose nations had to submit to painful austerity measures imposed by Brussels drove people into the arms of far-right, nationalist, anti-EU organizations. The surge in ethnonationalism in light of the refugee crisis was hardly limited to Eastern or even continental

Europe. In the United Kingdom, parties such as the UK Independence Party (UKIP) capitalized on anti-migrant sentiments to pass a 2016 referendum on Brexit, thereby divorcing the United Kingdom from the rest of the European Union.

Refugee crises provide living examples of how Islamophobia is simply one manifestation of xenophobia and racism. This becomes evident when one compares the rhetoric surrounding predominantly Muslim refugees in Europe with that surrounding the predominantly Christian Central American refugees trekking across Mexico to the southern US border. In the United States, the exact same issues have been raised as in Europe—lack of housing, overcrowded schools, rising crime, and overwhelmed welfare services. In some ways, fear of drugs replaces fear of terrorism, but not entirely, as there has been endless hype over the hypothetical possibility that Middle Eastern terrorists might be hiding among Central American refugees in order to gain entry into the United States. A fact sheet distributed in 2021 by Republican Representative John Katko, the ranking member of the House Homeland Security Committee, warned that "known or suspected terrorists are crossing the border at a level we have never seen before."[14] Eventually, Donald Trump threatened to apply tariffs to imports from Mexico if the Mexicans would not crack down on Central American migrants. The Mexicans complied.[15]

The outsourcing of refugees is becoming ever more commonplace. As discussed earlier, Turkey and Libya were bribed into preventing refugees from reaching Europe. Australia has been holding refugees arriving on boats from Muslim-majority countries in concentration camps— formally referred to as "processing centers"—in Nauru and Papua New Guinea.[16] Boris Johnson came to terms with Rwanda to take asylum-seekers arriving in Britain in return for a cash payment of 120 million pounds. He is merely mimicking a similar move by Israel in 2014 that led to the widespread enslavement of refugees by human traffickers.[17] Such plans result in heart-wrenching atrocities carried out against refugees being outsourced from first-world countries where the media might report on unfolding humanitarian catastrophes to developing nations where human rights abuses are easier to hide.

Chapter 25

If You're Not Happy Here, then Leave

A common refrain of the right is that if minorities are not happy with the west, they should simply leave. Donald Trump used this line of reasoning against "the Squad," four freshman congresswomen of color—Alexandria Ocasio-Cortez, Rashida Tlaib, Ilhan Omar and Ayanna Pressley. Addressing them, he said, "If you're not happy here, then you can leave,"[1] and "Why don't they go back... [to] the totally broken and crime infested places from which they came."[2] This sort of ill-logic, especially when used against someone like Ilhan Omar, a Somali American Muslim, resonates heavily among certain sectors of the population and is used as a thought-terminating cliché to end serious discussions of America's social ills.

That it appears rational for someone who is not happy with how certain things are in the US to just leave highlights pervasive racism when it comes to the concepts of who belongs, who is a real citizen, and who deserves freedom of speech. When someone of color bemoans voter restrictions, mass shootings, military adventurism, income inequality, racism, corporate greed, climate inaction, the disdainful treatment of refugees, an ever-expanding prison-industrial complex, lack of access to universal healthcare, and any number of other serious societal issues, the thought is, "Well, if America is so bad, go back to where you came from." Yet, when white Republicans express anger over completely fictitious issues such as President Obama not being a natural-born American, pervasive electoral fraud handing victories to Democrats, the US having open borders that allow anyone to cross unhindered, an expansive welfare state that provides generous benefits to undocumented immigrants, shariah law's encroachment into the justice system, and the infiltration of the government by Muslim subversives, no one seems to suggest that they should just leave the US if they're so unhappy. This is because the innate right to be American is culturally assigned to whites; the true Americanness of other groups is always in question. Non-whites don't truly belong in America; they belong to somewhere else and perhaps should return there.

This mindset does not exist in a vacuum; it arises from a long history in which white Protestants were seen as the only rightful citizens of the land. In the colonial era, many states outlawed Catholicism altogether. Later, in its 1857 *Dred Scott* ruling, the Supreme Court made it clear that the Constitution did not confer citizenship rights and hence any benefits thereof to people of African descent, be they enslaved or free. The Fourteenth Amendment finally granted citizenship to all native-born Americans, but it excluded Native Americans on the grounds that they were not subject to the jurisdiction of the United States. They were not granted citizenship until 1924. The right of a citizen to vote was not recognized until 1957, and this right is hardly universal today. People with even non-violent criminal convictions are routinely disenfranchised, and we see relentless ongoing efforts to limit minority voting.

The American concept of emancipation was never about treating blacks on equal footing. As Abraham Lincoln put it, "I have no purpose to introduce political and social equality between the white and the black races. There is physical difference between the two, which in my judgment will probably forever forbid their living together upon the footing of perfect equality."[3] He was an ardent supporter of colonization—sending American blacks to Africa or the Caribbean so they would no longer burden white society with their presence. A similar mindset today sees non-whites as essentially foreign and hence removable; this pervasive cultural assumption underlies why the concept of "if you're not happy here, then leave" resonates only when applied to non-whites.

The reality is that minority groups in western countries are constantly reminded of their being different, of their not genuinely belonging, and of their not being entirely American or French or Australian, while ignoring the fact that they are not of another place either. A third generation Iranian American who grows up in the US might hardly speak any Farsi, has little concrete ties to Iran, is likely to be culturally more American than Iranian, and would struggle to fit in if deported. We never talk of sending English Americans back to England, even though adapting to life in London might be less challenging, if only because they speak the same language.

Denmark recently enshrined into law a two-tiered citizenship system in which citizenship is irrevocable for native whites but revocable for others. Hence, white Danes who joined Daesh would retain their Danish citizenship, whereas many second-generation immigrants born in Denmark could be stripped of their citizenship at the behest of the minister for immigration and integration, without any trial.[4] Perhaps the democracy with the most blatant two-tiered citizenship system is Israel. Palestinian homes are demolished for lacking proper permits, whereas illegal Jewish settlements are protected by the state; Jews are allowed to claim ownership of property based on deeds predating 1948, whereas Arabs are not; and Jews from around the globe are allowed to move to Israel, whereas Palestinian refugees are not granted the right to return to their own homes.[5] Like other liberal democracies, Israel has a difficult time allowing ethnic minorities equal rights of citizenship.

The reality is that first- and subsequent-generation citizens are grateful for being able to reside in peace in western nations. Some of them might express their patriotism by demanding that their societies embrace social justice and their stated humanist ideals. That this type of free speech is vilified instead of celebrated reflects how freedom of speech is not valued in a race-blind fashion.

Chapter 26

Muslims Don't Want to Integrate

A 2018 Danish law promised to raze dwellings in "ghettoes," which are neighborhoods that meet a number of specific criteria, such as having inhabitants who are more than 50% "non-western." The law was purportedly passed to combat the formation of "parallel societies."[1] In the name of combating urban crime, the government doubled punishments for crimes committed in neighborhoods it classified as ghettoes.[2] Offenses normally subject to fines became punishable by imprisonment. Children as young as one were to be taken away from their parents for at least 25 hours a week to be taught "Danish values,"[3] in a move reminiscent of the "reeducation camps" China has set up for Uyghurs and the "residential schools" Canada ran for decades for indigenous children. Dr. Ferruh Yilmaz, an expert on Muslim immigration, said,

> Maybe it isn't the culture but discrimination that is the problem... If you look at any country on earth, you'll see that crime is concentrated in areas with poverty, which in turn is commonly the product of racial, ethnic, or religious discrimination, rather than their inhabitants' lack of Western reasoning.[1]

Criminalization of the ghetto is hardly going to succeed when one considers how ineffective using the strong arm of law enforcement has been in handling poverty and crime in urban neighborhoods in the United States. Instead of waging a war on the ghetto by emptying poverty-stricken neighborhoods and filling prisons, there should be a war on poverty, racism, and discrimination. There need to be efforts to provide adequate employment, not displacement. Furthermore, social connections are crucial to human well-being. Displacing poor immigrants to white neighborhoods will not improve integration. The lack of integration is invariably due to the racism of whites, not the stubborn rejection of integration by minority groups. This should be evident in societies such as the United States. It was not the blacks who refused to go to swimming pools with white patrons; it was not blacks who wanted to attend all-black schools; and it was not blacks who wanted to live in poverty-stricken urban ghettoes. White racism and misguided social policies are what have led to these forms of segregation. The fact that the Danish policies are inherently racist is reflected in how a crime is punished more severely when committed in a neighborhood of color. The same exact crime committed in an equally poor white-majority neighborhood would potentially not be subject to the same punitive measures.

How breaking up marginalized minorities will contribute to their socioeconomic wellbeing is hard to see. Friends and families will be torn apart and the connections that are the lifeblood of poor communities will crumble. As Asif, who moved to Denmark from Pakistan in 1994, said,

> I really like Mjolnerparken. Here, you never sleep hungry, you're never alone. If you forget your wallet when you go to the store, someone will let you take the food home, because we know each other here. You can never do that in the city centre... I'm very dependent on people here. If I'm at work and my wife or daughters have a small problem, I can call one of my friends to come help out. It's a huge support network. People can call it what they want, but it's not a "ghetto". They're [the government] the ones who built this place and now they're starting to call it a "ghetto". That's not fair. Now that it's become this hip place, they want people to move out and they use criminality as an excuse.[3]

Much like in Denmark where the displacement of minorities is deemed necessary to improve neighborhoods, "urban renewal" in the United States has served merely as a euphemism for "Negro removal."[4] After all, the problem is seen as the presence of too many racialized bodies within a specific enclave. Hence, the remedy for ghettoization is gentrification— i.e., the increased presence of white bodies within the neighborhood.

The narrative that ghettoes are hotbeds of intolerance and insularity is based on the racial homogenization of diverse Muslim communities. It is assumed that these people are all the same and want to stick to one another. In reality, Mjølnerparken is a diverse neighborhood with 2,500 residents who immigrated to Denmark from over three dozen different countries. The racial homogenization of Muslims in the popular imagination is similar to how all East Asians are seen as "Asian" or "Oriental" even though they come from nations with thousands of years of distinct languages, cultures, and religious traditions. Chinese, Koreans, Japanese, and Vietnamese might be dismissed as all-the-same through the lens of racial homogenization, but they hardly are. The ethnoracial heterogeneity of Muslim populations in the west is highlighted by Pew research that found, "Foreign-born Muslim Americans are very diverse in their origins. They have come from at least 77 different countries, with no single country accounting for more than one-in-six Muslim immigrants." They have their origins in the Middle East, North Africa, South Asia, Europe, and Sub-Saharan Africa.[5]

In Mjølnerparken, the unemployment rate is 43.5%, and 2.5% of its residents have been convicted of a crime.[6] The problem lies neither in the alleged intolerance of its residents nor in the erroneous concept that everyone there speaks the same foreign language; the issue is unemployment. Unemployment is often seen by the dominant group as laziness, a lack of desire to work, or being happy receiving welfare benefits. In reality, unemployment is due to discrimination in hiring. In Europe, this discrimination is particularly harsh when it comes to Muslim job applicants. One study based in France compared the outcome of job applications that differed only with respect to whether the applicant had a Christian- or Muslim-sounding Senegalese name. Employers were two-and-a-half times more likely to offer an interview to the applicant with a Christian name than the one with a Muslim name. When hired, a Muslim Senegalese will be paid, on average, 400 euros per month less than his or her Christian counterpart. This egregious discrimination prevents many Muslims from entering the middle class, cements intergenerational poverty, and contributes to a chronic mistrust of French institutions.[7] This is similar to the stubbornly persistent discrimination in employment African Americans in the United States face, which has led to intergenerational poverty, reduced social mobility, and difficulties in leaving poverty-stricken neighborhoods.

It is important to recognize that ghettoes are not formed by minority groups seeking to congregate as much as by "white flight," which occurs when whites abandon neighborhoods with ethnic minorities in search of a "white" neighborhood. In the United States, a neighborhood having a mere 8% black population has been found to be sufficient to trigger an irreversible pattern of white flight that would eventually leave the neighborhood entirely black. According to Jim Myers, author of *Afraid of the Dark*,

> For example, in the Detroit study, 7 percent of whites said they will leave when the neighborhood is 8 percent black, and 24 percent of whites will not move into a neighborhood that is 8 percent black. This is how the 8 percent figure came to be known as the *tipping point* at which white flight begins. Then, once the neighborhood is 8 percent black, the factors are present that will eventually make the neighborhood all black. Whites start to leave, then when the neighborhood becomes 21 percent black, 24 percent of the whites will leave. Then when it becomes 57 percent black, 64 percent of whites will try to leave. And other whites will not replace them, because by that point, 84 percent of whites would refuse

to move into a neighborhood that is 57 percent black. Eventually, the neighborhood becomes almost all black, and integration will have been seen, as a Chicago alderman once reportedly claimed, "the hiatus between when the first blacks arrive and the last whites leave."[8]

Until white intolerance is addressed, breaking up a "ghetto" will merely create new ones, as whites will leave whatever new neighborhoods the minority communities settle in. Even when mixed neighborhoods are achieved, as is seen with more recent gentrification, the white population puts in significant efforts to segregate certain spaces, particularly schools. In the United States, rapidly-proliferating, taxpayer-subsidized charter schools serve to allow whites residing in racially mixed neighborhoods to ensure that their children attend a predominantly white school.[9] This is hardly limited to racialized fears of black crime or hypersexuality, as top Silicon Valley high schools with outstanding academic reputations are experiencing white flight in response to an increase in their Asian student population.[10]

Similarly, pervasive racial segregation in churches is hard to overlook, especially when compared to mosques. In contrast to the ethnic diversity one encounters at Friday prayers, Sunday morning remains perhaps the most segregated hour in the United States, as millions of people congregate in uniformly white or black churches. Growing up in this environment, Malcolm X had an epiphany when he completed his *hajj* pilgrimage and found the Kaaba "being circumambulated by thousands upon thousands of praying pilgrims, both sexes, and every size, shape, color, and race in the world."[11] Realizing that racial coexistence is possible, he rejected the black nationalism and segregation preached by Elijah Muhammad's Nation of Islam and instead embraced Islam.

No-Go Zones

Neighborhoods in western countries with significant Muslim populations are routinely labeled as "no-go zones." Right-wing politicians and pundits conjure images of Muslim ghettoes run by Islamic fundamentalists who actively impose shariah law, preach extremism, and harbor terrorists, while the police and law-abiding (i.e., white) citizens are either not allowed to or are too scared to enter because of the imagined fate that would befall them. As Louisiana governor Bobby Jindal put it,

> In the West, non-assimilationist Muslims establish enclaves and carry out as much of Sharia law as they can without regard for the laws of the democratic countries which provided them a new home... It is startling to think that any country would allow, even unofficially, for a so called "no-go zone." The idea that a free country would allow for specific areas of its country to operate in an autonomous way that is not free and is in direct opposition to its laws is hard to fathom.

When pressed on the topic, he could not name a single instance of a Muslim no-go zone.[12] The absence of any specific factual basis, however, has not made the rhetoric disappear. Donald Trump, speaking about Britain during his first presidential campaign, said, "We have places in London and other places that are so radicalised that police are afraid for their own lives." The British were so appalled by the inaccuracy of his statement that Parliament debated a motion to ban Trump from entering the United Kingdom.[13]

The fact that such neighborhoods don't exist is evident to pretty much anyone who has travelled to these supposed no-go-zones. Many are vibrant urban communities with thriving shops and businesses and a diverse population composed of immigrants from Asia, Africa, and Europe who live alongside their native neighbors. Armchair "experts" like Daniel Pipes, president of the Middle East Forum whose mission is to "protect Western civilization from the threat of Islamism,"[14] described the presence of France's Sensitive Urban Zones (*Zones Urbaines*

Sensibles) as proof "that the French state no longer has full control over its territory."[15] In reality, these neighborhoods are not state-designated no-go zones but rather areas that have been selected for urban renewal and further infrastructure investment.[16] When Pipes actually visited some of these communities, he had to recant his earlier position:

> I had an opportunity today to travel at length to several *banlieues* (suburbs) around Paris, including Sarcelles, Val d'Oise, and Seine-Saint-Denis. This comes on the heels of having visited over the years the predominantly immigrant (and Muslim) areas of Brussels, Copenhagen, Malmö, Berlin, and Athens... For a visiting American, these areas are very mild, even dull... The immigrant areas are hardly beautiful, but buildings are intact, greenery abounds, and order prevails. These are not full-fledged no-go zones but, as the French nomenclature accurately indicates, "sensitive urban zones." ... Having this first-hand experience, I regret having translated what the French government terms *Zones Urbaines Sensibles* as no-go zones. One can indeed "go" in them.[15]

Similarly, Fox News issued an apology for its erroneous reporting on no-go zones in Birmingham. They had claimed that England's second largest city was "totally Muslim" and constituted a no-go zone for non-Muslims; in reality, Muslims comprised 22% of the city's population and there were no no-go zones to be found.[17] The apologies hardly helped because the fake news genie was already out of the bottle; the frightening image of Muslims having taken over a European city had already solidified in the minds of their viewership; and a simple verbal apology would do little to undo the rhetoric. If anything, the apology would make the viewers imagine that Fox News has succumbed to political correctness. Proper redress would require honest and accurate reporting, which is a tall order for an organization whose business model thrives off of fanning the flames of xenophobia, Islamophobia, and right-wing conspiracy theories.

Linguistic Integration

One of the most common charges laid against immigrants, including Muslim ones, is that it is obvious that they do not want to integrate because so many of them don't speak the language of their host nation. There is no question that it is more of a challenge to get a well-paying job if you don't know a country's language. However, the stereotype of the immigrant who doesn't want to learn the country's language raises several problems.

First, the woman wearing a niqab who doesn't speak a word of English at the department store might just be a tourist. To assume anyone who doesn't speak the language is a long-term resident who refuses to do so is rather presumptuous. Second, the immigrant might be relatively new to the country and will learn the language in due time. Third, immigrants who arrive as adults will never speak as fluently or unaccentedly as native-born speakers, so even if they learn the language, they will not entirely shed their "foreignness." It is this foreignness that, more than anything, irks xenophobes who hone in on the slightest difference in accent, attire, or cuisine to classify others as outsiders who do not belong. Fourth, some immigrants arrive at older ages when learning a new language is extremely difficult. Fifth, language classes are often not readily available and can be cost-prohibitive,[18] especially as cuts in government funding makes them less accessible.[19]

Sixth, some immigrants will have to work several jobs to survive and do not have enough free time to dedicate to learning the language. Many of these jobs will be in economic sectors where language skills are not paramount. If you work in the kitchen of a restaurant or your job entails cleaning hotel rooms, language skills may not be critical to employability.

Seventh, not learning a new language is not a rejection of that language or culture; it is reflective of being content with one's own specific situation, even if that situation appears intolerable to others. To see not learning a language as a sign of radicalization or laziness presupposes that everyone ought to aspire to be as European as possible.

Eighth, for white people to demand that foreign-born residents speak their language is fundamentally racist. White South Africans are somehow not expected to speak Swazi or Zulu despite having lived in South Africa for generations. Furthermore, numerous westerners live and work in countries all over the world and never gain proficiency in the language of their country of residence. They live in walled enclaves, their children attend English or French schools, they head back "home" to attend college in the United States or Europe, and they never integrate no matter how many decades they have lived there. If integrating within the culture of the country one lives in is so critical, then these westerners should be seen as problematic. The language of racism that surrounds migration is evident in how citizens from developing nations seeking better paying jobs in the west are referred to as "immigrants," whereas westerners who seek better paying jobs in developing nations are called "expatriates," even if they plan on living there for the rest of their lives. No amount of economic desperation can turn a modern-day person of Western European descent living in a developing nation into an "immigrant."

Ninth, failure of a minority ethnic group to linguistically integrate over many generations reflects segregation imposed by a dominant society, not the minority community's refusal to integrate. Segregation explains why many African Americans have retained linguistic distinctions emanating from Southern rural dialects even when they have lived in cities in the Northeast or California for generations. The distinct dialect, in turn, provides a basis for justifying ongoing discrimination. As with other instances of racial segregation and non-integration, the problem lies with the racism of the dominant race, not the insularity of the subjugated one.

Tenth, even though some xenophobes assume that immigrant children growing up in the west won't learn western languages because they grow up in ethnic enclaves, this is hardly the case. In the United States, nine-in-ten second-generation Hispanic and Asian American immigrants are "proficient English speakers." Conversely, among Asian Americans, only four-in-ten can speak their parents' native language fairly well, highlighting the rapid loss of native languages among immigrant populations.[20] Considering the centrality of language to culture, one ought to wonder in what way this linguistic loss is of benefit.

Complaining about immigrants who do not speak English or French or Dutch is merely a linguistic manifestation of racism. It allows someone to say, "I am not racist; I just don't like that they don't speak my language." This is hardly different than the one who says, "I am not racist; I just don't like that their women cover their hair," or the one who says, "I am not racist; I just don't want a mosque built in my backyard." In such instances, language, clothing, and architecture serve as mere proxies for racialized religio-cultural bigotry. This should be contrasted with the Islamic view of linguistic integration. Bilal was an Abyssinian slave in Mecca and an early convert to Islam who remained steadfast in his faith despite being tortured repeatedly by his master. He became the Prophet's (S) treasurer and *muezzin*—the one who recites the call to prayer (*adhan*)—even though he reportedly had difficulty pronouncing Arabic words. Similarly, Salman, a Persian enslaved by the pagans, was among the closest and most loyal of the Prophet's (S) companions. The moral is clear—one is to look past linguistic differences and instead value personal qualities.

Chapter 27

Fear of the Great Replacement

In 2011, French author Renaud Camus published a book entitled *Le Grand Remplacement (The Great Replacement)*.[1] Recycling old, nationalistic fears, he argues that French people will be replaced by non-Europeans, mostly Muslims immigrating from Africa and the Middle East, in what he terms a "genocide by substitution."[2] This fear, which is inseparable from Islamophobia, features prominently among Europe's right-wing populists. Muslims, the eternal other, are more numerous, eagerly outbreed Europeans, and will eventually become a majority population that will electorally control these democratic countries and impose shariah law on their host nations. In some iterations, this is portrayed as a deliberate process, part of a global Muslim conspiracy to take over western nations.

In the United States, the fear of population replacement has historically targeted Catholics, Japanese, blacks, and Hispanics, but Muslims have not been entirely spared. The slogans, "They will not replace us!" and "The Jews will not replace us!" were heard at the August 2017 Unite the Right Rally in Charlottesville, Virginia.[3] A year later, 46-year-old Robert Bowers killed eleven people and wounded six at a Pittsburgh synagogue. He was consumed with fear that white America and western civilization were "headed towards certain extinction," and that Jews were bringing Muslims and other immigrants to America to "kill our people (i.e., white Americans)."[4] What do the Jews have to do with bringing Muslims to America? Eric Ward, an African American scholar at the Southern Poverty Law Center, explains why Jews are often seen as the ones behind progressive civil rights and immigration policies that are feared to negatively affect white status and power:

> How could a race of inferiors have unseated this power structure through organizing alone? ... Some secret cabal, some mythological power, must be manipulating the social order behind the scenes. This diabolical evil must control television, banking, entertainment, education and even Washington D.C. It must be brainwashing white people, rendering them racially unconscious. What is this arch-nemesis of the white race, whose machinations have prevented the natural and inevitable imposition of white supremacy? It is, of course, the Jews.[5]

One iteration of this conspiracy theory asserts that "the Jewish financier George Soros has funded mass immigration of Muslims to Europe in order to destroy European society."[6] These fears highlight what has been shown repeatedly throughout this book, that Islamophobia, racism, xenophobia, and antisemitism are all products of the same ill-logical mental process inherent to all forms of bigotry. Conspiracy theories, irrational fears, and imagined us-versus-them dichotomies are par for the course of this type of pseudo-rationalism.

That the fear of population replacement has traction with the populace is evident in how the concept appears in widely disseminated Islamophobic memes. One titled "How Europeans Disappeared" shows a white couple and their son and daughter with the caption, "1 wife, 2 children." Below that is a lineup of stereotypically dressed Muslims and the caption, "4 wives, 12 children. Outbred - outnumbered - out voted - out."[7] Stereotypes of polygyny and high fertility are combined with fears of population replacement to generate fear, anxiety, xenophobia, Islamophobia, and calls for political action.

Another meme shows a lineup of infants in newborn nursery bassinets. They are all wearing black burqas except for the one white baby. The caption reads, "Europe in 2060. In

2060, 99% of all newborns will be ninjas."[8] "Ninja," needless to say, is a derogatory term used for women who wear a niqab. The idea is clear—soon enough, whites will be outbred by Muslims into oblivion. This type of fear is hardly new. In the 1920's, the United States was gripped with fear that overly fertile Japanese immigrants would outbreed American whites and soon dominate.[9] There was a similar fear of a Catholic takeover due to the allegedly high fertility rate of Italian, Irish, and Polish immigrants;[10] this fear was only compounded by the perception of Irish, Italians and German immigrants as being terrorists.[11] It is hardly surprising that immigrants have higher birth rates per capita, since immigrant and refugee populations tend to skew younger than native populations. What seem like strikingly different fertility rates among different ethnic groups tend to even out over time. This is evident in Israel, where fertility rates among Jewish and Palestinian women is currently 3.11 and 3.17 children per woman, respectively, in contrast to the 1990s when these values were 2.6 and 4.7. This has helped ease Israel's concern of a "demographic time bomb" that would turn Jews into a minority population.[12]

Other memes push economics into the equation also. One portrays five white men who appear to be miners or occupied in some similarly grueling and hazardous occupation. Below them is a couple who are to be recognized as Muslim by the husband's beard and the wife's hijab. They have five young children. The caption reads, "Men like this are forced to work until they're 70. Because the government is bringing in more and more people like this."[13] This meme portrays the stereotype of immigrants as economic leeches in contrast to hard-working whites and promotes the misperception that Muslim immigrants live off of the welfare system without contributing to the economy.

The stereotype of the welfare-leech immigrant exists alongside an equally strong fear that the immigrant will actually work and hence rob natives of jobs. The reality is that immigrants are often employed in positions not sought by or in geographic locations not popular with natives. In other instances, they fill specialized positions for which there is an inadequate supply of properly trained natives. Furthermore, the fact that the job market expands proportionately to population growth and that immigrants therefore create jobs is completely overlooked. These fears reflect the reality that in a democracy that provides equal rights to all its citizens and a pathway to citizenship for its long-term residents, dominant ethnic groups fear losing their hegemonic grip on power. Israel is a prime example of trying to balance its desire for being a democratic nation with its need to exclude Christian and Muslim Arabs from voter registries to ensure that the country can be both Jewish and democratic at the same time. As such, even though Jerusalem is claimed as Israel's indivisible and eternal capital, East Jerusalem's Arab residents are not allowed to vote in national elections.[14] Similarly, Israel opts for a permanent occupation of the West Bank without annexation to ensure that Palestinians are disenfranchised, while it allows illegal settlers in the occupied territories to vote in Israeli elections. Meanwhile, displaced Palestinian refugee populations are completely disenfranchised with respect to Israeli national elections.

Democratization is intricately linked to violent backlashes against suppressed minority groups. According to Kate Cronin-Furman, a political scientist at University College London, "Horrible violence against the Rohingya [was] breaking out at a time of increased democratization in Burma."[15] More generally, tolerating poverty-stricken and politically disenfranchised ethnic minorities is easier for dominant groups than allowing them to be treated as equal citizens. The system of Jim Crow laws and mob violence only became necessary after the emancipation of American blacks and their being granted the nominal constitutional right to vote. As discussed by Michelle Alexander in *The New Jim Crow: Mass Incarceration in the Age of Color Blindness*, felony convictions handed out with little compunction to predominantly black and brown citizens permanently disenfranchises many of them.[16] This large-scale disenfranchisement is supplemented by blatant gerrymandering and a variety of increasingly complex voter restriction laws that target communities of color, stripping them of political power. Anti-immigrant sentiments overlook the reality that much of human history is the history of human migration. This history includes the migration of humans to Europe, the migrations and conquests that created Europe's present ethnic geography, and the widespread migration of Europeans to the Americas, Australasia, Southern Africa, and elsewhere. Historically, migrants were not held back by having the wrong passport or lacking the right visa. These are relatively new inventions that have helped maintain global colonial and postcolonial white supremacy by heavily regulating the right to economic migration. Economic prosperity in one region is maintained through strict border controls.

The fear of population replacement also assumes that one ethnic population has an inherent right to a certain geographic location over any other. This is particularly ludicrous when one considers countries like the United States, where whites have felt that they are more entitled to the land than Native Americans. I know Hispanics in Texas whose families have lived here prior to Anglo settlement. Yet, they continue to be seen as foreign to the land. This explains why over a million American citizens of Mexican descent were deported to Mexico in the twentieth century.[17] Just recently, the Trump administration revoked the citizenship of thousands of Mexican Americans born in border regions, claiming that an American birth certificate does not provide sufficient proof of citizenship.[18] When Barack Obama ran for president, Trump became a prominent cheerleader for the "birther movement," claiming that Obama was not a natural-born citizen of the United States. His birth certificate issued by the state of Hawaii was dismissed as a forgery, and he was alleged to have been born in Kenya.[19] Even if that were the case, he would still be a natural-born citizen because he was born to a mother who was an American citizen at the time of his birth. Meanwhile, there was no real controversy over whether John McCain, Obama's opponent, was a natural-born citizen, even though he had been born in Coco Solo, Panama. McCain simply fit the stereotype of a "real" American in a way that Obama did not.

Denying citizenship to native-born minorities is an inherent consequence of seeing minority groups as essentially foreign, regardless of how long they have lived in an area. This is evident in the US Supreme Court's *Dred Scott* decision that stripped African Americans of US citizenship because blacks were declared to be innately foreign and unfit to be Americans. Similarly, the Buddhist-supremacists in Myanmar have declared Rohingya Muslims to be foreign Bangladeshis, despite their having lived in Rakhine State for close to a millennium.

More recently, Narendra Modi's Hindu-supremacist BJP party stripped two million mostly Muslim citizens of Assam, a state which lies to the north and east of Bangladesh, of their Indian citizenship. The claim is that they are illegal Bangladeshis, even though many of them have lived in Assam for generations, and some moved to Assam not from Bangladesh but from West Bengal, India. It is worth noting that India and Bangladesh were one country prior to the partition of India and Pakistan in 1947. Bangladesh, which was then known as East Pakistan, gained independence from Pakistan in 1971. The Bengali language, which is the official language of Bangladesh, is also the second most commonly spoken language in India; it constitutes the dominant language spoken in the Indian province of West Bengal. Many West Bengalis living in Assam were declared to be foreign Bangladeshis and were hence stripped of citizenship.[20]

Stripping Indian Muslims of citizenship helps cement the narrative of Muslim foreignness in Indian society, a concept that has formed the bedrock of the Hindu nationalism (Hinduvta) that has increasingly gripped Indian society. Theoretically, there is a right to appeal the revocation of citizenship, but the process is cumbersome and costly, particularly considering the meager means of many of those who have been targeted. Judges who act fairly and rule in favor of Muslims who provide proof of their Indian citizenship are targeted for elimination.[21] When it turned out that some Hindus were left off the national registry of citizens, the government changed the laws so that Hindus, Sikhs,

Buddhists, Jains, Parsis, and Christians would be fast-tracked for citizenship, whereas Muslims would remain stripped thereof.[22] The government has responded to protests against these discriminatory laws by carrying out mass arrests and by killing peaceful protesters.[23]

The fear of population replacement is entirely misplaced. What western nations should fear is what would happen to them without immigration. Capitalist economies would collapse under the weight of aging populations and inadequate workforces to fuel economic expansion. According to Pew, "93% of the growth of the working-age population between now and [2050] will be accounted for by immigrants (43%) or their US-born children (50%)."[24] Curtailing immigration would lead to drastic labor shortages that would grind the economy into permanent stagnation. Economic survival, not sheer magnanimity, is likely a main motivation for why many western governments accept immigrants.

Curtailing immigration would cause the west to lose its technological and scientific advantage. Innovation would stagnate with loss of access to the exceptional talent that has been drawn from other nations in what is commonly referred to as "brain drains." In the United States, nearly 60% of computer and mathematical engineers and scientists are foreign-born.[25] American universities and corporations are kept internationally competitive thanks to a steady stream of brilliant students and accomplished experts immigrating from all over the world. Nevertheless, immigration is commonly seen as a one-way favor to immigrants who are constantly reminded that they must be grateful to the "true Americans" for granting them the privilege of living in America. Yet, one hardly ever hears "true Americans" thanking immigrants for the scientific, financial, and cultural prosperity they contribute to America.

Chapter 28

Conspiracy Theories of Muslim Takeovers

Whereas the Great Replacement might see the demographic replacement of people of white European descent as an inevitable consequence of immigration and differences in fertility rates, such demographic projections do not necessarily require a conscious effort on behalf of the expanding minority community. As such, the United States can someday become a majority Hispanic country without any insidious master plan to bring about this eventuality. In Europe, the main demographic concern has been the growth of the Muslim population. According to Czech Prime Minister Andrej Babiš, the Netherlands and Sweden will become Muslim-majority countries by 2044 and 2065, respectively.[1] Most of these projections are exaggerated and do not consider anticipated declines in both immigration and immigrant fertility rates. Nevertheless, this sort of fear can help the political fortunes of those who run for office promising to maintain the ethnic purity of a nation state.

In contrast to demographic projections, conspiracy theories see the impending collapse of European populations as part of a master plan orchestrated by Islamists and sometimes involving the active participation of other vested interest groups (e.g., liberals, George Soros, Jews). For the growth of a minority population to be particularly concerning, it has to be tied to fears of cultural and religious imposition that will upend not only the dominance of whites but also their way of life. As such, Islamophobic rhetoric typically portrays Muslims as intending to take over the host nations and aspiring to impose shariah law onto the entire population. The logic is simple—Islam wants shariah law to be implemented and for everyone to be Muslim; Muslims want to implement what Islam wants; hence, in a democratic society, once Muslims attain a majority, they will impose Islam onto the population. This type of ill-logic almost makes sense, except for a number of problems.

First, Islam being singled out overlooks the fact that the same logic can be used in regard to any other religious group. This was, indeed, a big part of the anti-Catholic racism that predominated in the United States. It was alleged that Irish and Italian Americans would take over the country demographically because of their higher birth rates, and that they would eventually turn the United States into a Catholic state subservient to the Vatican. That the Pope, even in medieval times, could barely control the Papal States around Rome was somehow overlooked.

Second, it assumes that Muslims are monolithic and all share the exact same political and religious views. Even if 51% of the population of Sweden were to someday be Muslim, a political party seeking to impose shariah would struggle electorally even among Muslim voters. This is evident when one considers that not a single Muslim country implements traditional shariah law. If the aim of every Muslim was to force Islam onto established political systems, one would see a very different type of governance across Muslim lands. In the secular dictatorships that define most Muslim states, those who seek Islamic values reflected in the political system are far more likely to be found occupying prison cells than seats of power.

Third, among immigrants from Muslim-majority countries, there are many who are Muslim in name only, "ethnic Muslims" so to speak. Rather unfortunately from the standpoint of Islamic law, they drink alcohol, eat *haraam* food, watch pornography, and fornicate. It is hardly conceivable that they will show up in large numbers to oppose the secular order.

Fourth, the fear is misplaced. Consider, for example, the fact is that most Muslim women who immigrate to western countries do not wear hijab due to a personal lack of adherence to strict religious precepts, a preference not to stand out, a yearning to blend in as much as possible, a desire to avoid being stereotyped, a fear of bigoted violence, concern about state persecution, or any other combination of reasons. Why would anyone imagine that these women would seek to impose hijab onto non-Muslim women when they don't even wear hijab themselves?

Fifth, countries like the United States have systems of checks and balances that prevent one religious group from dominating others. If anything, these institutions have aggressively protected a system of white secular and white Christian supremacy. Institutions like the Supreme Court would knock down any imposition of Islam. Of course, the constitution can be changed. Yet, it is realistically inconceivable for enough Muslim voters who support an imposition of shariah to be found in enough states for a constitutional amendment allowing the imposition of Islam as a federal religion to be ratified.

Nevertheless, the caricaturized zombie-like Muslim who has only one mission in life—to make Islam dominate—persists. Seen through this lens, everything a Muslim does serves this one ultimate purpose. In a theological sense, it is true that everything a Muslim does ought to be to please God. From gaining an education to engaging in the labor force to marrying and rearing children, a Muslim's intention should be to please the Lord. This individual devotion and sense of greater purpose does not mean that Muslims seek to force their beliefs onto others. In reality, Muslims could more easily be faulted for not proselytizing enough.

Dissimulation (Taqiyya)

Many westerners do not personally know any Muslims and if they do, the interactions are typically distant and transactional. Nevertheless, there are plenty who work with, live with, befriend, date, or marry Muslims. They would see that the Muslims they know hardly fit the stereotype of people whose sole purpose in life is seeking to take over the west. The concept of dissimulation (*taqiyya*) is used to fill the gap between the imagined stereotype and observed reality. The Quran mentions *taqiyya* when it addresses "anyone who disbelieves in God after having believed, except for the one who is under compulsion while his heart remains secure in faith."[2] As such, pretending to disbelieve to save one's life is permitted in times of severe persecution. *Taqiyya* became particularly integral to the survival of minority sects, such as the Shia, during episodes of heightened persecution.

In another verse, the Quran says, "Let not the believers take disbelievers as their allies in lieu of believers. Whoever does this shall have no relation left with God, except if you are guarding yourselves out of fear."[3] This verse is used by Islamophobes to claim that any Muslim who demonstrates friendship towards non-Muslims is only performing *taqiyya* and hence pretending. However, the Quran is clear that having good relations with people of all faiths is the norm, and that it is only prohibited with respect to those who are actively persecuting Muslims:

> O believers! Do not take My enemy and your enemy as allies, offering them affection even though they deny what has come to you of the Truth [and] have driven out the Prophet and you because you believed in God as your Lord... [But] God does not forbid you from showing kindness to and dealing justly with those who have not fought against you because of your faith and who have not expelled you from your land. Verily God loves those who act justly.[4]

Despite such verses, Muslim governments routinely conspire with non-Muslim powers against Muslim populations. When China targets its Muslim Uyghur population with what many have classified as ethnic genocide, Muslim governments, ever-eager to cozy up to Beijing, appear mute. Sadly, we have heard the loudest protests from the likes of Pompeo and Pence.

Any conspiracy theory assumes or insinuates that those carrying out the conspiracy would not openly admit to it. No antisemite expects Jews to run around saying they are all part of a grand, secret plan to take over the world. Instead, they fall back on works of antisemitic fiction like *The Protocols of the Elders of Zion* to prove that such a conspiracy exists. With respect to Muslims, the concept of *taqiyya* is used to assert that Muslims are always hiding their true intentions. Regardless of how friendly one's Muslim neighbor is, one ought to be aware that they might just be practicing *taqiyya* while plotting the next 9/11. With this sort of thought in mind, Sam Harris exclaims, "There is, therefore, no future in which aspiring martyrs will make good neighbors for us."[5] Seeing every member of an ethnic or religious group as equally guilty of a past crime or equally suspicious of an imagined future crime epitomizes racism. Moreover, in western societies Muslims are not severely persecuted and hence the conditions for performing *taqiyya* do not exist.

This fear that Muslim are always practicing dissimulation was reflected in the widespread fear of sleeper cells that became particularly prominent after the September 11 attacks. One is made to imagine a population of Muslims who somehow blend in within society, lying dormant while waiting for an order to strike to come from some shadowy foreign nation or organization intent on global domination. The idea of a sleeper cell is quite powerful in laying the foundations of anti-Muslim racism, as any Muslim could be part of a sleeper cell and hence ought to be viewed with suspicion. There is no realistic way to prove that someone is not part of a sleeper cell or a secret organization plotting the subversion of society and the dawn of a new world order.

That sleeper cells existed was taken for granted in the aftermath of 9/11. *The Washington Times* published an article titled, "5,000 in US Suspected of Ties to Al-Qaeda."[6] George Tenet, the former CIA director, said, "It was inconceivable to us that Bin Laden had not already positioned people to conduct second, and possibly third and fourth waves of attacks inside the United States."[7] Shows like *Homeland*, in which a US prisoner of war was turned into a sleeper agent for global jihadists, and *The Americans*, in which Soviet agents would blend in perfectly while carrying out numerous missions, only reassert the concept that any foreigner might be a secret agent of an external adversary. Fomenting irrational fears of sleeper cells has helped justify bloated national security budgets while wasting resources and causing the homeland security apparatus to lose sight of the far larger terrorist threat emanating from far-right white supremacists.

Fear of Muslims in Government Positions

The rapid rise of Barack Obama from a community organizer to an Illinois state senator to a US senator from Illinois to the president of the United States was accompanied by conspiratorial claims that he was a secret Muslim who had been trained in a "*madrasa*" in Indonesia, who served the Muslim Brotherhood, and who was furthering the cause of the Islamization of America.[8] Well, technically, they were right about one thing—Obama did indeed attend a *madrasa* in Indonesia. *Madrasa* simply means "school," but in common English usage, it carries the connotation of a place in which Islamic extremists brainwash children. That Muslim children are actually taught subjects like mathematics and chemistry seems too far-fetched.

Numerous social media posts claim that Muslims have either infiltrated or are planning to infiltrate the government. A tweet by a Republican women's group titled, "Muslims Running in 2020 U.S. Elections," shows a picture of fifteen Muslims campaigning for office, and explains, "They know the drill—infiltrate American government and institute shariah law. It's all part of the Islamic faith and practice of jihad. Yet, we keep importing these people."[9]

A book by Paul Sperry entitled, *Infiltration: How Muslim Spies and Subversives have Penetrated Washington*, explains how Muslims have infiltrated federal and state prisons, the US military, the FBI, the Department of Homeland Security, and even the White House.[10] These sorts of ideas became prevalent in the American talk radio world during Barack Obama's presidency and became increasingly mainstream among members the Republican Party, helping fuel Donald Trump's ascendancy. That Muslims, as a minority that constitutes 1% of the US population, have minimal political clout in the United States is completely overlooked. These overhyped conspiracies resemble the fears of Catholic and Jewish takeovers that have plagued American white supremacists and nativists for generations. The same type of racist ill-logic gets recycled time and again.

Chapter 29

Fear of Encroaching Shariah

The rhetoric of "the great replacement" is often intertwined with the fear that native populations will soon have to live under "shariah law." The logic is simple—once Muslims attain a majority in a democratic state, they will be empowered to impose shariah on the population. "Shariah law" is often portrayed as nothing but a system of brutal punishments, the end of freedom of speech as we know it, and the subjugation of women and non-Muslims. It is perhaps ironic that aspects of Islamic jurisprudence that are least relevant to the lived experiences of Muslims are what have come to define Islam in its western conceptualization.

Defining Shariah

The simplest way to think of shariah is that it "is the way of God."[1] In this sense, shariah is inherently infallible since it is merely what God would want us to do. Shariah can also be conceptualized as the distinctive beliefs and practices of Islam. Hence, the word "shariah" can be replaced by "Islam" or "Islamic" in virtually any context. Anyone trying to follow shariah recognizes that there are innumerable debates over what shariah stipulates for any given situation. Jurisprudence (*fiqh*) is the fallible and relatively flexible human endeavor to determine what shariah entails. *Fiqh* constitutes the scholarly codification of laws based on the Quran, hadith, and depending on the school of law, reason (*aql*), juristic consensus (*ijma*), the use of analogies (*qiyas*), juristic preference (*istihsan*), and pragmatic public interest (*istislah*). Whereas shariah is divinely ordained, *fiqh* is the fallible human interpretation of shariah based on a combination of divine and human sources.[2] *Fiqh* is derived through the process of *ijtihad*, which is the scholarly attempt to determine what shariah stipulates for a given situation based on aforementioned juristic principles. A person who has the knowledge, skills, and personal qualities to perform *ijtihad* is known as a *mujtahid* or *faqih*. The fact that *ijtihad* and *mujtahid* are derived from the same root as *jihad* is due to the struggle needed to arrive at such rulings, which requires intense scholarly research and insight. Those who lack the training to perform *ijtihad* follow the rulings of a *mujtahid* in what is known as *taqlid* (imitation).

Shariah is not merely a set of punitive laws. It broadly encompasses acts of worship and transactions. The former include rituals such as prayer, fasting, and the hajj pilgrimage, whereas the latter encompass topics such as family relations, economic affairs, and criminal justice. Shariah divides acts into mandatory (e.g., five daily prayers), recommended (e.g., brushing your teeth), neutral (the majority of acts), disfavored (e.g., divorce), and forbidden (e.g., fornication).

There is no such thing as a book of shariah law.[3] *Fiqh*, similarly, is not one set of codified laws, but rather a diverse amalgamation of arguments, opinions, and rulings (fatwas). As such, the imposition of shariah law as a rigid set of laws is not realistic when there has always been an active debate over what shariah entails. Take a simple example, such as halal food. It might appear that legislating halal dietary laws would be easy enough, but in reality scholars from different legal schools have widely different opinions on issues such as whether it is permissible to eat lobsters, octopuses, or sea turtles. Perhaps other than pork and grape wine being forbidden under most circumstances, there is little else of juristic consensus with regard to food. Even these are permitted to Muslims at times of duress and can be produced and consumed by non-Muslims living in a Muslim state. In contrast to the image of Muslims as dogmatic, a hallmark of Muslim societies is the generally widespread tolerance of a wide array of legal opinions and rulings.

Another common misperception of shariah is that it is the law of the land in Muslim countries. As discussed by Ali-Karamali in her work *Demystifying Shariah*, the reality is that laws in Muslim countries might including shariah-sounding elements, but they far more closely resemble the rigid system of colonial laws imposed by Europeans.[4] Surprising as it might sound, traditional *fiqh*-based justice is antithetical to the strict, codified laws imposed by the colonial authorities. *Fiqh* allows a judge to rule in accordance with a wide array of historical rulings and with sensitivity to the sociocultural realities of the situation at hand; codified laws strip the judge of any leeway and deprive *fiqh* of the flexibility it historically enjoyed that allowed it to flourish over the centuries in a wide range of cultures and geographies. With codification, disagreements over the law are no longer tolerated, and the erudition needed to reach judgments is replaced with a judicial system based on looking up laws with little judicial leeway. In this context, *fiqh* progressively turned into an abstract exercise, detached from the real world.[5]

Furthermore, shariah-based justice traditionally provided some element of juristic independence from political rulers and created a system of Islamic education and meritocratic promotion that provided checks and balances against the ruling class.[6] The demise of traditional Islamic courts has handed autocrats complete control over both the formulation and the implementation of the law.

Punishments in Shariah

Shariah-based punishments can be divided into three broad categories—*hudud*, *tazir*, and *qisas*. *Hudud* are crimes for which specific punishments have been ordained—for example, lashing or stoning for fornication and adultery when the proper conditions are met. *Tazir* encompasses punishments for crimes for which no specific punishment has been ordained, such as for public masturbation. *Tazir* is extremely flexible and gives a judge broad leeway to consider both the alleged crime and any mitigating circumstances to craft an appropriate punishment, without being bound by any specific injunction. As discussed earlier, *qisas* and *diya* pertain to retributive punishment and financial compensation for injuries, respectively.

Hudud punishments are ordained for a very limited number of crimes. Indeed, the vast majority of sins and crimes have no specific earthly punishment. For example, someone who skips the daily prayers, isn't quite observant of Ramadan, forgoes the hajj pilgrimage, and who eats pork isn't subject to any specific punishment. The most commonly cited crimes for which punishments are specified include: (1) apostacy: capital punishment for men, imprisonment for women; (2) armed banditry and terrorism: execution, crucifixion, cutting off hands and feet from opposite sides, or exile; (3) theft: severing of the four smaller fingers of the right hand in the Shia Ja'fari school and amputation of the right hand at the wrist in Sunni schools; (4) adultery: stoning; (5) fornication: 100 lashes; (6) sexual defamation: 80 lashes; (9) drinking alcohol: 80 lashes. These specific punishments tend to be what are most commonly cited when trying to portray shariah as harsh and barbaric. There are multiple problems with this narrow view of what shariah is.

First, the aspects of shariah law that ensure social justice, economic prosperity, and universal human rights are completely ignored, as are the majority of shariah rulings which pertain to personal acts of cleanliness and worship. Essentially, a highly discriminatory process is used that entails sifting through thousands of pages of *fiqh* literature and handpicking a few items that will most shock a modern western audience. Nuance, context, contravening juristic opinions, and similar rulings in other religions including Judaism and Christianity are invariably omitted.

Second, *hudud* serve more as deterrents than punishments, as they convey the gravity of the sins or crimes, while setting such an unrealistic burden of proof that convictions are virtually impossible. This reality is evident with respect to the two punishments that appear to be most commonly cited in the Islamophobic context—extramarital sex and theft.

As for extramarital sex, there is a need for four "just" male witnesses to see a man's penis penetrate the vagina or anus all the way to the prepuce. All four witnesses must clearly see the penetration occur. Even if two people fornicate in a crowded public park under a blanket, the conditions would not be met. All four witnesses must withstand any attack on their character, otherwise they would not be considered "just" (*adil*). If four witnesses do see the act in detail and they appear to testify, but it turns out that one of the witnesses drinks alcohol on occasion (i.e., is not "just"), not only is the punishment waived on the adulterer, but the four witnesses are whipped eighty times each for bearing inadequately substantiated testimony of a sexual crime.[7] The fact that witnesses are so harshly punished if anything falls short provides the clearest evidence that shariah wants to discourage people from coming forth with allegations of sexual impropriety. Circumstantial evidence, such as an unmarried woman becoming pregnant, is not an indication for punishment. In fact, it is impermissible to even question the woman as to the circumstances of her pregnancy.[8] Similarly, the punishment of stoning is dropped if someone does not have sexual access to a spouse every morning and evening, claims that he or she believed the intercourse was legitimate (e.g., "it was dark and I thought the woman was my wife"), or claims that the intercourse was non-consensual.[9] Suppose someone does commit adultery and four just male witnesses of the utmost moral character happen to witness it and appear before a properly qualified judge to testify. Three of them have testified and the fourth one is about to. All the accused has to do is say, "Yes, I committed adultery, but I have repented." There would be no punishment.[10] One can only imagine what American criminal justice would look life if a perpetrator who is dragged in front of a judge could just say, "Sure, I was caught red-handed dealing drugs, but I repent," and have all charges instantly dismissed. In essence, it is virtually impossible to prove illicit intercourse and the perpetrator can claim any number of defenses to escape punishment. Hence, *hadd* punishments are designed to be exceedingly rare.

As for theft, there are a similarly large number of criteria that have to be met. The person must be a sane adult who commits theft without any external force or compulsion, such as hunger. The item stolen must be in a protected place that necessitates a break-in to steal it. Given the requirement for breaking and entering, common types of theft like shoplifting would not qualify. The value of what is stolen must be more than one-fourth of a gold *dinar*. Furthermore, the judge would have to forgo amputation in the presence of any question or doubt on behalf of the thief as to whether what he was committing constituted theft. Two just male witnesses must also testify that they saw the theft occur.[11] These conditions are clearly not easy to meet, and that is by design. It is hardly surprising that colonial officials in Muslim countries found shariah law to be too lenient and hence agitated for stricter punishments. As Sumbul Ali-Karamali put it,

> Colonial powers were not only suspicious of shariah; they were hostile to it and considered it too soft. Yes, *soft*. The British governor Warren Hastings, in eighteenth-century India, complained that Islamic law was too lenient and flexible. Hastings denounced shariah because it was founded on an "abhorrence of bloodshed" and too easily allowed criminals to escape without punishment. The British legal understanding of crime and punishment, especially in the eighteenth century, differed dramatically from that of Muslims. In England at the time, some two hundred crimes were punishable by death, including minor theft (worth five shillings, which equaled one-fourth of a pound). In contrast, the primary goal of shariah was to avoid zero-sum solutions and provide workable compromises whenever possible.[12]

Nevertheless, Disney's 1992 animated film *Aladdin* portrays the stereotypical view of Islamic punishments. When Princess Jasmine hands an apple to a hungry child, the apple seller grabs her hand and pulls out his blade to chop her hand off, exclaiming, "Thief! Do you know what the penalty is for stealing?!" Clearly, an apple taken from an open cart to feed a hungry child in the absence of proper witnesses would hardly qualify for *hadd*. But such technicalities are beside the point; the image of instant barbaric punishments being doled out by Muslims for the most banal of transgressions is what is imprinted on the western and indeed global imagination. It is the lack of nuance of these media representations that promote overly simplistic and highly inflammatory views of shariah.

Third, it is not clear whether the conditions for doling out *hudud* punishments are met today. Every obligation in Islam has preconditions. For example, five daily prayers are obligatory, but only when conditions such as maturity, sanity, and consciousness are satisfied. Similarly, the obligation to fast during Ramadan is waived if one is sick or travelling. As such, one must determine what the societal conditions are for implementing *hudud*. It is hard to dispute that a properly functioning Islamic judicial system with a cadre of adequately trained judges would be a prerequisite to implementing *hudud* punishments. *Hudud* punishments are not acts of lynching carried out by the whims of citizens based on rumors. Rather, they require judges trained adequately in Islamic jurisprudence, a proper judicial process, and the fulfillment of strict evidentiary requirements. These conditions are virtually never met in courts in Muslim countries today. It is worth nothing that historically, Shia scholars claimed consensus that *hudud* punishments leading to death or permanent injury could only be implemented in the presence of a divinely-appointed prophet or imam.[13] Considering the general Shia rejection of the authority of temporal Muslim rulers, it hardly made sense for them to grant these rulers the authority to oversee the punitive aspects of Islamic justice.

Finally, equating Islam with specific punishments that would only be carried out in exceedingly rare circumstances is inherently discriminatory. Other religions have injunctions that are far more severe. According to the New Testament, Jesus said, "And if your eye causes you to stumble, gouge it out and throw it away. It is better for you to enter life with one eye than to have

two eyes and be thrown into the fire of hell."[14] Old Testament
laws are similarly brutal. Stoning to death is ordained for
gathering firewood on the Sabbath,[15] summoning spirits,[16] and
being a stubborn child who doesn't obey his parents.[17] Similarly,
people are to be put to death for blasphemy,[18] murder,[19]
kidnapping,[20] bestiality,[21] adultery,[22] homosexuality,[23] working
on the Sabbath,[24] and making idolatrous human sacrifices.[25]
Forty-two boys were mauled to death by a bear for jeering a
prophet, highlighting the lack of divine tolerance for dissenting
views.[26] For Bible-thumpers to portray the Quran as particularly
cruel in terms of its punishments is rather disingenuous.

The Barbarity of the Prison-Industrial Complex

The criticism of Islamic *hudud* punishments is predicated on the
assumption that western punishments are humane whereas
shariah-based ones are barbaric. Michel Foucault, a prominent
twentieth century French philosopher, addresses this myth in
Discipline and Punish. Medieval punishments were severe and
savage and were carried out in plain sight. They both
demonstrated the power of the sovereign and turned people into
participants in the judicial process. The risk, however, was that
if the verdict was seen as unjust or the punishment was taken to
be too severe, the victim would become a hero or martyr and the
sovereign would be demonized or even overthrown. As such, the
sovereign had a general incentive to maintain a proper balance
between projecting power and appearing just. Gradually,
punishments were moved from the front of a church to its
backyard, and they were eventually hidden away from the public
eye in dungeons which later morphed into prisons.

   As punishments went from relatively quick public
floggings or hangings to eternities spent out-of-sight in prisons,
they could be doled out more liberally and with far less political
backlash. An ever-enlarging list of crimes was devised to
criminalize every minor aspect of life, with the threat of sovereign
force becoming an ever-more-constant aspect of modern life.

Whereas on a trip to a Muslim country one will pretty much never encounter someone whose hand has been chopped off for stealing, in the United States 2.3 million people, predominantly men of color, are incarcerated, more than in any other country on the planet. You can list every punishable crime in Islamic law on one page; an encyclopedia-length work would not suffice to enumerate every punishment on the book in western liberal democracies.

Islamic law is meant to dole out punishment and move on, with the crime erased once the punishment has been carried out. In contrast, the American criminal "justice" system labels people as "criminals" and "felons" for life, stripping them of numerous rights and privileges, such as the right to vote, to live in public housing, or to receive welfare benefits.[27] Considering the inherent racial injustice in American law enforcement and criminal "justice" system, a permanent underclass of black and brown "criminals" has been created, with being a criminal seen as an inseparable aspect of their human essence.

Furthermore, the Islamic punishment system is one of diminution, in that harsh punishments on paper are hardly ever administered. In American justice, a simple arrest for selling fake watches in New York City can turn into a months-long prison sentence because the "criminal" lacks the two hundred dollars to post bail and hence remains incarcerated white awaiting a repeatedly-delayed court date. Similarly, a simple parking ticket can end up with one's car booted, suspension of one's vehicle registration and driver's license, and a warrant for one's arrest. In light of worsening income disparity, the most minor infractions can have serious financial and legal ramifications for poor Americans. The United States has managed to harbor the world's largest prison population, with a thriving prison-industrial complex funded by taxpayers who appear more concerned about the imagined brutality of shariah punishments that are virtually never carried out while supportive of the very real brutalities of their own criminal justice system. As pointed out by Professor Peter Moskos, a Harvard- and Princeton-educated sociologist and author of *In Defense of Flogging*, given a choice between many years in prison and a handful of lashes, which would anyone sensible choose?[28]

Anti-Shariah Laws

In more recent years, Islamophobes have pushed for the passing of legislation outlawing any consideration of shariah in American courts. According to the Southern Poverty Law Center, between 2010 and 2018, 201 anti-shariah law bills were introduced in 43 states, 14 of which have been enacted. To avoid constitutional scrutiny over religious discrimination, such laws are typically passed under the guise of keeping "foreign laws" out of American courts, with *foreign* serving as a euphemism for *shariah*.[29] Considering that the entire American legal system is based on British common law—with the exception of Louisiana whose legal system is partly based on French civil law—the concern is not about laws being foreign per se, but rather about any laws that are perceived as being non-white in origin.

On face value, it seems reasonable to keep religious laws out of "secular" American courtrooms. However, civil courts are drawn into myriad cases involving religious affairs. For example, if someone draws up a will in accordance with shariah principles, does the court act in accordance with the deceased's wishes or does it dismiss the will because it is based on "foreign" laws and then proceed to divide the estate in accordance with the judge's wishes instead? If a Muslim couple is divorced in a Muslim country based on shariah principles, would they still be considered married in the United States because the foreign laws governing divorce would be inadmissible and hence render the divorce invalid? If a man guarantees his wife a sizeable dower at the time of marriage, is an American court obligated to uphold the agreement or to invalidate it? Would a loan agreement based on non-usurious shariah principles be upheld? If not, which part would be invalidated—the loan itself or the absence of interest?

Aside from such legal challenges, there are several other problems with anti-shariah legislation. First, it shows that absurd fears of shariah takeovers have become so mainstream that state legislators take up such bills. Second, constitutional rights to freedom of religion are hollowed out with one specific religion in mind. Freedom of religion is not guaranteed if followers of any one religion are not guaranteed the freedom to practice their religion. Third, it shows how the political system has been usurped as a tool to promote Islamophobia. Fourth, these laws overlook the reality that following shariah is just as American a thing to do as following Talmudic, canon, or Amish laws and customs. Finally, some of these bills effectively incriminate Islam as an entire religion.

A Tennessee bill pretty much reads like passages out of the bible of Islamophobia as it seeks to legislate the concept that "Islam equals *jihad* equals terrorism."[30] Among its stipulations are: (1) "'Sharia' means the set of rules, precepts, instructions, or edicts which are said to emanate directly or indirectly from the god of Allah or the prophet Mohammed;" (2) "Jihad and sharia are inextricably linked, with sharia formulating and commanding jihad, and jihad being waged for the purpose of imposing and instituting sharia;" (3) "Sharia requires all its adherents to actively and passively support the replacement of America's constitutional republic, including the representative government of this state with a political system based upon sharia;" (4) "Any rule, precept, instruction, or edict arising directly from the extant rulings of any of the authoritative schools of Islamic jurisprudence of Hanafi, Maliki, Shafi'i, Hanbali, Ja'afariya, or Salafi, as those terms are used by sharia adherents, is prima facie sharia without any further evidentiary showing." The bill essentially taints with criminality banal acts such as flossing one's teeth, bathing, fasting, marrying, and opening a business, all of which are performed by many Muslims in accordance with edicts arising from their respective schools of jurisprudence. It goes on to say, "Any person who knowingly provides material support or resources to a designated sharia organization, or attempts or conspires to do so, shall commit an offense... punishable by fine, imprisonment of not less than fifteen (15) years or both."[31]

It is worth nothing that the fearmongering one sees with respect to the encroachment of Islam and shariah law does not exist in a vacuum. It is a highly profitable enterprise that is well funded by a variety of interest groups. According to a 2018 article by John Esposito and Natana DeLong-Bas,

> As documented by organizations such as the Center for American Progress and islamophobianetwork.com, this fear was deliberately stoked between 2001 and 2012 by eight donors who contributed more than $57 million to promote fear of Islam, Muslims, and Shariah, claiming that they were working to overthrow the US Constitution and legal system and install a radical Islamic caliphate that will punish and subordinate all non-Muslims. In 2016, the Council on American-Islamic Relations (CAIR) and the Center for Race and Gender at the University of California, Berkeley, examined support for radical organizations. Their report, "Confronting Fear," based on tax filings, showed that between 2008 and 2013, a US-based Islamophobia Network of some 33 groups received $205,838,077 in total revenue.[32]

Anti-shariah bills are often quite formulaic in nature as their texts are drafted by the same cadre of Islamophobes. According to the Southern Poverty Law Center, "The majority of anti-Sharia legislation introduced across the country incorporates the American Laws for American Courts model legislation published on the American Public Policy Alliance's (APPA) website."[33] An exposé by *The New York Times* explains,

> The anti-Shariah movement... is the product of an orchestrated drive that began five years ago in Crown Heights, Brooklyn, in the office of a little-known lawyer, David Yerushalmi, a 56-year-old Hasidic Jew with a history of controversial statements about race, immigration and Islam. Despite his lack of formal

training in Islamic law, Mr. Yerushalmi has come to exercise a striking influence over American public discourse about Shariah."

Yerushalmi openly admits that the purpose of the bills he drafts is not so much to actually pass laws that will likely not withstand constitutional scrutiny, but rather to inflame tensions. As he put it, "If this thing passed in every state without any friction, it would have not served its purpose... The purpose was heuristic—to get people asking this question, 'What is Shariah?'"[34] The answer to the question is clearly not meant to be complex or nuanced, but rather an Islamophobic caricature meant to denigrate. Considering that the aspects of shariah that are portrayed as most offensive with respect to women's rights, sexual freedom, and punishments bear striking resemblance to traditional Jewish laws, it seems disingenuous at best for an ultra-Orthodox Hasidic to engage in this sort of race-baiting.

Shariah Courts in Western Countries

A lot of drama surrounds the idea that "shariah courts" are being set up in western countries, particularly in the United Kingdom, and that these courts create a parallel legal system that eludes the authority of the state. According to a report by *The Guardian*,

> Almost all the sharia councils, which first appeared in the UK in the 1980s, were founded to facilitate Islamic divorces for Muslim women who need a religious scholar to end their marriage where their husbands don't consent (they may also offer religious advice on inheritance, wills or issue religious rulings). They are not the only religious councils—there are also the Jewish Orthodox Beth Din, and Catholic tribunals. The sharia councils are often accused of operating a "parallel legal system" in the UK, but their rulings have no legal standing here or abroad, and they have no enforcement powers. As unofficial

bodies, they also have no jurisdiction over custody or financial issues. What they rely on is the weight that religious rulings carry in the Muslim community.[35]

These religious arbitration councils raise two types of concerns—right-wing Islamophobes ring the alarm that shariah is taking hold,[36] while feminists raise concerns that Muslim women are being pressured into reconciling with their husbands who allegedly abuse and rape them.[37] Both are merely succumbing to racist stereotypes—the stereotype of the Muslim invader who is determined to dominate and impose his religion and the stereotype of the abusive Muslim man whose helpless wife needs saving. The same type of outrage is not seen with respect to Jewish Halakha courts, which serve very similar functions. Under Jewish law, women cannot divorce their husbands, which creates a situation in which an estranged husband can withhold a divorce to prevent the woman from moving on with her life and marrying someone else. Furthermore, some Christian denominations such as Catholics and Copts do not allow for divorce at all, which arguably pressures many couples to remain in unhappy or abusive marriages. Yet, one hardly sees any widespread obsession with freeing Irish and Italian women or Coptic Egyptians from their unhappy marriages.

One should also consider the reality that civil courts have zero jurisdiction when it comes to religious law. A court can grant a civil divorce, but it cannot compel a Catholic bishop to annul a marriage, to sanctify the remarriage of someone whose previous union has not been annulled, or to officiate same-sex-marriages. Furthermore, the state has a limited ability to enforce its position vis-à-vis a citizen who does not recognize the state's authority over religious matters. Even if the state grants a person a divorce, he or she might feel obligated to have the divorce religiously sanctioned prior to remarriage. A secular state should divest itself of any interest in becoming bogged down in the intricacies of canon law, in deciphering competing Talmudic interpretations, or in deciding between opinions held by scholars from different schools of Islamic jurisprudence. Instead of singling out "shariah courts," one must set aside stereotypes and accept the role religious tribunals play in the lives of the followers of many different faiths. After all, unlike civil and criminal courts whose decisions are binding regardless of whether one believes in them or not, the decisions of these religious arbitration panels are only applicable to those who actually believe in them and freely choose to follow their rulings.

Chapter 30

Why so Few Muslim Nobel Prize Winners?

Among the central features of the Muslim stereotype is an innate backwardness that has frozen Muslim societies in time, making them a relic of a distant past and impervious to change. As Edward Said put it, Islam "represents a fundamental case of arrested human development."[1] Hence, Muslims are seen as incapable of innovation and unable to contribute to the advancement of a modern society. This mindset is reflected in the tweet by Richard Dawkins, a prominent British evolutionary biologist, that said, "All the world's Muslims have fewer Nobel Prizes than Trinity College, Cambridge. They did great things in the Middle Ages, though."[2,3] When one considers that nearly a quarter of the world's population is Muslim, the paucity of Muslim Nobel prize winners is a staggering reality indeed.

The question cloaks Islamophobia and white supremacy under the façade of a simple observation. While the question singles out Muslims, one has to realize that although blacks have won several Nobel Prizes in peace and literature as well as one in economics, there have been no black Nobel Prize winners in medicine, physics, or chemistry. Similarly, considering the large populations of China, India, and Southeast Asia, remarkably few people residing in these regions have won Nobel Prizes as well.

This seemingly simple question insinuates that Islam is antithetical to innovation and research and that the entirety of Muslim mental efforts, assuming that there are any, is to be dedicated to religious trivia. Such assumptions are patently false. In what Al-Bayhaqi classified as a "famous" hadith, the Prophet (S) said, "Seek knowledge, even if you have to go as far as China, for the seeking of knowledge is mandatory for every Muslim."[4]

Clearly, this is not referring to religious knowledge, as no Muslim from Arabia would travel to China for Islamic religious indoctrination. Indeed, the Quran repeatedly urges believers to travel the earth in search of understanding and knowledge.[5] Furthermore, the Quran does not expect all Muslims to specialize in theology and jurisprudence:

> The believers should not all go forth [to receive religious instruction], but rather some people from each group of them should go forth to gain religious knowledge, so that they may advise their people when they return to them, so that they may beware.[6]

As such, advanced religious education is seen as a specialized field that some but not all Muslims ought to pursue. This is not to the exclusion of other fields such as mathematics, natural sciences, medicine, social sciences, and humanities or professions such as blacksmithing, carpentry, plumbing, etc. Furthermore, the Quran repeatedly commands people to contemplate. It states that it and other signs from God have been revealed so that people think.[7] It pushes people to ponder the origins of the heavens and the earth,[8] astronomy,[9] geography,[10] meteorology,[11] navigation,[12] zoology,[13] human anatomy,[14] plant biology,[15] human history,[16] introspective psychology,[17] social relations,[18] and many other fields. Humans are told to ponder not just the hereafter but also this world.[19] The Quran also points out that anyone who thinks rationally wouldn't fall for insults leveled against the Prophet (S).[20] Accordingly, the role of reason was seen as central to faith in all three major schools of Islamic theology—Mu'tazilite, Ash'arite, and Shia. Indeed, books of jurisprudence mandate that a believer must come to accept the correctness of his or her faith through reason and not blind imitation.[21]

The Golden Age of Islam

The achievement of relative political stability in Muslim lands in the 8th century led to what has been called the Golden Age of Islam. A nation that valued individual human virtues and renounced discrimination based on race and ethnicity opened its doors to people of various backgrounds and faiths from across the vast multicontinental empire to come together and bring about the most astonishing advances humanity had ever witnessed. Underpinning the Islamic Golden Age was an unquenchable thirst for acquiring all the knowledge held by other civilizations from across the world.

Upon acquiring the technology to make paper from the Chinese, a mass translation movement was started that sought to translate and preserve the works of Greek, Persian, Indian, and other civilizations. The House of Wisdom was created in Baghdad to serve as the center of this global enterprise. Hunayn ibn Ishaq, a Nestorian Christian physician, was put in charge of the House of Wisdom and personally translated numerous works. A thirst for all types of knowledge was not limited to the Sunni Abbasid Caliphate in Baghdad, as the Shia Fatimid Dynasty in Egypt as well as the Umayyads ruling in Cordoba led similar endeavors. Much of this knowledge was passed on to the Europeans through Spain, and many of the seminal works of ancient Greece have only survived through their Arabic translations.

This period saw massive advances in a variety of fields. Al-Khwarizmi developed algebra in part to help solve complex situations that arose from Islamic inheritance laws. Through his works, "Arabic" (originally Indian) numerals were introduced to Europe, saving Europeans from the cumbersome task of carrying out mathematical calculations using Roman numerals. He also made great strides in cartography and developed many maps of remarkable geographic accuracy.[22]

Significant advances were made in the Muslim world in astronomy, spherical geometry, and trigonometry, which were needed to determine the direction of prayer, the times of prayer, and the dates of the Islamic calendar.[23] Al-Biruni used trigonometry and a hill to calculate the earth's radius so precisely that even centuries later, our estimation lies within 81 miles of his.[24] Meanwhile, Ismail al-Jazari became the father of robotics and modern engineering. His seminal work, *The Book of Knowledge of Ingenious Mechanical Devices*, describes how to construct some fifty different mechanical devices:

> The inventions he mentions in his book include the crank mechanism, connecting rod, programmable automaton, humanoid robot, reciprocating piston engine, suction pipe, suction pump, double-acting pump, valve, combination lock, cam, camshaft, segmental gear, the first mechanical clocks driven by water and weights, and especially the crankshaft, which is considered the most important mechanical invention in history after the wheel. Not bad for a guy who lived 800 years ago![25]

Whereas Adam Smith is commonly known as the father of modern economics, the title is more befitting of Ibn Khaldun, who four centuries earlier had "explored supply and demand, how population growth affects the economy, and tax theory—all ideas that were thought to be groundbreaking when western economists wrote on them several centuries later."[26] According to Dr. Ibrahim Oweiss, a professor of economics at Georgetown University, "Not only did Ibn Khaldun plant the germinating seeds of classical economics, whether in production, supply, or cost, but he also pioneered in consumption, demand, and utility, the cornerstones of modern economic theory."[27] Ibn Khaldun has also been considered the father of modern sociology, as his *Muqaddimah* "addressed all the fields of contemporary sociology."[28] He specifically analyzed issues of social cohesion, tribal identity, and social conflict, and he described the cyclicity seen in the rise and fall of empires.

This period also saw numerous advances in the medical sciences. Ibn al-Haytham, an early proponent of experimentation and scientific methodology, described ocular anatomy and neuroanatomy and proved that vision results from light entering the eye, not from the eye emanating rays that enable vision.[29] In the thirteenth century, Ibn al-Nafis described pulmonary circulation, debunking Galen's hypothesis that blood directly passes through the interventricular septum. In the west, this discovery has been credited to William Harvey's identical discovery some three centuries later.[30] Avicenna's 11th century medical treatise served as the foundation of medical education in Europe until the seventeenth century.[31] While modern vaccines have been attributed to Edward Jenner, he merely coopted techniques that had been in use in the Ottoman Empire. According to Alexandra Fleming's article "The origins of vaccination,"

> Edward Jenner (1749–1823), a physician from Gloucestershire in England, is widely regarded as the 'father of vaccination'. ... At the time Jenner reported his famous story about inoculating young James Phipps with cowpox and then demonstrating immunity to smallpox, the procedure of 'variolation' (referred to then as 'inoculation'), by which pus is taken from a smallpox blister and introduced into a scratch in the skin of an uninfected person to confer protection, was already well established. Variolation had been popularized in Europe by the writer and poet Lady Mary Wortley Montagu, best known for her 'letters from the Ottoman Empire'. As wife of the British ambassador to Turkey, she had first witnessed variolation in Constantinople in 1717, which she mentioned in her famous 'letter to a friend'. The following year, her son was variolated in Turkey, and her daughter received variolation in England in 1721. The procedure was initially met with much resistance—so much so that the first experimental variolation in England (including subsequent smallpox challenge) was carried out on condemned prisoners, who were promised freedom if they survived (they did).[32]

Despite Muslims being at the forefront of scientific and technological advances for centuries, one cannot overlook the reality that this period was far from idyllic. The caliphate left the population at the mercy of mercurial monarchs. Political freedoms were rather limited, and there were periods of intellectual crackdowns, such as during Caliph al-Ma'mun's *Mihna*. Nevertheless, the scholarship, experimentation, and intellectual debates that occurred during this period highlight the reality that Islam and Muslims are not innately antithetical to rational thought and scientific progress. However, as in any society, there are those who promote rational and experimental approaches as well as those who advocate for limiting human understanding to simple-minded analysis of religious texts.

Precolonial and Colonial Decline

The decline of the Golden Age started with internal strife, Crusader attacks that constituted a constant military threat, and the sacking of Baghdad by Mongol invaders. The breakdown of the Abbasid Empire and the ensuing political instability did not bode well for scientific inquiry. Despite such challenges, many Muslim scholars continued to contribute to fields such as astronomy, medicine, and philosophy. It can be argued that the end of the Islamic Golden Age was not due to any particular event in the Muslim world but rather due to changes in Europe. Rising European supremacy turned the continent from one that sought to learn from the Muslim world into one that sought to study the Muslim world from an angle of cultural supremacy.

In Africa, the transatlantic slave trade deprived large swaths of the continent from its intelligent and capable young men and women. They were either captured and shipped off to build colonial economies in the Americas, or they fled into the bush to reduce the risk of capture. Neither fate was well suited to promoting scientific discovery and academic scholarship. Entire regions became depopulated, leading to economic collapse.[33] The end of the transatlantic slave trade cut off a main source of revenue for the continent, compounding its dire economic situation.[34]

Colonial interventions throughout Africa, Asia, and Latin America drastically hindered the economic and scientific development of these continents. Entire nations were effectively enslaved and their economies were redrawn to benefit local colonial settler communities and distant European colonial powers. Traditional trade routes that served as the lifeblood of vibrant and interconnected economies and cultures were replaced with a system of colonial borders. Trade became effectively limited to the exportation of raw materials and the importation and forced consumption of manufactured goods. The pervasiveness of colonial economic control is highlighted by how the British forbade Indians from evaporating sea water to make their own sea salt; they had to purchase overpriced and overtaxed salt from the British. Mahatma Gandhi's 1930 march to the Arabian Sea coast to extract salt from seawater served as a pivotal moment in helping to bring about the end of British rule in India.

To this day, one hears echoes of how colonialism was to the benefit of the colonized lands, and that these "third world" citizens are ungrateful for the modernizing influence of Europeans. Utsa Patnaik, an economist at Jawaharlal Nehru University, estimates that between 1765 and 1938, Britain drained nearly $45 trillion from India alone through manipulation of its taxation and banking systems. The wealth extracted from India was used to industrialize western countries like England, Canada, and Australia and to wage wars of imperial expansion across the globe. During the second half of the nineteenth century, which marked the height of British colonial rule, India saw its per capita income drop in half, and between 1870 and 1920, its life expectancy dropped by a fifth.[35] Clearly, colonialism was to the detriment of India.

To understand how the west went from monopolies on salt, opium, sugar, and tobacco to a monopoly on Nobel Prizes, one must consider the economic realities laid bare by Belgian economist Paul Bairoch. In 1750, China's share of world GDP was 33% and India's was 24.5%; the combined share of Britain and its American colonies at that time was a meager 2%. By

1800, India's share fell to 20%. By 1900, the shares of India and China dropped to 1.7% and 6.2%, respectively. During the same period, the British and American share rose to over 41% of global GDP. As late at the mid-nineteenth century, westerners had a lower standard of living than Asians.[36] It was not lack of intelligence, following the wrong religions, or cultural deficiencies that held the Global South back; it was colonialism.

Postcolonial Interventions

The end of colonialism did not end western economic and military interventions in postcolonial societies. John Perkins, author of *The New Confessions of an Economic Hit Man*, details how leaders in country after country in the developing world were offered the same deal. Accept personal enrichment bribes and hand over control of your nation's resources, economy, banking, and foreign reserves to multinational (i.e., western) corporations or you will be ousted in a manufactured revolt (e.g., Mossadegh in Iran), deposed in a coup d'état (e.g., Arbenz in Guatemala), forced to "commit suicide" (e.g., Allende in Chile), blown out of the sky (e.g., Torrijos in Panama), kidnapped by US Marines and dumped off in a remote land (e.g., Aristide in Haiti), or hauled away to prison by the American military (e.g., Noriega in Panama). These neocolonial crimes are not a relic of ancient history. In 2009, President Manuel Zelaya of Honduras was ousted in an American-backed coup to prevent him from raising the minimum wage. The United States was concerned that a hike in the Honduran minimum wage would not only raise the price of Honduran exports to the US but also have a domino effect through enticing other Latin American countries to follow suit by raising their minimum wages also. This followed the 2004 ousting of Haiti's first democratically-elected president Jean-Bertrand Aristide due to his support for an increased minimum wage.[37] Aristide was literally "kidnapped by US Marines" and dumped off in the Central African Republic.[38]

When such methods fail to bring a "rogue" leader in line, the solution is all-out war, as we have seen with the disastrous invasions of Vietnam, Grenada, Iraq, Somalia, Afghanistan, and Libya, among many other countries. When war is not the best option, then sanctions are utilized to inflict misery on civilians in countries such as Iran, Iraq, North Korea, and Venezuela. That sanctions primarily affect civilian populations is hardly of concern. Madeleine Albright, former US Secretary of State, was asked on *60 Minutes* about Iraqi sanctions, "We have heard that half a million children have died. I mean, that's more children than died in Hiroshima, and, and, you know, is the price worth it?" She coldly replied, "We think the price is worth it."[39] Two years later, she further explained, "If we have to use force, it is because we are America; we are the indispensable nation. We stand tall and we see further than other countries into the future... I know that the American men and women in uniform are always prepared to sacrifice for freedom, democracy and the American way of life."[40] One must wonder how well American policymakers saw into the futures of Vietnam, Iraq, and Afghanistan when they decided to invade.

The absolute shock that is rightly expressed at civilian suffering under brutal Daesh and Taliban rule must be contrasted with the complete apathy towards far greater levels of civilian suffering under western occupation and sanctions regimes. Racist assumptions that the west is innately noble and well-intentioned whereas others are innately savage explain the discrepancy in outrage. That countries subject to colonialism, military interventions, and sanctions do not have the same scientific and economic output as wealthy nations who have benefited heavily from the exploitation inherent in colonialism and the neocolonial global economic system is hardly surprising.

Chapter 31

The Dangers of Islamophobia

As pointed out by the United Nations Special Rapporteur on Freedom of Religion or Belief, anti-Muslim hatred has reached "epidemic proportions" and has led states to adopt "measures which disproportionately target Muslims."[1] This is hardly surprising. As with any form of racism, Islamophobia is not limited to mere personal prejudice, but rather underpins national and global social, political, and economic structures. Like other forms of racism, Islamophobia constitutes a dangerous social phenomenon that has dire and pervasive consequences that should not be overlooked. A few of these consequences will be discussed here.

Discrimination, Poverty, Marginalization, and Extremism

The proliferation of anti-Muslim bigotry invariably leads to overt discrimination against Muslims. According to Pew Research, 82% of Americans believe that Muslims are subject to some (37%) or a lot of (45%) discrimination.[2] This becomes a rather striking problem when it comes to employment. In France, the chance of a Muslim man getting a job interview is one-quarter that of an equally qualified Catholic man. In fact, Muslims were found to be far more discriminated against in employment in France than African Americans are in the United States.[3] In Germany, a Turkish job applicant named "Meryem Ozturk" who wears a headscarf has to send an average of 4.5 times as many applications to receive one job interview as a woman named "Sandra Bauer."[4]

The problem with job discrimination is that it closes the door to economic prosperity, contributes to persistent and multigenerational poverty, and creates a perpetual colored underclass. If the American experience with four centuries of systemic racism and the lost opportunities at the founding of the Republic and during Reconstruction provide any lesson, it is that it is imperative to act early and decisively to stem the formation, solidification, and continuation of an ethnoracial caste system.

There is no better recruitment tool for extremists than a significant population that feels marginalized. Disgruntled youth whose culture and religion are derided and who lack any job prospects are far more likely to be drawn to extremist organizations. According to a presentation given by Sarah Lyons-Padilla of Stanford University at the American Psychological Association's 125th Annual Convention,

> We found that immigrants who identify with neither their heritage culture nor the culture they are living in feel marginalized and insignificant... Experiences of discrimination make the situation worse... In what has also been referred to as a vicious cycle of prejudice, we find that lower levels of openness to diversity are associated with lower levels of cultural integration... Difficulty integrating, in turn, shapes support for extremism. Our findings therefore suggest that radicalization is not merely a process that takes place within individuals, but that the larger context of reception plays a crucial role.[5]

According to a *Haaretz* article based on an interview with Olivier Roy, a leading French terrorism expert, "An estimated 60 percent of those who espouse violent jihadism in Europe are second-generation Muslims who have lost their connection with their country of origin and have failed to integrate into Western societies." They develop an "identity vacuum" in which they feel "detached from both the European society and the one of their origins." This creates a situation in which "violent extremism thrives." Third-generation Muslims who are generally better integrated account for no more than 15 percent of extremists. "Converts, who also have an approach to Islam decontextualized from any culture, account for about 25 percent of those who fall prey to violent fundamentalism."[6]

That marginalization and decontextualization constitute leading causes of extremism in Muslim youth growing up in the west is hardly surprising. To tell someone growing up in Tehran, Jeddah, or Cairo that Islam calls for terrorism against civilians would be a hard sell. They would have known plenty of devout Muslims who are the most peace-loving people they have ever known. In contrast, it is much easier to sell the idea that Islam calls for terrorism to someone growing up in the west whose understanding of Islam is based on popular media stereotypes without any cultural counter-narrative.

Even western concepts such as that of "the moderate Muslim" only further promote negative stereotypes of Islam by implying that only a "moderate" Muslim—i.e., one who barters parts of his or her faith for "modernity"—can be peaceful. It assumes that a true believer who accepts Islam in its entirety would not be able to live in peace with others. This could not be further from the truth. Someone who wants to be a good Muslim but lacks proper Islamic education would be easy prey for extremists who preach what the media consistently assures everyone true Islam really is. As such, we must be cognizant of the dangers posed by the perpetuation of Islamophobic stereotypes in the media.

Indeed, a question one often hears is, "Where is the moderate Muslim voice?"[7] This either implies that they do not exist or that they are too afraid to speak up because of the pervasiveness of extremists within Muslim communities. Yet, for the media to constantly repeat this question is rather disingenuous because the media is in charge of deciding which voices are heard. If the media thinks that moderate Muslims are those who forgo hijab and drink and party in nightclubs, they wouldn't have a hard time finding plenty of Muslims like that. If moderate Muslims are those who are quite religious and follow the precepts of Islam but have zero inclination towards terrorism, they'd be quite easy to find as well. If the message put forth by Muslims appears too extremist, it is only because the media chooses to disseminate those specific messages. At the end, one has to wonder if airing extremist messages are just better for ratings and earnings than featuring someone intelligent, educated, and erudite with a nuanced understanding of the richness of the Islamic religion and Muslim societies.

Anti-Muslim Violence

Rising Islamophobia has contributed to outbreaks of hate crimes targeting Muslims. According to Brown University's Watson Institute for International and Public Affairs, "The total number of reported hate crime incidents in the U.S. decreased by over 18 percent between 2000 and 2009, but during the same period, the percentage of hate crime incidents directed towards Muslims increased by over 500 percent."[8] Internationally, Islamophobia has been used to justify the mass internment of Uyghurs in China's Xinjiang province, the systematic ethnic cleansing of Rohingyas in Myanmar's Rakhine State, the massacre and mass-rape of Bosnians after the breakup of Yugoslavia, and the stripping of citizenship from millions of Indian Muslims in Assam.

Aside from state-sponsored brutalities, Islamophobia also leads to mob violence. In Sri Lanka, anti-Muslim riots broke out in at least 24 towns in 2019, leading to widespread looting, arson, and assault.[9] In India, mobs hunt down Muslims accused of waging "love jihad" or alleged to be involved with the slaughter of cattle.[10] The 2002 Gujarat pogrom led to the death of 790 Muslims and 254 Hindus.[11] The United States, United Kingdom, and European Union issued travel bans against Narendra Modi, who at the time was the Chief Minister of Gujarat, because of his role in fueling the violence. Given his continued electoral success, these restrictions have since been lifted.[12] Western capitals now roll out the red carpet for him even as he continues to fan the flames of anti-Muslim bigotry throughout India.[13] In

2020, in response to peaceful protests against Modi's citizenship law targeting Muslims in Assam, an anti-Muslim "pogrom" broke out in Delhi that left 53 dead.[14]

Political discourse has a significant impact on violence targeting Muslims. The starkly Islamophobic tone of Donald Trump's 2016 campaign was associated with a 91% rise in anti-Muslim hate crimes between the first half of 2016 and 2017 in the United States.[15] In 2016, there were more anti-Muslim attacks in the US than in 2001 when the September 11 attacks occurred.[16] The victory of Donald Trump helped energize Islamophobes worldwide. In Germany, there were nearly 1,000 anti-Muslim crimes committed in 2017. There was an average of over one attack targeting a mosque per week, with Nazi symbols and pig's blood used to desecrate German mosques.[17]

Individual hate crimes against Muslims are far too numerous to enumerate and reflect the violent extremism that Islamophobia has spawned in the west. The Christchurch shooter killed 51 and injured 40 Muslim worshipers in New Zealand. The perpetrator was obsessed with the Great Replacement theory and believed in fighting for Christian supremacy.[18] He was particularly fond of Pope Urban II who led the First Crusade.[19] In 2011, Anders Behring Breivik placed a car bomb in Oslo, Norway that killed eight and injured over 200 people. He then drove to a summer camp where he killed another 69 civilians, mostly children. His manifesto described his motive as combating the Islamization of Europe. In the aftermath of the killings, he claimed to be a commander of a secret Christian miliary order that was plotting an anti-Muslim revolution.[20]

In 2015, in neighboring Sweden, a masked swordsman killed two in a school that he targeted for its high immigrant population.[21] In 2017, a mass shooting in the Islamic Cultural Center of Quebec City resulted in the loss of six lives. The perpetrator was not charged with terrorism.[22] In Ontario, Nathaniel Veltman drove his pickup truck and ran over a Pakistani family walking on a sidewalk, killing four, including the 74-year-old grandmother; only the 9-year-old son survived.[23] In Germany, on February 19, 2020, Tobias Rathjen, a far-right extremist, killed nine and severely injured five in a shooting spree targeting two shisha bars frequented by Muslims.[24] In Chapel Hill, North Carolina, three Muslim students were killed in their own home by Craig Stephen Hicks, their avowedly atheist neighbor in 2015.[25] In 2016, a local imam and his assistant were shot execution-style while on their way home from the Al-Furqan Jame Mosque in New York City.[26] In the 2017 Portland, Oregon train attack, a man went on an Islamophobic tirade after seeing a woman in hijab and stabbed two passengers to death.[27] These and numerous other acts of Islamophobic violence quite tangibly demonstrate the dangers of Islamophobia.

When societal discourse defines a religious or ethnic minority population as a "problem," calls for exclusion or genocide targeting that population gain traction. The "Jewish Problem" of the early twentieth century that led to Hitler's "Final Solution" has now been replaced by discussions of the "Muslim Problem."[28] The danger of labeling any minority group as a problem cannot be overstated.

Focusing on Only Muslim Terrorism

The Islamophobic stereotype that paints terrorism as a specifically Muslim problem causes a state's security apparatus to lose sight of the larger problem of far-right extremism. Indeed, acts of terror against civilian populations carried out by Muslims should be classified as one manifestation of global far-right extremism.

In a long-delayed 2020 report, the US Department of Homeland Security admitted that violent white supremacy constitutes the "most persistent and lethal threat in the homeland." Chad Wolf, the acting secretary said, "I am particularly concerned about white supremacist violent extremists who have been exceptionally lethal in their abhorrent, targeted attacks in recent years."[29]

The impunity with which white supremacist groups operate in the US is highlighted by the Capitol insurrection in which far-right rioters tried to forestall the peaceful transition of power from Donald Trump to Joe Biden. That there is relatively little outrage over the incident highlights societal tolerance for far-right vigilantism. Seeing a crowd that was mostly white and Christian, Capitol police pretty much just stood by while the mob broke into and ransacked Congress. One can only imagine the police reaction and societal backlash had Muslims invaded Congress to stop Donald Trump from assuming office in 2017. Islamophobia has created a distorted view of dangerous white extremists as "very fine people,"[30] while peaceful Muslims are seen as a potential danger.

Rightwing pundits and politicians obsess over the risk posed by potential terrorists who might enter the United States by hiding among Syrian and Central American refugees, even though the risk of a refugee becoming a "terrorist" (defined broadly) is a mere 0.00062 percent. Between 1975 and 2015, terrorists who entered the US as refugees have killed a total of three Americans.[31] In the meanwhile, in the United States there are 45,000 firearm-related,[32] 95,000 alcohol-related,[33] and 480,000 tobacco-related fatalities per year.[34] This is why irrational fears cause an immense waste of resources on nearly non-existent problems while overlooking far more pernicious social ills. A report from Brown University's Cost of War Project estimates the price tag of the 20-year War on Terror to be $8 trillion and its human toll to be 900,000 deaths.[35] Had that kind of financial investment been made in infrastructure, education, and healthcare, we would have seen lasting dividends in terms of social prosperity and longevity, while avoiding such needless loss of life.

Similarly, the federal air marshal program, whose purpose was to keep airline passengers safe from Muslim terrorists, merely squandered taxpayer funds. At its peak, it arrested four passengers in one year at a cost of $200 million per arrest.[36] There was never any proof that the program stopped any terrorist attack; after all, an air marshal would hardly be able to prevent a bomb being detonated on a plane. It also led to the tragic shooting death of an agitated Hispanic American passenger who decided to disembark a plane that was boarding passengers for a flight from Miami to Orlando.[37] But the program wasn't entirely without benefits, as it provided free customized travel to marshals pursuing personal sexual trysts.[38]

Similarly, focusing on how prevalent extremism might be in Muslim populations makes us lose focus on the fact that nearly one-third of Republicans believe that "true American patriots may have to resort to violence in order to save our country."[39] Considering that extremism, at least by the definition I have used throughout this book, is believing in the use of extrajudicial violence to achieve political aims, this alarming statistic should receive far more attention than it does.

The Formulation of Wrong Policies

Islamophobia hampers the ability of politicians and social policymakers to understand the root causes of extremism, terrorism, and violence. By blaming Islam or something innate to Muslims, it is easy to overlook the postcolonial social, political, and economic realities that fuel extremist ideologies. As such, the response to Muslim terrorism has almost invariably been through a security lens— more surveillance, more crackdowns, and more war. Yet, this is exactly what drives the violence in the first place.

Iraq was a country reduced to starvation through a brutal United Nations sanctions regime. Yet, it did not have a problem with Islamic extremism until the United States invaded the country under the false pretext that Saddam Hussein was harboring weapons of mass destruction. An ensuing power vacuum, the political marginalization of Sunni Arabs, and callous disregard for civilian life created an environment in which violent extremism flourished. In an occupied land where the only currency is force, the most brutal groups thrive. Entities like Daesh appeared seemingly out of nowhere. According to Noam Chomsky,

[William] Polk reveals [in his book *Violent Politics*] a pattern that has been replicated over and over. The invaders—perhaps professing the most benign motives— are naturally disliked by the population, who disobey them, at first in small ways, eliciting a forceful response, which increases opposition and support for resistance. The cycle of violence escalates until the invaders withdraw—or gain their ends by something that may approach genocide.[40]

It is not hard to see how western invasions of Muslim-majority countries fuel extremism. Imagine someone sitting by and watching on television how sanctions imposed by the UN Security Council starve as many as 576,000 of Iraqi children to death,[41] how American aircraft destroy civilian infrastructure such as power plants and transmission lines,[42] how US missiles strike Al Jazeera's offices in Baghdad so they can't cover the brutality of the invasion,[43] how American soldiers gang rape a 14-year-old Iraqi girl in ear-shot of her parents and her 6-year-old sister and then proceed to kill them,[44] how children as young as 14 are detained and subsequently held without trial at Guantanamo,[45] how prisoners in Abu Ghraib are subjected to torture and sexual abasement,[46] and how countless other atrocities are carried out with utter impunity. It can hardly be shocking that a small portion of the Muslim population would empathize with the plight of the invaded country and be moved to fight against whomever they perceive as the aggressor. This is not unlike the Jewish volunteers from all over the world who rushed to Israel to help during the 1967 Six-Day War.[47] The fact that some Muslims are drawn to "terrorist" organizations is more a symptom of the savage brutality repeatedly unleashed on the Middle East than anything innate to Islam or Muslims. Just imagine if the United States was in Iraq's place. Imagine that a consortium of Middle Eastern Muslim nations has invaded and occupied the country, has laid ruin to civilian infrastructure, and has displaced and killed what proportionately would be tens of millions of American civilians. To expect that this would not drive extremist ideology among Americans and indeed sympathetic people from other nations would be inconceivable. To debate what it is about Americans and Christians and their cultures and religious texts that leads to such extremism would be ridiculous. This is why the entire framework of the debate on Islamic extremism is fundamentally misguided and highly discriminatory. Accepting that western military interventions constitute one of the main causes of, not the solution to, Islamic extremism is key to reducing terrorism carried out by Muslims.

Meanwhile, the stereotype that Muslims want to live under a medieval autocracy has led to the erroneous policy of propping up brutal dictators and monarchs throughout the Muslim world, most notably in the Persian Gulf region. With western political backing, the Saudi monarchy has spread its virulent Wahhabi ideology, becoming the world's main exporter of Islamic extremism. In many countries, western-backed autocrats effectively buoy *takfiri* Salafi extremists who appeal to the disillusioned masses by offering what seems like the only alternative to the well-entrenched despots. A better way to combat extremism would be to stop supporting and arming regimes that oppress their citizenry and that contribute to regional and global instability.

Viewing Muslims as monolithic makes it hard for western policymakers to engage with Muslim societies. After all, in a world in which Islam equals terrorism, constructive engagement with any Muslim group can become politically unpalatable in the west. In the aftermath of the Iranian Revolution and the overthrow of the Shah, there was a struggle for power between different factions: clerics, liberal Islamists, liberals, and non-Islamic leftists. As Edward Said put it, "So strong was the ideological commitment to the idea of a monolithic and unchanging Islam that no note was taken of the political process *within* this or any other particular Islamic country."[48] Indeed, organizations as diverse as Hezbollah, the Muslim Brotherhood, the Taliban, and Daesh have vast differences in terms of politics, cultures, and ideology. They originate from different conflicts—the Israeli occupation of

Lebanon, European colonialism, the Soviet occupation of Afghanistan, and the American occupation of Iraq. They have inherently different visions for society and cater to quite distinct populations for their base of support. Lumping them all together as "Islamists" is hardly going to make for great policymaking. At the end, the word "Islamist" means nothing but "a group of Muslims we don't like," which begs the question, "Which is the group of Muslims we do like in the west?" This type of homogenized view of Muslims is what repeatedly paralyzes American foreign policy. When George Bush defeated Iraq, he found himself dealing with Sunnis (the bad guys who carried out 9/11 and who supported Saddam Hussein) and Shias (the ones supported by the bad guys in Iran). His administration became paralyzed, unable to engage constructively with the diverse factions within Iraqi society. The paralysis caused by his administration's Islamophobia is what contributed heavily to the vicious and unprecedented sectarian meltdown in Iraq. Similarly, when CIA agent Robert Ames gave a detailed and nuanced presentation to Ronald Reagan on ways to mediate between the Israelis and Palestinians, Raegan mused about the latter, "But they are all terrorists, aren't they?" His bigoted stereotyping paralyzed his ability to carry out diplomacy that would benefit the Israelis, Palestinians, and Americans, as well as the security of the entire world.[49]

There is also a myopic focus on the Quran and works of hadith and *fiqh* as constituting the causes of the problems seen in Muslim societies. In this vein, Sam Harris openly daydreams of having a group of atheists sit down to re-write the Quran to his liking.[50] Not only is this highly insulting, but it also would be a futile task—who would read an edited Quran after all? And why does he think that Muslims should follow the dictates of western white men? That such concepts are openly discussed by people claiming to be western intellectual elites only highlights the pervasiveness of neocolonial attitudes. Furthermore, even if one were to imagine a world with no Quran, no hadith, no *fiqh*, and indeed no Muslims, there would still be war, terrorism, domestic violence, and misogyny. To blame Islam for these problems is completely fallacious.

What we need instead is to embrace Islam as a living religion and to be open to the voices of the countless scholars who tirelessly strive to use *ijtihad* to understand how Islamic principles relate to the latest social and technological realities. Theological and intellectual battles will be fought along the way, as they have been for centuries, but at the end Islam has only survived the test of time because of its malleability not because of its rigidity. Furthermore, a more intricate understanding of Islam and Muslim societies would allow meaningful and supportive engagement with constructive elements within Muslim societies, as opposed to dismissing them all as monolithic radicals.

Seeing Muslims as Irrational Hampers Diplomacy

The stereotype of Muslims as distinctly irrational and inspired only by martyrdom flies in the face of any objective examination of Muslims, including Muslim extremists. Even Daesh was not run as an irrational suicidal cult, but rather as a well-calculated and media-savvy propaganda machine that exploited Sunni political grievances arising from the American occupation of Iraq and the civil war in Syria to create a pseudo-caliphate.

It is not uncommon to run across questions of rationality posed in the context of dealing with Muslims. Jon Alterman, who holds the Zbigniew Brzezinski Chair in Global Security and Geostrategy and who is director of the Middle East Program at the Center for Strategic and International Studies in Washington, asks the question, "Is Iran merely hostile, or is it irrational?"[51] Israel's former defense minister Moshe Ya'alon answers this question by declaring that Iran's government is a "messianic and apocalyptic regime." Benjamin Netanyahu, Israel's former prime minister, similarly assures us that, you can't "bet on their rationality."[52] The idea is that that nuclear weapons in the hands of the Iranians would be particularly dangerous because, as Muslims, they are innately suicidal and irrational and won't be deterred by sensible concepts like mutual assured destruction, which served well to avoid nuclear war with the Soviet Union.[53] The reality is that Iran did not survive eight years of war with Iraq, which was supported by the US and the Soviet Union and virtually all Arab and European states, as well as four decades of brutal western and United Nations sanctions through irrationality or a desire for self-destruction or mass suicide. Moreover, it is hard not to point out that there has only been one country in history whose level of disregard for civilian life allowed it to unleash nuclear bombs against civilian targets.

The problem is that policymakers and politicians waste time debating whether an adversary is rational or not as opposed to accepting them as rational humans and engaging with them constructively. As pointed out by Edward Said, the entire concept of the "Islamic mind (an inability to employ 'step-by-step thinking')... would be considered either racist or nonsensical if used to described any other language, religion, or ethnic grouping."[54] Somehow overt racism is distasteful except when dealing with Muslims. When Muslims are deemed irrational, then avenues for engagement become drastically limited. Daniel Pipes, an avid Islamophobe and self-proclaimed Middle East expert, explains,

> I would say Muslims only understand the language of force. Any peaceful dialogue with them is a sign of weakness. It's like: either you dominate them or they will dominate you. For them there is no in between and a peaceful co-existence with non-Muslims. It's our choice, what will it be?[55]

This mindset is distinctly dangerous because if Muslims are irrational and only understand force, then the only way to deal with them is through endless military conflict. This is where racism toes the line of genocide. The real problem is that this exact type of thinking has plagued American policymaking for decades.

It is worth noting that, according to Falguni Sheth, the accusation of irrationality is a central part of racist discourse. By dismissing a racialized group as "not fully rational, and therefore possibly not capable of utilizing their rights appropriately," the stage is set for "objective grounds for political inferiority."[56] As such, the curtailment of civil rights becomes justified. After all, no society allows its mad people the same rights and privileges as its sane ones. In *Killers of the Flower Moon*, David Grann describes how Native Americans were assigned white guardians to overlook their wealth, since they were seen as imbeciles. Historically, Catholics were seen as incapable of rational decision making, as they were mere automatons blindly carrying out the wishes of the Pope. Blacks and women were seen as lacking the rational faculties to pursue higher education or to vote. Today, it is Muslims who are seen as innately irrational. They are irrationally angry, irrationally violent, and irrationally intent on seeking martyrdom. At the very least, as pointed out by Edward Said, Muslims are "unwilling to accept reality, or at least that part of reality in which the West's superiority was demonstrable."[57]

The ascription of irrationality is dehumanizing. After all, what sets humans apart from lesser creatures is its purported sense of rationality. At the very least, irrational people are unpredictable and hence dangerous. No one would want a paranoid schizophrenic who is actively hallucinating sitting next to them on a flight, so why would they want an irrational Muslim who could, at any moment, choose martyrdom in that seat instead? It is imperative to recognize that allegations of irrationality are purely racist constructs and to call them out as overtly racist. Any credence given to debates over Muslim rationality must be seen as indicative of the pervasiveness of Islamophobic racism within society and in no way reflective of "the Muslim mind."

Islamophobic Racism Afflicts Political and Academic Circles

A major problem with racist stereotypes is that they form the backbone of a cultural narrative and leave hardly anyone unaffected, including academics and policymakers. Just as racism led to racial pseudosciences that squandered mental and financial resources on finding objective biological differences between blacks and whites, Islamophobia lends itself to academic inquiries that merely try to substantiate the stereotypes without ever discovering anything useful or real. Funding "armchair anthropologists" and "car-window sociologists" to help us understand Islam and Muslims will only lead to further indoctrination with what were, from the beginning, false premises. As Edward Said put it, "Today Islam is defined negatively as that with which the West is radically at odds, and this tension establishes a framework radically limiting knowledge of Islam."[58] So-called "experts" do not concentrate on actually understanding Islam but rather work "reactively in answer to what [the vested] interests seem to require of him or her."[59] As such, there is an inadequate quest for a nuanced and broad-based understanding of the diversity of Muslim thought, cultures, and societies, but rather "suitable Islamic topics are hewn out of an enormous mass of Islamic details, and these topics (extremism, violence, and so forth) define both Islam and the proper study of Islam so as to exclude everything not fitting neatly."[60]

In this milieu, one can hardly expect academic inquiries into Islam to bear much fruit other than to perpetuate a form of racism that, today, is only acceptable when dealing with Islam. "It is still possible to say things about Islam that are simply unacceptable for Judaism, for other Asians, or for blacks."[61] One can hardly imagine the type of expert advice that policymakers receive from academic experts of this sort. This is not to say that genuine academicians do not exist. Rather, their voices have historically been drowned out by the pseudoscientific study of Islam. This is compounded by the proliferation of self-proclaimed experts on Islam who are heavily favored by television and talk radio shows. How many of them know Arabic or Farsi or Pashto; how many have lived in the Islamic world; and how many have close familiarity with Muslim societies? Speaking authoritatively on Islam without having mastered classical Arabic is akin to claiming expertise on French literature without knowing a word of French. The only thing these experts have mastered is the spewing of rhetoric based on racist stereotypes.

More worrisome is that the political class in western countries are by no means immune to racialized stereotypes of Muslims. These are the people who make decisions regarding immigration, foreign relations, trade, and war. When such momentous decisions are based on erroneous and entirely racist assumptions, one can only imagine that decisions are made that do not serve overall societal interests. The likes of Donald Trump, Boris Johnson, and Viktor Orban hardly hide their Islamophobia, but the bigger danger might lie in the pervasive racism that is neatly covered up under a façade of liberalism and the preaching of tolerance. This is, in fact, a concern with all forms of racism. As Eduardo Bonilla-Silva, a professor at Duke University and author of *Racism Without Racists*, put it, "The main problem nowadays is not the folks with the hoods, but the folks dressed in suits... The more we assume that the problem of racism is limited to the Klan, the birthers, the tea party or to the Republican Party, the less we understand that racial domination is a collective process and we are all in this game."[62] Indeed, you hardly need overtly bigoted Islamophobes for commonplace Islamophobic stereotypes to have widespread social, political, and economic ramifications. It is perhaps ironic that the likes of Trump actually help bring attention to Islamophobia by their bluntly racist rhetoric. It takes a lot more to dissect out the type of Islamophobia that is rather subtle but quite pervasive.

Chapter 32

Towards a Brighter Future

Discussing the racial paradigms (ill-logic, so to speak) that underlie Islamophobia is not particularly useful if it is limited merely to a mental exercise dissecting out modes of thought that justify stereotypes about Islam or Muslims. Discussing the perverted logic of racism would be merely academic if racism is simply accepted as a rigid and immutable subconscious mental framework. The reality is that awareness of how racist ill-logic works is helpful for several reasons.

First, considering that racism is based on a system of pervasive stereotypes, promoting a conscious understanding that these stereotypes are not factual is a worthwhile endeavor. In this vein, seeing how groups such as Catholics, Jews, Japanese, and women were perceived in the past as opposed to how they are accepted now helps us see that groups that we perceive similarly now are likely to be seen differently in the future. This simple realization can help expedite the process through which conscious awareness of stereotypes helps undo them.

Second, stereotypes do not just exist. They are created and actively maintained through common discourse, media representations, "expert" opinion, discriminatory laws, and governmental policies. Having an active counternarrative and accepting Muslims as a population that is far from monolithic will help break this monopoly on racist stereotyping. The counternarrative, at the very least, will demote Islamophobic assumptions to the sphere of debatable opinions from its status as facts assumed to be universal truths. The ultimate goal should be for someone spewing anti-Muslim bigotry to just look ridiculous and not be granted any credence.

Third, conflicts should not be seen void of historical contexts. Western pundits and academics ought to be called out when they exercise hegemonic control over history itself. The image of an angry mass of Iranian revolutionaries chanting "death to America," when stripped of historical context, fuels the stereotype of Muslims as an innately and perpetually angry mob. Jimmy Carter dismissed their grievances as "ancient history."[1] Within this framework, the west is always the innocent victim being wronged. In the meanwhile, these angry protesters, stripped of any historical context, become perpetualized as the image of all Muslims from all times and in all places. Monopolizing history has led to a situation in which the geographic claims of European Jews based on ancient history are granted credence, whereas Palestinians who have resided in the same land much more recently are denied the right to return. Furthermore, it is often the same far-right Europeans who vilify Muslims as a backward people trapped in ancient history who are the ones celebrating ancient historical victories over Ottoman Turks.

Finally, the only realistic options facing us are confrontation, segregation, or accommodation. The confrontational approach sees the post-Cold War world as portrayed by Samuel Huntington's *The Clash of Civilizations*. This view entails endless and fundamentally unavoidable hostilities between clashing civilizations. Such a paradigm leaves either subjugation or genocide as the west's only options. Subjugation itself is not lasting, as it leads to renewed conflict when subjugated populations rebel. Segregation in today's interconnected world is increasingly difficult to maintain, often just serves as a proxy for subjugation, and at the end is a temporary solution that leads to confrontation and/or accommodation. Accommodation sees it possible for humans of different faiths, cultures, and ethnicities to co-exist. In reality, one can point to examples of confrontation (e.g., the War on Terror and laws restricting religious practice), segregation (e.g., strict border policies and ghettoization), and accommodation (e.g., social justice movements and anti-discrimination laws) all concomitantly at play.

I personally believe that both Islam and western liberalism have within them the innate capacity for coexistence, which is the only stable, viable, long-term solution. Within the context of Muslim societies, it is evident that Muslims have coexisted with other religious groups both as dominant and as minority communities for centuries. Other societies, meanwhile, must hone positive aspects of the liberal framework to foster a universal system of accommodation and tolerance.

Selected Bibliography

Aaronson, Trevor. *The Terror Factory: Inside the FBI's Manufactured War on Terrorism*. New York: Ig Publishing, 2014.

Alexander, Michelle. *The New Jim Crow: Mass Incarceration in the Age of Colorblindness*. New York: New Press, 2020.

Ali, Ayaan Hirsi. *Heretic: Why Islam Needs a Reformation Now*. New York: Harper, 2015.

Ali-Karamali, Sumbul. *Demystifying Shariah: What It Is, How It Works, and why It's not Taking Over Our Country*. Boston: Beacon Press, 2020.

Anderson, Carol. *The Second: Race and Guns in a Fatally Unequal America*. New York: Bloomsbury Publishing, 2021.

Aslan, Reza. *Zealot: The Life and Times of Jesus of Nazareth*. New York: Random House, 2013.

Dekker, Ted and Carl Medearis. *Tea with Hezbollah: Sitting at the Enemies' Table, Our Journey Through the Middle East*. New York: Doubleday Religion, 2010.

DiAngelo, Robin. *White Fragility: Why It's so Hard for White People to Talk About Racism*. Boston: Beacon Press, 2018.

Elnoury, Tamer and Kevin Maurer. *American Radical: Inside the World of an Undercover Muslim FBI Agent*. New York City: Dutton, 2017.

Fish, Stanley. *There's no such Thing as Free Speech... and it's a good thing too*. New York: Oxford University Press, 1994.

Foucault, Michel. *Discipline & Punish: The Birth of the Prison*. Translated by Alan Sheridan. New York: Random House, Inc., 1995.

Foucault, Michel. *The History of Sexuality: Volume 1: An Introduction*. Translated by Robert Hurley. New York: Vintage Books, 1990.

Grann, David. *Killers of the Flower Moon: The Osage Murders and the Birth of the FBI*. New York: Doubleday, 2017.

Herman, Edward and Noam Chomsky. *Manufacturing Consent: The Political Economy of the Mass Media*. New York: Pantheon, 2002.

Huntington, Samuel. *The Clash of Civilizations and the Remaking of World Order*. New York: Simon & Schuster Touchstone, 1996.

Kendi, Ibram X. *How to Be an Antiracist*. New York: One World, 2019.

Khan, Maryam, editor. *It's Not About the Burqa*. London: Picador, 2020.

Khomeini, Ayatollah Ruhollah. *Tahrir al-Wasilah*. Translated by Sayyid Muhammad Baqir Musavi Hamedani. Isfahan: Dar ul-Elm. Published digitally by Ghaemiyeh.

Perkins, John. *The New Confessions of an Economic Hit Man*. Oakland, California: Berrett-Koehler Publishers, Inc, 2016.

Rothstein, Richard. *The Color of Law: A Forgotten History of How Our Government Segregated America*. New York: Liveright Publishing Corporation, 2017.

Rushdie, Salman. *The Satanic Verses*. New York: Picador, 1988.

Said, Edward W. *Covering Islam*. New York: Penguin Vintage Books, 1997.

Said, Edward W. *Orientalism*. United Kingdom: Penguin Random House, 2003.

Shaheen, Jack G. *Reel Bad Arabs: How Hollywood Vilifies a People*. Northampton, Massachusetts: Olive Branch Press, 2009.

Sheth, Falguni A. *Toward a Political Philosophy of Race*. Albany: State University of New York Press, 2009.

Vance, J.D. *Hillbilly Elegy: A Memoir of a Family and Culture in Crisis*. New York: Harper, 2016.

Wilkerson, Isabel. *Caste: The Origins of Our Discontents*. New York: Random House, 2020.

Zakaria, Rafia. *Against White Feminism: Notes on Disruption*. New York: W. W. Norton & Company, 2021.

Endnotes

Introduction

1. W. E. Burghardt DuBois, *Soul of Black Folk* (Electronic Text Center, University of Virginia Library, 1996), 107.
   http://etext.lib.virginia.edu/toc/modeng/public/DubSoul.html
2. Aya Batrawy, Paisley Dodds and Lori Hinnant, "'Islam for Dummies': IS recruits have poor grasp of faith," *AP News*, August 15, 2016.
   https://apnews.com/article/lifestyle-middle-east-africa-europe-religion-9f94ff7f1e294118956b049a51548b33

Chapter 1
Islamophobia as a Form of Racism

1. Eduardo Bonilla-Sivla, *Racism without Racists: Color-Blind Racism and the Persistence of Racial Inequality in America*, Sixth Edition, (Lanham: Rowman & Littlefield Publishers, 2021).
2. Robin DiAngelo, *White Fragility*, 123-4.
3. Robin DiAngelo, *White Fragility*, 112.
4. Haroon Moghul, "Flying While Muslim: The unapologetic racial profiling of Muslims has become America's new normal," *Quartz*, April 20, 2016.
   https://qz.com/665317
5. Falguni A. Sheth, *Toward a Political Philosophy of Race*, 22.
6. "Racism, Law, & Politics (Race Part 1)," Philosophy Tube, January 29, 2016.
   https://www.youtube.com/watch?v=BGIetWAds6A&t=488s
7. Quran 49:13.
8. Falguni A. Sheth, *Toward a Political Philosophy of Race*, 23.
9. Ibid., 25
10. Ibid., 45.
11. Ibid., 113.
12. Ibid., 117.
13. Crenshaw, Kimberle, "Demarginalizing the Intersection of Race and Sex: A Black Feminist Critique of Antidiscrimination Doctrine, Feminist

Theory and Antiracist Politics," *University of Chicago Legal Forum* 1989, no. 1 (1989): 139-167. https://chicagounbound.uchicago.edu/cgi/viewcontent.cgi?article=105 2&context=uclf

14. "Kimberlé Crenshaw at Ted + Animation," Kate Anderson, May 17, 2017. https://www.youtube.com/watch?v=JRci2V8PxW4

15. Salim Al-Hassani, "Baghdad Clock in Aachen: Harun al Rashid's Gift to Charlemagne," Muslim Heritage: Discover the golden age of Muslim civilisation, May 7, 2021. https://muslimheritage.com/baghdad-clock/

16. Simon Sebag Montefiore, *Jerusalem: The Biography* (United States: Vintage Books, 2011), 198. https://books.google.com/books/about/Jerusalem.html?id=KC4xXItRkwC

17. Rachel Moss, "Saracen Go Home: Modern Islamophobia in Medieval Context," History at Northampton, April 1, 2019. https://historyatnorthampton.com/2019/04/01/saracen-go-homemodern-islamophobia-in-medieval-context/

18. David L. Johnston, "American Evangelical Islamophobia: A History of Continuity with a Hope for Change," Fuller Studio, accessed August 3, 2022. https://fullerstudio.fuller.edu/american-evangelical-islamophobia-history-continuity-hope-change/

19. Edward W. Said, *Orientalism*, 60.

20 Denise Spellberg, *Thomas Jefferson's Qur'an: Islam and the Founders* (New York: Vintage Books, 2014).

21 Peter Manseau, "Why Thomas Jefferson Owned a Qur'an," *Smithsonian Magazine*, January 31, 2018. https://www.smithsonianmag.com/smithsonian-institution/why-thomas-jefferson-owned-qur-1-180967997/

22. Edward W. Said, *Orientalism*, 39.

23. Ibid., 40.

24. Ibid., 42.

25. Ibid., 40.

26. Ibid., 43.

27. Ibid., 46.

28. Ibid., 7.

29. H.R. 40, "Naturalization Bill," March 4, 1790. https://www.visitthecapitol.gov/exhibitions/artifact/h-r-40-naturalization-bill-march-4-1790

30. *In re Ross*, 140 U.S. 453 (1891).

https://supreme.justia.com/cases/federal/us/140/453/

31. Khaled A. Beydoun, "America banned Muslims long before Donald Trump," *The Washington Post*, August 18, 2016.
https://www.washingtonpost.com/opinions/trumps-anti-muslim-stance-echoes-a-us-law-from-the-1700s/2016/08/18/6da7b486-6585-11e6-8b27-bb8ba39497a2_story.html

32. Taylor Eubanks, "The Global Racialization of Muslims: An Interview with Associate Professor Saher Selod," Simmons University Faculty Spotlight, April 1, 2021.
https://www.simmons.edu/news/global-racialization-muslims-interview-associate-professor-saher-selod

33. Wheeler, Nicholas, "Chechnya: Anti-Terrorist Operation or Human Rights Disaster?" Wilson Center, accessed April 30, 2022.
https://www.wilsoncenter.org/publication/chechnya-anti-terrorist-operation-or-human-rights-disaster

34. Kristian Petersen, "How 9/11 helped China wage its own false 'war on terror,'" *Al Jazeera*, September 8, 2021.
https://www.aljazeera.com/opinions/2021/9/8/how-9-11-helped-china-wage-its-own-false-war-on

35. Sahar Khan, "The Danger of Linking the Rohingya Crisis to Terrorism," *The Diplomat*, October 13, 2017.
https://thediplomat.com/2017/10/the-danger-of-linking-the-rohingya-crisis-to-terrorism/

36. Andrea Malji and Syed Tahseen Raza, "The Securitization of Love Jihad," *Religions* 12, no. 12 (2021): 1074.
https://doi.org/10.3390/rel12121074

37. Jack G. Shaheen, *Reel Bad Arabs*, 56-60.

38. Edward Said, *Covering Islam*, 101.

39. Rafia Zakaria, *Against White Feminism*, 7.

40. YouGov, February 3-6, 2017.
https://big.assets.huffingtonpost.com/tabsHPIslam20170206.pdf

41. Edward Said, *Covering Islam*, 77.

42. Craig Considine, "The Racialization of Islam in the United States: Islamophobia, Hate Crimes, and 'Flying while Brown,'" *Religions* 8, no. 9 (2017): 165.
https://doi.org/10.3390/rel8090165

43. Jack G. Shaheen, *Reel Bad Arabs*, 25.

44. Ibid., 28-30.

45. Ibid., 34-40.

46. Ibid., 37.

47. Marilyn Elias, "Sikh Temple Killer Wade Michael Page Radicalized in Army," Southern Poverty Law Center, November 11, 2012.

https://www.splcenter.org/fighting-hate/intelligence-report/2012/sikh-temple-killer-wade-michael-page-radicalized-army

48. The Sikh Coalition, Fact Sheet on Post-9/11 Discrimination and Violence against Sikh Americans," accessed August 3, 2022.
https://www.sikhcoalition.org/images/documents/fact%20sheet%20o n%20hate%20against%20sikhs%20in%20america%20post%209-11%201.pdf

Chapter 2
Why Are All Terrorists Muslim?

1. European Network Against Racism, "Frequently Asked Questions," accessed March 10, 2022.
https://www.enar-eu.org/Frequently-asked-questions-1160

2. Mark Potokm, "Remembering Oklahoma," *Intelligence Report*, June 10, 2015.
https://www.splcenter.org/fighting-hate/intelligence-report/2015/remembering-oklahoma

3. Paul Queary, "Government Defends Man's Detainment in Bombing Investigation," *AP News*, November 10, 1995.
https://apnews.com/article/279cb6a9d08c2ea097d1e3d65a2d8fbc

4. Keon West and Joda Lloyd, "The role of labelling bias in the portrayals of acts of 'terrorism': representations of Muslims versus non-Muslims," *Journal of Muslim Minority Affairs* 37, no. 2 (2017): 211-222.
https://doi.org/10.1080/13602004.2017.1345103

5. Connor Huff and Joshua D. Kertzer, "How the Public Defines Terrorism," *American Journal of Political Science* 62, no. 1 (2018): 55-71.
https://www.jstor.org/stable/26598750

6. Shmuel Bar, "The Religious Sources of Islamic Terrorism," *Policy Review* 125 (2004, June/July): 27-37.
https://www.aclu.org/sites/default/files/field_document/ACLURM00 1331.pdf

7. David C. Henley, "9/11 hijackers visits to Nevada remain a mystery," *The Record-Courier*, September 16, 2020.
https://www.recordcourier.com/news/2020/sep/16/david-c-henley-911-hijackers-visits-to-nevada-rema/

8. Edward Said, *Covering Islam*, 53-54.

9. Samuel R. Sommers, Evan P. Apfelbaum, Kristin N. Dukes, Negin Toosi and Elsie J. Wang, "Race and Media Coverage of Hurricane Katrina: Analysis, Implications, and Future Research Questions," *Analyses of Social Issues and Public Policy* 6, no. 1 (2006): 39-55.

https://spssi.onlinelibrary.wiley.com/doi/epdf/10.1111/j.1530-2415.2006.00103.x

10.   Craig Considine, "Why White Men Are 'Gunmen' and Muslim Men Are 'Terrorists,'" *HuffPost*, December 3, 2015, updated December 2, 2016. https://www.huffpost.com/entry/why-white-men-are-gunmen-_b_8704740

11.   Erin M. Kearns, Allison E. Beatus and Anthony F. Lemieux, "Why Do Some Terrorist Attacks Receive More Media Attention Than Others?" *Justice Quarterly* 36, no. 6 (2019): 985-1022. https://doi.org/10.1080/07418825.2018.1524507 https://www.erinmkearns.com/uploads/2/4/5/5/24559611/9._kearns_betus___lemieux_2019.jq.pdf

12.   "Yearly Worldwide Shark Attack Summary: The ISAF 2021 shark attack report," accessed March 10, 1022. https://www.floridamuseum.ufl.edu/shark-attacks/yearly-worldwide-summary/

13.   Boris Worm, Brendal Davis, Lisa Kettemer, Christine A. Ward-Paige, Demian Chapman, Michael R. Heithaus, Steven T. Kessel and Samuel H. Gruber, "Global catches, exploitation rates, and rebuilding options for sharks," *Marine Policy* 40 (2013):194-204. doi: 10.1016/j.marpol.2012.12.034

14.   Leila Shahid, "The Sabra and Shatila Massacres: Eye-Witness Reports," *Journal of Palestine Studies* 32, no. 1 (2002): 36-58. doi: 10.1525/jps.2002.32.1.36 https://palestinalibre.org/upload/Sabra-Chatila-Eye-Witness-Reports.pdf

15.   FBI, "Terrorism," accessed on March 10, 2022. https://www.fbi.gov/investigate/terrorism

16.   Alex P. Schmid, *The Routledge Handbook of Terrorism Research* (Abingdon, Oxon: Routledge, 2011), 39-40. https://books.google.com/books?id=_PXpFxKRsHgC&pg

17.   "Noam Chomsky: US is world's biggest terrorist," Global Conversation, April 17, 2015. https://www.youtube.com/watch?v=vRbnPA3fd5U&t=570s

18.   Edward S. Herman, "US Sponsorship of International Terrorism: An Overview," *Crime and Social Justice* 27/28 (1987): 1-31. https://www.jstor.org/stable/29766326

19.   U.S. Agency for International Development, "Uganda—Complex Emergency," September 15, 2006. https://web.archive.org/web/20111030105505/http://www.usaid.gov/our_work/humanitarian_assistance/disaster_assistance/countries/uganda/fy2006/uganda_ce_sr03_09-15-2006.pdf

20. "Full Text of Eric Rudolph's Confession," *NPR*, April 14, 2005.
    https://www.npr.org/templates/story/story.php?storyId=4600480
21. "Views of Violence," *Gallup*, accessed March 10, 2022.
    https://news.gallup.com/poll/157067/views-violence.aspx
22. Baruch Goldstein, "Israel Needs No New Enemy State at Its Border,"
    The New York Times, July 9, 1981.
    https://www.nytimes.com/1981/07/09/opinion/l-israel-needs-no-
    new-enemy-state-at-its-border-187347.html
23. "Price Tag and Extremist Attacks in Israel," Anti-Defamation League,
    accessed March 20, 2022.
    https://www.adl.org/resources/backgrounders/price-tag-and-
    extremist-attacks-in-israel
24. Joseph Rhee, Tahman Bradley and Brian Ross, "U.S. Military Weapons
    Inscribed With Secret 'Jesus' Bible Codes," *ABC News*, January 15, 2020.
    https://abcnews.go.com/Blotter/us-military-weapons-inscribed-secret-
    jesus-bible-codes/story?id=9575794
25. Iain Overton, "How a 13-year-old boy became the first modern suicide
    bomber," *GQ*, April 13, 2019.
    https://www.gq-magazine.co.uk/article/the-price-of-paradise-iain-
    overton-extract
26. "A timeline of disaster and displacement for Iraqi Christians," *AP News*,
    March 5, 2021.
    https://apnews.com/article/middle-east-islamic-state-group-saddam-
    hussein-baghdad-iraq-296b5588995cf7be62b49619bf1a7bb6
27. Abubakar Abid, Maheen Farooqi and James Zou, "Persistent Anti-
    Muslim Bias in Large Language Models," *Arxiv*, January 18, 2021.
    https://doi.org/10.48550/arXiv.2101.05783
28. "Chomsky says US is world's biggest terrorist," *Euronews*, April 17,
    2015.
    https://www.euronews.com/2015/04/17/chomsky-says-us-is-world-s-
    biggest-terrorist
29. Quran 5:33.
30. *Jami` at-Tirmidhi*, hadith #1663.
    https://sunnah.com/tirmidhi:1663
31. *Jami` at-Tirmidhi*, hadith #2562.
    https://sunnah.com/tirmidhi:2562
32. Shmuel Bar, "The Religious Sources of Islamic Terrorism," *Policy
    Review* 125 (2004, June/July): 27-37.
    https://www.aclu.org/sites/default/files/field_document/ACLURM00
    1331.pdf

33. Muhammad H. Hassan, "Mobilization of Muslims for Jihad: Insights from the Past and Their Relevance Today," *Counter Terrorist Trends and Analyses* 5, no. 8 (2013): 10–15. http://www.jstor.org/stable/26351173.

34. Aaron Klein, "Hillary Clinton snagged in Benghazi cover-up," *Socio-Political-Journal*, March 13, 2013. https://www.socio-political-journal.com/2013/03/?m=1

35. Andrew P. Napolitano, "Hillary's secret war," *Washington Times*, July 1, 2015. https://www.washingtontimes.com/news/2015/jul/1/andrew-napolitano-hillarys-secret-war/

Chapter 3
Is Islam a Religion of Peace or War?

1.   Quran 2:190.
2.   Quran 8:65.
3.   Quran 9:5.
4.   Quran 2:191.
5.   Quran 2:190-1.
6.   Quran 2:192.
7.   Quran 5:45.
8.   Quran 9:12.
9.   Quran 8:39. A similarly phrased verse can be found in Quran 2:193.
10. *Sahih Bukhari*, hadith #4513. https://sunnah.com/bukhari:4513
11. *Sahih Bukhari*, hadith #7095. https://sunnah.com/bukhari:7095
12. *Tafsir Nur al-Thaqalayn*, verse 8:39.
13. Rudolph Ware, "Timbuktu: The Ink of Scholars and the Blood of Martyrs," *HuffPost*, August 31, 2012. https://www.huffpost.com/entry/timbuktu-the-ink-of-schol_b_1847749
14. Quran 2:143.
15. Adam Blenkov, "Boris Johnson said that Islamophobia is a 'natural reaction' to Islam and that 'Islam is the problem,'" *Business Insider*, November 27, 2019. https://www.businessinsider.com/boris-johnson-islam-is-the-problem-and-islamophobia-is-a-natural-reaction-2018-8
16. Todd Hertz, "Riots, Condemnation, Fatwa, and Apology Follow Falwell's CBS Comments," *Christianity Today*, October 1, 2002.

https://www.christianitytoday.com/ct/2002/octoberweb-only/10-14-41.0.html

17. Deuteronomy 20:16-18, New International Version.
18. 1 Samuel 15:3, New International Version.
19. Deuteronomy 20:13-14, New International Version.
20. Psalm 137:9, New International Version.
21. Revelation 21:8, New International Version.
22. Matthew 7:14, New Revised Standard Version.
23. Matthew 10:34-36, New International Version.
24. Luke 14:26, English Standard Version.
25. Andrew Brown, "Bush, Gog and Magog," *The Guardian*, August 10, 2009.
    https://www.theguardian.com/commentisfree/andrewbrown/2009/aug/10/religion-george-bush
26. Quran 3:7.
27. Quran 5:2.
28. Quran 2:158.
29. Quran 2:191.
30. Quran 4:34.
31. Quran 2:26.
32. Quran 5:6.
33. Muhammad Baqir Majlisi, *Haqq al-Yaqin* (Shirazi Bazar, Iran: Entesharat Elmiyyeh Eslamiyyeh), 225.
34. Sumbul Ali-Karamali, *Demystifying Shariah*, 154.
35. "Catechism of the Catholic Church," 82nd Catechism.
    http://www.catholic-catechism.com/ccc_81-82.htm
36. Luke 10:29-37, New International Version.
37. Bayhaqi, *Sunan al-Kubra*, hadith #20571.
    http://islamport.com/w/mtn/Web/2996/25051.htm
38. Quran 2:177.
39. Quran 3:37.
40. Quran 5:66.
41. Quran 5:69.
42. Quran 5:45.
43. Quran 2:237.
44. Quran 2:280.
45. Quran 5:8.
46. Quran 5:2.
47. Drake Baer, "A software engineer analyzed the Quran and the Bible to see which was more violent — here's what he found," *Business Insider*, February 10, 2016.

https://www.businessinsider.com/quran-and-bible-which-is-more-violent-2016-2

48. Barbara B. Hagerty, "Is The Bible More Violent Than The Quran?" *NPR*, March 18, 2010.
https://www.npr.org/templates/story/story.php?storyId=124494788

49. Garrett M. Graff, "After 9/11, the U.S. Got Almost Everything Wrong," *The Atlantic*, September 8, 2021.
https://www.theatlantic.com/ideas/archive/2021/09/after-911-everything-wrong-war-terror/620008/

50. Jim Hoagi, "Figures in a Persian Carpet," *The Washington Post*, May 1, 1988.
https://www.washingtonpost.com/archive/entertainment/books/1988/05/01/figures-in-a-persian-carpet/e94764aa-4335-49f7-bde8-9f51ba821360/

51. Bernard Lewis, "The Roots of Muslim Rage," *The Atlantic*, September 1, 1990.
https://www.theatlantic.com/magazine/archive/1990/09/the-roots-of-muslim-rage/304643/

52. Alison Lovell, "An Outsider's Guide to Iranian Hospitality," accessed March 10, 2022.
https://iran.1stquest.com/blog/guide-to-iranian-hospitality/

53. Richard Gunderman, "I'm a US doctor just back from Sudan, where hospitality from Muslims greeted me everywhere," *The Conversation*, January 30, 2017.
https://theconversation.com/im-a-us-doctor-just-back-from-sudan-where-hospitality-from-muslims-greeted-me-everywhere-72158

54. "Mehdi Hasan | Islam Is A Peaceful Religion," Oxford Union, July 3, 2013.
https://www.youtube.com/watch?v=Jy9tNyp03M0&t=684s

55. "Islam is a Religion of Peace," Intelligence Squared Debates, July 20, 2011.
https://www.youtube.com/watch?v=rh34Xsq7D_A

56. "Christopher Hitchens and Tariq Ramadan Debate: Is Islam a Religion of Peace?" 92nd Street Y, February 4, 2013.
https://www.youtube.com/watch?v=mMraxhd9Z9Q&t=16s

Chapter 4
Why Don't Muslims Condemn Terrorism?

1. Scroll Staff, "'Let's be honest here, Islam has a problem,' claims Indian-American politician Bobby Jindal," *Scroll.in*, January 16, 2015.

https://scroll.in/article/700796

2. B. A. Robinson, "Statements by Muslim individuals and groups condemning terrorist attacks," Ontario Consultants on Religious Tolerance, accessed March 10, 2022.
    http://www.religioustolerance.org/islfatwa.htm

3. "Candle Power: Iran mourns America's dead," *Time Europe*, September 18, 2001.
    https://web.archive.org/web/20101115094604/http://www.time.com/time/europe/photoessays/vigil/2.html

4. James Bennet, "A Day of Terror: The Israelis; Spilled Blood Is Seen as Bond That Draws 2 Nations Closer," *The New York Times*, September 12, 2001.
    https://www.nytimes.com/2001/09/12/us/day-terror-israelis-spilled-blood-seen-bond-that-draws-2-nations-closer.html

5. Imtiyaz Delawala, "What ABC News Footage Shows of 9/11 Celebrations," *ABC News*, December 4, 2015.
    https://abcnews.go.com/Politics/abc-news-footage-shows-911-celebrations/story?id=35534125

6. MEE Staff, "French-Algerian police officer killed in Charlie Hebdo attacks buried," *Middle East Eye*, February 13, 2015.
    https://www.middleeasteye.net/news/french-algerian-police-officer-killed-charlie-hebdo-attacks-buried

7. Anne Penketh, "Policeman Ahmed Merabet mourned after death in Charlie Hebdo attack," *The Guardian*, January 8, 2015.
    https://www.theguardian.com/world/2015/jan/08/ahmed-merabet-mourned-charlie-hebdo-paris-attack

8. Associated Press, "Muslims hailed for protecting Christians during terror attack on Kenyan bus," *The Guardian*, December 22, 2015.
    https://www.theguardian.com/world/2015/dec/22/kenya-al-shabaab-attack-muslims-protect-christians-mandera

9. "Kenyan Muslims shield Christians in Mandera bus attack," *BBC News*, December 21, 2015.
    https://www.bbc.com/news/world-africa-35151967

10. Khaled Diab, "Egypt's Christians in the cross-hairs," *Al Jazeera*, December 14, 2016.
    https://www.aljazeera.com/opinions/2016/12/14/egypts-christians-in-the-cross-hairs

11. Aijaz Ansari, "Mumbai cemetery won't bury gunmen," *The San Diego Union-Tribune*, December 1, 2018.
    https://www.sandiegouniontribune.com/sdut-india-shooting-no-burial-120108-2008dec01-story.html

12. Jack Hunter, "Who's a terrorist? It starts with assigning collective guilt," *Austin American-Statesman*, September 4, 2016. https://www.statesman.com/story/news/2016/09/04/hunter-whos-a-terrorist-it-starts-with-assigning-collective-guilt/9985574007/

13. Antiwar.com, "WikiLeaks reveals Atrocities by US forces," *Daily Mirror*, September 1, 2011. https://web.archive.org/web/20111101120621/http://print.dailymirro r.lk/news/front-page-news/54943.html

14. Dan Collyns, "Letters support claim Assange would not face death penalty," *The Guardian*, April 15, 2019. https://www.theguardian.com/media/2019/apr/15/letters-support-claim-julian-assange-would-not-be-extradited-to-us

15. Associated Press, "Troops cleared in Ishaqi deaths," *Deseret News*, June 3, 2006. https://www.deseret.com/2006/6/3/19956791/troops-cleared-in-ishaqi-deaths

16. Martin Asser, "What happened at Haditha?" *BBC News*, March 10, 2008. http://news.bbc.co.uk/2/hi/middle_east/5033648.stm

17. Jeanne Meserve, Richard Quest, Nic Robertson and Elise Labott, "Source: Terror suspect's father tried to warn authorities," *CNN*, December 27, 2009. http://www.cnn.com/2009/CRIME/12/26/airline.attack/index.html

18. Paul Harris, "The ex-FBI informant with a change of heart: 'There is no real hunt. It's fixed,'" *The Guardian*, March 20, 2012. https://www.theguardian.com/world/2012/mar/20/fbi-informant

19. Leela Jacinto, "Left in limbo by the state, Paris attacks informant awaits new identity," *France 24*, December 2, 2016. https://www.france24.com/en/20161202-france-paris-attacks-informant-witness-sonia-temoine-andrieux

20. "Charleston shooting: Dylann Roof named as suspect," *BBC News*, June 19, 2015. https://www.bbc.com/news/world-us-canada-33189325

21. Flavia Cresswel, "Several charges dropped against Nigerians in murder case," *The Italian Insider*, June 7, 2018. http://www.italianinsider.it/?q=node/6863

22. "Italy: failed Northern League candidate held over migrant shootings," *The Guardian*, February 3, 2018. https://www.theguardian.com/world/2018/feb/03/driver-opens-fire-african-migrants-italian-city-macerata

23. Jamie Wilson, "US admits using white phosphorus in Falluja," *The Guardian*, November 16, 2005.

https://www.theguardian.com/world/2005/nov/16/iraq.usa#
24. Ruth Alexander and Hannah Moore, "Are most victims of terrorism Muslim?" *BBC News*, January 20, 2015.
    https://www.bbc.com/news/magazine-30883058
25. W. E. Burghardt DuBois, *Soul of Black Folk* (Electronic Text Center, University of Virginia Library, 1996), 1-2.
    http://etext.lib.virginia.edu/toc/modeng/public/DubSoul.html
26. Ibid., 10-11.
27. Ezra Klein and Max Fisher, "Ben Carson's bizarre comments about Muslims and the Constitution, explained," *VOX*, September 21, 2015.
    https://www.vox.com/2015/9/21/9362989
28. Kelly Cohen, "Bobby Jindal: 'Let's be honest here, Islam has a problem,'" *Washington Examiner*, January 16, 2015.
    https://www.washingtonexaminer.com/bobby-jindal-lets-be-honest-here-islam-has-a-problem
29. Lionel Du Cane, "Boris Johnson: 'Islam is The Problem,' Islamophobia a 'Natural Reaction' to Islam," *National File*, December 16, 2019.
    https://nationalfile.com/boris-johnson-islam-is-the-problem-islamophobia-a-natural-reaction-to-islam/
30. Greg Heffer, "Tory Islamophobia inquiry: Boris Johnson says he would not use 'offending language' again now he's PM," *Sky News*, May 25, 2021.
    https://news.sky.com/story/tory-islamophobia-inquiry-boris-johnson-says-he-would-not-use-offending-language-again-now-hes-pm-12316699

Chapter 5
Racial Profiling of Muslims

1. Sabrina Siddiqui, "Americans' Attitudes Toward Muslims And Arabs Are Getting Worse, Poll Finds," *HuffPost*, July 29, 2014.
   https://www.huffpost.com/entry/arab-muslim-poll_n_5628919
2. Christina Carrega, "Four Brooklyn men claim they were kicked off flight for looking too Muslim in lawsuit," *Daily News*, January 18, 2016.
   https://www.nydailynews.com/new-york/lawsuit-claims-flight-ejected-men-muslim-article-1.2499843
3. Liam Stack, "College Student Is Removed From Flight After Speaking Arabic on Plane," *New York Times*, April 17, 2016.
   https://www.nytimes.com/2016/04/17/us/student-speaking-arabic-removed-southwest-airlines-plane.html

4. Associated Press, "2 Muslim men say American Airlines canceled flight after crew 'didn't feel comfortable,'" *USA Today*, September 21, 2019. https://www.usatoday.com/story/travel/news/2019/09/20/two-muslim-men-texas-say-american-airlines-racially-profiled-them/2395830001/

5. Chary A. Chandrasekhar, "Flying While Brown: Federal Civil Rights Remedies to Post-9/11 Airline Racial Profiling of South Asians," *Asian Law Journal* 10 (2003): 215-252. doi:10.15779/Z381Z9Q

6. Mark Hicks, "Mich. man says he was kicked off bus for speaking Arabic," *The Detroit News*, December 12, 2018. https://www.detroitnews.com/story/news/local/michigan/2018/12/12/man-civil-rights-complaint-kicked-off-bus-arabic/2296253002/

7. Tom Dart, "'My crime was wearing a turban': Sikh man arrested on US bus pursues justice," *The Guardian*, April 29, 2016. https://www.theguardian.com/us-news/2016/apr/29/sikh-man-arrested-bus-terrorist-bomb-islamophobia

8. "Muslim Americans: No Signs of Growth in Alienation or Support for Extremism," Pew Research Center, August 30, 2011. https://www.pewresearch.org/politics/2011/08/30/section-1-a-demographic-portrait-of-muslim-americans/

9. Bart Schuurman, Peter Grol and Scott Flower, "Converts and Islamist Terrorism: An Introduction," *The International Centre for Counter-Terrorism – The Hague* 7, no. 3 (2016). doi:10.19165/2016.2.03 https://www.icct.nl/app/uploads/2016/06/ICCT-Schuurman-Grol-Flower-Converts-June-2016.pdf

10. Peter Bergen and David Sterman, "Terrorism in America After 9/11," *New America*, September 10, 2021. https://www.newamerica.org/international-security/reports/terrorism-in-america/who-are-the-terrorists

11. F. Brinley Bruton, Lawahez Jabari and Paul Goldman, "Holy Land Christians feel abandoned by U.S. evangelicals," *NBC News*, May 5, 2018. https://www.nbcnews.com/news/world/holy-land-christians-feel-abandoned-u-s-evangelicals-n867371

12. Steven Erlanger, "Spitting incident fuels debate on intolerance," *The New York Times*, October 19, 2004. https://www.nytimes.com/2004/10/19/world/africa/spitting-incident-fuels-debate-on-intolerance.html

13. Harriet Sherwood, "Christians in Jerusalem's Old City 'under threat' from settlers," *The Guardian*, May 1, 2018.

https://www.theguardian.com/world/2018/may/01/christians-in-jerusalems-old-city-under-threat-from-settlers

14. "Nation of Islam," Southern Poverty Law Center, accessed July 31, 2022. https://www.splcenter.org/fighting-hate/extremist-files/group/nation-islam

15. Amber Phillips, "Donald Trump calls profiling Muslims 'common sense,'" *The Washington Post*, June 19, 2016. https://www.washingtonpost.com/news/post-politics/wp/2016/06/19/donald-trump-calls-profiling-muslims-common-sense/

16. Louis Nelson, "Trump's Muslim registry wouldn't be illegal, constitutional law experts say," *Politico*, November 17, 2016. https://www.politico.com/story/2016/11/donald-trump-muslim-registry-constitution-231527

17. Jessica Taylor, "Trump Calls For 'Total And Complete Shutdown Of Muslims Entering' U.S.," *NPR*, December 7, 2015. https://www.npr.org/2015/12/07/458836388/trump-calls-for-total-and-complete-shutdown-of-muslims-entering-u-s

18. Alex Horton, "Trump said to study General Pershing. Here's what the president got wrong," *The Washington Post*, August 18, 2017. https://www.washingtonpost.com/news/retropolis/wp/2017/08/18/after-barcelona-attack-trump-said-to-study-general-pershing-heres-what-the-president-got-wrong/

19. Peter Wade, "Trump Thinks the United States Needs to Profile Muslims," *Esquire*, June 19, 2016. https://www.esquire.com/news-politics/news/a45985/trump-profile-muslims/

20. Nadeem Muaddi, "The Bush-era Muslim registry failed. Yet the US could be trying it again," *CNN*, December 22, 2016. https://www.cnn.com/2016/11/18/politics/nseers-muslim-database-qa-trnd/index.html

21. Tessa Stuart, "Why Trump Calls for Racial Profiling After Attacks," *Rolling Stone*, September 19, 2016. https://www.rollingstone.com/politics/politics-features/why-trump-calls-for-racial-profiling-after-attacks-103371/

22. Jan Ransom, "Trump Will Not Apologize for Calling for Death Penalty Over Central Park Five," *The New York Times*, June 18, 2019. https://www.nytimes.com/2019/06/18/nyregion/central-park-five-trump.html

23. Joe Parkin Daniels, "Colombia tribunal reveals at least 6,402 people were killed by army to boost body count," *The Guardian*, February 19, 2021.

https://www.theguardian.com/global-development/2021/feb/19/colombia-farc-tribunal-false-positives

24. Aylish O'Driscoll, "Colombian soldiers paid $500 for victims to boost kill counts: Testimony," *Colombia Reports*, December 5, 2011. https://colombiareports.com/false-positives-recruiter-received-500-per-victim

25. Trevor Aaronson, "The Sting: How the FBI Created a Terrorist," *The Intercept,* March 16, 2015. https://theintercept.com/2015/03/16/howthefbicreatedaterrorist/

26. Trevor Aaronson, "How this FBI strategy is actually creating US-based terrorists," TED2015, March 2015. https://www.ted.com/talks/trevor_aaronson_how_this_fbi_strategy_is_actually_creating_us_based_terrorists/transcript?language=en

27. Rob Gillies and Charmaine Noronha, "Terror suspect's father worried about radicalization," *Newsday*, April 24, 2013. https://www.newsday.com/news/world/terror-suspect-s-father-worried-about-radicalization-1.5135751

28. Phil Hirschkorn, "The Newburgh Sting," *HuffPost*, April 29, 2014. https://www.huffpost.com/entry/the-newburgh-sting_b_5234822

29. Ben Ryder Howe, "13,000 Pounds at 118 Miles Per Hour," *New York Magazine,* January 19, 2022. https://nymag.com/intelligencer/article/limo-crash-ny-fbi-informant.html

30. ACLU Southern California, "*Fazaga v. FBI,*" accessed March 14, 2022. https://www.aclusocal.org/en/cases/fazaga-v-fbi

31. Teresa Watanabe and Paloma Esquivel, "L.A. area Muslims say FBI surveillance has a chilling effect on their free speech and religious practices," *Los Angeles Times*, March 1, 2009. https://www.latimes.com/archives/la-xpm-2009-mar-01-me-muslim1-story.html

32. "Robert Spencer," Southern Poverty Law Center, accessed March 14, 2022. https://www.splcenter.org/fighting-hate/extremist-files/individual/robert-spencer

33. Spencer Ackerman, "FBI 'Islam 101' Guide Depicted Muslims as 7th-Century Simpletons," *Wired*, July 27, 2011. https://www.wired.com/2011/07/fbi-islam-101-guide/

34. Alexander, Michelle, *The New Jim Crow: Mass Incarceration in the Age of Colorblindness* (New York: New Press, 2020).

35. Malcolm X, *AZ Quotes*, accessed August 3, 2022. https://www.azquotes.com/quote/1546676

Chapter 6
Freedom of Speech

1. Theo van Gogh and Ayaan Hirsi Ali, "*Submission*," NativeEuropean, December 14, 2007.
https://www.youtube.com/watch?v=aGtQvGGY4S4&t=32s

2. Slim Allagui, "Danish business feels the pain of cartoon boycotts," *Middle East Online*, February 20, 2006.
https://web.archive.org/web/20060717193324/http://www.middle-east-online.com/english/business/?id=15795

3. Marie Louise Sjølie, "The Danish cartoonist who survived an axe attack," *The Guardian*, January 4, 2010.
https://www.theguardian.com/world/2010/jan/04/danish-cartoonist-axe-attack

4. Brian Love, "French paper reprints Mohammad cartoon after firebomb," *Reuters*, November 3, 2011.
https://www.reuters.com/article/us-france-fire-magazine-idUSTRE7A26MO20111103

5. Mark Memmott, "France On Alert, Closing Embassies, After Magazine Publishes Muhammad Cartoons," *NPR*, September 19, 2012.
https://www.npr.org/sections/thetwo-way/2012/09/19/161394146

6. Norimitsu Onishi, "Charlie Hebdo Republishes Cartoons That Prompted Deadly 2015 Attack," *The New York Times*, September 1, 2020.
https://www.nytimes.com/2020/09/01/world/europe/charlie-hebdo-cartoons-trial-france.html

7. European Parliamentary Research Service, "Holocaust denial in criminal law: Legal frameworks in selected EU Member States," European Parliament, January 2022.
https://www.europarl.europa.eu/RegData/etudes/BRIE/2021/698043/EPRS_BRI(2021)698043_EN.pdf

8. Ishaan Tharoor, "Iran revs up for its latest Holocaust cartoon contest," *Washington Post*, May 12, 2016.
https://www.washingtonpost.com/news/worldviews/wp/2016/05/12/iran-revs-up-for-its-latest-holocaust-cartoon-contest/

9. Elizabeth Dias, "Pope Francis Speaks Out on Charlie Hebdo: 'One Cannot Make Fun of Faith,'" *Time*, January 15, 2015.
https://time.com/3668875

10. Sam Schechner and Stacy Meichtry, "Demonstrations Pay Homage to French Teacher Beheaded After Lesson on Charlie Hebdo," *The Wall Street Journal*, October 18, 2020.

https://www.wsj.com/articles/french-officials-identify-chechen-man-as-suspect-in-teacher-beheading-11602938009

11. Philippe Wojazer, "'Our compatriot was killed for teaching children freedom of speech': French president Macron over beheading of teacher," *The Free Press Journal*, October 17, 2020. https://www.freepressjournal.in/world/our-compatriot-was-killed-for-teaching-children-freedom-of-speech-french-president-macron-over-beheading-of-teacher

12. Dwight Garner, "A Study of Edward Said, One of the Most Interesting Men of His Time," *The New York Times*, March 22, 2021. https://www.nytimes.com/2021/03/22/books/review-places-of-mind-edward-said-timothy-brennan.html

13. Lydia O'Connor, "Gun-Toting Islamophobic Group Protests Outside Texas Mosque," *HuffPost*, November 22, 2015. https://www.huffpost.com/entry/irving-texas-armed-mosque-protest_n_5651eddfe4b0d4093a581d14

14. "ACLU Statement on Killing of Anwar al-Aulaqi," American Civil Liberties Union, September 30, 2011. https://www.aclu.org/press-releases/aclu-statement-killing-anwar-al-aulaqi

15. Jason Burke, "'Anti-Semitic' satire divides liberal Paris," *The Guardian*, August 2, 2008. https://www.theguardian.com/world/2008/aug/03/france.pressandpublishing

16. Stanley Fish, *There's no such thing as free speech*, 105-6.

17. Vincent Blasi, "Milton's *Areopagitica* and the Modern First Amendment," National Humanities Center, accessed March 14, 2022. https://web.archive.org/web/20071214064554/http://nationalhumanitiescenter.org/ideasv42/blasi4.htm

18. John Milton, "Areopagitica," accessed March 14, 2022. https://milton.host.dartmouth.edu/reading_room/areopagitica/text.html
Please note that the spelling of some words were changed to more modern spellings for ease of reading.

19. Michael Gerson, "Catholics, contraceptives and John Locke," *The Washington Post*, March 15, 2012. https://www.washingtonpost.com/opinions/catholics-contraceptives-and-john-locke/2012/03/15/gIQAb477ES_story.html

20. Lisa Wade, "Irish Apes: Tactics of De-Humanization," Sociological Images, January 28, 2011. https://thesocietypages.org/socimages/2011/01/28/irish-apes-tactics-of-de-humanization/

21. Asma Barlas, "Reprinting the Charlie Hebdo cartoons is not about free speech," *Al Jazeera*, September 10, 2020. https://www.aljazeera.com/opinions/2020/9/10/reprinting-the-charlie-hebdo-cartoons-is-not-about-free-speech

22. Editorial Board, "Metro should end its delay of running 'Defeat Jihad' ad," *The Washington Post*, September 24, 2012. https://www.washingtonpost.com/opinions/metro-should-end-its-delay-of-running-defeat-jihad-ad/2012/09/24/1465c75c-0664-11e2-afff-d6c7f20a83bf_story.html

23. "France protects flag after bottom-wiping photograph," *BBC News*, July 23, 2010. https://www.bbc.com/news/world-europe-10744040

24. Yasco Horsman, "What was *Charlie Hebdo*? Blasphemy, laughter, politics," *Patterns of Prejudice* 54, no. 1-2 (2020): 168-181. https://doi.org/10.1080/0031322X.2020.1735722

25. Edward Said, *Covering Islam*, 75.

26. "The Guardian view on Shireen Abu Aqleh: press freedom under attack," *The Guardian*, May 13, 2022. https://www.theguardian.com/commentisfree/2022/may/13/the-guardian-view-on-shireen-abu-aqleh-press-freedom-under-attack

27. Anne Penketh, "Policeman Ahmed Merabet mourned after death in Charlie Hebdo attack," *The Guardian*, January 8, 2015. https://www.theguardian.com/world/2015/jan/08/ahmed-merabet-mourned-charlie-hebdo-paris-attack

Chapter 7
Apostasy and Blasphemy in Islam

1. Quran 3:90.
2. Quran 4:137.
3. Quran 2:217.
4. Quran 15:6, 26:27, 37:36, 44:14, 51:39, 51:52, 68:2, 68:51, 81:22.
5. Quran 21:5, 37:36, 52:30, 69:41.
6. Quran 51:39, 51:52.
7. Quran 25:5, 44:14, 16:103.
8. Quran 6:25, 8:31, 16:24, 23:83, 25:5, 27:68, 46:17, 68:15, 83:13.
9. Quran 4:140.
10. Quran 6:108.
11. Quran 16:125.
12. Quran 9:6.
13. Quran 3:20.

14. Quran 2:256.
15. Javaid Rehman, Freedom of expression, apostasy, and blasphemy within Islam: *Sharia*, criminal justice systems, and modern Islamic state practices, *Criminal Justice Matters* 79, no. 1 (2010): 4-5. doi.org/10.1080/09627250903569841
16. Quran 18:29.
17. Quran 109:6.
18. "Despite Danish repeal, blasphemy laws still common in Europe," *International Press Institute*, July 13, 2017. https://ipi.media/despite-danish-repeal-blasphemy-laws-still-common-in-europe/
19. Samirah Majumdar and Virginia Villa, "Globally, Social Hostilities Related to Religion Decline in 2019, While Government Restrictions Remain at Highest Levels," Pew Research Center, September 30, 2021. https://www.pewforum.org/2021/09/30/globally-social-hostilities-related-to-religion-decline-in-2019-while-government-restrictions-remain-at-highest-levels/
20. "Ben Affleck, Sam Harris and Bill Maher Debate Radical Islam," Real Time with Bill Maher (HBO), October 6, 2014. https://www.youtube.com/watch?v=vln9D81eO60
21. Andrea Elliott, "In Kabul, a Test for Shariah," *The New York Times*, March 26, 2006. https://www.nytimes.com/2006/03/26/weekinreview/in-kabul-a-test-for-shariah.html
22. "Dozens killed as US-backed strike hits Afghan wedding," *DW*, September 23, 2019. https://p.dw.com/p/3Q6Ei
23. "5 Things More Likely to Kill You than a Shark Attack," RUSHKULT, accessed March 15, 2022. https://rushkult.com/eng/scubamagazine/things-more-likely-to-kill-you-than-a-shark
24. Agence France-Presse in Islamabad, "Mob stones mentally ill man to death for 'desecrating Qur'an,'" *The Guardian*, February 13, 2022. https://www.theguardian.com/world/2022/feb/13/man-stoned-to-death-in-pakistan-after-desecrating-quran
25. Joshua Rhett Miller, "Instagram model killed in suspected murder-suicide in Texas: cops," *New York Post*, August 31, 2021. https://nypost.com/2021/08/31/miss-mercedes-morr-dead-in-suspected-murder-suicide-cops-say/
26. "Treason," 18 U.S. Code § 2381, accessed March 15, 2022. https://www.law.cornell.edu/uscode/text/18/2381
27. "Desertion," 10 U.S. Code § 885 - Art. 85., accessed March 15, 2022.

https://www.law.cornell.edu/uscode/text/10/885

28. Deuteronomy 13:6-9, New International Version.
29. Deuteronomy 17:2-5, New International Version.
30. 2 Chronicles 15:13, New International Version.
31. Romans 1:25-32, New International Version.
32. Peter Walker, "Ukip's Gerard Batten reiterates his belief that Islam is a 'death cult,'" *The Guardian*, February 18, 2018. https://www.theguardian.com/politics/2018/feb/18/ukip-gerard-batten-islam-muslims-quran
33. Sam Harris, "It's real, it's scary, it's a cult of death," *Los Angeles Times*, September 18, 2006. https://www.latimes.com/archives/la-xpm-2006-sep-18-oe-harris18-story.html
34. "Newcastle UKIP election candidate calls Islam 'satanic cult,'" *BBC News*, April 14, 2018. https://www.bbc.com/news/uk-england-tyne-43718014
35. Tim Alberta, "Tenn. pol: Islam may be a 'cult,'" *Politico*, July 28, 2010. https://www.politico.com/story/2010/07/tenn-pol-islam-may-be-a-cult-040328
36. Quran 29:46.
37. Gabriel Said Reynolds, "Is Allah a Different God Than the Biblical God?" *Church Life Journal*, May 26, 2020. https://churchlifejournal.nd.edu/articles/is-the-quranic-god-the-same-god-as-the-biblical-god/
38. Joachim Martillo, "Islamic Marcionism in Malaysia: Is Allah Equivalent to God?" *The American Muslim*, January 25, 2008. http://www.theamericanmuslim.org/tam.php/features/articles/islamic_marcionism_in_malaysia_is_allah_equivalent_to_god/
39. "Malaysia High Court rules Christians can use 'Allah,'" *BBC News*, March 11, 2021. https://www.bbc.com/news/world-asia-56356212
40. Ruth Graham, "The Professor Wore a Hijab in Solidarity — Then Lost Her Job," *The New York Times*, October 13, 2016. https://www.nytimes.com/2016/10/16/magazine/the-professor-wore-a-hijab-in-solidarity-then-lost-her-job.html
41. Mike Tisdell, "Is Allah the God of the Bible?" *Journal of Biblical Missiology*, September 30, 2020. https://biblicalmissiology.org/2020/09/30/is-allah-the-god-of-the-bible/

Chapter 8

Secularism: Freedom of Religion or Freedom from Religion?

1. Frederick Douglass, "The Meaning of July Fourth for the Negro," in: Philip S. Foner, *The Life and Writings of Frederick Douglass, Volume II: Pre-Civil War Decade 1850-1860* (New York: International Publishers Co., Inc., 1950).
https://www.pbs.org/wgbh/aia/part4/4h2927t.html

2. Hafsa Lodi, "French Senate Votes to Ban the Hijab for Muslim Women Under the Age of 18," *Vogue*, April 4, 2021.
https://en.vogue.me/culture/french-senate-votes-hijab-ban/

3. "French senators vote to ban hijab in sports competitions," *Al Jazeera*, January 19, 2022.
https://www.aljazeera.com/news/2022/1/19/french-senators-vote-to-ban-the-hijab-in-sports-competitions

4. Lucy Williamson, "France Islam: Muslims under pressure to sign French values charter," *BBC News*, December 1, 2020.
https://www.bbc.com/news/world-europe-55132098

5. Rose George, "Ghetto warrior," *The Guardian*, July 16, 2006.
https://www.theguardian.com/world/2006/jul/17/france.politicsphilosophyandsociety

6. 1 Peter 3:3-4, New Revised Standard Version.

7. Zahra Mila Elmi, "Educational Attainment in Iran," Middle East Institute, January 2009.
https://www.mei.edu/publications/educational-attainment-iran

8. Catherine Phipps, "France's ban on the veil looks far more sinister in historical context," *Washington Post*, April 13, 2021.
https://www.washingtonpost.com/outlook/2021/04/13/frances-ban-veil-looks-far-more-sinister-historical-context/

9. Alf Andrew Heggoy, "Education in French Algeria: An Essay on Cultural Conflict," *Comparative Education Review* 17, no. 2 (1973): 180-197.
www.jstor.org/stable/1186812

10. Branche Raphaëlle, "Rape During the Algerian War," in *Vingtième Siècle: Revue d'histoire* 75 (2002/2003): 123-132.
doi: 10.3917/ving.075.0123

11. Lara Marlowe, "Breaking silence," *The Irish Times*, March 16, 2002.
https://www.irishtimes.com/news/breaking-silence-1.1053989

12. Frantz Falon, "Algeria Unveiled," in *Decolonization: Perspectives from now and then*, edited by Prasenjit Duara (London: Routledge, 2003), 42-56.
https://academics.skidmore.edu/blogs/transnationals19/files/2014/08/Fanon-Algeria-Unveiled.pdf

13. Ben Quinn, "French police make woman remove clothing on Nice beach following burkini ban," *The Guardian*, August 23, 2016. https://www.theguardian.com/world/2016/aug/24/french-police-make-woman-remove-burkini-on-nice-beach

14. Myriam François, "Meet the 'Muslim Rosa Parks': How France's pools have become the latest site of a civil right battle," *ABC*, August 19, 2021. https://www.abc.net.au/religion/muslim-women-and-french-pools-myriam-fran%C3%A7ois/13499338

15. Janine Marsh, "Speedos v Trunks in swimming pools in France," The Good Life France, accessed March 16, 2022. https://thegoodlifefrance.com/speedos-versus-trunks-in-swimming-pools-in-france/

16. Victoria W. Wolcott, "The forgotten history of segregated swimming pools and amusement parks," *The Conversation*, July 9, 2019. https://theconversation.com/the-forgotten-history-of-segregated-swimming-pools-and-amusement-parks-119586

17. Rachel Martin (Host), Interview with Jeff Wiltse, "Racial History of American Swimming Pools," *NPR*, May 6, 2008. https://www.npr.org/templates/story/story.php?storyId=90213675

18. Rose Hackman, "Swimming while black: the legacy of segregated public pools lives on," *The Guardian*, August 4, 2015. https://www.theguardian.com/world/2015/aug/04/black-children-swimming-drownings-segregation

19. Jayshree Bajoria, "CoronaJihad is Only the Latest Manifestation: Islamophobia in India has Been Years in the Making," Human Rights Watch, May 1, 2020. https://www.hrw.org/news/2020/05/01/coronajihad-only-latest-manifestation-islamophobia-india-has-been-years-making

20. Nazia Parveen, "Police investigate UK far-right groups over anti-Muslim coronavirus claims," *The Guardian*, April 5, 2020. https://www.theguardian.com/world/2020/apr/05/police-investigate-uk-far-right-groups-over-anti-muslim-coronavirus-claims

21. "A Jewish Movement to Shroud the Female Form," *NPR*, March 17, 2008. https://www.npr.org/templates/story/story.php?storyId=88381958

22. "When Jews Wore Burkas: Exhibition Showcases 19th Century Jewish Fashion," *Haaretz*, October 2, 2017, updated April 24, 2018. https://www.haaretz.com/israel-news/culture/when-jews-wore-burkas-an-exhibition-of-jewish-fashion-1.5454896

23. Miriam Jordan, "Secret Mission Rescues Yemen's Jews," *The Wall Street Journal*, October 31, 2009. https://www.wsj.com/articles/SB125693376195819343

24. Emanuela Campanella, "People share photos of nuns on the beach in response to burkini ban in France," *Global News*, August 25, 2016. https://globalnews.ca/news/2903036/
25. 1 Corinthians 11:5-6, New Catholic Bible.
26. Romans 12:12, English Standard Version.
27. Vishwanath Petkar, "European Court of Justice rules headscarves can be banned at work," *Jurist*, July 17, 2021. https://www.jurist.org/news/2021/07/european-court-of-justice-rules-headscarves-can-be-banned-at-work/
28. "The Effect of the British Raj on Clothing in India," Strand of Silk, August 11, 2013. https://strandofsilk.com/indian-fashion-blog/driven-curiosity/effect-british-raj-clothing-india
29. History.com Editors, "Zoot Suit Riots," History, September 27, 2017. https://www.history.com/topics/world-war-ii/zoot-suit-riots
30. Kate Connolly and Jack Shenker, "The headscarf martyr: murder in German court sparks Egyptian fury," *The Guardian*, July 7, 2009. https://www.theguardian.com/world/2009/jul/07/german-trial-hijab-murder-egypt
31. "Angela Merkel endorses burka ban 'wherever legally possible,'" *BBC News*, December 6, 2016. https://www.bbc.com/news/world-europe-38226081

Chapter 9
Bans on Islamic Architecture

1. "Stopp, Ja zum Minarett verbot," Vintage Posters, Chisholm Larsson Gallery, accessed April 3, 2022. https://www.chisholm-poster.com/posters/CL49726.html
2. "Inside Story - Switzerland's minaret ban," *Al Jazeera English*, December 2, 2009. https://www.youtube.com/watch?v=pWjGYSQdX2I
3. Alexandra Wey, "'Importing' foreign-trained imams can cause problems," *SWI swissinfo.ch*, November 5, 2019. https://www.swissinfo.ch/eng/religious-report_-importing--foreign-trained-imams-can-cause-problems/45348768
4. Edward Said, *Covering Islam*, lviii.
5. Elizabeth Schumacher, "Germans tolerant of LGBT neighbors, but not Muslim ones," *DW*, August 16, 2018. https://www.dw.com/en/germans-tolerant-of-lgbt-neighbors-but-not-muslim-ones/a-45078938

6. Adapted from Robin DiAngelo, *White Fragility*, 71.
7. Kathleen E. Foley, "Building Mosques in America: Strategies for Securing Municipal Approvals," Institute for Social Policy and Understanding, October 2010, 9-10. https://www.ispu.org/wp-content/uploads/2016/08/ISPU_Building_Mosques_Report.pdf?x2629 7
8. Alain Jocard, "Why France Is Banning Muslim Prayer on the Country's Streets," *Newsweek*, November 20, 2017. https://www.newsweek.com/why-france-banning-muslim-prayer-countrys-streets-716494
9. Rush Limbaugh, "Why This Mosque on This Spot?" *The Rush Limbaugh Show*, August 17, 2010. https://web.archive.org/web/20100820020856/http://www.rushlimba ugh.com/home/daily/site_081710/content/01125111.guest.html
10. "Public Remains Conflicted Over Islam," Pew Research Center, August 24, 2010. https://www.pewforum.org/2010/08/24/public-remains-conflicted-over-islam/
11. Chris Hawley, "NYPD monitored Muslim students all over Northeast," *The Associated Press*, February 18, 2012. https://www.ap.org/ap-in-the-news/2012/nypd-monitored-muslim-students-all-over-northeast
12. Daniel Pipes, "Embry-Riddle MSA and Paintball," October 15, 2006. https://www.danielpipes.org/comments/60504
13. Daniel Marans, "Smear Campaign Against Michigan Candidate Shows How Hard It Is For Muslims To Run For Office," *HuffPost*, May 3, 2018. https://www.huffpost.com/entry/democrat-abdul-el-sayed-michigan-muslim-candidates-conspiracy-theories_n_5aeb27f6e4b0ab5c3d62baa7
14. Agence France-Presse, "Chinese city bans Islamic beards, headwear and clothing on buses," *The Guardian*, August 6, 2014. https://www.theguardian.com/world/2014/aug/06/chinese-city-bans-islamic-beards-headwear-and-clothing-on-buses
15. "China Uighurs: Xinjiang ban on long beards and veils," *BBC News*, April 1, 2017. https://www.bbc.com/news/world-asia-china-39460538
16. Gerry Shih and Dake Kang, "Muslims forced to drink alcohol and eat pork in China's 're-education' camps, former inmate claims," *The Independent*, May 19, 2018. https://www.independent.co.uk/news/world/asia/china-re-education-muslims-ramadan-xinjiang-eat-pork-alcohol-communist-xi-jinping-a8357966.html

17. Matthew Hill, David Campanale and Joel Gunter, "'Their goal is to destroy everyone': Uighur camp detainees allege systematic rape," *BBC News*, February 2, 2021.
https://www.bbc.com/news/world-asia-china-55794071

18. David Brunnstrom, "U.S. congressmen call on Hilton to cut link to Xinjiang project," *Reuters*, July 29, 2021.
https://www.reuters.com/world/asia-pacific/us-congressmen-call-hilton-cut-link-xinjiang-project-2021-07-29/

19. Cate Cadell, "Mosques disappear as China strives to 'build a beautiful Xinjiang,'" *Reuters*, May 13, 2021.
https://www.reuters.com/world/china/mosques-disappear-china-strives-build-beautiful-xinjiang-2021-05-13/

20. Lucy Jenkins, "Muslims ordered to sell alcohol in China's Xinjiang region," *The Drinks Business*, May 8, 2015.
https://www.thedrinksbusiness.com/2015/05/muslims-ordered-to-sell-alcohol-in-chinas-xinjiang-region/

21. Ted Regencia, "Uighurs forced to eat pork as China expands Xinjiang pig farms," *Al Jazeera*, December 4, 2020.
https://www.aljazeera.com/news/2020/12/4/holduighurs-forced-to-eat-pork-as-hog-farming-in-xinjiang-expands

22. Cresa Pugh, "Rohingya Crisis: Rakhine's Fallen Mosques," Harvard University: The Lakshmi Mittal and Family South Asia Institute, January 17, 2018.
https://mittalsouthasiainstitute.harvard.edu/2018/01/rohingya-crisis-rakhines-fallen-mosques/

23. Dan Milmo, "Rohingya sue Facebook for £150bn over Myanmar genocide," *The Guardian*, December 6, 2021.
https://www.theguardian.com/technology/2021/dec/06/rohingya-sue-facebook-myanmar-genocide-us-uk-legal-action-social-media-violence

24. Todd Pitman, "Myanmar attacks, sea voyage rob young father of everything," *AP News*, October 27, 2017.
https://apnews.com/article/ap-top-news-international-news-asia-bangladesh-oceans-8972bde7517d4e7aba770fb124a40726

25. Sarah Hagi, "The Dangerous Normalization of Islamophobia," *GQ*, March 19, 2019.
https://www.gq.com/story/islamophobia-christchurch-attack

26. Peter Cluskey, "Amsterdam refuses mosque's request for loudspeaker call to prayer," *The Irish Times*, October 30, 2019.
https://www.irishtimes.com/news/world/europe/amsterdam-refuses-mosque-s-request-for-loudspeaker-call-to-prayer-1.4067260

27. Lahav Harkov, "Ministers approve bill muffling muezzin's call to prayer," *The Jerusalem Post*, November 13, 2016. https://www.jpost.com/Israel-News/Ministers-approve-bill-muffling-muezzins-call-to-prayer-472519

28. Umar Farooq, "Call to prayer is a daily reminder of Turkey's religious and political shift," *Los Angeles Times*, November 25, 2018. https://www.latimes.com/world/la-fg-turkey-adhan-call-to-prayer-20181121-story.html

29. Susan Svrluga and Michelle Boorstein, "Duke University reverses decision, cancels weekly Muslim call to prayer," *The Washington Post*, January 15, 2015. https://www.washingtonpost.com/news/grade-point/wp/2015/01/15/duke-university-reverses-decision-cancels-weekly-muslim-call-to-prayer/

30. Krishnadev Calamur, "After Saying Yes, Duke Nixes Muslim Call To Prayer From Chapel Bell Tower," *NPR*, January 15, 2015. https://www.npr.org/sections/thetwo-way/2015/01/15/377535894/duke-reverses-course-on-muslim-call-to-prayer-from-chapel-bell-tower

31. CAIR California, "Campus Climate Report 2019-2020," The Council on American-Islamic Relations, accessed August 3, 2022. https://static.ca.cair.com/reports/downloads/CAIR-2019-2020-Campus-Climate-Report.pdf

32. Ed Pilkington, "US campuses become a growing front in Israeli-Palestinian conflict," *The Guardian*, May 21, 2021. https://www.theguardian.com/us-news/2021/may/21/us-campuses-sraeli-palestinian-conflict-universities

33. Gail Kaplan Guttman, "Rocks, Pebbles And Edward Said," *The New York Times*, March 13, 2001. https://www.nytimes.com/2001/03/13/opinion/l-rocks-pebbles-and-edward-said-373397.html

34. Sunnie Kim, "Edward Said Accused of Stoning in South Lebanon," *Columbia Spectator*, July 19, 2000. https://www.columbiaspectator.com/2000/07/19/edward-said-accused-stoning-south-lebanon/ An image of the front page can be accessed at: https://spectatorarchive.library.columbia.edu/?a=d&d=cs20000719-01.2.4

35. Cleve R. Wootson Jr. and Herman Wong, "After calling Barbara Bush an 'amazing racist,' a professor taunts critics: 'I will never be fired,'" *The Washington Post*, April 19, 2018.

https://www.washingtonpost.com/news/gradepoint/wp/2018/04/18/after-calling-barbara-bush-an-amazing-racist-a-professor-taunts-critics-i-will-never-be-fired/

36.   Chris Bell, "A professor spoke ill of the dead. What happened next?" *BBC News*, July 29, 2019.
      https://www.bbc.com/news/blogs-trending-47147778

37.   Surita Basu and Pareesay Afzal, "Uyghur Graduate Student Raises Brother's Detention at Cornell Event, Chinese Students Walk Out," *Cornell Sun*, March 16, 2022.
      https://cornellsun.com/2022/03/16/uyghur-graduate-student-raises-brothers-detention-at-cornell-event-chinese-students-walk-out/

Chapter 10
The War on Halal Food

1.   John R. Bowen, "What Does Europe Have Against Halal?" *Boston Review*, June 11, 2021.
     https://bostonreview.net/articles/what-does-europe-have-against-halal/

2.   Azeezah Kanji, "Kosher and Halal bans: Fur-washing factory farming's brutality," *Al Jazeera*, November 3, 2021.
     https://www.aljazeera.com/opinions/2021/11/3/kosher-and-halal-bans-fur-washing-factory-farmings-brutality

3.   "EU Court backs ban on animal slaughter without stunning," *BBC News*, December 17, 2020.
     https://www.bbc.com/news/world-europe-55344971

4.   Azeezah Kanji, "Kosher and Halal bans: Fur-washing factory farming's brutality," *Al Jazeera*, November 3, 2021.
     https://www.aljazeera.com/opinions/2021/11/3/kosher-and-halal-bans-fur-washing-factory-farmings-brutality

5.   "How are Factory Farms Cruel to Animals?" The Humane League, January 4, 2021.
     https://thehumaneleague.org/article/factory-farming-animal-cruelty

6.   Febe Armanios and Bogac Ergene, *Halal Food: A History* (New York: Oxford University Press, 2018), 190-210.

7.   JTA, "Marine Le Pen: Ban halal and all ritual slaughter," *Times of Israel*, April 25, 2017.
     https://www.timesofisrael.com/marine-le-pen-ban-halal-and-all-ritual-slaughter/

8.   Angelique Chrisafis, "Pork or nothing: how school dinners are dividing France," *The Guardian*, October 13, 2015.

https://www.theguardian.com/world/2015/oct/13/pork-school-dinners-france-secularism-children-religious-intolerance

9. Jack Malvern, "Racist far right finds a home on Facebook," *The Times*, March 17, 2018.
https://www.thetimes.co.uk/article/racist-far-right-finds-a-home-on-facebook-fggjdrg8p

10. "Terror-Free Slovakia Completely Refuses Islam and Won't Allow a Single Mosque," *S4C News: Stand for Christians*, November 17, 2018.
https://en.s4c.news/2018/11/17/terror-free-slovakia-completely-refuses-islam-and-wont-allow-a-single-mosque/

11. "Slovakia effectively bans Islam from country, forbids mosques," *Remix News*, February 20, 2020.
https://rmx.news/article/slovakia-effectively-bans-islam-from-country-forbids-mosques/

12. Linda Alvarez, "Colonization, Food, and the Practice of Eating," Food Empowerment Project, accessed March 18, 2022.
https://foodispower.org/our-food-choices/colonization-food-and-the-practice-of-eating/

13. J. Weston Phippen, "'Kill Every Buffalo You Can! Every Buffalo Dead is an Indian Gone,'" *The Atlantic*, May 13, 2016.
https://www.theatlantic.com/national/archive/2016/05/the-buffalo-killers/482349/

Chapter 11
Muslim Intolerance vs Intolerance of Muslims

1. Mohsin H. Khan, Hamedi M. Adnan, Surinderpal Kaur, Rashid A. Khuhro, Rohail Asghar and Sahira Jabeen, "Muslims' Representation in Donald Trump's Anti-Muslim-Islam Statement: A Critical Discourse Analysis," *Religions* 10, no. 2 (2019): 115.
doi: 10.3390/rel10020115

2. Jenna Johnson and Abigail Hauslohner, "'I think Islam hates us': A timeline of Trump's comments about Islam and Muslims," *The Washington Post*, May 20, 2017.
https://www.washingtonpost.com/news/post-politics/wp/2017/05/20/i-think-islam-hates-us-a-timeline-of-trumps-comments-about-islam-and-muslims/

3. Ibtihaj Muhammad, *Proud: My fight for an unlikely American dream* (New York: Hachette Books, 2018, eBook edition), 184-192.

4. Andrew Rosenthal, "Foes Accuse Bush Campaign of Inflaming Racial Tension," *The New York Times*, October 24, 1988.

https://www.nytimes.com/1988/10/24/us/foes-accuse-bush-campaign-of-inflaming-racial-tension.html

5. Martin Pengelly, "Ben Carson says no Muslim should ever become US president," *The Guardian*, September 20, 2015.
    https://www.theguardian.com/us-news/2015/sep/20/ben-carson-no-muslim-us-president-trump-obama

6. Sabrina Siddiqui, "Americans' Attitudes Toward Muslims And Arabs Are Getting Worse, Poll Finds," *HuffPost*, July 29, 2014.
    https://www.huffpost.com/entry/arab-muslim-poll_n_5628919

7. Rick Wyatt, "Native American Party (U.S.)," CRW Flags, September 18, 2015.
    https://www.crwflags.com/fotw/flags/us%7Dnap.html

8. Matthew Cooper, "Why Have There Been No Catholic Presidents Since John F. Kennedy?" *Newsweek*, September 23, 2015.
    https://www.newsweek.com/why-have-there-been-no-catholic-presidents-john-f-kennedy-375401

9. Falguni A. Sheth, *Toward a Political Philosophy of Race*, 42.

10. Ishaan Tharoor, "When the West wanted Islam to curb Christian extremism," *The Washington Post*, October 16, 2014.
    https://www.washingtonpost.com/news/worldviews/wp/2014/10/15/when-the-west-wanted-islam-to-curb-christian-extremism/

11. Glenn Kessler, "The 'very fine people' at Charlottesville: Who were they?" *The Washington Post*, May 8, 2020.
    https://www.washingtonpost.com/politics/2020/05/08/very-fine-people-charlottesville-who-were-they-2/

12. Sumbul Ali-Karamali, *Demystifying Shariah*, 34-5.

13. Alex Nowrasteh, "More Americans Die in Animal Attacks than in Terrorist Attacks," Cato Institute, March 8, 2018.
    https://www.cato.org/blog/more-americans-die-animal-attacks-terrorist-attacks

14. Peter Bergen and David Sterman, "Terrorism in America After 9/11," *New America*, September 10, 2021.
    https://www.newamerica.org/international-security/reports/terrorism-in-america/who-are-the-terrorists

15. Kieran Pender, "History will judge IOC and Fifa as opportunistic hypocrites over Russia," *The Guardian*, March 3, 2022.
    https://www.theguardian.com/sport/2022/mar/03/history-will-judge-ioc-and-fifa-as-opportunistic-hypocrites-over-russia

Chapter 12
Islamophobia without Muslims

1. Eugénie Bastié, "'Que serait devenu le petit Aylan s'il avait grandi?':
   Charlie Hebdo choque," *Le Figaro*, January 14, 2016.
   https://www.lefigaro.fr/actualite-france/2016/01/14/01016-
   20160114ARTFIG00112-que-serait-devenu-le-petit-aylan-s-il-avait-
   grandi-charlie-hebdo-choque.php

2. Kerri Bartlett, "Trump says must deter Syrian-refugee 'Trojan Horse,'
   preserve Second Amendment and Christmas to 'make America great,'"
   Williamson Herald, October 8, 2015.
   https://www.williamsonherald.com/news/trump-says-must-deter-
   syrian-refugee-trojan-horse-preserve-second-amendment-and-
   christmas-to-make/article_be721d22-6a25-11e5-9dcb-
   f380e0cd4d43.html

3. Libby Nelson, "The strange history and ugly core of Donald Trump Jr.'s
   Skittles tweet, explained," *Vox*, September 20, 2016.
   https://www.vox.com/2016/9/20/12987202/skittles-tweet-donald-
   trump-syrian-refugees

4. "Germany convicts soldier who posed as refugee, plotted attack," *Al
   Jazeera*, July 15, 2022.
   https://www.aljazeera.com/news/2022/7/15/germany-convicts-
   soldier-who-posed-as-refugee-plotted-attack

5. "Page from the Antisemitic Children's Book The Poisonous Mushroom,"
   Holocaust Sources in Context, accessed March 18, 2022.
   https://perspectives.ushmm.org/item/page-from-the-antisemitic-
   childrens-book-the-poisonous-mushroom

6. Ishaan Tharoor, "Yes, the comparison between Jewish and Syrian
   refugees matters," *The Washington Post*, November 19, 2015.
   https://www.washingtonpost.com/news/worldviews/wp/2015/11/19/
   yes-the-comparison-between-jewish-and-syrian-refugees-matters/

7. Chris Cillizza, "Democrats say GOP politicians are immoral for opposing
   Syrian refugees in the U.S. That's not entirely fair," *The Washington Post*,
   November 19, 2015.
   https://www.washingtonpost.com/news/the-
   fix/wp/2015/11/19/republican-voters-dont-want-to-let-syrian-
   refugees-in-what-should-gop-politicians-
   do/?postshare=9911447946405016

8. PRRI Staff, "The 2020 Census of American Religion," Public Religion
   Research Institute, July 7, 2021.
   https://www.prri.org/research/2020-census-of-american-religion/

9. "Educational attainment of U.S. religious groups," Pew Research Center,
   November 3, 2016.

https://www.pewresearch.org/fact-tank/2016/11/04/the-most-and-least-educated-u-s-religious-groups/ft_16-10-06_educationreligiousgroups/

10. Katarzyna Górak-Sosnowska, "Islamophobia without Muslims? The Case of Poland", *Journal of Muslims in Europe* 5, no. 2 (2016): 190-204. doi: 10.1163/22117954-12341326

11. Agnieszka Dudzińska and Michał Kotnarowski, "Imaginary Muslims: How the Polish right frames Islam," The Brookings Institution, July 24, 2019. https://www.brookings.edu/research/imaginary-muslims-how-polands-populists-frame-islam/

12. Makana Eyre and Martin Goillandeau, "Poland's two-faced immigration strategy," *Politico*, June 6, 2019. https://www.politico.eu/article/poland-two-faced-immigration-strategy-ukraine-migrants/

13. Eric Reidy, "Is Poland's smooth reception of Ukrainian refugees heading for trouble?" *The New Humanitarian*, August 4, 2022. https://www.thenewhumanitarian.org/news-feature/2022/08/04/Poland-Ukraine-refugee-concern-grows

14. *TRT World*, "Here's why Poland takes in millions of migrants... just not Muslim ones," The Newsmakers, April 2, 2019. https://www.youtube.com/watch?v=TYSX2vI7oPk

15. "Eastern Europe braces for refugees as Ukraine tensions simmer," *Al Jazeera*, February 14, 2022. https://www.aljazeera.com/news/2022/2/14/eastern-europe-braces-for-refugees-as-ukraine-crisis-simmers

16. Liv Stroud, "International students 'dying by the side of the road' trying to flee Ukraine, say refugees," *The Telegraph*, March 2, 2022. https://www.telegraph.co.uk/global-health/terror-and-security/international-students-dying-side-road-trying-flee-ukraine-say/

17. Lorenzo Tondo and Emmanuel Akinwotu, "People of colour fleeing Ukraine attacked by Polish nationalists," *The Guardian*, March 2, 2022. https://www.theguardian.com/global-development/2022/mar/02/people-of-colour-fleeing-ukraine-attacked-by-polish-nationalists

18. Al Jazeera Staff, "'Double standards': Western coverage of Ukraine war criticized," *Al Jazeera*, February 27, 2022. https://www.aljazeera.com/news/2022/2/27/western-media-coverage-ukraine-russia-invasion-criticism

19. "Polish MP: 'For me, multiculturalism is not a value' | UpFront (Headliner)," *Al Jazeera English*, November 9, 2019.

https://www.youtube.com/watch?v=ccOp0I8ZPho

20. Péter Krekó, Bulcsú Hunyadi and Patrik Szicherle, "Anti-Muslim populism in Hungary: From the margins to the mainstream," The Brookings Institution, July 24, 2019. https://www.brookings.edu/research/anti-muslim-populism-in-hungary-from-the-margins-to-the-mainstream/#cancel

Chapter 13
How Social Media Fuels Islamophobia

1. Lawrence Pintak, Brian J. Bowe and Jonathan Albright, "Influencers, Amplifiers, and Icons: A Systematic Approach to Understanding the Roles of Islamophobic Actors on Twitter," Journalism and Mass Communication Quarterly (July 2021). doi: 10.1177/10776990211031567

2. Saif Shahin, "How social media – aided by bots – amplifies Islamophobia online," The Conversation, September 9, 2021. https://theconversation.com/how-social-media-aided-by-bots-amplifies-islamophobia-online-166080

3. Johan Farkas, Jannick Schou and Christina Neumayer, "Cloaked Facebook Pages: Exploring Fake Islamist Propaganda in Social Media," New Media & Society 20, no. 5 (2018): 1850–67. doi: 10.1177/1461444817707759

4. Adam Taylor, "The lies told about refugees, city by city," The Washington Post, February 17, 2016. https://www.washingtonpost.com/news/worldviews/wp/2016/02/17/the-lies-told-about-refugees-city-by-city/

5. "Liberals don't care Hirsi Ali lied to get asylum in 1992," Expatica, May 12, 2006. https://www.expatica.com/nl/uncategorized/liberals-dont-care-hirsi-ali-lied-to-get-asylum-in-1992-36759/

6. Soraya S. Nelson, "For Some Muslim Asylum-Seekers In Germany, Christianity Beckons," NPR Morning Edition, November 9, 2015. https://www.npr.org/sections/parallels/2015/11/09/454670739

7. Mike Mariani, "Nativism, Violence, and the Origins of the Paranoid Style," Slate, March 22, 2017. https://slate.com/news-and-politics/2017/03/the-awful-disclosures-of-maria-monk-and-the-origins-of-the-paranoid-style.html

8. Nitasha Tiku, "Tech Platforms Treat White Nationalism Different From Islamic Terrorism," Wired, March 20, 2019.

https://www.wired.com/story/why-tech-platforms-dont-treat-all-terrorism-same/

9.   Sharon Pulwer and Elihay Vidal, "Facebook Complying With 95% of Israeli Requests to Remove Inciting Content, Minister Says," *Haaretz*, April 10, 2018. https://www.haaretz.com/israel-news/business/facebook-removes-inciting-content-at-israel-s-request-minister-says-1.5432959

10. Adam Smith, "Palestinians' Digital Rights 'Violated' by Censorship on Facebook, Twitter, and Instagram, New Report Claims," *Independent*, May 21, 2021. https://www.independent.co.uk/life-style/gadgets-and-tech/palestine-israel-censorship-facebook-twitter-instagram-7amleh-b1851328.html

11. Rahul Mukherjee, "Mobile witnessing on WhatsApp: Vigilante virality and the anatomy of mob lynching," *South Asian Popular Culture* 18, no. 1 (2020): 79-101. https://www.tandfonline.com/doi/abs/10.1080/14746689.2020.1736810

12. Tommy Wilkes and Roli Srivastava, "Protests held across India after attacks against Muslims," *Reuters*, June 28, 2017. https://www.reuters.com/article/india-protests-muslims-beef-idINKBN19J2BV

13. Suhasini Raj, "Hindu Cow Vigilantes in Rajasthan, India, Beat Muslim to Death," *The New York Times*, April 5, 2017. https://www.nytimes.com/2017/04/05/world/asia/india-cow-mob-hindu-vigilantes.html

14. Muniba Saleem, Sara Prot, Craig A. Anderson and Anthony F. Lemieux, "Exposure to Muslims in Media and Support for Public Policies Harming Muslims," *Communication Research* 44, no. 6 (2017): 841–69. doi: 10.1177/0093650215619214.

15. Jane Lytvynenko, "Anti-Muslim Hate Speech Is Absolutely Relentless On Social Media Even As Platforms Crack Down On Other Extremist Groups," *BuzzFeed News*, March 18, 2019. https://www.buzzfeednews.com/article/janelytvynenko/islamophobia-absolutely-relentless-social-media

16. Sarah Laskow, "Salacious Convent Exposés Were the Most Popular Books in Antebellum America," Atlas Obscura, July 13, 2017. https://www.atlasobscura.com/articles/19th-century-covent-exposes-protestants-catholics-nuns-sin

17. Tiffany Hsu, "The Sandy Hook defamation cases have put Alex Jones's finances under scrutiny," *The New York Times*, August 22, 2022. https://www.nytimes.com/2022/08/05/us/alex-jones-finances.html

Chapter 14
The Place of Non-Muslims in a Muslim State

1. Quran 2:256.
2. Quran 9:29.
3. "Converts And Social Integration," Encyclopedia.com, accessed March 19, 2022. https://www.encyclopedia.com/history/news-wires-white-papers-and-books/converts-and-social-integration
4. Kelly P. Erb, "Islamic State Warns Christians: Convert, Pay Tax, Leave Or Die," *Forbes*, July 19, 2014. https://www.forbes.com/sites/kellyphillipserb/2014/07/19/islamic-state-warns-christians-convert-pay-tax-leave-or-die/?sh=4aae70ba2c25
5. Les Picker, "Where Are ISIS's Foreign Fighters Coming From?" *The NBER (National Bureau of Economic Research) Digest*, no. 6 (June 2016). https://www.nber.org/digest/jun16/where-are-isiss-foreign-fighters-coming
6. Priyanka Boghani and Anjali Tsui, "Who's Who in the Fight Against ISIS?" *PBS Frontline*, October 11, 2016. https://www.pbs.org/wgbh/frontline/article/whos-who-in-the-fight-against-isis/
7. "Timeline: the Rise, Spread, and Fall of the Islamic State," Wilson Center, October 28, 2019. https://www.wilsoncenter.org/article/timeline-the-rise-spread-and-fall-the-islamic-state
8. Jaime Fuller, "'ISIS' vs. 'ISIL' vs. 'Islamic State': The political importance of a much-debated acronym," *The Washington Post*, January 20, 2015. https://www.washingtonpost.com/news/the-fix/wp/2015/01/20/isis-vs-isil-vs-islamic-state-the-political-importance-of-a-much-debated-acronym-2/
9. Patrick Garrity, "Paris Attacks: What Does 'Daesh' Mean and Why Does ISIS Hate It?" *NBC News*, November 14, 2015. https://www.nbcnews.com/storyline/isis-terror/paris-attacks-what-does-daesh-mean-why-does-isis-hate-n463551
10. Zack Beauchamp, "New study: people from French-speaking countries are more likely to become jihadists," *VOX*, March 29, 2016. https://www.vox.com/2016/3/29/11326120/jihadism-francophone
11. Musa al-Gharbi, "Don't Think of the 'Islamic State' in Religious Terms," Middle East Policy Council, accessed March 20, 2022. https://mepc.org/commentary/dont-think-islamic-state-religious-terms

12. Denise Aigle, "The Mongol Invasions of Bilād al-Shām by Ghāzān Khān and Ibn Taymīyah's Three 'Anti-Mongol' Fatwas," *Mamlūk Studies Review* 11, no. 2 (2007): 89-120.
https://knowledge.uchicago.edu/record/1129

13. "Ibn Taymiyyah—Scholar and Statesman Part 2," Dar al-Nicosia, May 28, 2013.
https://daralnicosia.wordpress.com/2013/05/28/ibn-taymiyyah-scholar-and-statesman-part-2/

14. Quran 4:94.

15. Mehmet B. Dorduncu, *The Yildiz Albums of Sultan Aldulhamid: Mecca-Medina*, Translated by Hakan Yesilova (Somerset, New Jersey: The Light, Inc., 2006).

16. Sumbul Ali-Karamali, *Demystifying Shariah*, 38.

17. Karen Armstrong, "Wahhabism to ISIS: how Saudi Arabia exported the main source of global terrorism," *New Statesman*, November 27, 2014.
https://web.archive.org/web/20141127132619/http://www.newstatesman.com/world-affairs/2014/11/wahhabism-isis-how-saudi-arabia-exported-main-source-global-terrorism

Chapter 15
The Rapefugee Crisis

1. Jessie Wingard, "'Islamic rape of Europe': Polish magazine sparks outrage," *DW*, February 18, 2016.
https://www.dw.com/en/islamic-rape-of-europe-polish-magazine-sparks-outrage/a-19056162

2. François Haas, "German science and black racism—roots of the Nazi Holocaust," *The FACEB Journal* 22, no. 2 (2008): 332-337.
doi: 10.1096/fj.08-0202ufm

3. Saskia Bonjour and Sarah Bracke, "Europe and the Myth of the Racialized Sexual Predator: Gendered and Sexualized Patterns of Prejudice," *Europe Now Journal*, December 7, 2020.
https://www.europenowjournal.org/2020/12/07/europe-and-the-myth-of-the-racialized-sexual-predator-gendered-and-sexualized-patterns-of-prejudice/

4. Ishaan Tharoor, "The so-called 'Islamic rape of Europe' is part of a long and racist history," *The Washington Post*, February 18, 2016.
https://www.washingtonpost.com/news/worldviews/wp/2016/02/18/the-so-called-islamic-rape-of-europe-is-part-of-a-long-and-racist-history/

5.   "100 Years Later, What's The Legacy Of 'Birth Of A Nation'?" *NPR*, February 8, 2015.
     https://www.npr.org/sections/codeswitch/2015/02/08/383279630
6.   Sheila Weller, "The Missing Woman: How Author Timothy Tyson Found the Woman at the Center of the Emmett Till Case," *Vanity Fair*, January 26, 2017.
     https://www.vanityfair.com/news/2017/01/how-author-timothy-tyson-found-the-woman-at-the-center-of-the-emmett-till-case?mbid=social_twitter
7.   Scott J. South and Richard B. Felson, "The Racial Patterning of Rape," *Social Forces* 69, no. 1 (1990):71-93.
     doi: 10.2307/2579608
8.   "Racism and Rape," National Alliance to End Sexual Violence, accessed March 20, 2022.
     https://endsexualviolence.org/where_we_stand/racism-and-rape/
9.   Aryn Baker, "The Secret War Crime: Ending the scourge of conflict rape," *Time*, March 10, 2016.
     https://time.com/magazine/south-pacific/4254115/march-21st-2016-vol-187-no-10-asia-europe-middle-east-and-africa-south-pacific/
10. Halime Pehlivan, "Genocidal rape and the invisible children of Bosnia," *TRT World*, July 12, 2021.
     https://www.trtworld.com/perspectives/genocidal-rape-and-the-invisible-children-of-bosnia-48312
11. Kate Connolly, "Tensions rise in Germany over handling of mass sexual assaults in Cologne," *The Guardian*, January 7, 2016.
     https://www.theguardian.com/world/2016/jan/06/tensions-rise-in-germany-over-handling-of-mass-sexual-assaults-in-cologne
12. "Germany sex assaults could be linked to criminal gang," *CBS News*, January 6, 2016.
     https://www.cbsnews.com/news/germany-police-cologne-sexual-assaults-criminal-network-refugees-migrants/
13. Yermi Brenner and Katrin Ohlendorf, "Time for the facts. What do we know about Cologne four months later?" *The Correspondent*, May 2, 2016.
     https://thecorrespondent.com/4401/time-for-the-facts-what-do-we-know-about-cologne-four-months-later/1073698080444-e20ada1b
14. Patrick Hinton, "New Survey Reveals 9 in 10 Female Students Have Been Groped in a Nightclub?" *MixMag*, November 21, 2016.
     https://mixmag.net/amp/new-survey-reveals-91-per-cent-of-female-students-have-experienced-sexual-harassment-in-clubs
15. Abby Young-Powell, "Sexual harassment is 'normal' in clubs, but are things about to change?" *The Guardian*, March 13, 2014.

https://amp.theguardian.com/education/2014/mar/13/sexual-harassment-normal-clubs-but-about-to-change

16. "Smart dress shows how often and where women are groped in clubs," She Mazing, accessed August 4, 2022. https://www.shemazing.net/smart-dress-shows-how-often-and-where-women-are-groped-in-clubs/

17. "Fake photos flood Internet after sexual assaults in Germany," *France 24*, January 13, 2016. https://amp.observers.france24.com/en/20160113-assaults-migrants-germany-rape-fake-photos

18. Melissa Eddy, "*Bild* Apologizes for False Article on Sexual Assaults in Frankfurt by Migrants," *The New York Times*, February 16, 2017. https://www.nytimes.com/2017/02/16/world/europe/bild-fake-story.html

19. Janosch Delcker, "Germany targets migrants from North Africa," *Politico*, December 30, 2016. https://www.politico.eu/article/after-berlin-terror-attack-germany-gets-tough-on-maghreb-countries-tunisia-morocco-algeria/

20. Moncef Slimi, "Germany and North Africa split over illegal migrants," *DW*, October 10, 2017. https://www.dw.com/en/germany-and-north-africa-split-over-illegal-migrants/a-37077844

21. Ministry of Justice, "Freedom of Information Request," June 2014, accessed August 3, 2022. https://assets.publishing.service.gov.uk/government/uploads/system/uploads/attachment_data/file/324097/number-males-rape-muslim.doc

22. Der Spiegel Staff, "Is There Truth To Refugee Rape Reports?" *Der Spiegel*, January 17, 2018. https://www.spiegel.de/international/germany/is-there-truth-to-refugee-sex-offense-reports-a-1186734.html

23. "Indicators of Integration 2012: Germany," Organisation for Economic Co-operation and Development (OECD), accessed March 20, 2022. https://www.oecd.org/migration/integration-indicators-2012/keyindicatorsbycountry/name,218330,en.htm#

24. Ami Sedghi, "UK Census: religion by age, ethnicity and country of birth," *The Guardian*, May 16, 2013. https://www.theguardian.com/news/datablog/2013/may/16/uk-census-religion-age-ethnicity-country-of-birth

25. Jessica Shaw and HaeNim Lee, "Race and the Criminal Justice System Response to Sexual Assault: A Systematic Review," *American Journal of Community Psychology* 64, no. 1-2 (2019): 255-276. doi: 10.1002/ajcp.12334

26. "Germany Murder/Homicide Rate 1990-2022," Macrotrends, accessed April 4, 2022. https://www.macrotrends.net/countries/DEU/germany/murder-homicide-rate
27. "U.S. Murder/Homicide Rate 1990-2022," Macrotrends, accessed April 4, 2022. https://www.macrotrends.net/countries/USA/united-states/murder-homicide-rate
28. Anil Kumar and Nikhil Dawar, "Fact Check: Claim linking Muslims to 96 per cent rapes in India falls flat," *India Today*, July 6, 2018. https://www.indiatoday.in/fact-check/story/fact-check-claim-linking-muslims-to-96-per-cent-rapes-in-india-falls-flat-1278750-2018-07-06 Commas were added and spacing was adjusted to enhance readability.
29. "Israeli Arab who 'raped' a woman says verdict 'racist,'" *BBC News*, July 21, 2010. https://www.bbc.com/news/world-middle-east-10717186
30. James Longman, "Norway teaches migrants about Western women," *BBC News*, June 7, 2016. https://www.bbc.com/news/world-europe-36469828
31. Jenny Kleeman, Tom Silverstone and Mustafa Khalili, "Norway's Muslim immigrants attend classes on western attitudes to women–video," *The Guardian*, August 1, 2016. https://www.theguardian.com/world/video/2016/aug/01/norway-muslim-immigrants-classes-western-attitudes-women-video
32. Nicholas D. Mirzoeff, "'Reckless Eyeballing': Why Freddie Gray Was Killed," How to See the World, May 30, 2015. https://wp.nyu.edu/howtoseetheworld/2015/05/30/auto-draft-46/
33. Alan Posener, "Germany after the sex attacks: fences are going up and the mood is ugly," *The Guardian*, January 9, 2016. https://www.theguardian.com/world/2016/jan/09/germany-sex-attacks-cologne-immigration
34. Lotta Brännström, Sara Nyhlén and Katja Gillander Gådin, "'You are so ugly, you whore'- girls in rural Sweden discuss and address gendered violence," *International Journal of Qualitative Studies on Health and Well-being* 15, no. 1 (2020): 1695308. doi: 10.1080/17482631.2019.1695308
35. Quran 24:30.
36. Quran 24:31.
37. "The Night That Changed Germany's Attitude To Refugees," Journeyman Pictures, April 4, 2016. https://www.youtube.com/watch?v=qm5SYxRXHsI

38. Carol Anderson, *The Second: Race and Guns in a Fatally Unequal America* (New York: Bloomsbury Publishing, 2021), 103-5.

39. Oklahoma Commission to Study the Tulsa Race Riot of 1921, "Tulsa Race Riot," February 28, 2001. https://www.okhistory.org/research/forms/freport.pdf

40. Rukmini Callimachi, "ISIS Enshrines a Theology of Rape," *New York Times*, August 13, 2015. https://www.nytimes.com/2015/08/14/world/middleeast/isis-enshrines-a-theology-of-rape.html

41. Sam Harris, "#23—Islam and the Future of Tolerance," Making Sense with Sam Harris, podcast audio, December 21, 2015.

42. HE the Sultan Muhammad Sa'ad Ababakar, et al. (126 authors), "Open Letter to Dr. Ibrahim Awwad al-Badri, Alias 'Abu Bakr al-Baghdadi', and to the Fighters and Followers of the Self-Declared 'Islamic State,'" September 19, 2014. https://issuu.com/openlettertobaghdadi/docs/arabic_english_open_lett er_to_baghd

43. Frederick Douglass, *The Frederick Douglass Papers: Series Three: Correspondence: Volume 1: 1842-1852*, John R. McKivigan, editor (New Haven:Yale University Press, 2009), 421. https://books.google.com/books?id=iD07x9v-CiEC

44. US Census Bureau, "America's Families and Living Arrangements: 2010: Table FG4," accessed March 21, 2022. https://www.census.gov/data/tables/2010/demo/families/cps-2010.html

Chapter 16
Economic Gender Inequality in Islam

1. Quran 4:32.

2. Quran 4:7.

3. Ayatollah Ruhollah Khomeini, *Tahrir al-Wasilah*, 607-611.

4. Ayatollah Ruhollah Khomeini, *Tahrir al-Wasilah*, 599.

5. Ayatollah Ruhollah Khomeini, *Tahrir al-Wasilah*, 598.

6. "Difference Between Dower And Dowry," Law Corner, July 19, 2019. https://lawcorner.in/difference-between-dower-and-dowry

7. Jone Johnson Lewis, "A Short History of Women's Property Rights in the United States," *ThoughCo.*, July 13, 2019. https://www.thoughtco.com/property-rights-of-women-3529578

8. "Married Women's Property Act 1882." https://www.legislation.gov.uk/ukpga/Vict/45-46/75/contents

9. Trista, "40 Basic Rights Women Did Not Have Until The 1970s,"
    History Collection, June 26, 2019.
    https://historycollection.com/40-basic-rights-women-did-not-have-
    until-the-1970s/30/
10. Urooba Jamal, "Danish minister's comment on sex before marriage
    angers Muslims," *Al Jazeera*, November 26, 2020.
    https://www.aljazeera.com/features/2020/11/26/danish-ministers-
    comment-on-sex-before-marriage-angers-muslims
11. Quran 4:20.
12. Sumbul Ali-Karamali, *Demystifying Shariah*, 199-200.
13. "More Danish teens are waiting to have sex," *The Local*, November 18,
    2016.
    https://www.thelocal.dk/20161118/more-danish-teens-waiting-to-
    have-sex/
14. Quran 4:11.
15. Quran 4:11.
16. Quran 4:12.
17. Quran 4:176.
18. Quran 4:11.
19. Nazir Khan, Tesneem Alkiek and Safiah Chowdhury, "Women in
    Islamic Law: Examining Five Prevalent Myths," Yaqeen Institute, July
    24, 2019.
    https://yaqeeninstitute.org/read/paper/women-in-islamic-law-
    examining-five-prevalent-myths#ftnt_ref113
20. Ayatollah Ruhollah Khomeini, *Tahrir al-Wasilah*, 611-14.
21. Quran 4:11 and 4:12.
22. Quran 2:180.
23. Ursula Lindsey, "Can Muslim Feminism Find a Third Way?" *The New
    York Times*, April 11, 2018.
    https://www.nytimes.com/2018/04/11/opinion/islam-feminism-third-
    way.html
24. Edward W. Said, *Orientalism*, 67.
25. It should be noted that many Shia scholars exclude land from a wife's
    inheritance, in which case the daughters would each get a third of the
    land. The cousin would, regardless, be excluded.
26. Numbers 27:8, New International Version.
27. Deuteronomy 25:5, New International Version.
28. Quran 4:19.

Chapter 17
Gender Inequality in Legal Affairs

1.   Quran 5:87.
2.   Spencer Wilking and Lauren Effron, "Snake-Handling Pentecostal Pastor Dies From Snake Bite," *ABC News*, February 17, 2014. https://abcnews.go.com/US/snake-handling-pentecostal-pastor-dies-snake-bite/story?id=22551754
3.   Quran 2:282.
4.   Ayatollah Ruhollah Khomeini, *Tahrir al-Wasilah*, 693.
5.   Sheryl G. Stolberg and Carl Hulse, "Joe Biden Expresses Regret to Anita Hill, but She Says 'I'm Sorry' Is Not Enough," *The New York Times*, April 25, 2019. https://www.nytimes.com/2019/04/25/us/politics/joe-biden-anita-hill.html
6.   Ayatollah Ruhollah Khomeini, *Tahrir al-Wasilah*, 693.
7.   Ayatollah Ruhollah Khomeini, *Tahrir al-Wasilah*, 600.
8.   Yuval Sinai, "Witness," Jewish Virtual Library, accessed March 21, 2022. https://www.jewishvirtuallibrary.org/witness
9.   Mark 16:9-11.
10. 1 Timothy 2:12, New International Version.
11. 1 Corinthians 14:34, Christian Standard Bible.
12. Quran 5:45.
13. Quran 2:237.
14. Quran 2:280.
15. Quran 4:92.
16. Quran 2:178.
17. Bureau of Democracy, Human Rights, and Labor, U.S. Department of State, "Iran: International Religious Freedom Report 2006," September 15, 2006. https://2001-2009.state.gov/g/drl/rls/irf/2006/71421.htm
18. Dariely Rodriguez and Hope Kwiatkowski, "How Race, Ethnicity, and Gender Impact Your Life's Worth: Discrimination in Civil Damage Awards," Lawyers' Committee for Civil Rights Under Law, July 2018: 6. https://lawyerscommittee.org/wp-content/uploads/2018/07/LC_Life27s-Worth_FINAL.pdf
19. Amanda Barroso and Anna Brown, "Gender pay gap in U.S. held steady in 2020," Pew Research Center, May 25, 2021. https://www.pewresearch.org/fact-tank/2021/05/25/gender-pay-gap-facts/
20. "Iranian sentenced to blinding for acid attack pardoned," *BBC News*, July 31, 2011.

https://www.bbc.com/news/world-middle-east-14356886
21. Pete, "How we know Islam is irrational," *News24*, August 1, 2013.
https://www.news24.com/News24/how-we-know-islam-is-irrational-20130801
22. Anthony Franc, Scott Hesketh and Ben Morgan, "London is 'acid attack hotspot of western world' with victims as young as 10," *Evening Standard*, August 28, 2019.
https://www.standard.co.uk/news/crime/london-is-acid-attack-hotspot-of-western-world-with-victims-as-young-as-10-a4222921.html
23. Lizzie Dearden, "John Tomlin: Man jailed for 16 years for acid attack on two cousins in east London," *The Independent*, April 20, 2018.
https://www.independent.co.uk/news/uk/crime/john-tomlin-acid-attack-car-jailed-resham-khan-jameel-muhktar-london-latest-updates-a8314101.html
24. "London Muslims 'scared to leave homes' amid online panic over acid attacks," *Al Arabiya News*, July 5, 2017, updated May 20, 2020.
https://english.alarabiya.net/features/2017/07/05/London-Muslims-scared-to-leave-homes-amid-online-panic-over-acid-attacks-
25. Ayatollah Ruhollah Khomeini, *Tahrir al-Wasilah*, 444 and 617.
26. "Priests' wives missing after converting to Islam in divorce bid," *Irish Examiner*, December 27, 2010.
https://www.irishexaminer.com/world/arid-30487090.html
27. Dov Lieber and Agencies, "Terror group Hamas condemns 'heinous' Egypt church bombing," *The Times of Israel*, April 9, 2017.
https://www.timesofisrael.com/terror-group-hamas-condemns-heinous-egypt-church-bombing/

Chapter 18
The Polygynous Muslim Man

1. "Special Ops TV: U.S. WELFARE PAYS FOR 4 'WIVES' PER HUSBAND," CleanTVcom, August 26, 2014.
https://www.youtube.com/watch?v=0R81h6rWgtU
2. Clayton Youngman, "A Muslim immigrant in Michigan can list his second, third or fourth wives as "extended family" and qualify for welfare," *PolitiFact*, December 7, 2015.
https://www.politifact.com/factchecks/2015/dec/07/chain-email/youtube-video-says-michigan-muslims-can-list-multi/
3. Quran 4:3.
4. Quran 4:129.

5.   Stephanie Kramer, "Polygamy is rare around the world and mostly confined to a few regions," Pew Research Center, December 7, 2020. https://www.pewresearch.org/fact-tank/2020/12/07/polygamy-is-rare-around-the-world-and-mostly-confined-to-a-few-regions/

6.   Exodus 21:10, Christian Standard Bible.

7.   1 Kings 11:3, New International Version.

8.   Patrick F. O'Hare, *The Facts about Luther* (New York: Frederick Pustet, Inc., 1916), 334. https://books.google.com/books?id=ndoPAAAAYAAJ

9.   Burcu Karakaş, "The fragility of Syrian refugee women in Turkey," *Osservatorio Balcani e Caucaso Transeuropa*, December 24, 2018. https://www.balcanicaucaso.org/eng/Areas/Turkey/The-fragility-of-Syrian-refugee-women-in-Turkey-191805

10. Stanley Fish, *There's No Such Thing as Free Speech*, 12.

11. Courtney Comstock, "Niall Ferguson Is Leaving His Wife For A Young Hot Feminist And Political War Refugee," *Business Insider*, February 8, 2010. https://www.businessinsider.com/niall-ferguson-is-ditching-his-wife-for-a-young-hot-feminist-and-politcal-war-refugee-2010-2

12. Jeevan Vasagar, "Niall Ferguson: admirable historian, or imperial mischief maker?" *The Guardian*, June 18, 2012. https://www.theguardian.com/books/2012/jun/18/niall-ferguson-bbc-reith-lecturer-radio4

13. Quran 33:4-5.

14. Kaleef K. Karim, "Zayd, Zaynab And Muhammed: Fabrications And Lies," Discover the Truth, August 18, 2016. https://discover-the-truth.com/2016/08/18/zayd-zaynab-and-muhammed-fabrications-and-lies/

Chapter 19
Portraying Muslims as Pedophiles

1.   Christina Cauterucci, "Why Republicans Have Become Obsessed With Accusing Their Opponents of Pedophilia," *Slate*, October 22, 2020. https://slate.com/news-and-politics/2020/10/republicans-baseless-pedophilia-accusations-explained.html

2.   Amanda Robb, "Anatomy of a Fake News Scandal," *Rolling Stone*, November 16, 2017. https://www.rollingstone.com/feature/anatomy-of-a-fake-news-scandal-125877/

3. Julia C. Wong, "QAnon explained: the antisemitic conspiracy theory gaining traction around the world," *The Guardian*, August 25, 2020. https://www.theguardian.com/us-news/2020/aug/25/qanon-conspiracy-theory-explained-trump-what-is

4. Ridhwan ibn Saleem, "Proof That Aisha Was Over 15 Years Old When She Married The Prophet (Peace Be Upon Him)," Ha Meem Foundation, February 11, 2019. https://hameem.org/2019/02/11/proof-that-aisha-was-over-15-years-old-when-she-married-the-prophet-peace-be-upon-him/

5. "Pakistan—Completeness Of Birth Registration, Rural," Trading Economics, accessed March 22, 2022. https://tradingeconomics.com/pakistan/completeness-of-birth-registration-rural-percent-wb-data.html

6. Scott Allen, "6 Athletes (and a Coach) Who Lied About Their Age," *Mental Floss*, February 25, 2009. https://www.mentalfloss.com/article/20971/6-athletes-and-coach-who-lied-about-their-age

7. Kaleef K. Karim, "Marriage of Mary To Joseph the Carpenter!" Discover the Truth, September 30, 2013. https://discover-the-truth.com/2013/09/30/marriage-of-mary-to-joseph-the-carpenter/

8. Judges 21:11, New International Version.

9. Numbers 31:17-18. King James Version.

10. Numbers 31:35, International Standard Version.

11. Judges 21:22-23.

12. Exodus 21:7.

13. "Niddah 45a," *The William Davidson Talmud*. https://www.sefaria.org/Niddah.45a

14. "Age of Consent in European & American History," Discover the Truth, September 9, 2013. https://discover-the-truth.com/2013/09/09/age-of-consent-in-european-american-history/

15. "Sexual Assault," Texas Penal Code, PENAL § 22.011, accessed March 22, 2022. https://statutes.capitol.texas.gov/Docs/PE/htm/PE.22.htm

16. "Marriage Age by State 2022," World Population Review, accessed March 22, 2022. https://worldpopulationreview.com/state-rankings/marriage-age-by-state

17. Max Roser, Esteban Ortiz-Ospina and Hannah Ritchie, "Life Expectancy," Our World in Data, October, 2019. https://ourworldindata.org/life-expectancy

18. Mohammed Jamjoom, "Yemeni child bride dies of internal bleeding," *CNN*, April 9, 2010. http://www.cnn.com/2010/WORLD/meast/04/09/yemen.child.bride.death/index.html

19. "Iran Reports Increase In Child Marriages," *Radio Farda*, August 20, 2021. https://www.rferl.org/a/iran-child-marriages/31420642.html

20. Maya Gebeily, "Syrian refugee girls face 'dangerous' child marriage trend, says charity," *Reuters*, June 25, 2021. https://www.reuters.com/article/us-refugees-mideast-children-trfn-idUSKCN2E11MS

21. Margaret Brennan, "U.S. investigates "child bride" cases among Afghan evacuees," *CBS News*, September 3, 2021. https://news.yahoo.com/u-investigates-child-bride-cases-001700012.html?fr=sycsrp_catchall

22. Michael Konopasek, "OKC Drug Addicts Prostitute Toddler For Meth," *News 9*, June 24, 2011. https://www.news9.com/story/5e34f9a2e0c96e774b366b58/okc-drug-addicts-prostitute-toddler-for-meth

23. Caitlin O'Kane, "Demi Moore: Man who raped me as teen said I was 'whored' by my mother for $500," *CBS News*, September 23, 2019. https://www.cbsnews.com/news/demi-moore-diane-sawyer-interview-opens-up-about-being-raped-by-a-man-who-paid-her-mother-500-book-inside-out/

24. Marissa B Esser, Adam Sherk, Yong Liu, Timothy S. Naimi, Timothy Stockwell, Mandy Stahre, Dafna Kanny, Michael Landen, Richard Saitz and Robert D. Brewer, "Deaths and Years of Potential Life Lost From Excessive Alcohol Use - United States, 2011-2015," *MMWR: Morbidity and Mortality Weekly Report* 69, no. 39 (2020): 1428–1433. doi: 10.15585/mmwr.mm6939a6

25. IANS, "84% Of 12 mn married children under 10 are Hindus," *Business Standard*, June 1, 2016. https://www.business-standard.com/article/news-ians/84-of-12-mn-married-children-under-10-are-hindus-special-to-ians-116060101132_1.html

26. *The Skanda Purana*, translated by G. V. Tagare, 1950, Book 3, Section 2, Chapter 30, verses 8-9. https://www.wisdomlib.org/hinduism/book/the-skanda-purana/d/doc423651.html

27. *The Skanda Purana*, translated by G. V. Tagare, 1950, Book 5, Section 3, Chapter 142.

https://www.wisdomlib.org/hinduism/book/the-skanda-purana/d/doc425871.html

28. *"Vamana Purana* 6.17.1 Mena gives birth to Uma," in *The Puranas: A compact, English-only version of the Major 18 Puranas in one document*, Dharmic Scriptures Team, October 3, 2002.
http://www.vcscsd.com/content/balabhavan/18-Puranas.pdf

29. Sulaiman Razvi, "Paedophilia in Hinduism," VedKaBhed.Com, January 3, 2014.
https://vedkabhed.com/index.php/2014/01/03/paedophilia-in-hinduism/

30. Daniel M. Filler and Kenneth M. Rosen, "Terrorism, Panic and Pedophilia," *Alabama Law Scholarly Commons*, September 12, 2003.
https://scholarship.law.ua.edu/cgi/viewcontent.cgi?article=1176&cont ext=fac_working_papers

31. Stephen Piggott, "ACT for America's 'March Against Sharia' Official Facebook Page Full of Racist Anti-Muslim Sentiment," Southern Poverty Law Center Hatewatch, May 23, 2017.
https://www.splcenter.org/hatewatch/2017/05/23/act-americas-march-against-sharia-official-facebook-page-full-racist-anti-muslim-sentiment

32. "Hmmm, That new wife smell," Sizzle, accessed March 22, 2022.
https://onsizzle.com/i/157710838-hmmm-that-new-wife-smell-11841501

33. Ayatollah Ruhollah Khomeini, *Tahrir al-Wasilah*, 563.

Chapter 20
Honor Killings and Wife Beatings

1. "Item 12 - Integration of the human rights of women and the gender perspective: Violence Against Women and 'Honor' Crimes," Human Rights Watch, April 5, 2001.
https://www.hrw.org/news/2001/04/05/item-12-integration-human-rights-women-and-gender-perspective-violence-against-women

2. Rafia Zakaria, *Against White Feminism*, 141.

3. Ibid., 155-6.

4. Ibid., 95-102.

5. Ibid., 152-3.

6. Ibid., 95.

7. Olga Kazan, "Nearly Half of All Murdered Women Are Killed by Romantic Partners," *The Atlantic*, July 20, 2017.

https://www.theatlantic.com/health/archive/2017/07/homicides-women/534306/

8.   National Coalition Against Domestic Violence, "Domestic Violence,"
     2020.
     https://assets.speakcdn.com/assets/2497/domestic_violence-
     2020080709350855.pdf?1596811079991

9.   "Homicide statistics by gender," Wikipedia, accessed March 22, 2022.
     https://en.wikipedia.org/wiki/Homicide_statistics_by_gender

10. Government of Canada, "Rights and Responsibilities of Citizenship,"
     accessed March 22, 2022.
     https://www.canada.ca/en/immigration-refugees-
     citizenship/corporate/publications-manuals/discover-canada/read-
     online/rights-resonsibilities-citizenship.html

11. Michelle Goodman, "'I Married for Health Insurance,'" *ABC News*, July
     17, 2008.
     https://abcnews.go.com/Business/CareerManagement/story?id=53799
     23

12. Sam Cabral, "'Sania Khan: She TikToked her divorce, then her husband
     killed her,'" *BBC News*, August 9, 2022.
     https://www.bbc.com/news/world-us-canada-62427084

13. Koenig, Sarah, "Season One," Serialpodcast.org, Fall 2014.
     https://serialpodcast.org/season-one

14. Mary C. McCauley, "Adnan Syed's story, as told by friend and advocate
     Rabia Chaudry," *The Baltimore Sun*, August 6, 2016.
     https://www.baltimoresun.com/opinion/columnists/zurawik/bs-ae-
     rabia-chaudry-adnan-syed-20160806-story.html

15. Quran 4:34.

16. Ayatollah Ruhollah Khomeini, *Tahrir al-Wasilah*, 308-320.

17. Quran 2:231.

18. *Sahih Muslim*, hadith #2328a.
     https://sunnah.com/muslim:2328a

19. *Sunan Abi Dawud*, hadith #2139.
     https://sunnah.com/abudawud:2144

20. 1 Peter 3:1, New International Version.

21. Ephesians 5:22-24, New International Version.

22. 1 Corinthians 11:3, New Revised Standard Version.

23. 1 Corinthians 14:34-35, New International Version.

24. Proverbs 10:13, New King James Version.

25. Proverbs 26:3, New King James Version.

26. Proverbs 20:30, New King James Version.

27. Quran 3:110.

Endnotes 379

28. Kim Elsesser, "The Truth About Women's Impact On Corporate Boards (It's Not Good News)," *Forbes*, June 23, 2016. https://www.forbes.com/sites/kimelsesser/2016/06/23/the-truth-about-womens-impact-on-corporate-boards-its-not-good-news/?sh=231933a95ecb
29. Adam Grant, "Who won't shut up in meetings? Men say it's women. It's not," *The Washington Post*, February 18, 2021. https://www.washingtonpost.com/outlook/2021/02/18/men-interrupt-women-tokyo-olympics/
30. Ayatollah Ruhollah Khomeini, *Tahrir al-Wasilah*, 607-11.
31. Ayatollah Ruhollah Khomeini, *Tahrir al-Wasilah*, 606.
32. "Iran Panel Backs Divorce Payments," *The New York Times*, December 17, 1992. https://www.nytimes.com/1992/12/17/world/iran-panel-backs-divorce-payments.html
33. Holly Dagres, "'Game of Thrones' fever grips Iran," *Al-Monitor*, July 12, 2017. https://www.al-monitor.com/originals/2017/07/why-iranians-love-game-of-thrones.html
34. Max Fisher, "Iran's Female Ninjas File a Lawsuit: Not Every Iranian Is Out to Kill Us," *The Atlantic*, March 29, 2012. https://www.theatlantic.com/international/archive/2012/03/irans-female-ninjas-file-a-lawsuit-not-every-iranian-is-out-to-kill-us/255237/
35. "Meet Iran's female ninja assassins: 3,000 women training to defend the Muslim state," *Daily Mail*, February 6, 2012. https://www.dailymail.co.uk/news/article-2097087/Irans-female-ninja-assassins-3-000-women-training-defend-Muslim-state.html

Chapter 21
Love Jihad

1. Anand Dibyesh, *Hindu Nationalism in India and the Politics of Fear* (United States: Palgrave Macmillian, 2011), 1.
2. Lalmani Verma, "BJP Unnao MP Sakshi Maharaj claims madrasas offering cash rewards for love jihad," *The Indian Express*, March 23, 2022. https://indianexpress.com/article/india/politics/bjp-unnao-mp-sakshi-maharaj-claims-madrasas-offering-cash-rewards-for-love-jihad/
3. "Govt directs CID to probe 'love jihad,'" *The Times of India*, October 27, 2009.

https://timesofindia.indiatimes.com/city/bengaluru/govt-directs-cid-to-probe-love-jihad/articleshow/5166639.cms?referral=PM

4.   "Jail term, fine for 'illegal' conversions in Uttar Pradesh," *The Hindu*, November 24, 2020.
     https://www.thehindu.com/news/national/uttar-pradesh-cabinet-clears-ordinance-against-love-jihad/article33170627.ece

5.   T. A. Johnson, "Karnataka's draft Bill has 10-year jail term for 'forced conversion,'" *The Indian Express*, December 17, 2021.
     https://indianexpress.com/article/cities/bangalore/bjp-stringent-law-against-conversion-in-karnataka-7676439/

6.   Lebo Diseko, "Interfaith marriage: Pew survey says most Indians oppose it," *BCC News*, June 29, 2021.
     https://www.bbc.com/news/world-asia-india-57647931

7.   M. G. Radhakrishnan, "Over 2500 women converted to Islam in Kerala since 2006, says Oommen Chandy," *India Today*, September 4, 2012.
     https://www.indiatoday.in/india/south/story/love-jihad-oommen-chandy-islam-kerala-muslim-marriage-115150-2012-09-04

8.   Josh Layton, "Sikh girls 'abused by grooming gangs for decades' says shock new report," *Birmingham Mail*, December 3, 2018.
     https://www.birminghammail.co.uk/news/midlands-news/sikh-girls-abused-grooming-gangs-15492360

9.   Ishita Mishra, "In UP, community bans mobiles for girls to fight 'love jihad,'" *The Times of India*, September 2, 2014.
     https://timesofindia.indiatimes.com/india/In-UP-community-bans-mobiles-for-girls-to-fight-love-jihad/articleshow/41472311.cms

10. Betwa Sharma and Ahmer Khan, "Hindu Vigilantes Work with Police to Enforce 'Love Jihad' Law in North India," *The Intercept*, July 3, 2021.
     https://theintercept.com/2021/07/03/love-jihad-law-india/

11. This is my adaptation of the quote, "when a white woman cries, a black man gets hurt," from Robin DiAngelo, *White Fragility*, 133.

12. Rahul Bhatia, "The Year of Love Jihad in India," *The New Yorker*, December 31, 2017.
     https://www.newyorker.com/culture/2017-in-review/the-year-of-love-jihad-in-india

13. Sut Jhally, "Edward Said: On 'Orientalism,'" (interview), Media Education Foundation 2005.
     https://issuu.com/mlfcham/docs/edwardsaidonorientalism

14. Julie H. Davis and Katie Rogers, "Donald Trump: Women at rallies see a hero protecting their way of life," *The Sydney Morning Herald*, November 4, 2018.

https://www.smh.com.au/world/north-america/donald-trump-
women-at-rallies-see-a-hero-protecting-their-way-of-life-20181104-
p50dwk.html

Chapter 22
Portraying Muslims as Homophobes

1. Allen West, "BRILLIANT cartoon highlights liberal LGBT hypocrisy,"
    Twitter, May 11, 2016.
    https://twitter.com/allenwest/status/730456770137579521
2. Quran 24:4.
3. Saskia Glas and Niels Spierings, "Rejecting homosexuality but tolerating
    homosexuals: The complex relations between religiosity and opposition
    to homosexuality in 9 Arab countries," *Social Science Research* 95 (2021):
    102533.
    doi: 10.1016/j.ssresearch.2021.102533
4. Michel Foucault, *The History of Sexuality*, 43.
5. Quran 49:12.
6. Quran 2:189.
7. Quran 24:27.
8. Jalal al-Din al-Suyuti, *Al-Durr al-Manthur Fi Tafsir Bil-Ma'thur*, verse
    49:12.
    https://www.altafsir.com/Tafasir.asp?tMadhNo=2&tTafsirNo=26&tSo
    raNo=49&tAyahNo=12&tDisplay=yes&Page=3&Size=1&LanguageId
    =1
9. Quran 49:12.
10. Quran 24:4.
11. Leviticus 18:22, New International Version.
12. Leviticus 20:13, New International Version.
13. Genesis 19.
14. 1 Corinthians 6:9, New International Version.
15. 1 Timothy 1:9-10, New International Version.
16. Romans 1:27-32, New International Version.
17. "Like Americans overall, Muslims now more accepting of
    homosexuality," Pew Research Center, July 25, 2017.
    https://www.pewforum.org/2017/07/26/political-and-social-
    views/pf_2017-06-26_muslimamericans-04new-06/
18. "Why Iran is a hub for sex-reassignment surgery," *The Economist*, April
    6, 2019.
    https://www.economist.com/middle-east-and-
    africa/2019/04/04/why-iran-is-a-hub-for-sex-reassignment-surgery

19. Robert Tait, "Sex change funding undermines no gays claim," *The Guardian*, September 25, 2007.
https://www.theguardian.com/world/2007/sep/26/iran.gender
20. Ali Hamedani, "The gay people pushed to change their gender," *BBC News*, November 5, 2014.
https://www.bbc.com/news/magazine-29832690
21. Zara Saeidzadeh, "Understanding Socio-Legal Complexities of Sex Change in Postrevolutionary Iran," *Transgender Studies Quarterly* 6, no. 1 (2019): 80-102.
doi: 10.1215/23289252-7253510

Chapter 23
Circumcision as Mutilation

1. "Circumcision (male)," Mayo Clinic, accessed March 23, 2022.
https://www.mayoclinic.org/tests-procedures/circumcision/about/pac-20393550
2. "CDC Provides Information to Male Patients and Parents Regarding Male Circumcision and the Prevention of HIV Infection, Sexually Transmitted Infections, and Other Health Outcomes," Centers for Disease Control and Prevention, accessed March 23, 2022.
https://www.cdc.gov/nchhstp/newsroom/docs/factsheets/MC-for-HIV-Prevention-Fact-Sheet_508.pdf
3. "Male circumcision for HIV control," World Health Organization, accessed March 23, 2022.
https://www.who.int/reproducwtivehealth/topics/rtis/male_circumcision/en/
4. Antoin Douglawi and Timothy A. Masterson, "Updates on the epidemiology and risk factors for penile cancer," *Translational Andrology and Urology* 6, no. 5 (2017): 785-90.
doi: 10.21037/tau.2017.05.19
5. Muhammad ibn Ya'qub al-Kulayni, *Al-Kafi*, 6:34.
http://lib.eshia.ir/11005/6/34
6. Maria Owings, Sayeedha Uddin and Sonja Williams, "Trends in Circumcision for Male Newborns in U.S. Hospitals: 1979–2010," Centers for Disease Control and Prevention, August 2013.
https://www.cdc.gov/nchs/data/hestat/circumcision_2013/circumcision_2013.pdf
7. "German court rules circumcision is 'bodily harm,'" *BBC News*, June 26, 2012.
https://www.bbc.com/news/world-europe-18604664

8. Stephen Evans, "German circumcision ban: Is it a parent's right to choose?" *BBC News*, July 13, 2012.
    https://www.bbc.com/news/magazine-18793842

9. CNE.news, "Danish parliament rejects ban on boys' circumcision," *Reformatorisch Dagblad*, May 19, 2021.
    https://www.rd.nl/artikel/927843-danish-parliament-rejects-ban-on-boys-circumcision

10. Lyssandra Sears, "Ban religious circumcision: Swiss," *The Local*, July 31, 2012.
    https://www.thelocal.ch/20120731/majority-of-swiss-want-religious-circumcision-banned/

11. JTA and TOI Staff, "Leading US House members urge Iceland to back down on circumcision ban," *Times of Israel*, April 13, 2018.
    https://www.timesofisrael.com/leading-us-house-members-urge-iceland-to-back-down-on-circumcision-ban/

12. "Sexual Medicine: Female Genital Anatomy," Boston University School of Medicine, accessed March 23, 2022.
    https://www.bumc.bu.edu/sexualmedicine/physicianinformation/female-genital-anatomy/

13. "Types of female genital mutilation," World Health Organization, accessed March 23, 2022.
    https://www.who.int/teams/sexual-and-reproductive-health-and-research-(srh)/areas-of-work/female-genital-mutilation/types-of-female-genital-mutilation

14. Emma Batha, "'Heartwrenching' study shows FGM prevalent among India's Bohra sect," *Reuters*, February 5, 2018.
    https://www.reuters.com/article/us-india-fgm-study/heartwrenching-study-shows-fgm-prevalent-among-indias-bohra-sect-idUSKBN1FP12D

15. Kevin Drum, "Female Genital Mutilation Is Not a Uniquely Muslim Problem," *Mother Jones*, February 6, 2016.
    https://www.motherjones.com/kevin-drum/2016/02/female-genital-mutilation-not-uniquely-muslim-problem/

16. "The Cut: Exploring FGM," *Al Jazeera English*, October 5, 2017.
    https://www.youtube.com/watch?v=TWIzaD4-_y4

17. Kat McQuade, "Cornflake Christians: Women Are Being Subjected To Female Genital Mutilation In The Heart Of America," *Bust*, accessed March 23, 2022.
    https://bust.com/feminism/195839-female-genital-mutilation-america-kentucky-woman-christian.html

18. *Sunan Abi Dawud*, hadith #5271
    https://sunnah.com/abudawud:5271

19. Muhammad ibn Ya'qub al-Kulayni, *Al-Kafi*, 6:38.
    http://lib.eshia.ir/11005/6/38
20. Muhammad ibn Ya'qub al-Kulayni, *Al-Kafi*, 6:37.
    http://lib.eshia.ir/11005/6/37
21. Bayhaqi, *Sunan al-Kubra*, hadith #17343-5.
    http://islamport.com/w/mtn/Web/969/3297.htm
22. Karaman, M. Ihsan, "Female circumcision debate: A muslim surgeon's perspective," *Turkish Journal of Urology* 47, no. 3 (2021): 193–198.
    doi:10.5152/tud.2021.20546
23. Laren Stover, "The Selfie That Dares to Go There," *The New York Times*, July 7, 2018.
    https://www.nytimes.com/2018/07/07/style/vagina-selfies.html
24. "Reduction of Clitoris," Gary J Alter, M.D., November 4, 2020.
    https://www.youtube.com/watch?v=P2YHC5L5hpU
25. Olga Khazan, "Why Some Women Choose to Get Circumcised," *The Atlantic*, April 8, 2015.
    https://www.theatlantic.com/international/archive/2015/04/female-genital-mutilation-cutting-anthropologist/389640/
26. "Fatwas against FGM," Stop FGM Middle East, accessed April 8, 2022.
    http://www.stopfgmmideast.org/fatwas-against-fgm/

Chapter 24
We Can't Take Any More Muslim Immigrants

27. WHO study group on female genital mutilation and obstetric outcome, Emily Banks, Olav Meirik, Tim Farley, Oluwole Akande, Heli Bathija and Mohamed Ali, "Female genital mutilation and obstetric outcome: WHO collaborative prospective study in six African countries," *Lancet* 367, no. 9525 (2006): 1835-41.
    doi:10.1016/S0140-6736(06)68805-3
28. Danny Hakim, "U.S. Chamber of Commerce Works Globally to Fight Antismoking Measures," *The New York Times*, June 30, 2015.
    https://www.nytimes.com/2015/07/01/business/international/us-chamber-works-globally-to-fight-antismoking-measures.html
1. Von Michael Bröcker and Eva Quadbeck, "'Grundrecht auf Asyl kennt keine Obergrenze,'" *RP Online*, September 11, 2015. Translated by Google Translate on March 24, 2022.
    https://rp-online.de/politik/deutschland/angela-merkel-das-grundrecht-auf-asyl-kennt-keine-obergrenze_aid-9533771
2. "What is the EU-Turkey deal?" International Rescue Committee, March 18, 2022.

https://eu.rescue.org/article/what-eu-turkey-deal

3.   Irene Dominioni, "Italy Refinances Immigration Agreement With Libya Amid Protests," *Forbes*, July 18, 2020.
     https://www.forbes.com/sites/irenedominioni/2020/07/18/italy-refinances-immigration-agreement-with-libya-amid-protests/?sh=27522e6a3c49

4.   "Polish MP: 'For me, multiculturalism is not a value' | UpFront (Headliner)," *Al Jazeera English*, November 9, 2019.
     https://www.youtube.com/watch?v=ccOp0I8ZPho

5.   Charlotte Lysa, "A Recent History of Refugees in Saudi Arabia," Refugee History, October 2020.
     http://refugeehistory.org/blog/2020/11/12/a-recent-history-of-refugees-in-saudi-arabia

6.   Dave Lawler, "Migrants freezing to death on EU frontier," *Axios*, November 22, 2021.
     https://www.axios.com/poland-belarus-border-freezing-9633aeee-7fb8-4fe3-aca8-56adc891a7c5.html

7.   Marlene Auer, "Witness: 'If You Scream, They Will Beat You More,'" Human Rights Watch, March 5, 2021.
     https://www.hrw.org/news/2021/03/05/witness-if-you-scream-they-will-beat-you-more

8.   Trine Villemann, "Denmark's daylight robbery of refugees," *DW*, January 25, 2016.
     https://www.dw.com/en/denmarks-daylight-robbery-of-refugees/a-19002215

9.   Kenan Malik, "Lukashenko is a handy villain to mask the cruelty of Fortress Europe," *The Guardian*, November 14, 2021.
     https://www.theguardian.com/commentisfree/2021/nov/14/fortress-europe-violent-pushbacks-exploit-people-pursue-policy

10. "Refugee Data Finder," UNHCR: The UN Refugee Agency, accessed February 22, 2022.
     https://www.unhcr.org/refugee-statistics/

11. "Refugees Around the World—Facts and Figures," Amnesty International, accessed February 22, 2022.
     https://www.amnesty.org/en/what-we-do/refugees-asylum-seekers-and-migrants/global-refugee-crisis-statistics-and-facts/

12. "List of countries by refugee population," Wikipedia, accessed February 22, 2022.
     https://en.wikipedia.org/wiki/List_of_countries_by_refugee_population

13. "Universal Declaration of Human Rights," United Nations, accessed February 22, 2022.

https://www.un.org/en/about-us/universal-declaration-of-human-rights

14.   John Katko, "Border Crisis: Startling Stats," October 25, 2021.
       https://republicans-homeland.house.gov/wp-content/uploads/2021/10/Startling-Stats-11.0-v1.pdf

15.   Julián Aguilar, "Trump backs off tariff threat, says Mexico will help stem
       tide of Central American migrants headed for the U.S.," *The Texas
       Tribune*, June 7, 2019.
       https://www.texastribune.org/2019/06/07/trump-tariff-threat-dropped-mexico-stem-tide-central-american-migrants/

16.   Virginia Harrison, "Nauru refugees: The island where children have
       given up on life," *BBC News*, September 1, 2018.
       https://www.bbc.com/news/world-asia-45327058

17.   Nosmot Gbadamosi, "Britain Seeks to Send Refugees to Rwanda,"
       Foreign Policy, April 20, 2022.
       https://foreignpolicy.com/2022/04/20/britain-rwanda-refugees-asylum-kagame-authoritarianism/

Chapter 25
If You're Not Happy Here, then Leave

1.   "President Trump: 'They want to leave they can leave,'" *C-Span*, July
       15, 2019.
       https://www.youtube.com/watch?v=dpJE5qd9CRM

2.   Bianca Quilantan and David Cohen, "Trump tells Dem congresswomen:
       Go back where you came from," *Politico*, July 14, 2019.
       https://www.politico.com/story/2019/07/14/trump-congress-go-back-where-they-came-from-1415692

3.   Stacy P. McDermott, "Lincoln & Race: The Great Emancipator didn't
       advocate racial equality. But was he a racist?" *NPR Illinois*, February 1,
       2004.
       https://www.nprillinois.org/statehouse/2004-02-01/lincoln-race-the-great-emancipator-didnt-advocate-racial-equality-but-was-he-a-racist

4.   "Denmark approves stripping IS fighters of citizenship," *DW*, October
       24, 2019.
       https://www.dw.com/en/denmark-approves-stripping-is-fighters-of-citizenship/a-50970297

5.   Hagai El-Ad, "Israel has chosen a two-tiered society. Violence is the
       inevitable result," *The Washington Post*, May 14, 2021.

https://www.washingtonpost.com/outlook/israel-has-chosen-a-two-tiered-society-violence-is-the-inevitable-result/2021/05/14/3ab35f2e-b424-11eb-a980-a60af976ed44_story.html

Chapter 26
Muslims Don't Want to Integrate

1. Lenora Chu and Brendan Sweeney, "Denmark evicts 'ghetto' residents to integrate them. Will it help?" *The Christian Science Monitor*, June 2, 2021.
https://www.csmonitor.com/World/Europe/2021/0602/Denmark-evicts-ghetto-residents-to-integrate-them.-Will-it-help
2. "Denmark plans double punishment for ghetto crime," *BBC News*, February 27, 2018.
https://www.bbc.com/news/world-europe-43214596
3. Jamila Versi, "Denmark's 'ghetto plan' and the communities it targets," *Al Jazeera*, January 15, 2020.
https://www.aljazeera.com/features/2020/1/15/denmarks-ghetto-plan-and-the-communities-it-targets
4. Brent Cebul, "Urban Renewal Meant Negro Removal," *LA Progressive*, July 29, 2020.
https://www.laprogressive.com/racism/urban-renewal
5. "Muslim Americans: No Signs of Growth in Alienation or Support for Extremism," Pew Research Center, August 30, 2011.
https://www.pewresearch.org/politics/2011/08/30/section-1-a-demographic-portrait-of-muslim-americans/
6. "Mjølnerparken, Copenhagen" TrekZone, accessed August 3, 2022.
https://trek.zone/en/denmark/places/872615/mjolnerparken-copenhagen
7. "The Struggle to Integrate Muslims in Europe," Stanford University Immigration Policy Lab, accessed March 24, 2022.
https://immigrationlab.org/project/the-struggle-to-integrate-muslims-in-europe/
8. Jim Myers, *Afraid of the Dark: What Whites and Blacks Need to Know About Each Other* (Chicago: Lawrence Hill Books, 2000), 80.
https://www.google.com/books/edition/Afraid_of_the_Dark/BgUWGDdErDoC
9. Erika K. Wilson, "The New White Flight," *Duke Journal of Constitutional Law & Public Policy* 14 (2019): 233-284.
https://scholarship.law.duke.edu/djclpp/vol14/iss1/5/

10. Suein Hwang, "The New White Flight," *The Wall Street Journal*, November 19, 2005. https://www.wsj.com/articles/SB113236377590902105

11. Pierre Tristam, "Malcom X in Mecca," *ThoughtCo*, January 17, 2021. https://www.thoughtco.com/malcom-x-in-mecca-2353496

12. David A. Graham, "Why the Muslim 'No-Go-Zone' Myth Won't Die," *The Atlantic*, January 20, 2015. https://www.theatlantic.com/international/archive/2015/01/paris-mayor-to-sue-fox-over-no-go-zone-comments/384656/

13. Rowena Mason, "'Hate crime is being inflamed': MPs debate banning Donald Trump from UK," *The Guardian*, January 19, 2016. https://www.theguardian.com/uk-news/2016/jan/18/donald-trump-should-be-banned-from-uk-for-inflaming-hate-mp-says

14. "MEF Uncovers Obama-era Scandal; Congress Investigates," Middle East Forum, October 16, 2018. https://www.meforum.org/7282/mef-uncovers-obama-era-scandal-congress

15. Daniel Pipes, "The 751 No-Go Zones of France," Middle East Forum, November 14, 2006. https://www.danielpipes.org/blog/2006/11/the-751-no-go-zones-of-france

16. Ovid, "French "Sensitive Urban Zones," *Daily Kos*, January 22, 2015. https://www.dailykos.com/stories/2015/1/22/1359402/-French-Sensitive-Urban-Zones

17. Erik Wemple, "Fox News corrects, apologizes for 'no-go zone' remarks," *The Washington Post*, January 18, 2015. https://www.washingtonpost.com/blogs/erik-wemple/wp/2015/01/18/fox-news-corrects-apologizes-for-no-go-zone-remarks/

18. Olga Khazan, "Americans Say Immigrants Should Learn English. But U.S. Policy Makes That Hard," *The Atlantic*, June 4, 2021. https://www.theatlantic.com/politics/archive/2021/06/why-cant-immigrants-learn-english/619053/

19. Jessica Shepherd, "Anger over English lesson funding cuts," *The Guardian*, April 14, 2011. https://www.theguardian.com/education/2011/apr/14/english-lessons-funding-immigrants

20. "Second-Generation Americans," Pew Research Center, February 7, 2013. https://www.pewresearch.org/social-trends/2013/02/07/second-generation-americans/

Chapter 27
Fear of the Great Replacement

1. Renaud Camus, *Le Grand Remplacement: Introduction au remplacisme global* (Paris: David Reinharc, 2011).
2. Lara Bullens, "How France's 'great replacement' theory conquered the global far right," *France 24*, November 8, 2021. https://www.france24.com/en/europe/20211108-how-the-french-great-replacement-theory-conquered-the-far-right
3. Sarah E. Bond, "The Origins of White Supremacists' Fear of Replacement," *Hyperallergic*, August 22, 2019. https://hyperallergic.com/514034/the-origins-of-white-supremacists-fear-of-replacement/
4. Lois Beckett, "Pittsburgh shooting: suspect railed against Jews and Muslims on site used by 'alt-right,'" *The Guardian*, October 27, 2018. https://www.theguardian.com/us-news/2018/oct/27/pittsburgh-shooting-suspect-antisemitism
5. Yair Rosenberg, "'Jews will not replace us': Why white supremacists go after Jews," *The Washington Post*, August 14, 2017. https://www.washingtonpost.com/news/acts-of-faith/wp/2017/08/14/jews-will-not-replace-us-why-white-supremacists-go-after-jews/
6. Katrine Fangen, "Why Did Muslims Become the New Enemy in Norway and Europe?" PRIO Blogs, July 9, 2021. https://blogs.prio.org/2021/07/why-did-muslims-become-the-new-enemy-in-norway-and-europe/
7. "How Europeans Disappeared," MEME, accessed March 24, 2022. https://me.me/i/how-europeans-disappeared-1-wife-2-children-4-wives-12-c3749434cb964e28b531e1e72f47ee2d
8. "Europe in 2060," imgflip, accessed March 24, 2022. https://imgflip.com/i/2j2iyl
9. Falguni A. Sheth, *Toward a Political Philosophy of Race*, 59-60.
10. Michael Scott Moore, "Panic, Pseudoscience and Muslim Immigration," *Pacific Standard*, June 14, 2017. https://psmag.com/social-justice/panic-pseudoscience-and-muslim-immigration-25717
11. Edward T. O'Donnell, "When Irish immigrants were America's most feared terrorist group," *The Washington Post*, March 17, 2019. https://www.washingtonpost.com/outlook/2019/03/17/when-irish-immigrants-were-americas-most-feared-terrorist-group/

12. Yaroslav Trofimov, "Jewish Baby Boom Alters Israeli-Palestinian Dynamic," *The Wall Street Journal*, July 14, 2016. https://www.wsj.com/articles/jewish-baby-boom-alters-israeli-palestinian-dynamic-1468499825

13. "Men Like This Are Forces to Work Until They're 70," America's best pics and videos, accessed March 24, 2022. https://americasbestpics.com/picture/30-88-in-search-men-like-this-are-forced-t-vuro4UHw8

14. Eetta Prince-Gibson, "Why There's No Palestinian Protest Vote in Jerusalem," *Foreign Policy*, November 19, 2018. https://foreignpolicy.com/2018/11/19/why-theres-no-palestinian-protest-vote-in-jerusalem-israel-municipal-palestinian-authority-ramadan-dabash-aziz-abu-sarah/

15. Max Fisher and Amanda Taub, "'Overrun,' 'Outbred,' 'Replaced': Why Ethnic Majorities Lash Out Over False Fears," *The New York Times*, April 30, 2019. https://www.nytimes.com/2019/04/30/world/asia/sri-lanka-populism-ethnic-tensions.html

16. Alexander, Michelle, *The New Jim Crow: Mass Incarceration in the Age of Colorblindness* (New York: New Press, 2020).

17. Jasmine Aguilera, "Citizens Facing Deportation Isn't New. Here's What Happened When the U.S. Removed Mexican-Americans in the 1930s," *Time*, August 2, 2019. https://time.com/5638586/us-citizens-deportation-raids/

18. Dara Lind, "Trump's stripping of passports from some Texas Latinos, explained," *Vox*, August 30, 2018. https://www.vox.com/2018/8/30/17800410/trump-passport-birth-certificate-hispanic-denial-citizens

19. Alana Abramson, "How Donald Trump Perpetuated the 'Birther' Movement for Years," *ABC News*, September 16, 2016. https://abcnews.go.com/Politics/donald-trump-perpetuated-birther-movement-years/story?id=42138176

20. Shaswati Das, "Assam and West Bengal spar over citizenship list," *Mint*, August 1, 2018. https://www.livemint.com/Politics/3tcODpTFsJKJgETnHVWKvJ/Assam-and-West-Bengal-spar-over-citizenship-list.html

21. "Modi Denies India Is Targeting Muslims. We Found a Different Reality," *The New York Times*, April 6, 2020. https://www.youtube.com/watch?v=7yCUIZVMVZQ

22. Soumya Shankar, "India Citizenship Law, in Tandem with National Registry, Could Make BJP's Discriminatory Targeting of Muslims Easier," *The Intercept*, January 30, 2020.

https://theintercept.com/2020/01/30/india-citizenship-act-caa-nrc-assam/

23. Ahmer Khan and Omar Khan, "Two killed in protests over controversial Indian citizenship bill," *CNN*, December 13, 2019.
https://www.cnn.com/2019/12/13/asia/india-assam-unrest-citizenship-bill-intl-hnk

24. "Second-Generation Americans," Pew Research Center, February 7, 2013.
https://www.pewresearch.org/social-trends/2013/02/07/second-generation-americans/

25. "Foreign-Born Students and Workers in the U.S. Science and Engineering Enterprise," National Science Board, 2020, accessed August 3, 2022.
https://www.nsf.gov/nsb/sei/one-pagers/Foreign-Born.pdf

Chapter 28
Conspiracy Theories of Muslim Takeovers

1. John Cody, "Czech PM: Majority of Dutch and Swedish society to be Muslims by 2044 and 2065," *Remix News*, June 16, 2021.
https://rmx.news/article/czech-pm-majority-of-dutch-and-swedish-society-to-be-muslims-by-2044-and-2065/

2. Quran 16:106.

3. Quran 3:28.

4. Quran 60:1 and 60:8.

5. Sam Harris, "It's real, it's scary, it's a cult of death," *Los Angeles Times*, September 18, 2006.
https://www.latimes.com/archives/la-xpm-2006-sep-18-oe-harris18-story.html

6. "5,000 in U.S. suspected of ties to al Qaeda," *The Washington Times*, July 11, 2002.
https://www.washingtontimes.com/news/2002/jul/11/20020711-033737-9875r/

7. John Mueller and Mark G. Stewart, *Chasing Ghosts: The Policing of Terrorism* (New York: Oxford University Press, 2016), 14.
https://books.google.com/books?id=rvOuCgAAQBAJ

8. Asawin Suebasaeng and Dave Gilson, "Chart: Almost Every Obama Conspiracy Theory Ever," *Mother Jones*, November 2, 2012.
https://www.motherjones.com/politics/2012/11/chart-obama-conspiracy-theories/

9. Ibrahim Hooper, "CAIR-Kansas Calls on Kansas GOP to Condemn GOP Women's Club's Defense of Anti-Muslim Speaker, Anti-Muslim Facebook Post," Council on American-Islamic Relations, June 17, 2020. https://www.cair.com/press_releases/cair-kansas-calls-on-kansas-gop-to-condemn-gop-womens-clubs-defense-of-anti-muslim-speaker-anti-muslim-facebook-post/

10. Paul Sperry, *Infiltration: How Muslim Spies and Subversives Have Penetrated Washington* (Nashville: Thomas Nelson Inc, 2005).

Chapter 29
Fear of Encroaching Shariah

1. Sumbul Ali-Karamali, *Demystifying Shariah*, 9.
2. Ibid., 9.
3. Ibid., 10.
4. Ibid., 107-8.
5. Ibid., 91-92.
6. Sumbul Ali-Karamali, *Demystifying Shariah*, 63-66.
7. Quran 24:4.
8. Ayatollah Ruhollah Khomeini, *Tahrir al-Wasilah*, 701.
9. Ibid., 698-700.
10. Ibid., 708.
11. Ibid., 4:715-22.
12. Sumbul Ali-Karamali, *Demystifying Shariah*, 92-93.
13. Shaykh Tusi, *Al-Tibyan Fi Tafsir al-Quran*, commentary on Quranic verse 2:24.
   https://www.altafsir.com/Tafasir.asp?tMadhNo=4&tTafsirNo=39&tSoraNo=24&tAyahNo=2&tDisplay=yes&UserProfile=0&LanguageId=1
14. Matthew 18:9, New International Version.
15. Numbers 15:32-36.
16. Leviticus 20:27.
17. Deuteronomy 21:18-21.
18. Leviticus 24:16.
19. Leviticus 24:17.
20. Exodus 21:16.
21. Exodus 22:19.
22. Leviticus 20:10.
23. Leviticus 20:13.
24. Exodus 31:15.
25. Leviticus 20:2.
26. 2 Kings 2:23-24.

27. Alexander, Michelle, *The New Jim Crow: Mass Incarceration in the Age of Colorblindness* (New York: New Press, 2020).
28. Peter Moskos, *In Defense of Flogging* (New York: Basic Books, 2011).
29. Swathi Shanmugasundaram, "Anti-Sharia law bills in the United States," Southern Poverty Law Center, February 5, 2018. https://www.splcenter.org/hatewatch/2018/02/05/anti-sharia-law-bills-united-states
30. The quoted phrase is from Edward W. Said, *Covering Islam*, 77.
31. "House Bill 1353 by Matheny; Senate Bill 1028 by Ketron: AN ACT to amend Tennessee Code Annotated, Title 38; Title 39; Title 40; Title 45; Title 55 and Title 58, relative to terrorism," Tennessee General Assembly, accessed March 26, 2022. https://www.capitol.tn.gov/Bills/107/Bill/SB1028.pdf
32. John L. Esposito and Natana Delong-Bas, "Shariah: myths vs. realities," Oxford University Press Blog, July 14, 2018. https://blog.oup.com/2018/07/shariah-myths-vs-realities/
33. Swathi Shanmugasundaram, "Anti-Sharia law bills in the United States," Southern Poverty Law Center, February 5, 2018. https://www.splcenter.org/hatewatch/2018/02/05/anti-sharia-law-bills-united-states
34. Andrea Elliott, "The Man Behind the Anti-Shariah Movement," *The New York Times*, July 30, 2011. https://www.nytimes.com/2011/07/31/us/31shariah.html
35. Homa Khaleeli, "Inside Britain's sharia councils: hardline and anti-women – or a dignified way to divorce?" *The Guardian*, March 1, 2017. https://www.theguardian.com/law/2017/mar/01/inside-britains-sharia-councils-hardline-and-anti-women-or-a-dignified-way-to-divorce
36. ACLU Program on Freedom of Religion and Belief, "Nothing to Fear: Debunking the Mythical 'Sharia Threat' to Our Judicial System," American Civil Liberties Union, May 2011. https://www.aclu.org/sites/default/files/field_document/Nothing_To_Fear_Report_FINAL_MAY_2011.pdf
37. Leda Reynolds, "Sharia court told rape victim to RETURN to her attacker husband," *Express*, November 14, 2016. https://www.express.co.uk/news/uk/732064/Sharia-court-told-rape-victim-return-attacker-husband

Chapter 30
Why so Few Muslim Nobel Prize Winners?

1. Edward W. Said, *Covering Islam*, 137.
2. Heather Saul, "Richard Dawkins Muslim jibe sparks Twitter backlash," *Independent*, August 9, 2013. https://www.independent.co.uk/news/people/news/richard-dawkins-muslim-jibe-sparks-twitter-backlash-8753837.html
3. Richard Dawkins, Twitter, August 8, 2013. https://twitter.com/richarddawkins/status/365473573768400896
4. Al-Bayhaqi, *Shu'ab al-Iman*, hadith #1612. http://islamport.com/d/1/mtn/1/68/2446.html
5. Quran 3:137, 6:11, 12:109, 16:36, 22:46, 27:69, 29:20, 30:9, 30:42, 35:44, 40:21, 40:82, 47:10.
6. Quran 9:122.
7. Quran 2:219, 2:266, 16:44.
8. Quran 3:191.
9. Quran 2:164, 13:2-3, 16:12, 23:80, 45:4.
10. Quran 13:3.
11. Quran 2:164, 16:10, 45:5.
12. Quran 2:164.
13. Quran 2:164, 45:4.
14. Quran 23:78.
15. Quran 13:3, 16:11.
16. Quran 7:176.
17. Quran 30:8.
18. Quran 30:21.
19. Quran 2:219-20.
20. Quran 7:184.
21. Ayatollah Ruhollah Khomeini, *Resaleh Towzih al-Masa'il*, 1. http://www.imam-khomeini.ir/fa/c78_3141/
22. N. Akmal Ayyubi, "Contribution of Al-Khwarizmi to Mathematics and Geography," Muslim Heritage, December 27, 2006. https://muslimheritage.com/contribution-of-al-khwarizmi-to-mathematics-and-geography/
23. Owen Gingerich, "Islamic Astronomy," *Scientific Amcerican*, April 1986. https://www.scientificamerican.com/article/islamic-astronomy/
24. Amelia C. Sparavigna, "The Science of Al-Biruni," *International Journal of Sciences* 2, no. 12 (2013): 52-60. doi: 10.18483/ijSci.364
25. "Father of robotics?" Iowa State University: University Library, October 10, 2007. https://www.lib.iastate.edu/news/father-robotics
26. Olivia Goldhill, "An Arab thinker invented economic theory 400 years before Adam Smith did," *Quartz*, June 17, 2017.

https://qz.com/1008371/an-arab-thinker-invented-economic-theory-400-years-before-adam-smith-did/
27. Ibrahim M. Oweiss, Georgetown University, accessed August 3, 2022.
https://faculty.georgetown.edu/imo3/ibn.htm
28. Florian Zemmin, "How (Not) to Take 'Secularity' Beyond the Modern West: Reflections from Islamic Sociology," *Working Paper Series of the HCAS "Multiple Secularities—Beyond the West, Beyond Modernities"* no. 9 (Leipzig University, 2019): 34.
https://ul.qucosa.de/api/qucosa%3A36128/attachment/ATT-0/
29. "Who was Ibn al-Haytham," 1001 Inventions and the World of Ibn Al-Haytham, accessed April 10, 2022.
https://www.ibnalhaytham.com/discover/who-was-ibn-al-haytham/
30. M. Akma, M. Zulkifle and A. H. Ansari, "Ibn Nafis—A Forgotten Genius in the Discovery of Pulmonary Blood Circulation," *Heart Views* 11, no. 1 (2010): 26-30.
https://www.ncbi.nlm.nih.gov/pmc/articles/PMC2964710/
31. "Ibn Sina [Avicenna]," Stanford Encyclopedia of Philosophy, September 15, 2016.
https://plato.stanford.edu/entries/ibn-sina/
32. Alexandra Flemming, "The origins of vaccination," *Nature Milestones*, September 28, 2020.
https://www.nature.com/articles/d42859-020-00006-7
33. Albert Van Dantzig, "Effects of the Atlantic Slave Trade on Some West African Societies," In: *Revue française d'histoire d'outre-mer* 62, no. 226-7 (1975): 252-269.
https://doi.org/10.3406/outre.1975.1831
34. Toby Green, "After Slavery," *Aeon*, March 30, 2021.
https://aeon.co/essays/how-the-end-of-atlantic-slavery-paved-a-path-to-colonialism
35. Jason Hickel, "How Britain stole $45 trillion from India," *Al Jazeera*, December 19, 2018.
https://www.aljazeera.com/opinions/2018/12/19/how-britain-stole-45-trillion-from-india
36. S. Gurumurthy, "Boss, read the true history before speaking," *The New Indian Express*, April 6, 2013.
https://www.newindianexpress.com/opinions/columns/s-gurumurthy/2013/apr/06/boss-read-the-true-history-before-speaking-465400.html
37. Robert Naiman, "The Minimum Wage and the Coup in Honduras," *HuffPost*, September 7, 2009.
https://www.huffpost.com/entry/the-minimum-wage-and-the_b_254023

38. Andrew Buncombe and Andrew Gumbel, "Aristide: 'Marines forced me to leave,'" *Independent*, March 2, 2004. https://www.independent.co.uk/news/world/americas/aristide-marines-forced-me-to-leave-71698.html

39. "Albright: Iraq Sanctions 'Worth It' (Full Context)," Admin UncoverIraq, May 13, 2016. https://www.youtube.com/watch?v=UYagQuqK31s

40. Secretary of State Madeleine K. Albright, "Interview on NBC-TV 'The Today Show' with Matt Lauer," February 19, 1998. https://1997-2001.state.gov/statements/1998/980219a.html#

Chapter 31
The Dangers of Islamophobia

1. "Anti-Muslim hatred has reached 'epidemic proportions' says UN rights expert, urging action by States," *UN News*, March 4, 2021. https://news.un.org/en/story/2021/03/1086452

2. Laura Silver, Moira Fagan, Aidan Connaughton and Mara Mordecai, "Views About National Identity Becoming More Inclusive in U.S., Western Europe," Pew Research Center, May 5, 2021. https://www.pewresearch.org/global/2021/05/05/3-discrimination-in-society/

3. Karla Dieseldorff, "Islamophobia in France Affects Muslim Job Applicants: Study," *Morocco World News*, Oct. 10, 2015. https://www.moroccoworldnews.com/2015/10/170086/islamophobia-in-france-affects-muslim-job-applicants-study

4. Sarah G. Carmichael, "Study: Employers Are Less Likely to Hire a Woman Who Wears a Headscarf," *Harvard Business Review*, May 26, 2017. https://hbr.org/2017/05/study-employers-are-less-likely-to-hire-a-woman-who-wears-a-headscarf

5. Audrey Hamilton, "Can Discrimination Contribute to Feelings of Radicalization?" American Psychological Association, August 5, 2017. https://www.apa.org/news/press/releases/2017/08/discrimination-radicalization

6. Davide Lerner, "It's Not Islam That Drives Young Europeans to Jihad, France's Top Terrorism Expert Explains," *Haaretz*, August 20, 2017. https://www.haaretz.com/world-news/europe/it-s-not-islam-that-drives-young-europeans-to-jihad-terrorism-expert-says-1.5477000?v=1642636476901

7. Tehilla R. Goldberg, "Moderate Muslim voice," *Intermountain Jewish News*, April 10, 2022.
https://www.ijn.com/moderate-muslim-voice/
8. Neta C. Crawford, Lisa Graves and Jessica Katzenstein, "Racial Profiling and Islamophobia," Watson Institute, June 2021, accessed March 28, 2022.
https://watson.brown.edu/costsofwar/costs/social/rights/profiling
9. Lisa Fuller and Rukshana Rizwie, "In Sri Lanka, Muslims say Sinhala neighbours turned against them," *Al Jazeera*, May 21, 2019.
https://www.aljazeera.com/news/2019/5/21/in-sri-lanka-muslims-say-sinhala-neighbours-turned-against-them
10. Meenakshi Ganguly, "It's Not Just Cow Vigilantes. Mob Madness is Spreading and Undermining the Rule of Law in India," *Scroll.in*, July 26, 2017.
https://scroll.in/article/845002
11. PTI, "790 Muslims, 254 Hindus perished in post-Godhra," *The Times of India*, May 11, 2005.
https://timesofindia.indiatimes.com/india/790-muslims-254-hindus-perished-in-post-godhra/articleshow/1106699.cms
12. Mail Today Bureau, "After the UK, other European states set to join the Modi line," *India Today*, February 7, 2013.
https://www.indiatoday.in/india/west/story/eu-ends-embargo-against-narendra-modi-153607-2013-02-07
13. Annie Gowen, "Once banned from the U.S., India's Modi set for historic address to Congress," *The Washington Post*, June 6, 2016.
https://www.washingtonpost.com/news/worldviews/wp/2016/06/06/from-pariah-to-capitol-hill-narendra-modis-extraordinary-rise/
14. Adam Whitnall, "Delhi riots: Violence that killed 53 in Indian capital 'was anti-Muslim pogrom', says top expert," *Independent*, March 7, 2020.
https://www.independent.co.uk/independentpremium/world/delhi-riots-pogrom-violence-deaths-modi-bjp-india-police-a9384891.html
15. "CAIR: Hate crimes against Muslims spike after Trump win," *Al Jazeera*, July 18, 2017.
https://www.aljazeera.com/news/2017/7/18/cair-hate-crimes-against-muslims-spike-after-trump-win
16. Katayoun Kishi, "Assaults against Muslims in U.S. surpass 2001 level," Pew Research Center, November 15, 2017.
https://www.pewresearch.org/fact-tank/2017/11/15/assaults-against-muslims-in-u-s-surpass-2001-level/
17. Timothy Jones, "Germany sees almost 1,000 anti-Muslim crimes in 2017," *DW*, March 3, 2018.

https://www.dw.com/en/germany-sees-almost-1000-anti-muslim-crimes-in-2017/a-42810445

18. Lara Bullens, "How France's 'great replacement' theory conquered the global far right," *France 24*, November 8, 2021. https://www.france24.com/en/europe/20211108-how-the-french-great-replacement-theory-conquered-the-far-right

19. Rajiv Thind, "The crusaders' tropes in white supremacist violence and how Christchurch's own rugby team won't change its name," *Overland*, September 24, 2019. https://overland.org.au/2019/09/the-crusaders-tropes-in-white-supremacist-violence/

20. Peter Beaumont, "Norwegian mass killer Anders Breivik appears before parole hearing," *The Guardian*, January 18, 2022. https://www.theguardian.com/world/2022/jan/18/norwegian-mass-killer-anders-breivik-begins-parole-hearing

21. David Crouch, "Sweden school attack: horror as sword attacker kills teacher and pupil," *The Guardian*, October 22, 2015. https://www.theguardian.com/world/2015/oct/22/pupils-wounded-in-sword-attack-at-swedish-school?CMP=share_btn_gp

22. Postmedia News, "Why no terrorism charges in Quebec mosque shooting? It would place extra burden on prosecutors: experts," *National Post*, January 31, 2017. https://nationalpost.com/news/canada/quebec-mosque-shooting-terrorism-offences-are-complex-experts-say

23. The Canadian Press, "Man charged in fatal London, Ont., truck attack on Muslim family to head straight to trial," *CBC*, February 9, 2022. https://www.cbc.ca/news/canada/london/london-muslim-family-attack-trial-expected-1.6345113

24. Philip Oltermann and Kate Connolly, "Germany shooting: far-right gunman kills 10 in Hanau," *The Guardian*, February 20, 2020. https://www.theguardian.com/world/2020/feb/19/shooting-germany-hanau-dead-several-people-shisha-near-frankfurt

25. Adam B. Lerner, "Chapel Hill murders: Hate crime or parking dispute?" *Politico*, February 11, 2015. https://www.politico.com/story/2015/02/chapel-hill-muslim-deaths-north-carolina-115110#

26. Al Baker, "Imam's Killer Is Sentenced, but Motive Remains a Mystery," *The New York Times*, June 6, 2018. https://www.nytimes.com/2018/06/06/nyregion/queens-imam-murder-sentencing.html

27. Matthew Haag and Jacey Fortin, "Two Killed in Portland While Trying to Stop Anti-Muslim Rant, Police Say," *The New York Times*, May 27, 2017. https://www.nytimes.com/2017/05/27/us/portland-train-attack-muslim-rant.html

28. Adam BenSaid, "France's 'Muslim' problem and the unspoken racism at its heart," *TRT World*, February 19, 2020. https://www.trtworld.com/magazine/france-s-muslim-problem-and-the-unspoken-racism-at-its-heart-33939

29. Zolan Kanno-Youngs, "Delayed Homeland Security Report Warns of 'Lethal' White Supremacy," *The New York Times*, October 6, 2020. https://www.nytimes.com/2020/10/06/us/politics/homeland-security-white-supremacists-russia.html

30. Glenn Kessler, "The 'very fine people' at Charlottesville: Who were they?" *The Washington Post*, May 8, 2020. https://www.washingtonpost.com/politics/2020/05/08/very-fine-people-charlottesville-who-were-they-2/

31. Zack Beauchamp, "You're more likely to be killed by your own clothes than by an immigrant terrorist," *Vox*, June 26, 2017. https://www.vox.com/2016/9/13/12901950/terrorism-immigrants-clothes

32. John Gramlich, "What the data says about gun deaths in the U.S.," Pew Research Center, February 3, 2022. https://www.pewresearch.org/fact-tank/2019/08/16/what-the-data-says-about-gun-deaths-in-the-u-s/

33. "Deaths from Excessive Alcohol Use in the United States," Centers for Disease Control and Prevention, accessed March 28, 2022. https://www.cdc.gov/alcohol/features/excessive-alcohol-deaths.html

34. "Smoking and Tobacco Use," Centers for Disease Control and Prevention, accessed March 28, 2022. https://www.cdc.gov/tobacco/data_statistics/fact_sheets/fast_facts/index.htm

35. Jill Kimball, "Costs of the 20-year war on terror: $8 trillion and 900,000 deaths," Brown University: News from Brown, September 1, 2021. https://www.brown.edu/news/2021-09-01/costsofwar

36. Scott Simon Interview with Congressman John Duncan, "Should We End The Controversial Air Marshal Program?" *NPR Weekend Edition*, October 24, 2015. https://www.npr.org/2015/10/24/451403416/should-we-end-the-controversial-air-marshal-program

37. "White House backs air marshals' actions," *CNN*, December 9, 2005. http://www.cnn.com/2005/US/12/08/airplane.gunshot/index.html

38. Nathan Rubbelke, "Are air marshals keeping America safe?" *Washington Examiner*, July 20, 2015.
https://www.washingtonexaminer.com/tag/hillary-clinton?source=%2Fare-air-marshals-keeping-america-safe

39. Adam Gabbatt, "Almost one in three of Republicans say violence may be necessary to 'save' US," *The Guardian*, November 1, 2021.
https://www.theguardian.com/us-news/2021/nov/01/republicans-violence-save-us-poll

40. Noam Chomsky, "The US 'War on Terror' Is Playing Right Into ISIS's Hands," *The Nation*, May 10, 2016.
https://www.thenation.com/article/archive/the-us-war-on-terror-is-playing-right-into-isiss-hands/

41. Barbara Crossette, "Iraq Sanctions Kill Children, U.N. Reports," *The New York Times*, December 1, 1995.
https://www.nytimes.com/1995/12/01/world/iraq-sanctions-kill-children-un-reports.html

42. Thomas E. Griffith, Jr., "Strategic Attack of National Electrical Systems," (Alabama: Air University Press, 1994).
https://media.defense.gov/2017/Dec/29/2001861964/-1/-1/0/T_GRIFFITH_STRATEGIC_ATTACK.PDF

43. "Al Jazeera 'hit by missile,'" *BBC News*, April 8, 2003.
http://news.bbc.co.uk/2/hi/2927527.stm

44. "Lest We Forget Abeer Qassim al-Janabi," Geneva International Centre for Justice, February 21, 2017.
https://www.gicj.org/lest-we-forget/884-abeer-qassim-al-janabi

45. Olivia Snaije, "The true story of Mohammed El-Gharani, one of Guantanamo Bay's youngest prisoners," *The National News*, April 9, 2019.
https://www.thenationalnews.com/arts-culture/books/the-true-story-of-mohammed-el-gharani-one-of-guantanamo-bay-s-youngest-prisoners-1.845965

46. "Iraq Prison Abuse Scandal Fast Facts," *CNN*, October 30, 2013, updated March 11, 2022.
https://www.cnn.com/2013/10/30/world/meast/iraq-prison-abuse-scandal-fast-facts/index.html

47. Judy Maltz, "When an Embattled Israel Called Them in 1967, They Came—and Never Left," *Haaretz*, June 3, 2017.
https://www.haaretz.com/israel-news/they-came-in-1967-to-help-an-embattled-israel-and-never-left-1.5478360

48. Edward W. Said, *Covering Islam*, 100.

49. Cecilia D'Anastasio, "In Our Orbit: A Tolerance for Ambiguity," *The Nation*, July 29, 2014.

https://www.thenation.com/article/archive/our-orbit-tolerance-ambiguity/

50. Sam Harris, "#23—Islam and the Future of Tolerance," *Making Sense with Sam Harris*, podcast audio, December 21, 2015. https://www.samharris.org/podcasts/making-sense-episodes/islam-and-the-future-of-tolerance-a-dialogue

51. Tom Curry, "Is Iran irrational or 'merely hostile'?" *NBC News*, June 30, 2008. https://www.nbcnews.com/id/wbna25442607

52. Fareed Zakaria, "Is Iran rational?" *The Washington Post*, April 9, 2015. https://www.washingtonpost.com/opinions/is-iran-rational/2015/04/09/3c2cc5a8-def5-11e4-a500-1c5bb1d8ff6a_story.html

53. John Yemma, "Is Iran rational enough for MAD?" *The Christian Science Monitor*, February 17, 2012. https://www.csmonitor.com/Commentary/From-the-Editor/2012/0217/Is-Iran-rational-enough-for-MAD

54. Edward W. Said, *Covering Islam*, 91.

55. Daniel Pipes, "Muslims only understand brute force," July 5, 2008. https://www.danielpipes.org/comments/134460

56. Falguni A. Sheth, *Toward a Political Philosophy of Race*, 80.

57. Edward W. Said, *Covering Islam*, 30.

58. Ibid., 163.

59. Ibid., 150.

60. Ibid., 151.

61. Ibid., 148.

62. John Blake, "The new threat: 'Racism without racists,'" *CNN*, November 27, 2014. https://www.cnn.com/2014/11/26/us/ferguson-racism-or-racial-bias/

Chapter 32
Towards a Brighter Future

1. Edward W. Said, *Covering Islam*, lxv.

Index

418   The ill-Logic of Islamophobia